# From the Middle Ages to Milton

Theatrical activity virtually disappeared during the early Middle Ages, but the buried seeds of drama found new life in ritualistic Biblical performances known as miracle plays. Three anonymous works included in this text, two miracle plays and a morality play, show the combined influence of folklore and Christianity on the burgeoning art of English drama, which reached its full glory in the eloquence of Shakespeare, who has never been matched in any age or any language . . . and in Milton, who spoke to all men for all time.

This superb collection is enhanced by a group of critical essays. A medieval critic warns that miracle plays are so lighthearted that they are sinful. T. S. Eliot's essay on Shakespearian criticism offers valuable insight to the student of Shakespeare. As a contemporary note, James Agate criticizes in detail a London production of Ben Jonson's *Volpone*. These and other essays by important figures in English literature aid greatly in showing the development of English theater.

*The three editors of this book hold Ph.D.'s from Harvard University and now teach in the Boston area—Sylvan Barnet at Tufts University, Morton Berman at Boston University, and William Burto at Lowell State College.*

D1400694

# Plays in MENTOR and SIGNET CLASSIC Editions

# The Genius
## of the
# EARLY ENGLISH
# THEATER

EDITED *and with*
*an* INTRODUCTION *by*

Sylvan Barnet
Morton Berman
William Burto

A MENTOR BOOK from
## NEW AMERICAN LIBRARY
TIMES MIRROR
New York and Scarborough, Ontario
The New English Library Limited, London

Grateful acknowledgment is made to the following for permission to quote from the works listed:

Cambridge University Press (Cambridge and New York) for "Shakespearean Criticism: From Dryden to Coleridge" by T. S. Eliot from *A Companion to Shakespeare Studies,* ed. H. Granville-Barker and G. B. Harrison. Copyright © 1960 by G. B. Harrison.

Jonathan Cape Ltd. (London) for "Volpone; or the Fox" by James Agate from *Brief Chronicles.*

The Clarendon Press (Oxford) for *The Tragical History of the Life and Death of Doctor Faustus by Christopher Marlowe: a Conjectural Reconstruction* by W. W. Gregg.

Columbia University Press (New York) for a selection from *Shakespeare's Audience* by Alfred Harbage.

Ginn and Company for permission to translate "A Treatise against Miracle Plays" from *A Literary Middle English Reader,* ed. Albert S. Cook. Copyright 1915, 1943 by Ginn and Company.

The editors wish to thank Mr. Albert Gilman for his helpful comments on much of the manuscript.

NOTE: Application for reproducing the plays in this volume protected by copyright against any unauthorized performance, in whole or in part, in any medium, should be made to the copyright holders listed above. The translations of *The Second Shepherds' Play* and "A Treatise against Miracle Plays" are copyrighted by the editors.

LIBRARY OF CONGRESS CATALOG CARD NO. 62-18429

SIGNET, SIGNET CLASSICS, MENTOR, PLUME AND MERIDIAN BOOKS are published *in the United States* by The New American Library, Inc., 1301 Avenue of the Americas, New York, New York 10019, *in Canada* by The New American Library of Canada Limited, 81 Mack Avenue, Scarborough, 704, Ontario, *in the United Kingdom* by The New English Library Limited, Barnard's Inn, Holborn, London, E.C. 1, England.

7 8 9 10 11 12 13 14 15

PRINTED IN THE UNITED STATES OF AMERICA

# Contents

# Medieval and Renaissance English Drama:

❧

## An Introduction

In 1840, not long after Englishmen had become aware that they possessed an empire, Thomas Carlyle, looking at English achievements, suggested in a lecture that Shakespeare "is the grandest thing that we have done." True, the empire was still to grow, but even in Carlyle's day it was far-flung. Yet Carlyle insisted that Shakespeare was England's greatest achievement:

> For our honor among foreign nations, as an ornament to our English Household, what item is there that we would not surrender rather than him? Consider now, if they asked us, Will you give-up your Indian Empire or your Shakespeare, you English; never have had any Indian Empire, or never have had any Shakespeare? Really it were a grave question. Official persons would answer doubtless in official language; but we, for our part too, should not we be forced to answer: Indian Empire, or no Indian Empire; we cannot do without Shakespeare! Indian Empire will go, at any rate, some day; but this Shakespeare does not go, he lasts forever with us; we cannot give-up our Shakespeare!

The Indian Empire has gone, but Shakespeare remains, and it is, of course, Shakespeare who is most "The Genius of the English Theater." It is, however, no disservice to Shakespeare to say that if his drama is for all time it is also of his age. But there are dangers here. We may be tempted to reduce his predecessors and contemporaries to pygmies who had the good fortune to help Shakespeare in the turning of this phrase, or in the construction of that plot; or we may be tempted to elevate to immortality anyone who resembles Shakespeare in some way, even if he only supplied Shakespeare with a wretched plot that Shakespeare transformed utterly.

Roughly speaking, until the end of the eighteenth century neither danger existed, because medieval drama was virtually unknown, because only a few of Shakespeare's contemporaries were fairly well known, and because Shakespeare himself was produced in highly cut and revised versions. These factors effectively prevented much careful study of Shakespeare's relation to his predecessors and contemporaries, and in the late seventeenth and eighteenth centuries helped create the myth that Shakespeare's plays came into existence by a sort of literary spontaneous combustion. But the end of the eighteenth century saw the rise of antiquarian study of English literature, which has continued into the twentieth century, sometimes as scholarship and sometimes as pedantry. Enormous energy has been expended on the study of English drama from its beginnings, and a great deal has been learned. At its worst, pedantry has told us that if we will only read such-and-such an Elizabethan play, sermon, or medical treatise, we will understand *Hamlet*, as though Shakespeare could not rise higher than his sources. At its best, literary scholarship has enabled us to rediscover masterpieces by making texts available and by furnishing introductions and notes that help a reader see what is going on inside a play—especially reminding him that a play of the sixteenth century or earlier need not be doing badly what a nineteenth- or twentieth-century play does well. Even as late as 1923, when a good deal had been learned about early dramatic techniques, aims, and accomplishments, William Archer, who had put the English-speaking world deeply in his debt by his translations of Ibsen, saw, in *The Old Drama and the New*, all drama before the late nineteenth century as an imperfect manifestation of what was to come. Shakespeare, he granted, had managed to write masterpieces, but even Shakespeare worked in the "impure form" of poetic drama, mistakenly uniting realistic "imitation" with "lyrical passion." Archer, applauding the divorce of the two into, respectively, realistic prose drama and opera, concluded that "realism . . . is only the last term in an inevitable process of evolution." Archer's words were dated when he wrote them; in fact they had been outdated twenty or thirty years earlier by the symbolic dramas of Strindberg and Ibsen, and by the verse dramas of Yeats, all of which were newer than Archer's "new" drama, marking a departure from the realistic drama that had already showed signs of wear.

If realism is defined as the imitation of external nature, as the presentation of the illusion of nature, the most obvious thing about drama before the nineteenth century is that it is unrealistic. It cannot pass Archer's test for good drama, which begins by having the critic ask "Does it present a reasonably faithful imitation of what may be called the visible and audible surfaces of life?" Take its language. The language of virtually all tragedy, and of much comedy, is verse, sometimes interspersed with prose. Aeschylus, Sophocles, Euripides, Aristophanes, Plautus, Terence, Calderón, Corneille, Racine, Molière (not to mention Shakespeare and his contemporaries) are among those who made the public think that drama meant poetry. Realistic drama changed all that, and no one aware of the achievements of Ibsen, Chekhov, and Synge can deny that prose has produced dramatic masterpieces. (Still, it must at once be mentioned that the prose spoken in these plays is artful and not the incoherency that we daily talk.) Perhaps it is enough to mention that although the prose theater offers realistic imitations that please, it usually lacks two important qualities. First, it usually lacks, as earlier drama does not, the element of play, of fun. The awareness that a drama is a play, and an actor a player, tends to disappear in the nineteenth-century illusionistic theater. When, for example, Ibsen was congratulated because he created good parts, he replied, "Parts! I do not write parts. I create men and women." None of Ibsen's characters reminds the audience that it is sitting in a theater, as Shakespeare's characters occasionally do:

> If this were played upon a stage now, I would condemn it
> as an improbable fiction.          [*Twelfth Night*]

> Our wooing doth not end like an old play;
> Jack hath not Jill: these ladies' courtesy
> Might well have made our sport a comedy.
>                    [*Love's Labor's Lost*]

The illusionistic theater asks only that the audience forget itself and witness the world on the stage; Shakespearean theater asks for the more complicated response (not the more naïve one, as is sometimes charged) that the audience participate in the world on the stage and at the same time recognize that this world is a sort of playful adult make-believe that illuminates our world and yet vanishes when held against it. Archer, therefore, was quite right in charging (but he inadvertently praised where he meant to damn) that "the Elizabethan dramatist . . . called upon his audiences for an amount of make-believe from which a modern audience would recoil."

Second, realistic drama usually lacks not only a sense of play but also a sense of the exceptional, which gets us back to the use of verse. People don't usually speak verse outside of the theater, but verse cannot only be fun (children enjoy reciting "Pease porridge hot"), it can also be a correlate for the language of exceptional people. The world of *Macbeth*, say, presents in many ways the daily world, but it presents also the world of unusual people and unusual happenings; it is both a familiar world and a strange world, and few would want more familiarity and less strange beauty. We can no longer be as sure as Archer was that "the purification of drama by the expulsion of operatic and exaggerative elements is a mark not of decline, but of progress."

The very origin of drama, as Archer himself mentions, seems to involve both realism and beauty. Aristotle says that it arises from an instinct for imitation and an instinct for harmony. Mere mimicry can make drama, but combined with some sort of rhythm it gains potency. Very little (beyond Aristotle's hints) is known of the origin of Greek drama. Not a great deal is known of the rebirth of drama during the Middle Ages, after its virtual extinction by the barbarians and by the Church in the early Christian centuries, but a few things can be said.

In A.D. 400 Augustine observed with pleasure the collapse of the drama. "The theaters," he said, "are falling almost everywhere, the theaters, those sinks of uncleanness and public places of debauchery. And for what reason are they falling? They are falling because of the reformation of the age, because the lewd and sacrilegious practices for which they were built are out of fashion." That the theaters were falling is indisputable; that the age had reformed is less so. Doubtless the barbarian attacks on Italy had helped decimate the theater; equally doubtless, most men retained a fondness for mimicry and harmony, and delighted in the antics of strollers who enacted skits or jokes. Surely, too, the common people retained some of their ancient dramatic rituals, derived from pre-Christian celebrations and adapted to the Christian calendar. There are no early written texts for these simple folk-plays, but they are alluded to in the Middle Ages and must have been quite like the texts that folklorists recorded in the nineteenth century. In *The Return of the Native* Thomas Hardy describes one of these primitive plays, commonly performed by illiterate or barely literate rustics. Because the gist of such a play is a mock combat, a death, and a rebirth, folklorists are convinced that the play is a survival of ancient rituals celebrating the rebirth of the year (spring) after its death (winter). But although there were strolling entertainers and rustics who engaged in dramatic rituals, one can say that the barbarians weakened the theater and that the churchmen exterminated it. By the middle of the sixth century, the profession of dramatist ceased to exist.

Yet dramatic activity regained life within the church itself.

By the early ninth century the Mass was embellished with antiphonal singing of meaningless sounds (e.g., a prolongation of the final vowel of the *Alleluia*); later, words were fitted to the musical pattern. The most important of these elaborations or tropes runs as follows:

*Interrogatio:*
　[Question (of the angels):]
　*Quem quaeritis in sepulchro, o Christicolae?*
　[Whom do you seek in the sepulcher, o followers of Christ?]

*Responsio:*
　[Answer (of the Marys):]
　*Jesum Nazarenum crucifixum, o Coelicolae.*
　[Jesus of Nazareth, who was crucified, o celestial ones.]

*Angeli:*
　[Angels:]
　*Non est hic; surrexit, sicut praedixerat.*
　[He is not here; he is risen, as he foretold.]
　*Ite, nuntiate quia surrexit de sepulchro.*
　[Go, announce that he is risen from the sepulcher.]

This scrap of dialogue, closely based on Mark 16: 1-7, at first sung as part of the Introit of the Mass at Easter, was later inserted into the services preceding the Mass, where it was sung, with amplifications, by a priest who impersonated an angel and by three priests who impersonated the three Marys. The impersonation was aided by costume (the priest playing the angel wore a white garment) and by gesture. Here is a translation of the late tenth-century instructions written in Latin by Ethelwold, Bishop of Winchester, for performing this liturgical play:

While the third lesson is being chanted, let four brethren vest themselves. Let one of these, vested in an alb, enter as though to take part in the service, and let him approach the sepulcher without attracting attention and sit there quietly with a palm in his hand. While the third respond is chanted, let the remaining three follow, and let them all, vested in copes, bearing in their hands thuribles with incense, and stepping delicately as those who seek something, approach the sepulcher. These things are done in imitation of the angel sitting in the monument, and the women with spices coming to anoint the body of Jesus. When therefore he who sits there beholds the three approach him like folks lost and seeking something, let him begin in a dulcet voice of

medium pitch, to sing "Whom do you seek." And when he
has sung it to the end, let the three reply in unison "Jesus
of Nazareth." So he, "He is not here; he is risen, as he foretold. Go, announce that he has risen from the dead." At the
word of this bidding let those three turn to the choir and
say "Alleluia! The Lord is risen!" This said, let the one,
still sitting there and as if recalling them, say the anthem
"Come and see the place." And saying this, let him rise,
and lift the veil, and show them the place bare of the cross,
but only the cloths laid there in which the cross was
wrapped. And when they have seen this, let them set down
the thuribles which they bare in that same sepulcher, and
take the cloth, and hold it up in the face of the clergy, and
as if to demonstrate that the Lord has risen and is no
longer wrapped therein, let them sing the anthem "The Lord
is risen from the sepulcher," and lay the cloth upon the
altar. When the anthem is done, let the prior, sharing in
their gladness at the triumph of our King, in that, having
vanquished death, He rose again, begin the hymn "Praise
God." And this begun, all the bells chime out together.[1]

There is realistic imitation here ("stepping delicately as those
who seek something"), but there is a good deal of theatricalism
too; the lines are chanted, the costumes are symbolic, the final
joy is in part suggested by music.

In time, there were accretions: St. Peter and St. John, soldiers guarding the tomb, the risen Christ, etc. And there were
imitations of this imitation of what had happened a thousand
years earlier; at Christmas, for example, a play was performed
in which shepherds were asked whom they sought in the
manger. With the added episodes, the drama moved from the
choir down through the nave of the church. The scenery consisted of "multiple settings," temporary structures built in the
nave, representing, say, Pilate's palace, Calvary, the tomb,
Emmaus, etc. The performers moved from one setting to the
next, as the action demanded, but all the settings were present
from start to finish. By the early thirteenth century the drama,
which by now had begun to include passages in the vernacu-
lar, in some places moved out of the church, into the open air.
The increased number of roles, as well as the increased expense of producing these elaborate shows, resulted in the medieval guilds—basically commercial fraternities, but with strong
social and religious commitments—lending (or taking) a hand
in the performance of a play (consisting of numerous playlets)
that covered the whole of history, from the Creation to the
Judgment.

[1] Translated by E. K. Chambers, *The Mediaeval Stage* (Oxford University Press, 1903), II, 14-15.

Each playlet on a Biblical subject is commonly called a "miracle play." In England the term came to include plays on a saint's life, but some literary historians distinguishing between the two sorts call the Biblical plays "mysteries" and the saints' plays "miracles." Doubtless Chaucer's adventurous Wife of Bath, who went to "pleyes of myracles" when her husband was out of town, did not make this distinction. The collection of playlets is commonly called a cycle or a craft cycle. Probably because Easter weather was uncertain, these cycles usually came to be performed later in the year, early in June, on Corpus Christi Day. In some localities the system of "multiple settings" or "simultaneous settings," which had been used within the church, prevailed. In others, there developed the custom of performing the plays on wagons (called "pageants") that drew up, one by one, to an appointed place. The first pageant would present its play, the Creation (staged at dawn), and then would go on to another place where it would repeat the play for a new audience; meanwhile the second pageant had drawn up to the first place, and its performers presented the second play, the Fall. And so on, until the last pageant showed God passing judgment. On the pageant, doubtless there were multiple settings: if *The Second Shepherds' Play* (p. 38) was performed on a pageant, the pageant probably had three acting areas—the fields, Mak's house, and the manger.

The craft cycles, enormously popular in England in the late fourteenth century and in the first half of the fifteenth, had seriously fallen off by the close of the fifteenth. Perhaps some of the guilds found the cost burdensome. Perhaps a Protestant spirit weakened the popularity of the plays, which included representations of Christ and the Virgin (see p. 395). Perhaps some of the guildsmen who performed in the cycles found playing a congenial activity, and preferred to play on a professional or semiprofessional basis, touring the countryside. This last explanation has some facts to support it; it seems likely that the amateur drama declined largely because it had engendered a professional drama.

The medieval miracle play performed the immense service of accustoming men to dramatic representations in verse. More specifically, its influence on the greater drama of the Renaissance can perhaps be said to be a tendency toward inclusiveness. The cycles had covered the whole of history, presenting kings and shepherds, God and beggars, sorrow and joy, in an effort to dramatize the whole Christian view of life. In the main, the drama of Greece and Rome covered only a short period—a day or less—but the Elizabethan dramatists, even those who were familiar with ancient drama, tended to prefer a longer period. Sophocles' *Oedipus the King* begins almost at the last moment preceding the catastrophe, and the play is largely the revelation of what *had happened; Macbeth* begins at the beginning, and the play is a presentation of what *is happening*. Similarly, *Macbeth* ranges in space, from Scotland to England, and its range in character (from a king to a drunken porter who is given a scene to himself) is wider than that found in most ancient drama.

Although the miracle plays lasted, in some areas, into the late sixteenth century (they were performed at Coventry, fourteen miles from Stratford, during Shakespeare's boyhood), the most important plays of the late fifteenth and early sixteenth centuries were the morality plays, of which some sixty are extant. Basically, a morality play is an allegory that shows a man how to live: the commonest ones dramatize the conflict between virtues and vices, but some, notably *Everyman* (p. 66), dramatize the coming of death, and some dramatize religious and political controversies. That the Christian is engaged in a conflict had been stated by St. Paul, who in Ephesians 6: 11-12 urged him to

> Put on the whole armor of God, that ye may be able to stand against the wiles of the devil.
> For we wrestle not against flesh and blood, but against principalities, against powers, against the rulers of the darkness of this world, against spiritual wickedness in high places.

One of the earliest extant morality plays, *The Castle of Perseverance* (*c.* 1425), shows the battle waged for the soul of Humanum Genus (i.e., Mankind): Humanum Genus, seduced by a Bad Angel who tells him there is time to be virtuous in one's old age, partakes of what the World, the Flesh, and the Devil offer; urged by a Good Angel, he repents, and is taken into the Castle of Perseverance, which is inhabited by the seven virtues. But Covetousness (the sin of old age) entices him to leave, and Death strikes him down. At a trial before God, Mercy and Peace plead for him against Righteousness and Truth, and God judges mercifully. The untragic ending is typical. But although the morality plays are untragic, and although their allegoric personifications are something of a retreat from the people of the mystery plays, the morality plays brought medieval drama very close to Renaissance tragedy. The miracle plays concerned themselves for the most part with godly men, dramatizing not so much the probable as the miraculous. The heroes of the morality plays, Humanum Genus, Everyman, and Mankind, are close to the Renaissance tragic hero who struggles against his passions and his ignorance, and is finally confronted with death.

These native forms are fused, in the middle and late sixteenth century, with classical forms. There are some out-and-out imitations of ancient drama, but in most English Renaissance drama it is impossible to separate sharply the native and the classical elements. Yet one can make some rough generalizations about the classical influences. The Elizabethan tragic writers probably derived from the Latin tragedies of Seneca the motif of revenge, the inclusion of a vindictive ghost, the use of stichomythia (speeches of a single line each, thrusting at one another), and heroes who alternate between highly impassioned outbursts and quiet stoical meditations. If one combs medieval drama one can find most or all of these qualities somewhere or other, but there is no doubt that it was from Seneca rather than from earlier native drama that the Elizabethan dramatists derived the tragic hero who must revenge a relative, is exhorted by a ghost, has bloody thoughts yet is aware that man is a mere quintessence of dust, and sometimes engages in dialogue of this sort:

> *Queen.*    Hamlet, thou hast thy father much offended.
> *Hamlet.*    Mother, you have my father much offended.
> *Queen.*    Come, come, you answer with an idle tongue.
> *Hamlet.*    Go, go, you question with a wicked tongue.

An Elizabethan dramatist whose Latin was weak could read Seneca in a translation. Thomas Nashe, apparently alluding to a lost play of *Hamlet,* suggests (1589) that an uninspired dramatist composed with a translation in hand:

> English Seneca read by candlelight yields many good sentences, as "Blood is a beggar," and so forth; and if you entreat him fair in a frosty morning, he will afford you whole *Hamlets,* I should say handfuls, of tragical speeches.

Similarly, though medieval drama has plenty of comedy (see *The Second Shepherds' Play*), the Elizabethan writers derived from Plautus (254?–184? B.C.) and Terence (190?–159? B.C.) some character types and a sense of elaborate plot. The pairs of young lovers who, aided by disguises and a clever servant, stumble through two hours of confusion before they finally outwit their elders and marry, are unparalleled in early native drama. Stephen Gosson (1554–1624) uttered many lies in his puritanical attacks on the drama, but he spoke considerable truth when he said that English comedy "smelt of Plautus."

The plays of this period, the late sixteenth century, were performed in a variety of places—touring players would have to set up a platform in whatever street, house, hall, or inn would admit them—but the playing-area that especially concerns us is the theater just outside of London. In December 1574 the Common Council of London, representing bourgeois and puritanical influences, in an ordinance called attention to

sundry great disorders and inconveniences . . . to this City by the inordinate haunting of great multitudes of people, specially youth, to plays, interludes, namely occasion of frays and quarrels, evil practices of incontinency in great inns having chambers and secret places adjoining to their open stages and galleries, inveigling and alluring of maids, specially orphans and good citizens' children under age, to privy and unmeet contracts, the publishing of unchaste, uncomely, and unshamefast speeches and doings, withdrawing of the Queen's Majesty's subjects from divine service on Sundays and holidays, at which times such plays were chiefly used, unthrifty waste of the money of the poor and fond persons, sundry robberies by picking and cutting of purses, uttering of popular, busy, and seditious matters, and many other corruptions of youth and other enormities, besides that also sundry slaughters and maimings of the Queen's subjects have happened by ruins of scaffolds, frames, and stages, and by engines, weapons, and powder used in plays.

The ordinance went on to decree that

from henceforth no play, comedy, tragedy, interlude, nor public show shall be openly played or showed within the liberties of the City, wherein shall be uttered any words, examples, or doings of any unchastity, sedition, nor suchlike unfit and uncomely matter, upon pain of imprisonment . . . ; and that no innkeeper, tavernkeeper, nor other person whatsoever within the liberties of this City shall openly show or play, nor cause or suffer to be openly showed or played, within the house, yard, or any other place within the liberties of this City, any play, interlude, comedy, tragedy, matter, or show, which shall not be first perused and allowed . . . ; and that no person shall suffer any plays, interludes, comedies, tragedies, or shows to be played or showed in his house, yard, or other place whereof he then shall have rule or power, but only such persons and in such places as upon good and reasonable considerations showed shall be thereunto permitted and allowed by the Lord Mayor and Aldermen.

The restrictions proved a boon to the drama: James Burbage, to be free from them (and probably from innkeepers, who took a percentage of the admissions and could not always be counted on to let players use their inns), decided to erect a playhouse in a suburb north of London, outside of the jurisdiction of the Lord Mayor. His building, called "The Theater" (1576), was the first permanent structure in England designed for plays. Almost immediately it had competitors, but there is a good deal of uncertainty about the stages in all of these buildings. The chief evidence consists of a few drawings (only one of which is of much value), the contract for a theater called "The Fortune," and references within the plays. The significant drawing is the so-called De Witt drawing of the Swan Theater, which is actually a copy by a friend of a drawing De Witt, a Dutchman, made when he visited the theater in 1596 or thereabouts. The drawing shows an elevated stage jutting out into a yard. At the rear of the stage are two doors, behind which is the "tiring house" or dressing room; above the doors is a gallery; above the gallery is a projecting roof or awning supported by posts resting on the stage; above the awning is a roofed chamber or "hut." Encircling the stage is the building itself (the tiring house forms the rear of the building), consisting of three tiers for spectators. Though most Elizabethan theaters were round or polygonal (Shakespeare called the theater a "wooden O"), the Fortune contract specifies a square building, 80' outside and 55' inside, with three tiers of galleries and a stage 43' broad and 27½' deep. References, especially stage directions, within the plays (e.g., "above," "aloft," "Enter a Fairy at one door, and Robin Goodfellow at another") provide some facts, but their interpretation is much disputed. This much is certain: in one theater or another, a large elevated stage projected into a yard; some members of the audience stood at its front and sides, others sat in the three galleries; some exits and entrances were made through doors at the rear; there was a higher playing space for some scenes; the place beneath the stage (the "cellar") was occasionally used for supernatural music, for ghosts, etc. ("Why sinks that cauldron?" Macbeth asks, as a cauldron descends through a trap into the cellar.) There was also some means of "discovering" performers, i.e., revealing them by drawing back a curtain that was near the rear of the platform. Perhaps there was a curtained alcove at the rear of the stage, between the doors, but the Swan drawing shows no such thing. Perhaps (and this is more likely) a temporary curtained booth was erected there for those plays that required persons to be discovered in caves or rooms; it would serve, too, as a hiding place for Jonson's

Volpone, who in the last act "peeps from behind a traverse." Most performers, however, merely walked onto the stage through the doors. Probably (we have left the realm of fact) a character discovered at the rear would not stay there, but would come forward and would thus by his presence transform the bare stage into whatever locale the rear had represented. The higher playing area—probably windows above the doors, as well as the gallery above the alcove or booth—afforded Juliet a place to stand when Romeo asked "What light through yonder window breaks?" and replied, "It is the east, and Juliet is the sun"; it also afforded the citizens of Harfleur in *Henry V* the city walls on which to stand.[2]

The action in an Elizabethan play moved quickly, aided by the various playing places and by the absence of bulky scenery. Costumes, torches, and banners must have afforded a good deal of spectacle (the last act of *Macbeth* has five stage directions calling for "Drum and Colors"), but little use was made of built scenery: a bed or a throne was about as massive as the scenery got. (The throne, incidentally, could be lowered from above: in *Doctor Faustus,* V, ii, a stage direction orders "music while the throne descends." In this same scene "Hell is discovered"; perhaps it was a construction placed at the rear behind the curtain, perhaps it was a painted cloth.) There is a mysterious Elizabethan reference to something that represented "the city of Rome," but probably it was a painted curtain. On the whole, the Elizabethan dramatist set the stage with words:

> This is Illyria, lady.

> This castle hath a pleasant seat. The air
> Nimbly and sweetly recommends itself
> Unto our gentle senses.

> What wood is this before us?
>                 The Wood of Birnam.

[2] The theater described above is the typical "public" theater, but there were also "private" theaters, which led a precarious existence during the last quarter of the sixteenth century and the first decade of the seventeenth. The private theaters were within the city of London, in buildings on grounds that had belonged to the church; these grounds had been appropriated by Henry VIII and thus were not under the jurisdiction of the city. These private theaters used only boy actors (aged about eight to twelve), and catered to a courtly audience (the price of admission was six times that of the public theaters). When in 1608 the companies of boy actors were suppressed, one of the theaters (Blackfriars) was taken over by an adult company, of which Shakespeare was a member.

> In my chamber-window lies a book; bring it hither
> to me in the orchard.

The nineteenth century, with its fondness for elaborate and realistic scenery, could produce Elizabethan plays only by cutting or by reshuffling the scenes, bringing together, for example, two castle scenes that the dramatist had separated by a battle scene. To leave the scenes in the author's order would have produced interminable delays erecting, striking, and again erecting scenery, but the cutting and shuffling produced equally unpleasant results. It is pedantry to insist that we attempt to re-create Elizabethan staging (which would mean, for example, that plays would be done by daylight, and that boys would play the female parts), but it is only common sense to insist that the plays be presented as written, and that the stage designer yield to the author.

The last play in this volume was not written for the Elizabethan stage or for any other, but for the theater of the mind. Still, it belongs in a collection that includes English Renaissance drama. In 1642, the year that the Puritans forced King Charles I to accept the status of a limited monarch, an ordinance of the Lords and Commons declared:

> Whereas the distressed estate of Ireland, steeped in her own blood, and the distracted estate of England, threatened with a cloud of blood by a civil war, call for all possible means to appease and avert the wrath of God appearing in these judgments, . . . and whereas public sports do not well agree with public calamities, nor public stage-plays with the seasons of humiliation, this being an exercise of sad and pious solemnity, and the other being spectacles of, too commonly expressing lascivious mirth and levity. It is therefore thought fit, and ordained by the Lords and Commons in this Parliament assembled, that while these sad causes and set times of humiliation do continue, public stage-plays shall cease and be foreborne.

The theaters did not reopen until 1660, when the monarchy was restored; and the drama they then presented was of a different sort, intended primarily for a courtly circle. Milton's *Samson Agonistes* (1671), though chronologically belonging with the new drama and therefore in the second volume of *The Genius of the English Theater,* is printed here because Milton is essentially a man of the Renaissance who happened to live on into the "dissolute days" (*Samson Agonistes,* line 772) of the Restoration.

# Part One

❧

# THE PLAYS

❧❧❧

## Anonymous:
## *ABRAHAM AND ISAAC*

The story of Abraham and Isaac, set forth in Genesis 22, was dramatized in several medieval English plays. Each of the extant craft cycles (see p. 13) contains such a play, and in addition there are a Cornish version and the so-called Brome version, named for Brome Manor, in Suffolk, where the manuscript was preserved. The Brome version, printed here, and widely acknowledged as the best, is not part of a cycle; perhaps it was the sole survivor of a lost cycle, perhaps it was performed separately on some appropriate occasion. Nothing is known of the staging, though one may conjecture that when God spoke, He spoke from "above," i.e., from some sort of scaffolding above the other players. Perhaps "yon mount" (line 123) to which Abraham and Isaac go was represented by an altar at one side of the playing-area. Their journey (three days, according to Genesis) must have been represented merely by a walk across the playing area, at most by a circuitous walk. If this sounds naïve, one should remember that Shakespeare was satisfied with a similar representation of a trip: to get to Capulet's house, Romeo and his friends "march about the stage."

The popularity of plays about Abraham and Isaac was due not only to the dramatic potentialities of the story, but also to the fact that for centuries the story had been interpreted as a "figure" of God the Father's sacrifice of the Son. Figural interpretation held that the happenings recorded in the Old Testament were not merely historical but also prophetic of happenings in the New. The Church Fathers developed such interpretations in detail, but they did not invent the practice. Jesus saw in Jonah an anticipation of His descent into the realm of the dead: "For as Jonas was three days and three nights in the whale's belly; so shall the Son of man be three days and three nights in the heart of the earth" (Matthew 12:40). The New Testament several times associates Isaac with Christ, and the Church Fathers had little difficulty in finding resemblances. Isaac carrying the wood on his back was an anticipation of Christ carrying the Cross; the ram caught in the briers (see line 324), sacrificed as a substitute for Isaac, anticipated Christ crowned with thorns.

To understand a work of art, T. S. Eliot has said, "comes to the same thing as to enjoy it for the right reasons." *Abraham and Isaac* is a religious play, and one should take it for what it is. There is little point in admiring it only for its realistic details. Though it does have realistic details (e.g., Isaac's delight that the sheep will die for him), the play's merit is not merely that it holds the mirror up to nature and catches the minutiae of human behavior, but that it presents an image of what Christian behavior should be. In this play about a father who draws his sword against his own son we are near and yet far from tragedy. There is irony here—Abraham wonders what kind of a sacrifice would best please God, Isaac wonders where the beast is that Abraham will sacrifice—but on the whole there are not the "purposes mistook" (to quote Horatio's description of the happenings in *Hamlet*) that are associated with tragedy. Abraham fully understands what is expected of him and he fully intends to do it. Forced to decide between loyalty to God and loyalty to family, he decides for God, as the pious man must do:

> I am full sorry, son, thy blood for to spill,
> But truly, my child, I may not choose.

When the time comes to sacrifice Isaac, Abraham hesitates briefly, but then resolves to strike—and fortunately, an angel catches his arm. Abraham is scarcely a tragic figure, chiefly because the blow is prevented and the story ends happily, but also because his intention is—from his and the audience's point of view—unquestionably right. Nor is Isaac tragic. His utter innocence and his weakness mark him as pathetic, a victim free from guilt and complicity. The tragic figure is in some measure, however mysteriously, sensed to be at least the partial cause of his own destruction. For the pathetic figure, suffering comes from without, and is undeserved and largely unresisted.

*Abraham and Isaac* is basically a joyous story, setting forth the piety of a man and the mercy of his God. Like the Crucifixion, which is transfused by the joy of the Resurrection, like the craft cycles, which conclude with the salvation of the faithful, and like Dante's *Commedia*, which was so-called because it includes a vision of heaven, *Abraham and Isaac* passes through sorrow but concludes joyously. The Christian view of life goes beyond suffering, or bypasses tragedy, robbing death of its sting and moving to a happy ending. It is significant that a "doctor" speaks the epilogue. Perhaps he is a doctor of theology, but his title is quite possibly derived from the folk plays (see p. 10), which dramatized the death (winter) and rebirth (spring) of the year. In these primitive plays a doctor brings the dead protagonist back to life. Whatever the exact nature of the doctor who speaks the epilogue to *Abraham and Isaac*, his final words, moving from the pain and apparent death of Jesus to the joy of "heaven bliss," assert the renewal of life that is at the heart of Christian belief.

## A Note on the Text

The Brome *Abraham and Isaac* is found in a manuscript of about 1470. The play was probably composed earlier, perhaps as early as the late fourteenth century. Nothing is known of the author or authors. In the edition given below, the spelling has been modernized but the words are otherwise unchanged. The closeness of this edition to the original may be seen by comparing its first stanza with the following:

> Fader of heuyn omnipotent,
> With all my hart to the I call.
> Thow hast goffe me both lond and rent;
> And my lyvelod thow hast me sent.
> I thanke the heyly ever-more of all.

# *ABRAHAM AND ISAAC*

## *Characters*

GOD
ABRAHAM
ISAAC
ANGEL
DOCTOR

*Abraham.*    Father of heaven omnipotent,
    With all my heart to thee I call.
    Thou hast gave me both land and rent,[a]
    And my livelihood thou hast me sent.
    I thank thee highly evermore of all.

    First of the earth thou madest Adam,
    And Eve also to be his wife;
    All other creatures of them two came.
    And now thou hast grant to me, Abraham,
    Here in this land to lead my life.          10

    In my age thou hast granted me this,
    That this young child with me shall wone.[b]
    I love nothing so much, iwis,[c]
    Except thine own self, dear Father of bliss,
    As Isaac here, my own sweet son.

    I have divers children mo,[d]
    The which I love not half so well;
    This fair sweet child he cheers me so
    In every place where that I go,
    That no disease [e] here may I feel.          20

    And therefore, Father of heaven, I thee pray
    For his health and also for his grace;
    Now, Lord, keep him both night and day,
    That never disease nor no fray [f]
    Come to my child in no place.

    Now come on, Isaac, my own sweet child;
    Go we home and take our rest.
*Isaac.*    Abraham, mine own father so mild,
    To follow you I am full prest,[g]
    Both early and late.          30
*Abraham.*    Come on, sweet child. I love thee best
    Of all the children that ever I begat.

*[They walk to another place.]* *

[a] income   [b] dwell   [c] indeed   [d] more   [e] discomfort   [f] harm   [g] ready

* Stage directions not in brackets appeared in original texts. Those in brackets were added by later editors.

*God.*    Mine angel, fast hie [h] thee thy way,
    And onto middle-earth anon thou go;
    Abraham's heart now will I assay,
    Whether that he be steadfast or no.

    Say I commanded him for to take
    Isaac, his young son, that he loves so well,
    And with his blood sacrifice he make,
    If any of my friendship he will feel.          40

    Show him the way onto the hill
    Where that his sacrifice shall be.
    I shall assay, now, his good will,
    Whether he loveth better his child or me.
    All men shall take example by him
    My commandments how they shall keep.

*Abraham.*    Now, Father of heaven, that formed all thing,
    My prayers I make to thee again,
    For this day my tender-offering [i]
    Here must I give to thee, certain.          50
    Ah, Lord God, almighty King,
    What manner beast will make thee most fain? [j]
    If I had thereof very knowing, [k]
    It should be done with all my main,
    Full soon anon.
    To do thy pleasing on a hill,
    Verily it is my will,
    Dear Father, God in Trinity.

[Angel *enters.*]

*Angel.*    Abraham, Abraham, will thou rest?
    Our Lord commandeth thee for to take          60
    Isaac, thy young son that thou lovest best,
    And with his blood sacrifice that thou make.

    Into the Land of Vision thou go,
    And offer thy child unto thy Lord;
    I shall thee lead and show also.
    Unto God's hest, [l] Abraham, accord,
    And follow me upon this green.

*Abraham.*    Welcome to me be my Lord's sand, [m]

[h] hurry   [i] burnt-offering   [j] pleased   [k] true   knowledge   [l] command
[m] messenger

And his hest I will not withstand.
Yet Isaac, my young son in land,[n]       70
A full dear child to me have been.

I had liefer,[o] if God had be pleased,
For to a for-bore [p] all the good [q] that I have,
Than Isaac my son should a be diseased,
So God in heaven my soul mot[r] save!

I loved never thing so much in earth,
And now I must the child go kill.
Ah, Lord God, my conscience is strongly stirred.
And yet, my dear Lord, I am sore afeard
To grudge anything against your will.       80

I love my child as my life;
But yet I love my God much more.
For though my heart would make any strife,
Yet will I not spare for child nor wife,
But do after my Lord's lore.[s]

Though I love my son never so well,
Yet smite off his head soon I shall.
Ah, Father of heaven, to thee I kneel;
An hard death my son shall feel
For to honor thee, Lord, withal.       90

*Angel.*    Abraham, Abraham, this is well said.
And all these commandments look that thou keep.
But in thy heart be nothing dismayed.    [*Exit.*]
*Abraham.*    Nay, nay, forsooth, I hold me well paid
To please my God to the best that I have.
For though my heart be heavily set
To see the blood of my own dear son,
Yet for all this I will not let,[t]
But Isaac, my son, I will go fet,[u]
And come as fast as ever we can.       100

Now, Isaac, my own son dear,
Where art thou, child? Speak to me.
*Isaac.*    My father, sweet father, I am here,
And make my prayers to the Trinity.

*Abraham.*    Rise up, my child, and fast come hither,

---

[n] on earth   [o] rather   [p] have lost   [q] possessions   [r] may   [s] teaching
[t] stop  [u] fetch

My gentle bairn <sup>v</sup> that art so wise,
For we two, child, must go together
And unto my Lord make sacrifice.

*Isaac.*   I am full ready, my father, lo!
   Even at your hands I stand right here;                    110
   And whatsoever ye bid me do,
   It shall be done with glad cheer,
   Full well and fine.
*Abraham.*   Ah, Isaac, my own son so dear,
   God's blessing I give thee, and mine.

   Hold this faggot upon thy back
   And here myself fire shall bring.
*Isaac.*   Father, all this here will I pack;
   I am full fain to do your bidding.
*Abraham.* [*Aside.*]   Ah, Lord of heaven, my hands I     120
      wring,
   This child's words all to-wound <sup>w</sup> my heart.

   Now, Isaac, son, go we our way
   Onto yon mount, with all our main.
*Isaac.*   Go we, my dear father, as fast as I may;
   To follow you I am full fain,
   Although I be slender.
*Abraham.* [*Aside.*]   Ah, Lord, my heart breaketh in
      twain,
   This child's words, they be so tender.

[*They reach the mount.*]

   Ah, Isaac, son, anon lay it down;
   No longer upon thy back it hold,                          130
   For I must make ready bon <sup>x</sup>
   To honor my Lord God as I should.

*Isaac.*   Lo, my dear father, there it is.
   To cheer you always I draw me near.
   But, father, I marvel sore of this,
   Why that ye make this heavy cheer.<sup>y</sup>

   And also, father, evermore dread I:
   Where is your quick <sup>z</sup> beast that ye should kill?
   Both fire and wood we have ready,
   But quick beast have we none on this hill.               140

<sup>v</sup> child   <sup>w</sup> shatter   <sup>x</sup> quickly   <sup>y</sup> look   <sup>z</sup> alive

A quick beast, I wot <sup>a</sup> well, must be dead <sup>b</sup>
  Your sacrifice for to make.
*Abraham.* Dread thee nought, my child, I thee rede,<sup>c</sup>
  Our Lord will send me unto this stead <sup>d</sup>
  Some manner a beast for to take,
  Through his sweet sand.
*Isaac.* Yea, father, but my heart beginneth to quake
  To see that sharp sword in your hand.

  Why bear ye your sword drawn so?
  Of your count'nance I have much wonder.                150
*Abraham.* [*Aside.*] Ah, Father of heaven, so I am woe.
  This child here breaks my heart asunder.

*Isaac.* Tell me, my dear father, ere that ye cease,
  Bear ye your sword drawn for me?
*Abraham.* Ah, Isaac sweet son, peace, peace.
  For, iwis, thou break my heart in three.

*Isaac.* Now truly, somewhat, father, ye think,<sup>e</sup>
  That ye mourn thus more and more.
*Abraham.* [*Aside.*] Ah, Lord of heaven, thy grace let
    sink,
  For my heart was never half so sore.                  160

*Isaac.* I pray you, father, that ye will let me that wit,<sup>f</sup>
  Whether shall I have any harm or no.
*Abraham.* Iwis, sweet son, I may not tell thee yet,
  My heart is now so full of woe.

*Isaac.* Dear father, I pray you, hide it not from me,
  But some of your thought that ye tell me.
*Abraham.* Ah, Isaac, Isaac, I must kill thee!
*Isaac.* Kill me, father? Alas, what have I done?

  If I have trespassed against you aught,
  With a yard <sup>g</sup> ye may make me full mild;        170
  And with your sharp sword kill me nought,
  For, iwis, father, I am but a child.

*Abraham.* I am full sorry, son, thy blood for to spill,
  But truly, my child, I may not choose.
*Isaac.* Now I would to God my mother were here on this
    hill.
  She would kneel for me on both her knees

<sup>a</sup> know  <sup>b</sup> killed  <sup>c</sup> advise  <sup>d</sup> place  <sup>e</sup> i.e., you have something on your mind, father  <sup>f</sup> know  <sup>g</sup> rod

To save my life.
And sithin [h] that my mother is not here,
I pray you, father, change your cheer,
And kill me not with your knife.                          180

*Abraham.*   Forsooth, son, but if [i] I thee kill
I should grieve God right sore, I dread.
It is his commandment, and also his will,
That I should do this same deed.

He commanded me, son, for certain,
To make my sacrifice with thy blood.
*Isaac.*   And is it God's will that I should be slain?
*Abraham.*   Yea, truly, Isaac, my son so good;
And therefore my hands I wring.

*Isaac.*   Now, father, against my Lord's will            190
I will never grudge, loud nor still.
He might a sent me a better destiny
If it had a been his pleasure.

*Abraham.*   Forsooth, son, but if I did this deed,
Grievously displeased our Lord will be.
*Isaac.*   Nay, nay, father, God forbid
That ever ye should grieve him for me.

Ye have other children, one or two,
The which ye should love well by kind. [j]
I pray you, father, make ye no woe;                       200
For, be I once dead, and from you go,
I shall be soon out of your mind.

Therefore do our Lord's bidding,
And when I am dead, then pray for me.
But, good father, tell ye my mother nothing;
Say that I am in another country dwelling.
*Abraham.*   Ah, Isaac, Isaac, blessed mot thou be.

My heart beginneth strongly to rise,
To see the blood of thy blessed body.
*Isaac.*   Father, since it may be no other wise          210
Let it pass over as well as I.

But, father, ere I go unto my death,

[h] since   [i] unless   [j] by nature

I pray you bless me with your hand.
[*He kneels.*]
*Abraham.*    Now, Isaac, with all my breath
   My blessing I give thee upon this land,
   And God's also thereto, iwis.
   Isaac, Isaac, son, up thou stand,
   Thy fair sweet mouth that I may kiss.

*Isaac.*    Now farewell, my own father so fine;
   And greet well my mother on earth.       220
   But I pray you, father, to hide my eyne,[k]
   That I see not the stroke of your sharp sword,
   That my flesh shall defile.
*Abraham.*    Son, thy words make me to weep full sore;
   Now, my dear son Isaac, speak no more.
*Isaac.*    Ah, my own dear father, wherefore?
   We shall speak together here but awhile.

   And sithin that I must needs be dead,
   Yet, my dear father, to you I pray,
   Smite but few strokes at my head,       230
   And make an end as soon as ye may,
   And tarry not too long.
*Abraham.*    Thy meek words, child, make me affray;
   So, "Welaway!" may be my song,

   Except all only God's will.[1]
   Ah, Isaac, my own sweet child,
   Yet kiss me again upon this hill.
   In all this world is none so mild.

*Isaac.*    Now truly, father, all this tarrying
   It doth my heart but harm;       240
   I pray you, father, make an ending.
*Abraham.*    Come up, sweet son, unto my arm.

   I must bind thy hands two,
   Although thou be never so mild.
*Isaac.*    Ah, mercy, father, why should ye do so?
*Abraham.*    That thou shouldst not let,[m] my child.

*Isaac.*    Nay, iwis, father, I will not let you.
   Do on, for me, your will;
   And on the purpose that ye have set you,

---

[k] eyes    [1] i.e., my song is "Alas" except by God's will    [m] hinder

For God's love keep it for thee still.                    250

I am full sorry this day to die,
But yet I keep [n] not my God to grieve.
Do on your list for me hardly; [o]
My fair sweet father, I give you leave.

But, father, I pray you evermore,
Tell ye my mother no deal; [p]
If she wost [q] it, she would weep full sore,
For iwis, father, she loveth me full well.
God's blessing mot she have.

Now farewell, my mother so sweet.                    260
We two be like no more to meet.
*Abraham.*    Ah, Isaac, Isaac, son, thou makest me to
        greet,[r]
And with thy words thou distemperest me.

*Isaac.*    Iwis, sweet father, I am sorry to grieve you.
I cry you mercy of that I have done,
And of all trespass that ever I did move you.
Now, dear father, forgive me that I have done.
God of heaven be with me.

*Abraham.*    Ah, dear child, leave off thy moans;
In all thy life thou grieved me never once.                    270
Now blessed be thou, body and bones,
That ever thou were bred and born.
Thou hast be to me child full good.
But iwis, child, though I mourn never so fast,
Yet must I needs here at the last
In this place shed all thy blood.

Therefore, my dear son, here shall thou lie.
[*Places* Isaac *on the altar.*]
Unto my work I must me stead.[s]
Iwis I had as lief myself to die,
If God will be pleased with my deed,                    280
And mine own body for to offer.
*Isaac.*    Ah, mercy, father, mourn ye no more.
Your weeping maketh my heart sore,
As my own death that I shall suffer.

Your kerch,[t] father, about my eyes ye wind.

---

[n] desire   [o] boldly do what you will with me   [p] bit   [q] knew   [r] cry out
[s] set myself   [t] kerchief

*Abraham.*    So I shall, my sweetest child on earth.
*Isaac.*    Now yet, good father, have this in mind,
   And smite me not often with your sharp sword,
   But hastily that it be sped.[u]

*Here* Abraham *laid a cloth on* Isaac's *face, thus saying:*

*Abraham.*    Now farewell, my child, so full of grace.          290
*Isaac.*    Ah, father, father, turn downward my face
   For of your sharp sword I am ever adread.

*Abraham.* [*Aside.*]    To do this deed I am full sorry,
   But, Lord, thine hest I will not withstand.
*Isaac.*    Ah, Father of heaven, to thee I cry;
   Lord, receive me into thy hand.

*Abraham.* [*Aside.*]    Lo, now is the time come, certain,
   That my sword in his neck shall bite.
   Ah, Lord, my heart riseth thereagain; [v]
   I may not find it in my heart to smite;          300
   My heart will not now thereto.
   Yet fain I would work my Lord's will.
   But this young innocent lieth so still,
   I may not find it in my heart him to kill.
   Oh, Father of heaven, what shall I do?

*Isaac.*    Ah, mercy, father, why tarry ye so,
   And let me lie thus long on this heath?
   Now I would to God the stroke were do.[w]
   Father, I pray you heartily, short me of my woe,
   And let me not look after my death.          310

*Abraham.*    Now, heart, why wouldest not thou break in
    three?
   Yet shall thou not make me to my God unmild.[x]
   I will no longer let for thee,
   For that my God aggrieved would be.
   Now hold [y] the stroke, my own dear child.

*Here* Abraham *drew his stroke and the* Angel *took the
   sword in his hand suddenly.*

*Angel.*    I am an angel, thou mayst see blithe,[z]
   That from heaven to thee is sent.

[u] quickly done    [v] against it    [w] done    [x] ungracious    [y] receive    [z] gladly

Our Lord thank thee an hundred sithe [a]
For the keeping of his commandment.

He knoweth thy will, and also thy heart,                    320
That thou dreadest [b] him above all thing;
And some of thy heaviness for to depart
A fair ram yonder I gan [c] bring;
He standeth tied, lo, among the briers.
Now, Abraham, amend thy mood,
For Isaac, thy young son that here is
This day shall not shed his blood.

Go, make thy sacrifice with yon ram.
Now farewell, blessed Abraham,
For unto heaven I go now home;                              330
The way is full gain. [d]
Take up thy son so free. [e]                    [*Exit.*]

*Abraham.*    Ah, Lord, I thank thee of thy great grace,
    Now am I yeyed in divers wise. [f]
    Arise up, Isaac, my dear son, arise;
    Arise up, sweet child, and come to me.

*Isaac.*    Ah, mercy, father, why smite ye not?
    Ah, smite on, father, once with your knife.
*Abraham.*    Peace, my sweet son, and take no thought,
    For our Lord of heaven hath grant thy life         340
    By his angel now,

    That thou shalt not die this day, son, truly.
*Isaac.*    Ah, father, full glad then were I—
    Iwis, father, I say, iwis—
    If this tale were true.
*Abraham.*    An hundred times, my son fair of hue,
    For joy thy mouth now will I kiss.

*Isaac.*    Ah, my dear father, Abraham,
    Will not God be wroth that we do thus?
*Abraham.*    No, no, hardily, my sweet son,             350
    For yon same ram he hath us sent
    Hither down to us.

    Yon beast shall die here in thy stead,
    In the worship of our Lord alone.

[a] times  [b] reverest  [c] did  [d] direct  [e] noble  [f] eased  (i.e., comforted)
greatly

Go, fetch him hither, my child, indeed.
*Isaac.*   Father, I will go hent [g] him by the head,
   And bring yon beast with me anon.

[Isaac *goes to the sheep*.]

   Ah, sheep, sheep, blessed mot thou be,
   That ever thou were sent down hither.
   Thou shall this day die for me          360
   In the worship of the Holy Trinity.
   Now come fast and go we together
   To my Father of heaven.
   Though thou be never so gentle and good,
   Yet had I liefer thou sheddest thy blood,
   Iwis, sheep, than I.

[*He returns to* Abraham.]

   Lo, father, I have brought here full smart [h]
   This gentle sheep, and him to you I give.
   But, Lord God, I thank thee with all my heart,
   For I am glad that I shall live,        370
   And kiss once my dear mother.
*Abraham.*   Now be right merry, my sweet child,
   For this quick beast, that is so mild,
   Here I shall present before all other.

*Isaac.*   And I will fast begin to blow;
   This fire shall burn a full good speed.
   But, father, while I stoop down low,
   Ye will not kill me with your sword, I trow? [i]
*Abraham.*   No, hardily, sweet son, have no dread;
   My mourning is past.        380
*Isaac.*   Yea, but I would that sword were in a gled, [j]
   For, iwis, father, it make me full ill aghast.

*Here* Abraham *made his offering, kneeling and saying thus:*

*Abraham.*   Now, Lord God of heaven in Trinity,
   Almighty God omnipotent,
   My offering I make in the worship of thee,
   And with this quick beast I thee present.
   Lord, receive thou mine intent,
   As [thou] art God and ground of our grace.

[g] seize  [h] quickly  [i] know  [j] fire

*God.*    Abraham, Abraham, well mot thou speed,[k]
   And Isaac, thy young son thee by.           390
   Truly, Abraham, for this deed
   I shall multiply your bothers [l] seed
   As thick as stars be in the sky,
   Both more and less;
   And as thick as gravel in the sea,
   So thick multiplied your seed shall be.
   This grant I you for your goodness.

   Of you shall come fruit great [won],[m]
   And ever be in bliss without end,
   For ye dread [n] me as God alone         400
   And keep my commandments every one;
   My blessing I give, wheresoever ye wend.

*Abraham.*    Lo, Isaac, my son, how think ye
   By this work that we have wrought?
   Full glad and blithe we may be.
   Against the will of God that we grudged nought,
   Upon this fair heath.
*Isaac.*    Ah, father, I thank our Lord every dell,[o]
   That my wit served me so well
   For to dread God more than my death.     410

*Abraham.*    Why, dearworthy son, were thou adread?
   Hardily, child, tell me thy lore.[p]
*Isaac.*    Yea, by my faith, father, now have I red,[q]
   I was never so afraid before
   As I have been at yon hill.
   But, by my faith, father, I swear
   I will nevermore come there
   But it be against my will.

*Abraham.*    Yea, come on with me, my own sweet son,
   And homeward fast now let us gone.     420
*Isaac.*    By my faith, father, thereto I grant;
   I had never so good will to go home,
   And to speak with my dear mother.
*Abraham.*    Ah, Lord of heaven, I thank thee,
   For now may I lead home with me
   Isaac, my young son so free,
   The gentlest child above all other,
   This may I well avow.

---

   [k] well may you prosper   [l] both your   [m] number   [n] because you revere
[o] part   [p] thought   [q] now that I have thought

Now go we forth, my blessed son.
*Isaac.*    I grant, father, and let us gon;                    430
   For, by my troth, were I at home,
   I would never go out under that form.[r]
   I pray God give us grace everymo,
   And all those that we be holding to.[s]          [*Exeunt.*]


[*Enter* Doctor.]


*Doctor.*    Lo, sovereigns and sirs, now have we showed
   This solemn story to great and small.
   It is good learning to learned and lewd,[t]
   And the wisest of us all,
   Withouten any berring.[u]
   For this story showeth you [here]                    440
   How we should keep, to our power,
   God's commandments without grudging.


Trow ye, sirs, and God sent an angel
And commanded you [your child be slain],
By your troth, is there any of you
That either would grudge or strive thereagain?[v]
How think ye now, sirs, thereby?


I trow there be three or four or mo.
And these women, that weep so sorrowfully
When that their children die them fro,[w]                    450
As nature will and kind,[x]
It is but folly, I may well avow,
To grudge against God or to grieve you,
For ye shall never see him mischieved,[y] well I know,
By land nor water, have this in mind;


And grudge not against our Lord God
In wealth or woe, whether [z] that he you send,
Though ye be never so hard bestead;
For when he will, he may it amend,
His commandments truly if ye keep with good heart,                    460
As this story hath now showed you beforn,
And faithfully serve him while ye be quart,[a]
That ye may please God both even and morn.
Now Jesu, that weareth the crown of thorn,
Bring us all to heaven bliss.


[r] condition?   [s] are beholden to   [t] ignorant   [u] barring   [v] against
[w] from   [x] as is nature's way   [y] harmed   [z] whichever   [a] safe

# Anonymous:

# *The Second Shepherds' Play*

The second chapter of the Gospel according to Luke includes this passage (6-16):

And so it was, that, while they were there, the days were accomplished that she should be delivered.

And she brought forth her firstborn son, and wrapped him in swaddling clothes, and laid him in a manger; because there was no room for them in the inn.

And there were in the same country shepherds abiding in the field, keeping watch over their flock by night.

And, lo, the angel of the Lord came upon them, and the glory of the Lord shone round about them: and they were sore afraid.

And the angel said unto them, Fear not: for, behold, I bring you good tidings of great joy, which shall be to all people.

For unto you is born this day in the city of David a Savior, which is Christ the Lord.

And this shall be a sign unto you; Ye shall find the babe wrapped in swaddling clothes, lying in a manger.

And suddenly there was with the angel a multitude of the heavenly host praising God, and saying,

Glory to God in the highest, and on earth peace, good will toward men.

And it came to pass, as the angels were gone away from them into heaven, the shepherds said one to another, Let us now go even unto Bethlehem, and see this thing which is come to pass, which the Lord hath made known unto us.

And they came with haste, and found Mary, and Joseph, and the babe lying in a manger.

The other three gospels do not specify the presence of shepherds at the birth of Jesus, but it is not surprising that, in a country with a thriving wool industry, the shepherds would be

well represented in a dramatization of the Nativity. The growth
of medieval drama is outlined in the general introduction, but
not until one reads *The Second Shepherds' Play* (so called because in the manuscript of the thirty-two Wakefield plays it is
the second of two plays on the Nativity) can one see the freedom and yet the reverence with which the Bible was dramatized. About six-sevenths of the play can be described as a
mock nativity or a parody of the Nativity, and yet there is no
sacrilege. The assertion is not paradoxical: the saints have not
all been humorless. Among the Christian virtues is love, and
one feels that although the Wakefield Master had a sharp eye
for foibles, follies, and injustices, he had also a love for his
fellow men that enabled him to laugh good-naturedly and to
play with the holy mysteries.

The parallels between the parody and the Nativity scene are
worked out with considerable detail. Central, of course, is the
birth: in the first part there is the alleged birth of the sheep-
stealer's child; in the second there is the birth of Jesus. An-
nouncement of each birth is preceded by song, and gifts are
offered to each infant. The three innocent shepherds form a
contrast with what has been called the Unholy Trinity of Mak
the sheep-stealer, Gill the wife, and their stolen sheep, and
these three of course contrast with the angel, Mary, and the
Lamb of God. Doubtless there are corresponding contrasts in
the way in which the characters sing: Mak sings "out of tune,"
the angel sings clearly, and the good shepherds probably sing
heartily rather than villainously or angelically.

After paying homage to Jesus, the three shepherds leave,
and as they leave, concluding the play, the third suggests that
they sing. Their song is not given in the manuscript, but it must
have been a song of joy, for they have received the gospel—
the *gōdspel*, to use the Old English word meaning "good
story," "good tidings." The basic movement of the plot is from
sorrow and winter (the opening line is "Lord, but these weathers are cold! And I am ill wrapped"), through boisterous fun, to
joy and a miraculous new life. This birth of Christ, which re-
vitalizes the world, is a sort of spring; its analogue in the world
of nature is the "bob of cherries" that the First Shepherd offers.
The play thus is "comic" not only by virtue of the humor that
runs through most of it, but also by virtue of the joyous happening that it dramatizes. It is in the tradition of Dante's *Commedia*, which moves from sin to salvation, and it anticipates
Shakespeare's comedies, which move, from a shipwreck or
some such near-disaster, to reunion, marriage, and marriage
celebrations. Whether we look back to the tenth-century *Quem
Quaeritis* (see p. 11), which ended with bells joyously announc-

ing the resurrected Christ, or look forward to the comedies of
Shakespeare, we find that *The Second Shepherds' Play* is firmly
in the comic tradition.

In the first act of *As You Like It*, Rosalind, whose father
has been banished from his own dukedom, says: "O, how full
of briers is this working-day world." Her cousin replies: "They
are but burrs, cousin, thrown upon thee in holiday foolery."
The author of *The Second Shepherds' Play* clearly sees the
burrs, and has a more discerning eye for the poor man's condition than have most medieval writers. But he sees, too, the absurdity in things, and mingles his condemnations with humor.
In keeping with this genial, comic view, Mak's theft of the
sheep is punished not by the legal fifteenth-century punishment—death—but by a grotesque tossing in a canvas. In the
comic world "all's well that ends well"; if the sheep is recovered, Mak pays sufficiently by affording the others some mirth
when he is tossed. The opening wintry complaints having
yielded to the closing spirit of fun, we are ready for the final
development of the play, the move to joy suffused with reverence and awe.

## Biographical Note

Nothing is known for certain about the author of any of
the thirty-two plays thought to have been performed at
Wakefield about 1450. (They are sometimes called "the Towneley plays," because the Towneley family owned the manuscript
in which they are preserved.) In 1576 the townspeople, prohibited from representing God on the stage, abandoned the
cycle. In 1961 part of the cycle was successfully produced in
London. Five of the plays are sufficiently united by metrics,
vocabulary, social attitudes, and high quality to be attributed
to a single author customarily called the Wakefield Master,
who is sometimes thought to have had a hand in parts of other
plays in the cycle. His occasional use of Latin and his knowledge of the Bible suggest that he was a cleric.

The Wakefield Master invented a peculiar nine-line stanza:
the first four lines are long, with four stresses in each, and
rhyme not only at the ends but also—with a different rhyme—
in the middle; the fifth line is short, with one stress; the sixth,
seventh, and eighth lines have two stresses in each, and rhyme
with each other; the ninth line has two stresses, and rhymes
with the one-stress fifth line. The rhyme scheme (omitting the
internal rhymes in the first four lines) is thus *aaaabcccb*.
The complexity of the stanza sometimes drove the author to
obscure words and involuted phrases.

**A Note on the Translation**

The Middle English of the Wakefield Master presents diffi-
culties; some of his lines can be easily read when the spelling
is modernized, but some remain obscure. Therefore, not only
has the spelling of the whole been modernized, but also many
words, phrases, and lines have been translated or adapted. The
penultimate stanza provides a good idea of the clarity of the
original in some parts and its obscurity in others. Mary is speaking:

> The fader of heven, god omnypotent,
> That sett all on seven, his son has he sent.
> My name couth he neven and lyght or he went.
> I conceyvyd hym full even thrugh myght as he ment;
> And now is he borne.
> He kepe you fro wo!
> I shall pray hym so.
> Tell furth as ye go,
> And myn on this morne.

The first line causes no difficulty, and the second only a little,
in "That sett all on seven," which means "Who created all in
seven days." The third line, translated verbatim, runs: "My
name could he name and [he] alighted before he went."
(*Lyght* alludes to the Incarnation.) In the fourth line, *full
even* means "entirely," and *thrugh myght* means "by might."
The translation—or adaptation—of the third and fourth lines
tries to keep the internal rhyme (*neven, even*):

> My name did he mention; I conceived ere he went.
> I fulfilled God's intention through his might, as he meant.

The last five lines of the stanza are simple, except for *myn,*
which means "remember," "mind." The reader who wishes to
study the play in its original language will find it (with a helpful glossary) in *The Wakefield Pageants,* ed. A. C. Cawley
(Manchester University Press, 1958).

# THE SECOND SHEPHERDS' PLAY*

∾

## Characters

FIRST SHEPHERD    [Coll]
SECOND SHEPHERD  [Gib]
THIRD SHEPHERD  [Daw]
MAK    [a sheep-stealer]
HIS WIFE   [Gill]
ANGEL
MARY
CHRIST-CHILD

* Translated by the editors

*A field.*

*First Shepherd.*    Lord, but these weathers are cold! And I
       am ill wrapped.
  I am near-hand dold,ᵃ so long have I napped;
  My legs they fold, my fingers are chapped.
  It is not as I would, for I am all lapped
    In sorrow.
    In storms and tempest,
    Now in the east, now in the west,
    Woe is him has never rest
    Midday nor morrow!

  But we simple husbands ᵇ that walk on the moor,      10
  In faith we are near-hands out of the door.
  No wonder, as it stands, if we be poor,
  For the tilth of our lands lies fallow as the floor,
    As ye ken.ᶜ
    We are so lamed,
    O'ertaxed and maimed,
    We are made hand-tamed
    By these gentlery men.

  Thus they rob us our rest, our Lady them harry!
  These men that are lord-fast, they make the plough tarry.  20
  What men say is for the best, we find it contrary.
  Thus are husbands oppressed, about to miscarry
    In life.
    Thus hold they us under,
    Thus they bring us in blunder;
    It were great wonder
    If ever should we thrive.

  There shall come a swain as proud as a po; ᵈ
  He must borrow my wain, my plough also;
  Then I am full fain ᵉ to grant ere he go.      30
  Thus live we in pain, anger, and woe,
    By night, and day.
    He must have it for sure,

ᵃ nearly numb    ᵇ husbandmen, i.e., shepherds    ᶜ know    ᵈ peacock
ᵉ pleased

Though I remain poor;
I'll be pushed out of door
If I once say nay.

If he has braid on his sleeve or a badge nowadays,
Woe to him that him grieve or ever gainsays!
No complaint he'll receive, whatever his ways.
And yet may none believe one word that he says,          40
No letter.
He can make his demands
With boasts and commands,
And all because he stands
For men who are greater.

It does me good, as I walk thus by mine own,
Of this world for to talk in manner of moan.
To my sheep will I stalk, and hearken anon,[f]
And there will I halt and sit on a stone
Full soon.          50
For I trust, pardie,[g]
True men if there be,
We get more company
Ere it be noon.

[*Enter the* Second Shepherd, *who does not see the* First
    Shepherd.]

*Second Shepherd.*    Blessings upon us, what may this be-
    mean?
Why fares this world thus? Such we seldom have seen.
Lord, these weathers are spiteous, and the winds full keen,
And the frosts so hideous they water mine eyne,[h]
No lie!
Now in dry, now in wet,          60
Now in snow, now in sleet,
When my shoes freeze to my feet
It is not all easy.

But as far as I've been, or yet as I know,
We poor wedded-men suffer great woe;
We sorrow now and again; it falls oft so.
Silly Caple, our hen, both to and fro
She cackles;
But begins she to croak,

[f] soon   [g] by God   [h] eyes

To groan or to cluck,                                           70
Woe is him, our cock,
For he is in her shackles.

These men that are wed have not all their will;
When they're full hard bestead,[i] they sigh full still.
God knows they are led full hard and full ill;
In bower nor in bed they say nought theretil.[j]
This tide [k]
My part have I found,
I know my ground!
Woe is him that is bound,                                       80
For he must abide.

But now late in our lives—a marvel to me,
That I think my heart rives such wonders to see;
Whate'er destiny drives, it must so be—
Some men will have two wives, and some men three
In store;
Some are grieved that have any.
But so far ken I—
Woe is him that has many,
For he feels sore.                                              90

[*Addresses the audience.*]

But, young men, of wooing, for God who you bought,[l]
Be well ware of wedding, and think in your thought,
"Had I known" is a thing that serves us of nought.
Much constant mourning has wedding home brought,
And griefs,
With many a sharp shower;
For thou may catch in an hour
What shall savor full sour
As long as thou lives.

For, as e'er read I epistle, I have one for my dear             100
As sharp as thistle, as rough as a brier;
She is browed like a bristle, with a sour-looking cheer; [m]
Had she once wet her whistle, she could sing full clear
Her Paternoster.
She is as great as a whale,
She has a gallon of gall;
By Him that died for us all,

---

[i] oppressed   [j] thereto   [k] time   [l] redeemed   [m] face

I would I had run till I had lost her!

[*The* First Shepherd *interrupts him.*]

*First Shepherd.*    The like I never saw! Full deafly ye stand.
*Second Shepherd.*    Be the devil in thy maw, so tariand! [n]    110
Saw thou ought of Daw?
*First Shepherd.*                Yea, on pasture-land
Heard I him blaw.[o] He comes here at hand,
Not far.
Stand still.
*Second Shepherd.*    Why?
*First Shepherd.*    For he comes here, think I.
*Second Shepherd.*    He will tell us both a lie
Unless we beware.

[*Enter the* Third Shepherd, *a boy, who does not see the others.*]

*Third Shepherd.*    Christ's cross, my creed, and Saint
Nicholas!
Thereof had I need; it is worse than it was.
Whoso could take heed and let the world pass,    120
It is ever in dread and brittle as glass
And slides.
This world fared never sure,
With marvels more and more—
Now with rich, now with poor,
Nothing abides.

Never since Noah's flood were such floods seen,
Winds and rains so rude, and storms so keen—
Some stammered, some stood in fear, as I ween,[p]
Now God turn all to good! I say as I mean,    130
For, ponder:
These floods so they drown,
Both in fields and in town,
And bear all down;
And that is a wonder.

[*He sees the others.*]

We that walk in the nights, our cattle to keep,
We see sudden sights when other men sleep.

[n] for tarrying    [o] blow on his shepherd's pipe    [p] fear

Yet methinks my heart lights; I see rogues peep.
Ye are two tall wights <sup>q</sup>—I will give my sheep
A turn.                                                    140
But much ill have I meant;
As I walk on this bent,<sup>r</sup>
I may lightly repent,
My toes if I spurn.<sup>s</sup>

[*The other two advance.*]

Ah, sir, God you save, and master mine!
A drink fain would I have, and somewhat to dine.
*First Shepherd.*    Christ's curse, my knave, thou art lazy, I
    find!
*Second Shepherd.*    How the boy will rave! Wait for a time;
    You have fed.
Bad luck on your brow;                                     150
The rogue came just now,
Yet would he, I vow,
Sit down to his bread.
*Third Shepherd.*    Such servants as I, that sweats and
    swinks,<sup>t</sup>
Eats our bread full dry, a sorrow methinks.
We are oft wet and weary when master-men winks; <sup>u</sup>
Yet comes full tardy both dinners and drinks.
But truly.
Both our dame and our sire,
When we have run in the mire,                              160
They can nip at our hire,<sup>v</sup>
And pay us full slowly.

But hear my mind, master: for the bread that I break,
I shall toil thereafter—work as I take.
I shall do but little, sir, and always hold back,
For yet lay my supper never on my stomach
In fields.
Why should I complain?
With my staff I can run;
And men say, "A bargain                                    170
Little profit yields."
*First Shepherd.*    You'd be a poor lad to go a-walking
With a man that had but little for spending.
*Second Shepherd.*    Peace, boy, I said. No more jangling,
Or I shall make thee afraid, by the heaven's king!

---

<sup>q</sup> men   <sup>r</sup> heath   <sup>s</sup> perhaps: if I trip, I can easily expiate my evil
thoughts   <sup>t</sup> works   <sup>u</sup> sleeps   <sup>v</sup> reduce our wages

Thy joke—
Where are our sheep, boy?—we scorn.
*Third Shepherd.*   Sir, this same day at morn
I them left in the corn,[w]
When the dawn broke.                                     180

They have pasture good, they can not go wrong.
*First Shepherd.*   That is right. By the rood,[x] these nights
   are long!
Ere we went, how I would, that one gave us a song.
*Second Shepherd.*   So I thought as I stood, to mirth us
   among.
*Third Shepherd.*   I grant.
*First Shepherd.*   Let me sing the tenory.
*Second Shepherd.*   And I the treble so high.
*Third Shepherd.*   Then the mean falls to me.
   Let see how ye chant.

[*They sing.*]

*Then* Mak *enters with a cloak drawn over his tunic.*

*Mak.*   Now, Lord, for Thy names seven, that made both
   beast and bird,
Well more than I can mention, Thy will leaves me un-      190
   stirred.
I am all uneven; that upsets my brains.
Now would God I were in heaven, for there weep no
   bairns [y]
So still.[z]
*First Shepherd.*   Who is that pipes so poor?
*Mak.*   Would God ye knew how I were!
Lo, a man that walks on the moor,
And has not all his will.
*Second Shepherd.*   Mak, where hast thou gone? Tell us
   tiding.
*Third Shepherd.*   Is he come? Then each one take heed      200
   to his thing.

*He takes the cloak from* Mak.

*Mak.*   What! Ich [a] be a yeoman, I tell you, of the king,
The self and the same, agent of a lording,
And sich.

---

[w] wheat   [x] cross   [y] children   [z] continuously   [a] Mak here adopts a
Southern dialect, but slips back into the Northern dialect at times.

Fie on you! Go hence
Out of my presence!
I must have reverence.
Why, who be Ich?

*First Shepherd.*    Why make ye it so quaint? Mak, ye do
  wrong.

*Second Shepherd.*    Mak, play ye the saint? I think not for
  long.

*Third Shepherd.*    I think the rogue can feign, may the
  devil him hang!                                                210

*Mak.*    I shall make complaint, and make you all to
  thwang ᵇ
  At a word,
  And tell even how ye doth.

*First Shepherd.*    But, Mak, is that truth?
  Now take out that Southern tooth,
  And put in a turd!

*Second Shepherd.*    Mak, the devil in your eye! A stroke
  would I beat you.

*Third Shepherd.*    Mak, know ye not me? By God, I could
  grieve you.

*Mak.*    God save you all three! Me thought I had seen you.
  Ye are a fair company.                                         220

*First Shepherd.*                  What is it that mean you?

*Second Shepherd.*    Shrew,ᶜ peep!
  Thus late as thou goes,
  What will men suppose?
  Thou hast a good nose
  For stealing a sheep.

*Mak.*    And I am true as steel, all men state;
  But a sickness I feel that will not abate:
  My belly fares not well; it is out of estate.

*Third Shepherd.*    Seldom lies the devil dead by the gate.

*Mak.*    Therefore,                                             230
  Full sore am I and sick;
  May I stand like a stick
  If I've had a bit
  For a month and more.

*First Shepherd.*    How fares thy wife? By thy hood, what
  say you?

*Mak.*    Lies wallowing—by the rood—by the fire, lo!
  And a house full of brood. She drinks well, too;
  There's no other good that she will do!
  But she

---

ᵇ be flogged    ᶜ rogue

Eats as fast as may be,                                    240
And every year that we see
She brings forth a baby—
And, some years, two.

Were I even more prosperous and richer by some,
I were eaten out of house and even of home.
Yet is she a foul souse, if ye come near;
There is none that goes or anywhere roams
Worse than she.
Now will ye see what I proffer?
To give all in my coffer,                                  250
Tomorrow early to offer
Her head-masspenny.[d]
*Second Shepherd.*   I know so forwaked[e] is none in
    this shire;
I would sleep, if I taked less for my hire.[f]
*Third Shepherd.*   I am cold and naked, and would have a
    fire.
*First Shepherd.*   I am weary, all achèd, and run in the
    mire—
    Watch, thou.

[*Lies down.*]

*Second Shepherd.*   Nay, I will lie near by,
    For I must sleep, truly.

[*Lies down beside him.*]

*Third Shepherd.*   As good a man's son was I           260
    As any of you.

[*Lies down.*]

    But, Mak, come thou here. Between us you'll stay.
*Mak.*   Then could I stop you if evil you'd say,
    No dread.
    From my top to my toe,
    *Manus tuas commendo,*
    *Poncio Pilato;* [g]
    May Christ's cross me clear.

[d] payment for funeral mass   [e] worn out with watching   [f] even though
I accepted less wages   [g] "Into thy hands I commend, Pontius Pilate"

*Then he gets up, the shepherds still sleeping, and says:*

Now's the time for a man that lacks what he would
To stalk privily then into a fold,                        270
And nimbly to work then, and be not too bold,
For he might pay for the bargain, if it were told
At the end.
Only time now will tell;
But he needs good counsel
Who fain would fare well,
And has little to spend.

[Mak *casts a spell over them.*]

Here about you a circle, as round as a moon,
Till I have done what I will, till that it be noon,
May ye lie stone-still till that I have done;          280
And I shall say theretil a few good words soon:
A height,
Over your heads, my hand I lift.
Out go your eyes! Black out your sight!
But yet I must make better shift
If it go right.

[*The shepherds begin to snore.*]

Lord, how they sleep hard. That may ye all hear.
I was never a shepherd, but now will I lere.[h]
Though the flock be scared, yet shall I draw near.
How! Draw hitherward! Now mends our cheer         290
From sorrow;
A fat sheep, I dare say,
A good fleece, dare I lay.
Pay back when I may,
But this will I borrow.

[*He takes the sheep home.*]

How, Gill, art thou in? Get us some light.
*Wife.*   Who makes such din this time of the night?
I am set for to spin; I don't think there might
Be a penny to win; I curse them, all right!
So fares                                                   300
The housewife that has been

[h] learn

Called from her work by a din.
Thus I earn not a pin
For such small chores.
*Mak.*    Good wife, open the hatch! See'st thou not what I
  bring?
*Wife.*    I will let you draw the latch. Ah, come in, my sweet-
  ing.
*Mak.*    Thou care not a scratch of my long standing.
*Wife.*    By thy naked neck art thou like for to hang.
*Mak.*    Away!
I am worthy my meat,                                          310
For in a pinch can I get
More than they that swink and sweat
All the long day. [*Shows her the sheep.*]
Thus it fell to my lot, Gill; I had such grace.
*Wife.*    It were a foul blot to be hanged for the case.
*Mak.*    I have 'scaped, Jelott, oft as hard a place.
*Wife.*    "But so long goes the pot to the water," men says,
  "At last
Comes it home broken."
*Mak.*    Well know I the token,                              320
But let it never be spoken.
But come and help fast.


I would it were slain; I would well eat.
This twelvemonth was I not so fain of one sheep-meat.
*Wife.*    Come they ere it be slain, and hear the sheep
  bleat—
*Mak.*    Then might I be ta'en. That were a cold sweat!
·Go bar
The gate-door.
*Wife.*                              Yes, Mak,
And if they're close at thy back—
*Mak.*    Then might I get, from all the pack,               330
The devil and more.
*Wife.*    A good trick have I spied, since thou know none:
Here shall we him hide, till they be gone—
In my cradle abide. Let me alone,
And I shall lie beside in childbed, and groan.
*Mak.*    Good head!
And I shall say thou was light [1]
Of a boy-child this night.
*Wife.*    For sure was the day bright
On which I was bred!                                          340

_____
[1] delivered

This is a good guise and a fair cast;
A woman's advice helps at the last.
I fear someone spies; again go thou fast.
*Mak.*    If I'm gone when they rise, they'll blow a cold blast.
I will go sleep. [*Returns to the shepherds.*]
Still they sleep, these three men,
And I shall softly creep in,
As though I had not been
He who stole their sheep.

[*He resumes his place.*]

[*The* First *and* Second Shepherds *awake.*]

*First Shepherd.*    *Resurrex a mortruus!* ¹ Give me a hand.        350
*Judas carnas dominus!* ᵏ I can not well stand;
My foot sleeps, by Jesus, and I totter on land.
I thought that we laid us full near England.
*Second Shepherd.*    Ah, yea?
Lord, but I have slept well!
As fresh as an eel,
As light I me feel
As leaf on a tree.

[*The* Third Shepherd *awakes.*]

*Third Shepherd.*    Blessing be herein! My heart so quakes,
My heart is out of skin, hear how it shakes.        360
Who makes all this din? How my brow aches!
To the door will I spin. Hark, fellows, wake!
Four we were—
See ye ought of Mak now?
*First Shepherd.*    We were up ere thou.
*Second Shepherd.*    Man, I give God a vow,
That he did not stir.
*Third Shepherd.*    Methought he was lapped in a wolf-skin.
*First Shepherd.*    So are many wrapped now, namely
within.
*Third Shepherd.*    When we had long napped, methought
with a gin ¹        370
A fat sheep he trapped; but he made no din.
*Second Shepherd.*    Be still!
Thy dream makes thee wood; ᵐ
It is but phantom, by the rood.

---

ʲ garbled Latin: "Resurrection from the dead"  ᵏ Judas, lord of the
flesh  ¹ trap  ᵐ crazy

*First Shepherd.*     Now God turn all to good,
   If it be his will.

[*They awaken* Mak.]

*Second Shepherd.*     Rise, Mak, for shame! Thou liest right
      long.
*Mak.*   Now Christ's holy name be us among.
   What is this? For Saint Jame, I may not go strong.
   I trust I be the same. Ah, my neck has lain wrong          380
   Enough.

[*The others help him to his feet.*]

   Many thanks! Since yester-even,
   Now by Saint Steven,
   I was scared by a dream—
   That makes me full gruff.

   I thought Gill began to croak and travail full sad,
   Well-nigh at the first cock, of a young lad
   To add to our flock. Then be I never glad;
   I have more of my stock, more than ever I had.          390
   Ah, my head!
   A house full of young dolts,
   The devil cut up their throats!
   Woe is him has many colts,
   And only little bread.

   I must go home, by your leave, to Gill, as I thought.
   I pray look up my sleeve, that I steal nought:
   I am loath you to grieve, or from you take ought.
                                                    [*Leaves.*]

*Third Shepherd.*     Go forth, ill may'st thou 'chieve! Now
      would I we sought,
   This morn,
   That we had all our store.          400
*First Shepherd.*   But I will go before;
   Let us meet.
*Second Shepherd.*   Where?
*Third Shepherd.*   At the crooked thorn.   [*They go out.*]

[Mak *outside his own door.*]

*Mak.*   Undo this door! Who is here? How long shall I
      stand?

*Wife.*    Who is it that's near? Go walk in the quicksand!
*Mak.*    Ah, Gill, what cheer? It is I, Mak, your husband.
*Wife.*    Then may we see here the devil in a band,[n]
    Sir Guile.
    Lo, he comes with a roar,
    As he were chased by a boar!       440
    I may not work at my chore
    A little while.
*Mak.*    Will ye hear what fuss she makes to get her a
      glose?[o]
    And does naught but shirks, and claws her toes.
*Wife.*    Why, who wanders, who wakes? Who comes, who
      goes?
    Who brews, who bakes? Who makes us our hose?
    And then
    It is sad to behold—
    Now in hot, now in cold,
    Full woeful is the household       420
    What lacks a woman.

    What end has thou made with the shepherds, Mak?
*Mak.*    The last word that they said when I turned my back
    They would look that they had their sheep, all the pack.
    I think they will not be allayed when they their sheep
      lack,
    Pardie!
    But howso the ball fly,
    To me they will hie,
    And make a foul cry
    And shout out upon me.       430

    But thou must do it aright.
*Wife.*              I accord me theretil;
    I shall swaddle him right in my cradle.

[Gill *puts the sheep in the cradle.*]

    If it were a greater sleight, yet could I help still.
    I will lie down straight. Come wrap me.
*Mak.*             I will.

[*Covers her.*]

*Wife.*    Behind!

[n] i.e., bound up    [o] explanation

Come Coll and his mate,
They will nip us full straight.
*Mak.* But I may cry out, "Wait!"
The sheep if they find.
*Wife.* Harken well when they call; they will come anon. 440
Come and make ready all, and sing all alone;
Sing "Lullay" thou shall, for I must groan,
And cry out by the wall on Mary and John,
In pain.
Sing "Lullay" so fast
When thou hearest at last;
And if I play a false cast,
Don't trust me again.

[*The shepherds meet at the thorn tree.*]

*Third Shepherd.* Ah, Coll, good morn. Why sleepest
thou not?
*First Shepherd.* Alas, that ever was I born. We have a
foul blot— 450
Of a sheep we have been shorn.
*Third Shepherd.* The devil! Say what!
*Second Shepherd.* Who should do us that scorn? That
is a foul plot.
*First Shepherd.* Some shrew.
I have sought with my dogs
All Horbury bogs,
And of fifteen hogs ᴾ
Found all but one ewe.
*Third Shepherd.* Now trust me, if ye will—by Saint
Thomas of Kent,
Either Mak or Gill was at that assent.
*First Shepherd.* Peace, man, be still. I saw when he went. 460
Thou slanderest him ill; thou ought to repent
With speed.
*Second Shepherd.* Now as ever might thrive I,
Though I should even here die,
It were he, I'd reply,
That did that same deed.
*Third Shepherd.* Go we thither, let's tread, and run on
our feet.
I shall never eat bread, till the truth is complete.
*First Shepherd.* No drink in my head, till him I can meet.
*Second Shepherd.* I will rest in no stead till that I him 470
greet.

ᴾ young sheep

My brother,
One pledge I will plight:
Till I see him in sight,
Shall I never sleep one night
Where I do another.

[*As the shepherds approach* Mak's *cottage,* Mak's *Wife
    begins to groan, and* Mak *sings a tuneless lullaby.*]

*Third Shepherd.*    Will ye hear how they hack? ⁹ Our sire
    can croon.
*First Shepherd.*    Heard I never none crack ⁹ so clear out
    of tune.
    Call to him.
*Second Shepherd.*                Mak, undo your door soon!
*Mak.*    Who is that spake, as it were noon
    Aloft?                                                      480
    Who is that, I say?
*Third Shepherd.*    Good fellows, were it day!
*Mak.*    As much as ye can, [*Opens the door.*]
    Sirs, speak soft,

    Over a sick woman's head that is at malaise;
    I had rather be dead than she had any disease.
*Wife.*    Go elsewhere instead. I may not well wheeze;
    Each foot that ye tread makes my nose sneeze.
    Ah, me!
*First Shepherd.*    Tell us, Mak, if ye may,                   490
    How fare ye, I say?
*Mak.*    But are ye in this town today?
    Now how fare ye?

    Ye have run in the mire, and are wet yet;
    I shall make you a fire, if ye will sit.
    A nurse would I hire. Think ye on it?
    Well paid is my hire—my dream, this is it—
    In season. [*Points to the cradle.*]
    I have sons, if ye knew,
    Well more than a few;                                       500
    But we must drink as we brew,
    And that is but reason.

    Ere ye go take some food. Me think that ye sweat.
*Second Shepherd.*    Nay, neither mends our mood, drink
    nor meat.

---

⁹ split a note

*Mak.*   Why, sir, is something not good?
*Third Shepherd.*                Yea, our sheep that we get
  Were stolen as they stood. Our loss is great.
*Mak.*   Sirs, drink!
  Had I been there,
  Some should have felt it full dear.
*First Shepherd.*   Marry, some men hold that ye were,          510
  And that's what I think.
*Second Shepherd.*   Mak, some men propose that it were ye.
*Third Shepherd.*   Either ye or your spouse, so say we.
*Mak.*   Now, if ye suppose it of Gill or of me—
  Come and search our house, and then may ye see
  Who had it.
  If I any sheep got,
  Either cow or stot ʳ—
  And Gill, my wife, rose not
  And here she lies yet—          520
  As I am true in zeal, to God here I pray
  That this be the first meal that I shall eat this day.

[*Points to the cradle.*]

*First Shepherd.*   Mak, as have I weal, be careful, I say:
  "He learned early to steal who could not say nay."

[*The shepherds begin to search.*]

*Wife.*   I shake!
  Out, thieves, from our home.
  Ye come to rob us of our own.
*Mak.*   Hear ye not how she groans?
  Your hearts should break.

[*The shepherds approach the cradle.*]

*Wife.*   Off, thieves, from my son. Nigh him not there.          530
*Mak.*   Know ye how she had done, your hearts would
    have care.
  Ye do wrong, I you warn, that thus come before
  To a woman that has borne—but I say no more.
*Wife.*   Ah, my middle!
  I pray to God so mild,
  If ever I you beguiled,
  May I eat this child

ʳ heifer

That lies in this cradle.
*Mak.*   Peace, woman, for God's pain, and cry not so.
   You injure your brain, and make me great woe.                550

*Second Shepherd.*   I think our sheep be slain. What find
   ye two?
*Third Shepherd.*   Our work is in vain; we may as well go.
   But hatters! [s]
   I can find no meat,
   Salt nor sweet,
   Nothing to eat—
   But two bare platters.

   Livestock like this, tame or wild, [*Points to cradle.*]
   None, as have I bliss, has smelled so vile.
*Wife.*   No, so God me bliss, and give me joy of my child.   550
*First Shepherd.*   We have gone amiss; I hold us beguiled.
*Second Shepherd.*   We're done.
   Sir—our Lady him save—
   Is your child a knave? [t]
*Mak.*   Any lord might him have,
   This child, as his son.

   When he wakens he grips, such joy it's to see.
*Third Shepherd.*   May heirs spring from his hips, happy
   he be.
   But who were his gossips [u] so soon ready?
*Mak.*   Blessings on their lips.                                560
*First Shepherd.* [*Aside.*]   Hark now, a lie!
*Mak.*   So God them thanks,
   Parkin, and Gibbon Waller, I say,
   And gentle John Horne, in good play—
   He made us all gay—
   With his great shanks.
*Second Shepherd.*   Mak, friends will we be, for we are all
   one.
*Mak.*   We? No, I'm out for me, for help get I none.
   Farewell all three. [*Aside.*] I wish they were gone.
*Third Shepherd.*   Fair words may there be, but love is
   there none
   This year.                                                   570

[*The shepherds leave the cottage.*]

*First Shepherd.*   Gave ye the child anything?
*Second Shepherd.*   I swear not one farthing.

   [s] confound it   [t] boy   [u] godparents

*Third Shepherd.*   Quickly back will I fling;
   Abide ye me here. [*He runs back.*]

   Mak, take it to no grief if I come to thy son.
*Mak.*   Nay, thou dost me great mischief, and foul hast
      thou done.
*Third Shepherd.*   The child will it not grieve, that day-
      star one?
   Mak, with your leave, let me give your son
   But sixpence.
*Mak.*   Nay, go way! He sleeps.                                580
*Third Shepherd.*   Methinks he peeps.
*Mak.*   When he wakens he weeps.
   I pray you, go hence!

[*The others return.*]

*Third Shepherd.*   Give me leave him to kiss, and lift up the
      clout.ᵛ [*He lifts up the cover.*]
   What the devil is this? He has a long snout!
*First Shepherd.*   He is shapèd amiss. Let's not wait about.
*Second Shepherd.*   "Ill-spun weft," iwis, "aye comes foul
      out." ʷ
   A son! [*Recognizes the sheep.*]
   He is like to our sheep!
*Third Shepherd.*   How, Gib, may I peep?                        590
*First Shepherd.*   "How nature will creep
   Where it cannot run!"
*Second Shepherd.*   This was a quaint gaud and a far cast; ˣ
   It was a high fraud.
*Third Shepherd.*               Yea, sirs, was't.
   Let's burn this bawd and bind her fast.
   A false scold hangs at the last;
   So shalt thou.
   Will ye see how they swaddle
   His four feet in the middle?
   Saw I never in a cradle                                       600
   A horned lad ere now.
*Mak.*   Peace, bid I. What! Leave off your care!
   I am he that begat, and yond woman him bare.
*First Shepherd.*   How named is your brat? "Mak?" Lo,
      God, Mak's heir.
*Second Shepherd.*   Let be all that. Now God curse his
      fare,

   ᵛ cloth   ʷ "An ill-spun weft," indeed, "comes ever out foul," i.e., the
deformity of the parents appears in the offspring   ˣ a clever prank and
a sly trick

This boy.
*Wife.*    A pretty child is he
  As sits on a woman's knee;
  A dillydown, pardie,
  To give a man joy.                                      610
*Third Shepherd.*    I know him by the ear-mark; that is a
  good token.
*Mak.*    I tell you, sirs, hark!—his nose was broken.
  I was told by a clerk a spell had been spoken.
*First Shepherd.*    This is a false work; my vengeance is
  woken.
  Get weapon!
*Wife.*    He was taken by an elf,
  I saw it myself;
  When the clock struck twelve
  Was he misshapen.
*Second Shepherd.*    Ye two are most deft, but we're not    620
  misled.
*First Shepherd.*    Since they stand by their theft, let's see
  them both dead.
*Mak.*    If I trespass eft,ʸ strike off my head.
  With you will I be left.
*Third Shepherd.*            Sirs, let them dread:
  For this trespass
  We will neither curse nor fight,
  Strike nor smite;
  But hold him tight,
  And cast him in canvas.

[*They toss* Mak *in a sheet, and return to the field.*]

*First Shepherd.*    Lord, how I am sore, and ready to burst.
  Faith, I can do no more; therefore will I rest.         630
*Second Shepherd.*    As a sheep of seven score Mak
  weighed in my fist.
  For to sleep anywhere me think that I must.
*Third Shepherd.*    Now I pray you
  Lie on grass yonder.
*First Shepherd.*    On these thieves I still ponder.
*Third Shepherd.*    Wherefore should ye wonder?
  Do as I say.

[*They lie down and fall asleep.*]

*An* Angel *sings "Gloria in excelsis," and then says:*

  ʸ again

*Angel.*   Rise, herdsmen kind, for now is he born
  Who shall take from the fiend what from Adam was
      drawn;
  That warlock [z] to rend, this night is he born.          640
  God is made your friend now at this morn.
  He requests
  To Bethlehem haste
  Where lies that Grace
  In a crib low placed,
  Betwixt two beasts.

[*The* Angel *withdraws.*]

*First Shepherd.*   This was the finest voice that ever yet I
      heard.
  It is a marvel to rejoice, thus to be stirred.
*Second Shepherd.*   Of God's son so bright he spoke the
      word.
  All the wood in a light methought that he made          650
  Appear.
*Third Shepherd.*   He spoke of a bairn
  In Bethlehem born.
*First Shepherd.*   That betokens yon starn; [*Points to the
      star.*]
  Let us seek him there.
*Second Shepherd.*   Say, what was his song? Heard ye not
      how he cracked [a] it,
  Three breves to a long?
*Third Shepherd.*   Yea, marry, he hacked it:
  Was no crotchet wrong, nor nothing that lacked it.
*First Shepherd.*   For to sing us among, right as he knacked
      it,
  I can.          660
*Second Shepherd.*   Let see how ye croon!
  Can ye bark at the moon?
*Third Shepherd.*   Hold your tongues! Have done!
*First Shepherd.*   Hark after, then.

[*He sings.*]

*Second Shepherd.*   To Bethl'em he bade that we be gone;
  I am afraid that we tarry too long.

[z] devil   [a] In the next few lines the shepherds use technical musical
terms in describing the Angel's singing: *cracked*, split a note; *Three
breves to a long*, three short notes to one long one; *hacked*, split a
note; *crotchet*, a quarter note; *knacked*, trilled.

*Third Shepherd.*    Be merry and not sad—of mirth is our
     song.
   Now may we be glad and hasten in throng;
   Say not nay.
*First Shepherd.*    Go we thither quickly,         670
   Though we be wet and weary,
   To that child and that lady;
   We must never delay.

[*He begins to sing again.*]

*Second Shepherd.*    The olden prophets bid—let be your
     din—
   Isaiah and David and more than I min [b]—
   With great learning they said that in a virgin
   Should he light and lie, to atone for our sin,
   And slake it,
   Our kindred, from woe;
   Isaiah said so:                 680
   *Ecce virgo*
   *Concipiet* [c] a child that is naked.
*Third Shepherd.*    Full glad may we be, and abide that
     day
   That Glory to see, whom all things obey.
   Lord, well were me, for once and for aye,
   Might I kneel on my knee, some word for to say
   To that child.
   But the angel said
   In a crib was he laid;
   He was poorly arrayed,          690
   So meek and so mild.
*First Shepherd.*    Patriarchs that have been, and prophets
     beforn,
   They desired to have seen this child that is born.
   They are gone full clean—they were forlorn.
   We shall see him, I ween, [d] ere it be morn,
   As token.
   When I see him and feel,
   Then know I full well
   It is true as steel
   That prophets have spoken:        700
   To so poor as we are that he would appear,
   Find us, and declare by his messenger.
*Second Shepherd.*    Go we now, let us fare; the place is us
     near.

[b] remember    [c] "Behold, a virgin shall conceive" (Isaiah 7:14)
[d] know

*Third Shepherd.*    I am ready, I swear; go we with cheer
　　To that joy.
　　Lord, if thy will be—
　　We are simple all three—
　　Now grant us that we
　　May comfort thy boy.

[*They enter the stable. The* First Shepherd *kneels.*]

*First Shepherd.*    Hail, comely and clean! Hail, young        710
　　child!
　　Hail, maker, as I mean, of a maiden so mild!
　　Thou hast beaten, I ween, the warlock so wild:
　　The beguiler of men, now goes he beguiled.
　　Lo, he merries!
　　Lo, he laughs, my sweeting!
　　A welcome meeting.
　　I here give my greeting:
　　Have a bob ᵉ of cherries.

[*The* Second Shepherd *kneels.*]

*Second Shepherd.*    Hail, sovereign savior, for thou hast us
　　sought!
　　Hail, noble child, the flower, who all thing has wrought!   720
　　Hail, full of favor, that made all of nought!
　　Hail! I kneel and I cower. A bird have I brought
　　To my bairn.
　　Hail, little tiny mop! ᶠ
　　Of our creed thou art crop; ᵍ
　　I would drink of thy cup,
　　Little day-starn.

[*The* Third Shepherd *kneels.*]

*Third Shepherd.*    Hail, darling dear, full of Godhead!
　　I pray thee be near when that I have need!
　　Hail, sweet is thy cheer! My heart would bleed            730
　　To see thee sit here in so poor weed,ʰ
　　With no pennies.
　　Hail! Put forth thy hand small.
　　I bring thee but a ball:
　　Have it and play withal,
　　And go to the tennis.

　　ᵉ bunch    ᶠ moppet, babe    ᵍ head    ʰ clothing

*Mary.*   The father of heaven, God omnipotent,
  That made all in seven, his son has he sent.
  My name did he mention; I conceived ere he went.
  I fulfilled God's intention through his might, as he     740
    meant;
  And now is he born.
  He keep you from woe!
  I shall pray him so.
  Tell forth as ye go,
  And mind you this morn.


*First Shepherd.*   Farewell, lady, so fair to behold,
  With thy child on thy knee.
*Second Shepherd.*                 But he lies full cold.
  Lord, well is me. Now we go, thou behold.
*Third Shepherd.*   Forsooth, already it seems to be told
  Full oft.                                               750
*First Shepherd.*   What grace we have found.
*Second Shepherd.*   Come forth; now are we sound.
*Third Shepherd.*   To sing are we bound—
  Ring it aloft.                    [*They go out singing.*]

# Anonymous:

# *EVERYMAN*

One may as well admit at the outset that *Everyman* is an allegory; the reader would soon find out anyway. On the whole, interest in allegory, which reflected a habit of thinking deeply ingrained in the medieval and Renaissance mind, has declined since the seventeenth century developed the habit of thinking that things are not representative of other things but simply are what they are. Allegory came to be thought of as an outmoded way of thinking, or as a childish way of mystifying. Dickens, for example, has a little fun in *Bleak House* when he describes Mr. Tulkinghorn's chambers, with "its painted ceilings, where Allegory, in Roman helmet and celestial linen, sprawls among balustrades and pillars, flowers, clouds, and big-legged boys, and makes the head ache—as would seem to be Allegory's object always, more or less."

An allegory is basically a work that contains what can be called a system of equivalents: in Bunyan's *Pilgrim's Progress,* for example, Christian (the pilgrim of the title), the road, and the Heavenly City toward which he journeys are roughly equivalent to the good man, the years of one's life span, and the presence of God. Today we are so accustomed to protagonists called Tom Jones, Silas Marner, and Holden Caulfield, that we balk at Christian, Mr. Worldly Wiseman, and so on. We reject the work that explicitly guides our thinking. Yet, in a way, all good literature is at bottom allegorical, presenting items whose relationships in some degree we inevitably translate into equivalents. We read *Julius Caesar,* and find ourselves saying that Brutus, the basically honest and philosophic man, influenced by Cassius, the passionate egoist. . . . Or we say that in Hardy's *Return of the Native,* Egdon Heath is not simply the setting, but comes to stand for. . . . The novels of Dickens, too, often praised for giving a detailed picture of London life, catch life partly by presenting equivalents: the fog in *Bleak House* inevitably comes to stand for the suffocating nature of litigation. Put it this way: a good book adds up to something, and its detailed landscapes and fully rounded characters are valuable not only because they are detailed landscapes and fully rounded characters but also because they suffuse the edges of our minds with controlled suggestions of things other than themselves.

The morality plays, of which *Everyman* is the finest, overtly deal allegorically with human behavior, the conflict between virtues and vices, especially with the problem of how to live— which can be another way of saying how to die. In some the problem of how to die well is at the center, but even in these the conflict between virtues and vices is not far in the background. The plays, then, deal with the central issues of life, and their material is intensely dramatic. Some thirteen hundred years before *Everyman* was written, Tertullian exhorted Christians to turn their backs on the Roman theater (which he claimed showed only filth) and to observe real conflicts rather than imaginary ones:

> Would you have also fightings and wrestlings? Well, of these there is no lacking, and they are not of slight account. Behold unchastity overcome by chastity, perfidy slain by faithfulness, cruelty stricken by compassion, impudence thrown into the shade by modesty; there are the contests we have among us, and in these *we* win our crowns.

Much as it would have shocked Tertullian, many plays of the fifteenth and sixteenth centuries set out to present in allegory these contests and these crowns.

Part of the pleasure that allegory can afford is doubtless explained by man's delight in detecting resemblances in things different. Saint Augustine noticed this: "I feel greater pleasure in contemplating holy men, when I view them as the teeth of the Church, tearing men away from their errors. . . . It is with the greatest pleasure too that I recognize them under the figure of sheep that have been shorn." In some works the resemblances are so slight that the pleasure is largely at having solved a puzzle, at having broken past the obvious differences to the hidden similarities. But most of the memorable allegories are not puzzles, or at least were not puzzles in their day. The resemblances were easily, almost thoughtlessly, grasped; the artist's job was to make his work hold attention without baffling. The author of *Everyman* holds attention in several ways. First, he gives his characters a richness of texture, that does not distract from the basic allegory. Because Everyman is every man, he is not given, for example, a particular profession; he is not a role for a "character actor," an actor who specializes in eccentrics. Yet Everyman is not a bore. First of all, his appearance catches the spectators' attention. "Whither art

thou going/ Thus *gaily?*" asks Death. It is not fanciful to
imagine that Everyman's gait and his apparel (later he will put
on a garment of contrition, undoubtedly a less colorful habit)
suggest the worldling, who, though he be "never so gay" (in
the words of the Prologue), will be confronted at last with
Death. Everyman's reply is at first cagey ("Why askest thou?");
when Death explains that God desires a reckoning, Everyman's reply is intensely human:

> To give a reckoning longer leisure I crave;
> This blind matter troubleth my wit.

He goes on to protest that he is "unready," and (now very un-
comfortable) to imply distrust of the messenger: "I know thee
not. What messenger art thou?" When Death identifies himself, Everyman does what every man would do, but what we
had not thought he or we would do until we saw him do it; he
attempts to bribe Death:

> Yet of my good will I give thee, if thou will be kind;
> Yea, a thousand pound shalt thou have,
> And defer this matter till another day.

Similarly, Death, "thou mighty messenger," is given lines that
hold our attention. Worse than being a bogey-man, he is
businesslike. In Hamlet's words, "this fell sergeant, death,/ Is
strict in his arrest." The false friends to whom Everyman first
turns similarly have enough personality to engage our interest,
and yet they never go beyond their strictly limited functions to
become irrelevancies who can only be justified on the grounds
of intrinsic interest. Fellowship at first insists that he will not
forsake Everyman, but hearing of Everyman's plight, he re-
vises his statement:

> If thou wilt eat, and drink, and make good cheer
> Or haunt to women the lusty company,
> I would not forsake you while the day is clear.

Kindred and Cousin, similarly at first assure Everyman of
their services, but soon Cousin finds an excuse ("I have the
cramp in my toe") and Kindred offers his maid instead of himself. It was this dramatist's willingness not to attempt to rival
in his characters the complexities of human nature that caused
T. S. Eliot to praise him at the expense of his successors: "The
great vice of English drama from Kyd to Galsworthy has been
that its aim of realism was unlimited. In one play, *Everyman,*

and perhaps in that one play only, we have a drama within the limitations of art."

The details that animate a character but do not push it beyond its place in the work of art are not, of course, the only things that hold our interest. The conduct of the plot itself is equally skillful. When, for example, Everyman knows that the summons is inescapable, he turns in the wrong direction. Then, from Fellowship, Kindred, and Cousin he goes even farther afield, to Goods. Trust in mortals is unavailing, but trust in Goods is damnable. "Lay not up for yourselves treasures upon earth, where moth and rust doth corrupt, and where thieves break through and steal: But lay up for yourselves treasures in heaven, where neither moth nor rust doth corrupt, and where thieves do not break through nor steal: For where your treasure is, there will your heart be also" (Matthew 6:19-21). In despair, Everyman turns at last to Good Deeds. Like Goods (a nice touch), Good Deeds is bound up, but for a different reason. Good Deeds is pitiably weak, but Everyman's fortunes improve from this point, and he gains various friends. These friends—parts of himself—are more reliable than the earlier ones, and Everyman becomes jubilant. But again he must be disappointed: Strength, Discretion, Knowledge, and Five Wits will not pass with him through the grave. Even before Strength announces that he will "hie me from thee fast," Everyman has felt Strength's imminent departure:

> Alas, I am so faint I may not stand;
> My limbs under me doth fold.

Knowledge lasts a little longer: "I will not from hence depart/ Till I see where ye shall be come."

What we get, in short, are details and a plot that (to use Coleridge's idea) offer not surprise but expectation and then satisfaction. Elsewhere Coleridge puts it this way: "As the feeling with which we startle at a shooting star, compared with that of watching the sunrise at a pre-established moment, such and so low is surprise compared with expectation."

*Everyman* can stand on its own merits. But its importance is historical as well as intrinsic. Two other plays in this volume, *Doctor Faustus* and *Macbeth,* let the reader see what use the Renaissance made of the morality play.

## Biographical Note

The author of *Everyman* is unknown; probably he wrote the play about 1500. It was printed several times during the first

third of the sixteenth century. The stress on Good Deeds has led
some readers to conjecture that the author had a Protestant
bias, but the stress on Priesthood has led others to conjecture
a stanch Roman Catholic. The close resemblance of *Everyman*
to the Dutch play *Elckerlijk,* by Peter Dorland of Diest, has
caused some scholars to think that one play is a translation of
the other, or that both have a common source. *Everyman* has
had a considerable stage history since it was revived in 1901
by William Poel, but it is best known on the stage in the German
adaptation by Hugo von Hofmannsthal, *Jedermann* (1911),
performed annually at Salzburg since 1920, except 1937–45,
when the Nazis prohibited its production. *Elckerlijk* has been
done annually at Delft since 1950.

# *EVERYMAN*

### ❧

## *Characters*

GOD

| | |
|---|---|
| MESSENGER | KNOWLEDGE |
| DEATH | CONFESSION |
| EVERYMAN | BEAUTY |
| FELLOWSHIP | STRENGTH |
| KINDRED | DISCRETION |
| COUSIN | FIVE WITS |
| GOODS | ANGEL |
| GOOD DEEDS | DOCTOR |

*Here Beginneth a Treatise how the High Father of Heaven Sendeth Death to Summon Every Creature to Come and Give Account of their Lives in this World, and is in Manner of a Moral Play.*

[*Enter* Messenger *as a Prologue.*]

*Messenger.*   I pray you all give your audience,
    And hear this matter with reverence,
    By figure <sup>a</sup> a moral play.
    The *Summoning of Everyman* called it is,
    That of our lives and ending shows
    How transitory we be all day.
    This matter is wondrous precious,
    But the intent <sup>b</sup> of it is more gracious,
    And sweet to bear away.
    The story saith: Man, in the beginning                    10
    Look well, and take good heed to the ending,
    Be you never so gay!
    Ye think sin in the beginning full sweet,
    Which in the end causeth the soul to weep,
    When the body lieth in clay.
    Here shall you see how Fellowship and Jollity,
    Both Strength, Pleasure, and Beauty,
    Will fade from thee as flower in May;
    For ye shall hear how our Heaven King
    Calleth Everyman to a general reckoning.                  20
    Give audience, and hear what he doth say.     [*Exit.*]

God *speaketh.*

*God.*   I perceive, here in my majesty,
    How that all creatures be to me unkind,
    Living without dread in worldly prosperity.
    Of ghostly sight <sup>c</sup> the people be so blind,
    Drowned in sin, they know me not for their God.
    In worldly riches is all their mind;
    They fear not my rightwiseness,<sup>d</sup> the sharp rod.
    My law that I showed, when I for them died,
    They forget clean, and shedding of my blood red;          30

<sup>a</sup> in form   <sup>b</sup> mea**ning**   <sup>c</sup> spiritual insight   <sup>d</sup> righteousness
72

I hanged between two, it cannot be denied;
To get them life I suffered ᵉ to be dead;
I healed their feet, with thorns hurt was my head.
I could do no more than I did, truly;
And now I see the people do clean forsake me.
They use the seven deadly sins damnable,
As pride, covetise, wrath, and lechery
Now in the world be made commendable;
And thus they leave of angels, the heavenly company.
Every man liveth so after his own pleasure,                    40
And yet of their life they be nothing sure.
I see the more that I them forbear
The worse they be from year to year.
All that liveth appaireth ᶠ fast;
Therefore I will, in all the haste,
Have a reckoning of every man's person;
For, and ᵍ I leave the people thus alone
In their life and wicked tempests,
Verily they will become much worse than beasts;
For now one would by envy another up eat;                    50
Charity they do all clean forget.
I hoped well that every man
In my glory should make his mansion,
And thereto I had them all elect.
But now I see, like traitors deject,
They thank me not for the pleasure that I to them meant,
Nor yet for their being that I them have lent.
I proffered the people great multitude of mercy,
And few there be that asketh it heartily.
They be so cumbered with worldly riches                    60
That needs on them I must do justice,
On every man living, without fear.
Where art thou, Death, thou mighty messenger?

[*Enter* Death.]

*Death*.    Almighty God, I am here at your will,
     Your commandment to fulfill.
*God*.    Go thou to Everyman,
     And show him, in my name,
     A pilgrimage he must on him take,
     Which he in no wise may escape;
     And that he bring with him a sure reckoning                    70
     Without delay or any tarrying.          [God *withdraws*.]

     ᵉ allowed myself   ᶠ becomes worse   ᵍ if

*Death.*   Lord, I will in the world go run overall,[h]
 And cruelly outsearch both great and small.
 Every man will I beset that liveth beastly
 Out of God's laws, and dreadeth not folly.
 He that loveth riches I will strike with my dart,
 His sight to blind, and from heaven to depart [i]—
 Except that alms be his good friend—
 In hell for to dwell, world without end.
 Lo, yonder I see Everyman walking.     80
 Full little he thinketh on my coming;
 His mind is on fleshly lusts and his treasure,
 And great pain it shall cause him to endure
 Before the Lord, Heaven King.

[*Enter* Everyman.]

 Everyman, stand still! Whither art thou going
 Thus gaily? Hast thou thy Maker forget?
*Everyman.*   Why askest thou?
 Wouldest thou wit? [j]
*Death.*   Yea, sir; I will show you:
 In great haste I am sent to thee     90
 From God out of his majesty.
*Everyman.*   What, sent to me?
*Death.*   Yea, certainly.
 Though thou have forget him here,
 He thinketh on thee in the heavenly sphere,
 As, ere we depart, thou shalt know.
*Everyman.*   What desireth God of me?
*Death.*   That shall I show thee:
 A reckoning he will needs have
 Without any longer respite.     100
*Everyman.*   To give a reckoning longer leisure I crave;
 This blind [k] matter troubleth my wit.
*Death.*   On thee thou must take a long journey;
 Therefore thy book of count [l] with thee thou bring,
 For turn again [m] thou cannot by no way.
 And look thou be sure of thy reckoning,
 For before God thou shalt answer, and show
 Thy many bad deeds, and good but a few;
 How thou hast spent thy life, and in what wise,
 Before the chief Lord of paradise.     110
 Have ado that we were in that way,[n]
 For, wit thou well, thou shalt make none° attorney.

[h] everywhere [i] sunder [j] know [k] obscure [l] account [m] back [n] get
ready that we may be on that road ° have no

*Everyman.*    Full unready I am such reckoning to give.
　I know thee not. What messenger art thou?
*Death.*    I am Death, that no man dreadeth,[p]
　For every man I rest,[q] and no man spareth;
　For it is God's commandment
　That all to me shall be obedient.
*Everyman.*    O Death, thou comest when I had thee least
　　in mind!
　In thy power it lieth me to save;　　　　　　　　　120
　Yet of my good [r] will I give thee, if thou will be kind;
　Yea, a thousand pound shalt thou have,
　And defer this matter till another day.
*Death.*    Everyman, it may not be, by no way.
　I set not by gold, silver, nor riches,
　Ne [s] by pope, emperor, king, duke, ne princes;
　For, and I would receive gifts great,
　All the world I might get;
　But my custom is clean contrary.
　I give thee no respite. Come hence, and not tarry.　　130
*Everyman.*    Alas, shall I have no longer respite?
　I may say Death giveth no warning!
　To think on thee, it maketh my heart sick,
　For all unready is my book of reckoning.
　But twelve year and I might have abiding,
　My counting-book I would make so clear
　That my reckoning I should not need to fear.
　Wherefore, Death, I pray thee, for God's mercy,
　Spare me till I be provided of remedy.
*Death.*    Thee availeth not to cry, weep, and pray;　　140
　But haste thee lightly [t] that thou were gone that journey,
　And prove thy friends, if thou can;
　For, wit thou well, the tide [u] abideth no man,
　And in the world each living creature
　For Adam's sin must die of nature.[v]
*Everyman.*    Death, if I should this pilgrimage take,
　And my reckoning surely make,
　Show me, for [w] Saint Charity,
　Should I not come again shortly?
*Death.*    No, Everyman; and thou be once there,　　　150
　Thou mayst never more come here,
　Trust me verily.
*Everyman.*    O gracious God in the high seat celestial,
　Have mercy on me in this most need!
　Shall I have no company from this vale terrestrial

---

[p] dreads no man　[q] arrest　[r] wealth　[s] nor　[t] quickly　[u] time　[v] as a
natural thing　[w] in the name of

Of mine acquaintance, that way me to lead?
*Death.*     Yea, if any be so hardy
  That would go with thee and bear thee company.
  Hie ˣ thee that thou were gone to God's magnificence,
  Thy reckoning to give before his presence.                    160
  What, weenest ʸ thou thy life is given thee,
  And thy worldly goods also?
*Everyman.*     I had wend ᶻ so, verily.
*Death.*     Nay, nay; it was but lent thee;
  For as soon as thou art go,
  Another a while shall have it, and then go therefro,ᵃ
  Even as thou hast done.
  Everyman, thou art mad! Thou hast thy wits five,
  And here on earth will not amend thy life;
  For suddenly I do come.                                         170
*Everyman.*     O wretched caitiff,ᵇ whither shall I flee,
  That I might scape this endless sorrow?
  Now, gentle Death, spare me till tomorrow,
  That I may amend me
  With good advisement.ᶜ
*Death.*     Nay, thereto I will not consent,
  Nor no man will I respite;
  But to the heart suddenly I shall smite
  Without any advisement.
  And now out of thy sight I will me hie.                         180
  See thou make thee ready shortly,
  For thou mayst say this is the day
  That no man living may scape away.     [*Exit* Death.]
*Everyman.*     Alas, I may well weep with sighs deep!
  Now have I no manner of company
  To help me in my journey, and me to keep;
  And also my writing is full unready.
  How shall I do now for to excuse me?
  I would to God I had never be get! ᵈ
  To my soul a full great profit it had be;                      190
  For now I fear pains huge and great.
  The time passeth. Lord, help, that all wrought!
  For though I mourn it availeth nought.
  The day passeth, and is almost ago.ᵉ
  I wot ᶠ not well what for to do.
  To whom were I best my complaint to make?
  What and I to Fellowship thereof spake,
  And showed him of this sudden chance?
  For in him is all mine affiance; ᵍ

ˣ hurry   ʸ think   ᶻ thought   ᵃ from it   ᵇ base person   ᶜ notice   ᵈ been
born   ᵉ gone by   ᶠ know   ᵍ trust

We have in the world so many a day                    200
Be good friends in sport and play.
I see him yonder certainly.
I trust that he will bear me company;
Therefore to him will I speak to ease my sorrow.
Well met, good Fellowship, and good morrow!


Fellowship *speaketh.*


*Fellowship.*    Everyman, good morrow, by this day!
  Sir, why lookest thou so piteously?
  If any thing be amiss, I pray thee me say,
  That I may help to remedy.
*Everyman.*    Yea, good Fellowship, yea;                    210
  I am in great jeopardy.
*Fellowship.*    My true friend, show to me your mind;
  I will not forsake thee to my life's end
  In the way of good company.
*Everyman.*    That was well spoken, and lovingly.
*Fellowship.*    Sir, I must needs know your heaviness; [h]
  I have pity to see you in any distress.
  If any have you wronged, ye shall revenged be,
  Though I on the ground be slain for thee,
  Though that I know before that I should die.                    220
*Everyman.*    Verily, Fellowship, gramercy.[i]
*Fellowship.*    Tush! by thy thanks I set not a straw.
  Show me your grief, and say no more.
*Everyman.*    If I my heart should to you break,[j]
  And then you to turn your mind from me,
  And would not me comfort when ye hear me speak,
  Then should I ten times sorrier be.
*Fellowship.*    Sir, I say as I will do, indeed.
*Everyman.*    Then be you a good friend at need!
  I have found you true here before.                    230
*Fellowship.*    And so ye shall evermore;
  For, in faith, and thou go to hell,
  I will not forsake thee by the way.
*Everyman.*    Ye speak like a good friend; I believe you well.
  I shall deserve it, and I may.
*Fellowship.*    I speak of no deserving, by this day!
  For he that will say, and nothing do,
  Is not worthy with good company to go;
  Therefore show me the grief of your mind,
  As to your friend most loving and kind.                    240


[h] sorrow    [i] thanks    [j] open

*Everyman.*   I shall show you how it is:
   Commanded I am to go a journey—
   A long way, hard and dangerous—
   And give a strait count, without delay,
   Before the high Judge, Adonai.[k]
   Wherefore, I pray you, bear me company,
   As ye have promised, in this journey.
*Fellowship.*   That is matter indeed. Promise is duty;
   But, and I should take such a voyage on me,
   I know it well, it should be to my pain.          250
   Also it maketh me afeard, certain.
   But let us take counsel here as well as we can,
   For your words would fear [1] a strong man.
*Everyman.*   Why, ye said if I had need
   Ye would me never forsake, quick [m] ne dead,
   Though it were to hell, truly.
*Fellowship.* So I said, certainly,
   But such pleasures be set aside, the sooth [n] to say.
   And also, if we took such a journey,
   When should we come again?          260
*Everyman.*   Nay, never again, till the day of doom.
*Fellowship.*   In faith, then will not I come there!
   Who hath you these tidings brought?
*Everyman.*   Indeed, Death was with me here.
*Fellowship.*   Now, by God that all hath bought,[o]
   If Death were the messenger,
   For no man that is living today
   I will not go that loath journey—
   Not for the father that begat me!
*Everyman.*   Ye promised otherwise, pardie.[p]          270
*Fellowship.*   I wot well I said so, truly.
   And yet if thou wilt eat, and drink, and make good cheer,
   Or haunt to women the lusty company,[q]
   I would not forsake you while the day is clear,
   Trust me verily.
*Everyman.*   Yea, thereto ye would be ready!
   To go to mirth, solace, and play,
   Your mind will sooner apply,
   Than to bear me company in my long journey.
*Fellowship.*   Now, in good faith, I will not that way.          280
   But and thou will murder, or any man kill,
   In that I will help thee with a good will.
*Everyman.*   O, that is a simple advice, indeed.
   Gentle fellow, help me in my necessity!

[k] Hebrew name for God   [1] frighten   [m] alive   [n] truth   [o] redeemed
[p] by God   [q] frequent the pleasant company of women

We have loved long, and now I need;
And now, gentle Fellowship, remember me.
*Fellowship.*   Whether ye have loved me or no,
By Saint John, I will not with thee go.
*Everyman.*   Yet, I pray thee, take the labor, and do so
    much for me
To bring me forward,[r] for Saint Charity,                    290
And comfort me till I come without the town.
*Fellowship.*   Nay, and thou would give me a new gown,
I will not a foot with thee go;
But, and thou had tarried, I would not have left thee so.
And as now God speed thee in thy journey,
For from thee I will depart as fast as I may.
*Everyman.*   Whither away, Fellowship? Will you forsake
    me?
*Fellowship.*   Yea, by my fay![s] To God I betake[t] thee.
*Everyman.*   Farewell, good Fellowship; for thee my heart
    is sore.
Adieu for ever! I shall see thee no more.                     300
*Fellowship.*   In faith, Everyman, farewell now at the end,
For you I will remember that parting is mourning.
                                            [*Exit* Fellowship.]
*Everyman.*   Alack! shall we thus depart[u] indeed—
Ah, Lady, help!—without any more comfort?
Lo, Fellowship forsaketh me in my most need.
For help in this world whither shall I resort?
Fellowship here before with me would merry make,
And now little sorrow for me doth he take.
It is said, "In prosperity men friends may find,
Which in adversity be full unkind."                           310
Now whither for succor shall I flee,
Sith that[v] Fellowship hath forsaken me?
To my kinsmen I will, truly,
Praying them to help me in my necessity.
I believe that they will do so,
For "kind[w] will creep where it may not go."
I will go say,[x] for yonder I see them go.
Where be ye now, my friends and kinsmen?

[*Enter* Kindred *and* Cousin.]

*Kindred.*   Here be we now at your commandment.
Cousin, I pray you show us your intent                        320
In any wise, and do not spare.[y]

---

[r] accompany me   [s] faith   [t] commend   [u] separate   [v] since   [w] kinship,
family   [x] try   [y] hold back

*Cousin.*   Yea, Everyman, and to us declare
  If ye be disposed to go any whither;
  For, wit you well, we will live and die together.
*Kindred.*   In wealth and woe we will with you hold,
  For over his kin a man may be bold.ᶻ
*Everyman.*   Gramercy, my friends and kinsmen kind.
  Now shall I show you the grief of my mind:
  I was commanded by a messenger,
  That is a high king's chief officer;                          330
  He bade me go a pilgrimage, to my pain,
  And I know well I shall never come again;
  Also I must give a reckoning strait,
  For I have a great enemy ᵃ that hath me in wait,
  Which intendeth me for to hinder.
*Kindred.*   What account is that which ye must render?
  That would I know.
*Everyman.*   Of all my works I must show
  How I have lived and my days spent;
  Also of ill deeds that I have used ᵇ                           340
  In my time sith life was me lent;
  And of all virtues that I have refused.
  Therefore, I pray you, go thither with me
  To help to make mine account, for Saint Charity.
*Cousin.*   What, to go thither? Is that the matter?
  Nay, Everyman, I had leifer ᶜ fast ᵈ bread and water
  All this five year and more.
*Everyman.*   Alas, that ever I was bore! ᵉ
  For now shall I never be merry,
  If that you forsake me.                                        350
*Kindred.*   Ah, sir, what, ye be a merry man!
  Take good heart to you, and make no moan.
  But one thing I warn you, by Saint Anne—
  As for me, ye shall go alone.
*Everyman.*   My Cousin, will you not with me go?
*Cousin.*   No, by Our Lady! I have the cramp in my toe.
  Trust not to me, for, so God me speed,ᶠ
  I will deceive you in your most need.
*Kindred.*   It availeth not us to tice.ᵍ
  Ye shall have my maid with all my heart;                       360
  She loveth to go to feasts, there to be nice,ʰ
  And to dance, and abroad to start.ⁱ
  I will give her leave to help you in that journey,
  If that you and she may agree.
*Everyman.*   Now show me the very effect of your mind:

ᶻ a man may command his kinsmen   ᵃ i.e., the Devil   ᵇ practiced
ᶜ rather   ᵈ have nothing but   ᵉ born   ᶠ so may God cause me to prosper
ᵍ entice   ʰ wanton   ⁱ rush

Will you go with me, or abide behind?
*Kindred.*    Abide behind? Yea, that will I, and I may!
   Therefore farewell till another day.    [*Exit* Kindred.]
*Everyman.*    How should I be merry or glad?
   For fair promises men to me make,                         370
   But when I have most need they me forsake.
   I am deceived; that maketh me sad.
*Cousin.*    Cousin Everyman, farewell now,
   For verily I will not go with you.
   Also of mine own an unready reckoning
   I have to account; therefore I make tarrying.
   Now God keep thee, for now I go.    [*Exit* Cousin.]
*Everyman.*    Ah, Jesus, is all come hereto? [j]
   Lo, fair words maketh fools fain; [k]
   They promise, and nothing will do certain.             380
   My kinsmen promised me faithfully
   For to abide with me steadfastly;
   And now fast away do they flee.
   Even so Fellowship promised me.
   What friend were best me of to provide? [l]
   I lose my time here longer to abide.
   Yet in my mind a thing there is:
   All my life I have loved riches;
   If that my Good [m] now help me might,
   He would make my heart full light.                      390
   I will speak to him in this distress.
   Where art thou, my Goods and riches?
*Goods.*    [*Within.*]    Who calleth me? Everyman? What!
      hast thou haste?
   I lie here in corners, trussed and piled so high,
   And in chests I am locked so fast,
   Also sacked in bags. Thou mayst see with thine eye
   I cannot stir; in packs low I lie.
   What would ye have? Lightly me say.
*Everyman.*    Come hither, Good, in all the haste thou may,
   For of counsel I must desire thee.                       400

[*Enter* Goods.]

*Goods.*    Sir, and ye in the world have sorrow or adversity,
   That can I help you to remedy shortly.
*Everyman.*    It is another disease that grieveth me;
   In this world it is not, I tell thee so.
   I am sent for another way to go,

---

[j] to this   [k] glad   [l] to provide me with   [m] wealth

To give a strait count general
Before the highest Jupiter of all;
And all my life I have had joy and pleasure in thee,
Therefore, I pray thee, go with me;
For, peradventure, thou mayst before God Almighty          410
My reckoning help to clean and purify;
For it is said ever among [n]
That "money maketh all right that is wrong."

*Goods.*    Nay, Everyman, I sing another song.
I follow no man in such voyages;
For, and I went with thee,
Thou shouldst fare much the worse for me;
For because on me thou did set thy mind,
Thy reckoning I have made blotted and blind,
That thine account thou cannot make truly—          420
And that hast thou for the love of me.

*Everyman.*    That would grieve me full sore,
When I should come to that fearful answer.
Up, let us go thither together.

*Goods.*    Nay, not so! I am too brittle, I may not endure.
I will follow no man one foot, be ye sure.

*Everyman.*    Alas, I have thee loved, and had great pleasure
All my life-days on good and treasure.

*Goods.*    That is to thy damnation, without lesing,[o]
For my love is contrary to the love everlasting.          430
But if thou had me loved moderately during,
As to the poor to give part of me,
Then shouldst thou not in this dolor be,
Nor in this great sorrow and care.

*Everyman.*    Lo, now was I deceived ere I was ware,
And all I may wite [p] misspending of time.

*Goods.*    What, weenest thou that I am thine?

*Everyman.*    I had wend so.

*Goods.*    Nay, Everyman, I say no.
As for a while I was lent thee;          440
A season thou hast had me in prosperity.
My condition is man's soul to kill;
If I save one, a thousand I do spill.
Weenest thou that I will follow thee?
Nay, not from this world, verily.

*Everyman.*    I had wend otherwise.

*Goods.*    Therefore to thy soul Good is a thief;
For when thou art dead, this is my guise [q]—
Another to deceive in this same wise

n every now and then    o lying    p blame on    q practice

As I have done thee, and all to his soul's reprief.[r]                450
*Everyman.* O false Good, cursed may thou be,
   Thou traitor to God, that hast deceived me
   And caught me in thy snare!
*Goods.* Mary![s] thou brought thyself in care,
   Whereof I am right glad;
   I must needs laugh, I cannot be sad.
*Everyman.* Ah, Good, thou hast had long my heartly[t]
    love;
   I gave thee that which should be the Lord's above.
   But wilt thou not go with me indeed?
   I pray thee truth to say.                                  460
*Goods.* No, so God me speed!
   Therefore farewell, and have good day.   [*Exit* Goods.]
*Everyman.* O, to whom shall I make my moan
   For to go with me in that heavy journey?
   First Fellowship said he would with me gone—
   His words were very pleasant and gay,
   But afterward he left me alone.
   Then spake I to my kinsmen, all in despair,
   And also they gave me words fair—
   They lacked no fair speaking,                              470
   But all forsook me in the ending.
   Then went I to my Goods, that I loved best,
   In hope to have comfort, but there had I least;
   For my Goods sharply did me tell
   That he bringeth many into hell.
   Then of myself I was ashamed,
   And so I am worthy to be blamed.
   Thus may I well myself hate.
   Of whom shall I now counsel take?
   I think that I shall never speed                           480
   Till that I go to my Good Deed.
   But, alas, she is so weak
   That she can neither go [u] nor speak.
   Yet will I venture on her now.
   My Good Deeds, where be you?

[Good Deeds *speaks from the ground.*]

*Good Deeds.* Here I lie, cold in the ground.
   Thy sins hath me sore bound,
   That I cannot stir.
*Everyman.* O Good Deeds, I stand in fear!

---

[r] reproof   [s] by Mary (an expletive)   [t] hearty   [u] walk

*I* must you pray of counsel,                                490
  For help now should come right well.
*Good Deeds.*   Everyman, I have understanding
  That ye be summoned account to make
  Before Messias, of Jerusalem King;
  And you do by me,<sup>v</sup> that journey with you will I take.
*Everyman.*   Therefore I come to you, my moan to make.
  I pray you that ye will go with me.
*Good Deeds.*   I would full fain, but I cannot stand, verily.
*Everyman.*   Why, is there anything on you fall?
*Good Deeds.*   Yea, sir, I may thank you of <sup>w</sup> all;      500
  If ye had perfectly cheered me,
  Your book of count full ready had be.
  Look, the books of your works and deeds eke! <sup>x</sup>
  Behold how they lie under the feet
  To your soul's heaviness.
*Everyman.*   Our Lord Jesus help me!
  For one letter here I cannot see.
*Good Deeds.*   There is a blind reckoning in time of distress.
*Everyman.*   Good Deeds, I pray you help me in this need,
  Or else I am for ever damned indeed;                     510
  Therefore help me to make reckoning
  Before the Redeemer of all thing,
  That King is, and was, and ever shall.
*Good Deeds.*   Everyman, I am sorry of your fall,
  And fain would I help you, and I were able.
*Everyman.*   Good Deeds, your counsel I pray you give
    me.
*Good Deeds.*   That shall I do verily;
  Though that on my feet I may not go,
  I have a sister that shall with you also,
  Called Knowledge, which shall with you abide,            520
  To help you to make that dreadful reckoning.


[*Enter* Knowledge.]


*Knowledge.*   Everyman, I will go with thee, and be thy
    guide,
  In thy most need to go by thy side.
*Everyman.*   In good condition I am now in every thing,
  And am wholly content with this good thing,
  Thanked be God my creator.
*Good Deeds.*   And when she hath brought you there
  Where thou shalt heal thee of thy smart,<sup>y</sup>

<sup>v</sup> as I advise   <sup>w</sup> for   <sup>x</sup> also   <sup>y</sup> pain

Then go you with your reckoning and your Good Deeds
    together,
For to make you joyful at heart                                    530
Before the Blessed Trinity.
*Everyman.*    My Good Deeds, gramercy!
I am well content, certainly,
With your words sweet.
*Knowledge.*    Now go we together lovingly
To Confession, that cleansing river.
*Everyman.*    For joy I weep; I would we were there!
But, I pray you give me cognition
Where dwelleth that holy man, Confession?
*Knowledge.*    In the house of salvation:                   540
We shall find him in that place,
That shall us comfort, by God's grace.


[Knowledge *leads* Everyman *to* Confession.]

Lo, this is Confession. Kneel down and ask mercy,
For he is in good conceit ᶻ with God Almighty.
*Everyman.*    O glorious fountain, that all uncleanness doth
    clarify,
Wash from me the spots of vice unclean,
That on me no sin may be seen.
I come with Knowledge for my redemption,
Redempt with heart and full contrition;
For I am commanded a pilgrimage to take,                          550
And great accounts before God to make.
Now I pray you, Shrift,ᵃ mother of salvation,
Help my Good Deeds for my piteous exclamation.
*Confession.*    I know your sorrow well, Everyman.
Because with Knowledge ye come to me,
I will you comfort as well as I can,
And a precious jewel I will give thee,
Called penance, voider of adversity;
Therewith shall your body chastised be,
With abstinence and perseverance in God's service.               560
Here shall you receive that scourge of me,
Which is penance strong that ye must endure,
To remember thy Savior was scourged for thee
With sharp scourges, and suffered it patiently;
So must thou, ere thou scape that painful pilgrimage.
Knowledge, keep him in this voyage,
And by that time Good Deeds will be with thee.

ᶻ high esteem   ᵃ confession

But in any wise be siker [b] of mercy,
  For your time draweth fast; and [c] ye will saved be,
  Ask God mercy, and he will grant truly.                        570
  When with the scourge of penance man doth him [d] bind,
  The oil of forgiveness then shall he find.
*Everyman.*    Thanked be God for his gracious work!
  For now I will my penance begin;
  This hath rejoiced and lighted my heart,
  Though the knots be painful and hard within.
*Knowledge.*    Everyman, look your penance that ye fulfill,
  What pain that ever it to you be;
  And Knowledge shall give you counsel at will
  How your account ye shall make clearly.                        580
*Everyman.*    O eternal God, O heavenly figure,
  O way of rightwiseness, O goodly vision,
  Which descended down in a virgin pure
  Because he would every man redeem,
  Which Adam forfeited by his disobedience,
  O blessed Godhead, elect and high divine,
  Forgive my grievous offense;
  Here I cry thee mercy in this presence.
  O ghostly treasure, O ransomer and redeemer,
  Of all the world hope and conductor, [e]                       590
  Mirror of joy, and founder of mercy,
  Which enlumineth heaven and earth thereby,
  Hear my clamorous complaint, though it late be;
  Receive my prayers, unworthy of thy benignity.
  Though I be a sinner most abominable,
  Yet let my name be written in Moses' table.
  O Mary, pray to the Maker of all thing,
  Me for to help at my ending,
  And save me from the power of my enemy,
  For Death assaileth me strongly.                               600
  And, Lady, that I may by mean of thy prayer
  Of your Son's glory to be partner,
  By the means of his passion, I it crave.
  I beseech you help my soul to save.
  Knowledge, give me the scourge of penance;
  My flesh therewith shall give acquittance. [f]
  I will now begin, if God give me grace.
*Knowledge.*    Everyman, God give you time and space!
  Thus I bequeath you in the hands of our Savior.
  Now may you make your reckoning sure.                          610
*Everyman.*    In the name of the Holy Trinity,

---

[b] sure   [c] if   [d] himself   [e] guide   [f] atonement

My body sore punished shall be.
Take this, body, for the sin of the flesh! [*Scourges
    himself.*]
Also thou delightest to go gay and fresh,
And in the way of damnation thou did me bring;
Therefore suffer now strokes of punishing.
Now of penance I will wade the water clear,
To save me from purgatory, that sharp fire.

[Good Deeds *rises from the floor.*]

*Good Deeds.*   I thank God, now I can walk and go,
  And am delivered of my sickness and woe.             620
    Therefore with Everyman I will go, and not spare;
    His good works I will help him to declare.
*Knowledge.*   Now, Everyman, be merry and glad!
  Your Good Deeds cometh now; ye may not be sad.
  Now is your Good Deeds whole and sound,
  Going upright upon the ground.
*Everyman.*   My heart is light, and shall be evermore;
  Now will I smite faster than I did before.
*Good Deeds.*   Everyman, pilgrim, my special friend,
  Blessed be thou without end;                 630
  For thee is preparate [g] the eternal glory.
  Ye have me made whole and sound,
  Therefore I will bide by thee in every stound.[h]
*Everyman.*   Welcome, my Good Deeds! Now I hear thy voice,
  I weep for very sweetness of love.
*Knowledge.*   Be no more sad, but ever rejoice;
  God seeth thy living in his throne above.
  Put on this garment to thy behove,[i]
  Which is wet with your tears,
  Or else before God you may it miss,           640
  When ye to your journey's end come shall.
*Everyman.*   Gentle Knowledge, what do ye it call?
*Knowledge.*   It is a garment of sorrow;
  From pain it will you borrow;[j]
  Contrition it is,
  That getteth forgiveness;
  It pleaseth God passing well.
*Good Deeds.*   Everyman, will you wear it for your heal?
*Everyman.*   Now blessed be Jesu, Mary's Son,
  For now have I on true contrition.           650
  And let us go now without tarrying.

[g] prepared   [h] moment (i.e., in every fierce attack)   [i] benefit   [j] redeem

Good Deeds, have we clear our reckoning?
*Good Deeds.*    Yea, indeed, I have here.
*Everyman.*    Then I trust we need not fear.
　Now, friends, let us not part in twain.
*Knowledge.*    Nay, Everyman, that will we not, certain.
*Good Deeds.*    Yet must thou lead with thee
　Three persons of great might.
*Everyman.*    Who should they be?
*Good Deeds.*    Discretion and Strength they hight,[k]          660
　And thy Beauty may not abide behind.
*Knowledge.*    Also ye must call to mind
　Your Five Wits [1] as for your counselors.
*Good Deeds.*    You must have them ready at all hours.
*Everyman.*    How shall I get them hither?
*Knowledge.*    You must call them all together,
　And they will hear you incontinent.[m]
*Everyman.*    My friends, come hither and be present,
　Discretion, Strength, my Five Wits, and Beauty.

[*Enter* Beauty, Strength, Discretion, *and* Five Wits.]

*Beauty.*    Here at your will we be all ready.          670
　What will ye that we should do?
*Good Deeds.*    That ye would with Everyman go,
　And help him in his pilgrimage.
　Advise you, will ye with him or not in that voyage?
*Strength.*    We will bring him all thither,
　To his help and comfort, ye may believe me.
*Discretion.*    So will we go with him all together.
*Everyman.*    Almighty God, loved may thou be!
　I give thee laud that I have hither brought
　Strength, Discretion, Beauty, and Five Wits. Lack I          680
　　nought.
　And my Good Deeds, with Knowledge clear,
　All be in my company at my will here.
　I desire no more to [n] my business.
*Strength.*    And I, Strength, will by you stand in distress,
　Though thou would in battle fight on the ground.
*Five Wits.*    And though it were through the world round,
　We will not depart for sweet ne sour.
*Beauty.*    No more will I unto death's hour,
　Whatsoever thereof befall.
*Discretion.*    Everyman, advise you [o] first of all;          690
　Go with a good advisement and deliberation.
　We all give you virtuous monition [p]

　[k] are called    [1] senses    [m] immediately    [n] for    [o] consider the matter
[p] admonition

That all shall be well.

*Everyman.*   My friends, harken what I will tell:
  I pray God reward you in his heavenly sphere.
  Now harken, all that be here,
  For I will make my testament
  Here before you all present:
  In alms half my good I will give with my hands twain
  In the way of charity with good intent,                    700
  And the other half still shall remain
  In queth,<sup>q</sup> to be returned there <sup>r</sup> it ought to be.
  This I do in despite of the fiend of hell,
  To go quite out of his peril
  Ever after and this day.

*Knowledge.*   Everyman, harken what I say:
  Go to Priesthood, I you advise,
  And receive of him in any wise
  The holy sacrament and ointment together.
  Then shortly see ye turn again hither;                     710
  We will all abide you here.

*Five Wits.*   Yea, Everyman, hie you that ye ready were.
  There is no emperor, king, duke, ne baron,
  That of God hath commission
  As hath the least priest in the world being;<sup>s</sup>
  For of the blessed sacraments pure and benign
  He bareth the keys, and thereof hath the cure<sup>t</sup>
  For man's redemption—it is ever sure—
  Which God for our soul's medicine
  Gave us out of his heart with great pain                   720
  Here in this transitory life, for thee and me.
  The blessed sacraments seven there be:
  Baptism, confirmation, with priesthood good,
  And the sacrament of God's precious flesh and blood,
  Marriage, the holy extreme unction, and penance.
  These seven be good to have in remembrance,
  Gracious sacraments of high divinity.

*Everyman.*   Fain would I receive that holy body,
  And meekly to my ghostly <sup>u</sup> father I will go.

*Five Wits.*   Everyman, that is the best that ye can do.     730
  God will you to salvation bring,
  For priesthood exceedeth all other thing:
  To us Holy Scripture they do teach,
  And converteth man from sin heaven to reach;
  God hath to them more power given
  Than to any angel that is in heaven.

<sup>q</sup> bequest   <sup>r</sup> where   <sup>s</sup> living   <sup>t</sup> charge   <sup>u</sup> spiritual

With five words [v] he may consecrate,
God's body in flesh and blood to make,
And handleth his Maker between his hands.
The priest bindeth and unbindeth all bands,                    740
Both in earth and in heaven.
Thou ministers [w] all the sacraments seven;
Though we kissed thy feet, thou were worthy;
Thou art surgeon that cureth sin deadly;
No remedy we find under God
But all only [x] priesthood.
Everyman, God gave priests that dignity,
And setteth them in his stead among us to be.
Thus be they above angels in degree.

[*Exit* Everyman *to receive the last sacraments from the
        priest.*]

*Knowledge.*    If priests be good, it is so,[y] surely.        750
    But when Jesus hanged on the cross with great smart,
    There he gave out of his blessed heart
    The same sacrament in great torment.
    He sold them not to us, that Lord omnipotent.
    Therefore Saint Peter the apostle doth say
    That Jesu's curse hath all they
    Which God their Savior do buy or sell,
    Or they for any money do take or tell.[z]
    Sinful priests giveth the sinners example bad;
    Their children sitteth by other men's fires, I have heard;   760
    And some haunteth women's company
    With unclean life, as lusts of lechery:
    These be with sin made blind.
*Five Wits.*    I trust to God no such may we find.
    Therefore let us priesthood honor,
    And follow their doctrine for our souls' succor.
    We be their sheep, and they shepherds be,
    By whom we all be kept in surety.
    Peace, for yonder I see Everyman come,
    Which hath made true satisfaction.                           770
*Good Deeds.*    Methink it is he indeed.

[*Re-enter* Everyman.]

*Everyman.*    Now Jesu be your alder speed! [a]

[v] *Hoc est enim corpus meum* (For this is my body), from the sacrament of the Eucharist   [w] administer   [x] except   [y] i.e., "above angels in
degree"   [z] count   [a] Now may Jesus let you all prosper

I have received the sacrament for my redemption,
And then mine extreme unction.
Blessed be all they that counseled me to take it!
And now, friends, let us go without longer respite;
I thank God that ye have tarried so long.
Now set each of you on this rod [b] your hand,
And shortly follow me.
I go before there [c] I would be; God be our guide!                    780
*Strength.*    Everyman, we will not from you go
Till ye have done this voyage long.
*Discretion.*    I, Discretion, will bide by you also.
*Knowledge.*    And though this pilgrimage be never so
  strong,[d]
I will never part you fro.
*Strength.*    Everyman, I will be as sure by thee
As ever I did by Judas Maccabee.[e]

[*They go together to the grave.*]

*Everyman.*    Alas, I am so faint I may not stand;
My limbs under me doth fold.
Friends, let us not turn again to this land,                            790
Not for all the world's gold;
For into this cave must I creep
And turn to earth, and there to sleep.
*Beauty.*    What, into this grave? Alas!
*Everyman.*    Yea, there shall ye consume, more and less.[f]
*Beauty.*    And what, should I smother here?
*Everyman.*    Yea, by my faith, and never more appear.
In this world live no more we shall,
But in heaven before the highest Lord of all.
*Beauty.*    I cross out all this! Adieu, by Saint John!                 800
I take my cap in my lap, and am gone.
*Everyman.*    What, Beauty, whither will ye?
*Beauty.*    Peace, I am deaf; I look not behind me,
Not and thou wouldest give me all the gold in thy chest.
                                          [*Exit* Beauty.]
*Everyman.*    Alas, whereto may I trust?
Beauty goeth fast away from me;
She promised with me to live and die.
*Strength.*    Everyman, I will thee also forsake and deny;
Thy game liketh [g] me not at all.
*Everyman.*    Why, then, ye will forsake me all?                       810
Sweet Strength, tarry a little space.

[b] cross  [c] where  [d] hard  [e] ancient Jewish leader; see Apocrypha, I
Maccabees 3:19  [f] high and low (i.e., persons)  [g] pleases

*Strength*.    Nay, sir, by the rood of grace!
  I will hie me from thee fast,
  Though thou weep till thy heart to-brast.[h]
*Everyman*.    Ye would ever bide by me, ye said.
*Strength*.    Yea, I have you far enough conveyed.
  Ye be old enough, I understand,
  Your pilgrimage to take on hand;
  I repent me that I hither came.
*Everyman*.    Strength, you to displease I am to blame;          820
  Yet promise is debt, this ye well wot.
*Strength*.    In faith, I care not.
  Thou art but a fool to complain;
  You spend your speech and waste your brain.
  Go, thrust thee into the ground!          [*Exit* Strength.]
*Everyman*.    I had wend surer I should you have found.
  He that trusteth in his Strength
  She him deceiveth at the length.
  Both Strength and Beauty forsaketh me;
  Yet they promised me fair and lovingly.          830
*Discretion*.    Everyman, I will after Strength be gone;
  As for me, I will leave you alone.
*Everyman*.    Why, Discretion, will ye forsake me?
*Discretion*.    Yea, in faith, I will go from thee,
  For when Strength goeth before
  I follow after evermore.
*Everyman*.    Yet, I pray thee, for the love of the Trinity,
  Look in my grave once piteously.
*Discretion*.    Nay, so nigh will I not come;
  Farewell, everyone!          [*Exit* Discretion.] 840
*Everyman*.    O, all thing faileth, save God alone—
  Beauty, Strength, and Discretion;
  For when Death bloweth his blast,
  They all run from me full fast.
*Five Wits*.    Everyman, my leave now of thee I take;
  I will follow the other, for here I thee forsake.
*Everyman*.    Alas, then may I wail and weep,
  For I took you for my best friend.
*Five Wits*.    I will no longer thee keep;
  Now farewell, and there an end.          [*Exit* Five Wits.] 850
*Everyman*.    O Jesu, help! All hath forsaken me.
*Good Deeds*.    Nay, Everyman; I will bide with thee.
  I will not forsake thee indeed;
  Thou shalt find me a good friend at need.
*Everyman*.    Gramercy, Good Deeds! Now may I true
    friends see.

[h] burst to pieces

They have forsaken me, every one;
I loved them better than my Good Deeds alone.
Knowledge, will ye forsake me also?
*Knowledge.*    Yea, Everyman, when ye to Death shall go;
  But not yet, for no manner of danger.                              860
*Everyman.*    Gramercy, Knowledge, with all my heart.
*Knowledge.*    Nay, yet I will not from hence depart
  Till I see where ye shall be come.
*Everyman.*    Methink, alas, that I must be gone
  To make my reckoning and my debts pay,
  For I see my time is nigh spent away.
  Take example, all ye that this do hear or see,
  How they that I loved best do forsake me,
  Except my Good Deeds that bideth truly.
*Good Deeds.*    All earthly things is but vanity:             870
  Beauty, Strength, and Discretion do man forsake,
  Foolish friends, and kinsmen, that fair spake—
  All fleeth save Good Deeds, and that am I.
*Everyman.*    Have mercy on me, God most mighty;
  And stand by me, thou mother and maid, Holy Mary.
*Good Deeds.*    Fear not; I will speak for thee.
*Everyman.*    Here I cry God mercy.
*Good Deeds.*    Short [i] our end, and minish [j] our pain;
  Let us go and never come again.
*Everyman.*    Into thy hands, Lord, my soul I commend;     880
  Receive it, Lord, that it be not lost.
  As thou me boughtest, so me defend,
  And save me from the fiend's boast,
  That I may appear with that blessed host
  That shall be saved at the day of doom.
  *In manus tuas,* of might's most
  For ever, *commendo spiritum meum.*[k] [Everyman *and*
    Good Deeds *descend into the grave.*]
*Knowledge.*    Now hath he suffered that we all shall en-
    dure;
  The Good Deeds shall make all sure.
  Now hath he made ending.                                         890
  Methinketh that I hear angels sing,
  And make great joy and melody
  Where Everyman's soul received shall be.
*Angel.*    Come, excellent elect spouse, to Jesu!
  Here above thou shalt go
  Because of thy singular virtue.
  Now the soul is taken the body fro,

---

[i] shorten    [j] diminish    [k] "Into thy hands I commend my spirit" (Luke
23:46)

Thy reckoning is crystal clear.
Now shalt thou in to the heavenly sphere,
Unto the which all ye shall come                                    900
That liveth well before the day of doom.

                           [*Exit* Knowledge.]


*Enter* Doctor.


*Doctor.*    This moral men may have in mind.
Ye hearers, take it of worth,[1] old and young,
And forsake Pride, for he deceiveth you in the end;
And remember Beauty, Five Wits, Strength, and Discretion,
They all at the last do every man forsake,
Save [m] his Good Deeds there doth he take.
But beware, and they be small
Before God, he hath no help at all;
None excuse may be there for every man.                             910
Alas, how shall he do then?
For after death amends may no man make,
For then mercy and pity doth him forsake.
If his reckoning be not clear when he doth come,
God will say: *"Ite, maledicti, in ignem eternum."* [n]
And he that hath his account whole and sound,
High in heaven he shall be crowned;
Unto which place God bring us all thither,
That we may live body and soul together.
Thereto help the Trinity!                                           920
Amen, say ye, for Saint Charity.


*Thus Endeth this Moral Play of* Everyman.


[1] value it   [m] only   [n] "Depart from me, ye cursed, into everlasting fire"
(Matthew 25:41)

# Christopher Marlowe:

## *DOCTOR FAUSTUS*

Georg Faustus, a wandering scholar of the early Renaissance, has been fortunate in his career. Although his name has suffered by being confused with Johannes Fust, a sixteenth-century printer, and although he has been libeled (surely this wandering scholar was at worst a charlatan rather than an ally of the devil), any man whose exploits—even if only legendary—have been treated by Marlowe, Goethe, Heine, Valéry, and Mann can count himself blessed, however diabolic he is painted. Around him collected tales that had been told even in pre-Christian times of men who leagued themselves with the powers of evil, as well as tales engendered in early Christian times by the church's distrust of purely human wisdom ("Hath not God made foolish the wisdom of this world?"). Marlowe's Faustus lives in a world of both diabolic power and wisdom that is folly: he sells his soul to the devil for knowledge that is power, but his knowledge and power are as nothing in the light of God.

*Doctor Faustus,* the first great tragedy of the English Renaissance, is so steeped in the earlier drama that it can almost be said to be the last play of the English Middle Ages. Its resemblance to the morality plays is obvious. Take the basic theme, the choice of a way of life. As in *Everyman*, which dramatizes the fact that a man must choose between Goods and Good Deeds, Faustus must choose between lawful and unlawful knowledge. Though *Everyman* covers only a day, most morality plays show heroes submitting to temptation, recovering, submitting again, and so on, to their final salvation. Faustus' periodic glimpses of the right way, even after he has chosen the wrong, are clearly in this tradition. The presence in *Doctor Faustus* of the Seven Deadly Sins also marks the play's closeness to medieval drama. At the start of *Everyman*, God says that men "use the seven deadly sins damnable," and later in the play Goods (i.e., avarice) boasts that he has deceived Everyman and will go on to deceive others. But most medieval of all are the Good and Evil Angels, those counselors (along with the

Old Man, who earlier would have been called Faith or Good Counsel) standing by the side of numerous sinners in the old drama.

Faustus, however, is called Faustus rather than Everyman. His parentage is specified, as are his birthplace and alma mater. If the play is about the choice every man must make, it is also about the choice that one particular and unusual man makes. The Chorus reveals Faustus in his study, not yet the conjuror, still the scholar. The long soliloquy that follows is not simply a second prologue, in which Faustus reviews his past. In the theater each moment is *now*, and the soliloquy shows us Faustus mastering one branch of learning after another—logic, medicine, law, and theology. Dissatisfied with lawful knowledge and power, he turns his mind to forbidden arts, knowing that the consequences may be deadly:

> This night I'll conjure though I die thereof.

The line catches us, as it must have caught Marlowe's audience. There is something about it that makes us with half our minds want him to go on and conjure, not so that he will die but so that this unusual man will satisfy his hunger. For us he stands above his colleagues, dull people ("Come, let us go and inform the Rector") who have neither power nor imagination. Now the sinner has a kind of attractiveness that he lacked in medieval drama, where he was primarily a monster or a fool. He will now stir sympathy in the spectators, where his predecessors stirred fear or laughter. What we have in part is the sinner as hero, hero not only in the sense of protagonist but in the sense of admired (literally "wondered-at") person. It is impossible not to find something admirable in a man who speaks so well, whose taste is so keen and mind so insatiable.

> I'll have them fly to India for gold,
> Ransack the ocean for orient pearl.
>
> I'll have them read me strange philosophy.
>
> Have not I made blind Homer sing to me
> Of Alexander's love and Oenon's death?
> And hath not he, that built the walls of Thebes
> With ravishing sound of his melodious harp,
> Made music with my Mephostophilis?

His desires to see Vergil's tomb and to understand the planetary motions are also relevant here. At the same time, there is something ominous in Faustus' egotism. The Chorus has early warned us that Faustus was "swollen with cunning of a self-conceit." The exact meaning of "self-conceit" is debatable (probably it means "learning engendered by pride"), but "swollen" has sufficiently queasy associations to make us see Faustus as something less than admirable. Faustus himself in the first scene forces us to regard him with some distaste:

> Be a physician Faustus, heap up gold,
> And be eternized for some wondrous cure.

Between the desire to be a physician and the desire to effect a cure is the desire for gold. Similarly, his patriotism is mingled with egotism:

> I'll levy soldiers with the coin they bring
> And chase the Prince of Parma from our land
> And reign sole king of all our provinces.

Thus, however attractive Faustus may be aesthetically, morally he is reprehensible, and Marlowe never lets us forget it. This is not a play about a Renaissance man who has burst the alleged chains of medieval superstition; it is a play about a man whose desires are misdirected and whose quest for freedom entraps him in eternal slavery. Throughout, Christian words are used in secular contexts, because Faustus deifies earthly activity, but at the end of the play he sees that Hell is not a fable and that he must at his death reap the consequences of his life. Scholars have argued much about the nature of the Renaissance, and *Doctor Faustus* has sometimes been held to be a paean to Renaissance individualism, but a case can be made that it supports Etienne Gilson's belief that "the Renaissance . . . was not the Middle Ages plus man, but the Middle Ages minus God, and the tragedy is that in losing God the Renaissance was losing man himself."

Faustus' confusion—which will ultimately cost him eternal salvation—of the heavenly with the diabolic and the secular appears as early as the Chorus' first speech. Faustus' interest in magic is so deep that he prefers it "before his chiefest bliss." Shortly we hear Faustus assert that conjuring "cheers my soul." Throughout the play there are similar Christian expressions reminding us that Faustus is not merely expressing or fulfilling himself but is perverting the heavenly to the diabolic and the secular; two of the most notable of these expressions can be commented on here. When Faustus signs the bond with his blood, he say *"Consummatumt est"* ("It is finished"), quoting the dying words of Christ, who gave His blood so that man's soul might me saved from the damnation Faustus now willingly accepts. The second passage is in the famous address to Helen:

> Was this the face that launched a thousand ships
> And burnt the topless towers of Ilium?
> Sweet Helen, make me immortal with a kiss.
> Her lips suck forth my soul: see where it flies!
> Come Helen, come, give me my soul again.
> Here will I dwell, for heaven is in these lips
> And all is dross that is not Helena.
>
> *Enter* Old Man.

The splendor of the lines has justly engraved them in the minds of readers, but there is horror too. Like the images of Alexander and his paramour, Helen is a shadow, nothing substantial. Her kiss cannot make him "immortal," her lips cannot hold "heaven," and if her lips suck forth his soul it is to the devil that it flies. The line "all is dross that is not Helena" is wonderfully punctuated by the entrance of the Old Man. The Old Man may seem dross in comparison to Helen, but in fact he is armed with heavenly strength and he repulses the fiends as Faustus (a "miserable man") cannot.

That Faustus has chosen dross (though Marlowe shows us the strong appeal dross can make) is clear in the numerous comic scenes. For example, the Seven Deadly Sins. They had long established themselves not only as the misleaders of man but also as absurd things. The sinful life in one view is horrifying; in another, it is absurd. That a man should enjoy gorging himself or heaping up wealth is comic as well as tragic. Comedy, in fact, is filled with gluttons, misers, and other monomaniacs. The comedy, then, is integral in the play; it reminds us that although Faustus' choice can be viewed as heroic, this choice viewed more closely is absurd. Doubtless Faustus' antics in the Pope's court amused the anti-Roman Catholic audience; equally doubtless they reveal the degeneracy of Faustus' mind. Similarly, the clowns of the subplot remind us of Faustus' folly, for they travesty his conjurings. (That the comic scenes may be a collaborator's does not affect the point.) In Marlowe's source, a prose treatise, *The History of the Damnable Life, and Deserved Death of Doctor John Faustus*, the laughter is always directed at the conjuror's victims, but here it is sometimes directed at the conjuror himself. Wagner says that the clown is "so hungry that I know he would give his soul to the devil for a shoulder of mutton, though it were blood-raw." The clown insists on a somewhat better bargain: the mutton must be "well roasted, and good sauce to it." The clown, who has stolen one of Faustus' conjuring books, offers to get his friend Dick as much wine as he desires; one senses a parallel to Faustus' life of "belly-cheer":

I think my master means to die shortly;
He has made his will and given me his wealth,
His house, his goods, and store of golden plate,
Besides two thousand ducats ready coined.
And yet I wonder; for if death were nigh
He would not banquet and carouse and swill
Amongst the students as even now he doth,
Who are at supper with such belly-cheer
As Wagner ne'er beheld in all his life.

What Wagner does not understand is that Faustus now fran-
tically carouses partly because he knows his time is running
out. We see Faustus' collapse in such a speech as that in V. ii,
filled with repetitions: "Faustus . . . must remain in hell for ever.
Hell, ah hell for ever! Sweet friends, what shall become of
Faustus, being in hell for ever?" Again, Faustus' desperation is
evident in his final speech, when he unsuccessfully attempts
to hide in the earth, wildly hopes to be drawn into the clouds
as a vapor, and vainly wishes he were a beast. But Marlowe
must also make him heroic. This he has done partly by having
Faustus make a choice that, however foolish, calls forth
all his energies, partly by the magnitude of the punishment,
partly by letting him bid a dignified farewell to his friends
("Gentlemen, away, lest you perish with me! . . . Gentlemen
farewell. If I live till morning I'll visit you; if not, Faustus is
gone to hell"), partly by the second scholar's tribute at the end,
and partly by the magnificent verse he speaks—verse that Ben
Jonson characterized as "Marlowe's mighty line."

## Biographical Note

Christopher Marlowe (1564–1593) was born in Can-
terbury, the son of a cobbler. He attended Cambridge
University, and was awarded the A.B. and A.M. degrees.
At college he was suspected of Roman Catholicism and
of planning to flee to Rheims, but the Privy Council
somewhat cryptically informed the college authorities
that he had been "employed in matters touching the benefit of his country." In 1593 he was accused of atheism,
but before he was called on to answer the charge, he was
stabbed to death in a tavern controversy. His first play,
*Tamburlaine*, was written about 1587. He wrote four
other plays, as well as some nondramatic poetry, but the
dates are uncertain. A good guess for *Doctor Faustus* is
1592, partly because Marlowe's source was not a German
book but an English translation that apparently was not
published until 1592. Though tradition calls the play Marlowe's, it is widely believed he had a collaborator (especial-

ly in the comic scenes), perhaps Samuel Rowley. Neither man was Shakespeare.

## A Note on the Text

Marlowe's *Doctor Faustus* exists in two versions, one called A (1604), the other B (1616). B is some 600 lines longer, but the differences go even beyond the additional lines. Passages in one are sometimes paralleled by similar but not identical passages in the second (e.g., "Here Faustus try thy braines to gain a deity"; "Here tire my braines to get a deity"); other passages in one cannot be said to have verbally parallel lines in the other but only corresponding passages whose content of action is roughly similar. The late W. W. Greg, whose study of *Doctor Faustus* is a masterpiece of logic and learning, conjectured that A is a report from memory of a cut version, adapted to the needs of a touring company. B, Greg held, is based mostly on the author's drafts but (where these drafts were illegible) partly on A. In short, Greg believes that an editor should rely principally on B, though most modern editors reprint the shorter A with a few alterations. Greg discussed the problems at length in his *Marlowe's "Doctor Faustus"* (Oxford, 1950); his edition of *The Tragical History of the Life and Death of Doctor Faustus* (Oxford, 1950) is what he calls "a conjectural reconstruction" of the play as he supposed it was first acted. It is this text—doubtless the most scrupulously thought-out text of the play—that is here presented, by permission of the publisher. Greg explains his procedure thus:

Square brackets [ ] distinguish editorial additions: these include a few words perhaps accidentally lost, certain necessary stage directions, and the act and scene numbers that I have adopted from the edition by Dr. F. S. Boas (1932). I have enclosed within pointed brackets ⟨ ⟩ certain stage directions and sections of the text (I. iii. I, S.D.; v. i. I, S.D.; v. ii. 1–25, 85–130; v. iii), which, following a suggestion originally made by A. H. Bullen, I believe may have been rejected when the play reached authoritative shape in the prompt-book: they include the final scene, which on this view was replaced by the Epilogue. If these passages are omitted, a couple of stage directions, here added in round brackets ( ), will need to be supplied (from A). Lastly, I have enclosed in curly brackets { } one speech (v. i. 11–17), which, though it appears in both texts, almost certainly formed no part of the play as originally performed, but was subsequently inserted by the reporter of A, and from A taken over by the compiler of B.

# DOCTOR FAUSTUS

❧

## Characters

*in the order of their appearance*

CHORUS
JOHN FAUSTUS, *a doctor of divinity of Wittenberg*
WAGNER, *a student, his servant*
A GOOD ANGEL
A BAD ANGEL, *also called the Spirit*
VALDES,
CORNELIUS, } *friends of Faustus and would-be adepts*
THREE SCHOLARS, *students under Faustus*
LUCIFER, *prince of devils*
MEPHOSTOPHILIS, *a devil*
ROBIN, *called the Clown*
BEELZEBUB, *a devil*
PRIDE,
COVETOUSNESS,
ENVY,
WRATH, } *the Seven Deadly Sins*
GLUTTONY,
SLOTH,
LECHERY,
DICK, *a clown*
POPE ADRIAN
RAYMOND, *King of Hungary*
BRUNO, *rival Pope appointed by the Emperor*
THE CARDINALS OF FRANCE AND PADUA
THE ARCHBISHOP OF RHEIMS
A FRIAR
A VINTNER

MARTINO,
FREDERICK,    } *gentlemen at the Emperor's court*
BENVOLIO,
THE GERMAN EMPEROR CHARLES THE FIFTH
THE DUKE OF SAXONY
TWO SOLDIERS
A HORSE-CORSER [a]
A CARTER
THE HOSTESS OF A TAVERN
THE DUKE OF VANHOLT AND
HIS DUCHESS
AN OLD MAN
DARIUS, *King of Persia,*
ALEXANDER THE GREAT AND    } *spirits* (*mute*)
HIS PARAMOUR,
HELEN OF GREECE,

*Devils, a piper, cardinals, monks and friars, attendants,
    soldiers, two Cupids.*

*The scene is laid at Wittenberg, Rome, the Imperial
    Court (at Innsbruck), the Duchy of Vanhold
    (Anhalt), and in the country adjoining.*

*Time: The first half of the sixteenth century.*

[a] horse-trader

[PROLOGUE.] *Enter* Chorus.

Not marching in the fields of Trasimene <sup>b</sup>
Where Mars did mate<sup>c</sup> the warlike Carthagens,
Nor sporting in the dalliance of love
In courts of kings where state is overturned,
Nor in the pomp of proud audacious deeds
Intends our muse to vaunt his heavenly verse:
Only this, gentles; we must now perform
The form of Faustus' fortunes, good or bad;
And so to patient judgments we appeal,
And speak for Faustus in his infancy.                          10
Now is he born, of parents base of stock,
In Germany, within a town called Rhode;
At riper years to Wittenberg he went,
Whereas <sup>d</sup> his kinsmen chiefly brought him up.
So much he profits in divinity,<sup>e</sup>
The fruitful plot of scholarism <sup>f</sup> graced,
That shortly he was graced with doctor's name,
Excelling all whose sweet delight disputes<sup>g</sup>
In th' heavenly matters of theology;
Till, swollen with cunning of a self-conceit,<sup>h</sup>          20
His waxen wings<sup>i</sup> did mount above his reach,
And melting, heavens conspired his overthrow.
For, falling to a devilish exercise,
And glutted now with learning's golden gifts,
He surfeits upon cursèd necromancy; <sup>j</sup>
Nothing so sweet as magic is to him,
Which he prefers before his chiefest bliss.<sup>k</sup>
And this the man that in his study sits.

[*Draws the curtain to discover—*]


[I. i.] Faustus *in his study.*

*Faustus.*    Settle thy studies Faustus, and begin

<sup>b</sup> Lake Trasimene, where Carthaginians defeated Romans in 217 B.C.
<sup>c</sup> ally himself with   <sup>d</sup> where   <sup>e</sup> theology   <sup>f</sup> scholarship   <sup>g</sup> i.e., is to dispute   <sup>h</sup> intellectual pride engendered by arrogance (Greg)   <sup>i</sup> i.e., Icarus' wings, which melted as he flew too near the sun   <sup>j</sup> magic   <sup>k</sup> i.e., salvation

To sound the depth of that thou wilt profess;[1]
Having commenced, be a divine in show,
Yet level at the end [m] of every art,
And live and die in Aristotle's works.
Sweet Analytics,[n] 'tis thou hast ravished me!
*Bene disserere est finis logices.*
Is to dispute well logic's chiefest end?
Affords this art no greater miracle?
Then read no more, thou hast attained that end;                   10
A greater subject fitteth Faustus' wit.
Bid on *kai me on* [o] farewell, Galen [p] come,
Seeing *ubi desinit philosophus, ibi incipit medicus.*[q]
Be a physician Faustus, heap up gold,
And be eternized for some wondrous cure.
*Summum bonum medicinae sanitas,*
The end of physic is our body's health.
Why Faustus, hast thou not attained that end?
Is not thy common talk sound aphorisms?[r]
Are not thy bills [s] hung up as monuments,                        20
Whereby whole cities have escaped the plague
And divers desperate maladies been cured?
Yet art thou still but Faustus, and a man.
Couldst thou make men to live eternally
Or being dead raise them to life again,
Then this profession were to be esteemed.
Physic farewell! Where is Justinian?[t]
*Si una eademque res legatur duobus, alter rem, alter*
*ualorem rei, et cetera.*[u]
A petty case of paltry legacies!                                    30
*Exhereditare filium non potest pater, nisi* [v]—
Such is the subject of the Institute [w]
And universal body of the law.
This study fits a mercenary drudge
Who aims at nothing but external trash,
Too servile and illiberal for me.
When all is done, divinity is best.
Jerome's Bible,[x] Faustus, view it well.
*Stipendium peccati mors est.* Ha! *Stipendium* ... The
reward of sin is death: that's hard. *Si peccasse nega-*        40

---

[1] teach   [m] aim at the mastery   [n] Aristotle's works on logic   [o] Aristotle's "being and not being"   [p] Greek physician (A.D. 130–200?)   [q] "where the philosopher stops, there the physician begins"   [r] concise medical truths   [s] prescriptions   [t] Roman Emperor who codified Roman law   [u] "If one thing is willed to two people, one shall have the thing itself; the other its equivalent value, etc."   [v] "A father cannot disinherit his son, unless—"   [w] title of one of Justinian's treatises   [x] the Vulgate

*mus, fallimur, et nulla est in nobis ueritas.* If we say
that we have no sin, we deceive ourselves, and there's
no truth in us. Why, then belike, we must sin, and
so consequently die.
Ay, we must die an everlasting death.
What doctrine call you this? *Che serà, serà:*
What will be, shall be! Divinity, adieu!
These metaphysics ʸ of magicians
And necromantic books are heavenly;
Lines, circles, signs, letters, and characters:              50
Ay, these are those that Faustus most desires.
Oh, what a world of profit and delight,
Of power, of honor, of omnipotence
Is promised to the studious artisan!
All things that move between the quiet poles ᶻ
Shall be at my command: emperors and kings
Are but obeyed in their several provinces,
Nor can they raise the wind or rend the clouds;
But his dominion that excels in this
Stretcheth as far as doth the mind of man:                   60
A sound magician is a demi-god;
Here tire my braines ᵃ to get a deity!

                                   Wagner! *Enter* Wagner.
        Commend me to my dearest friends,
The German Valdes and Cornelius;
Request them earnestly to visit me.
*Wagner.*    I will sir.                          *Exit.*
*Faustus.*    Their conference will be a greater help to me
Than all my labors, plod I ne'er so fast.

*Enter the* Angel *and* Spirit.ᵇ

*Good Angel.*    O Faustus, lay that damnèd book aside
    And gaze not on it lest it tempt thy soul             70
    And heap God's heavy wrath upon thy head.
    Read, read the scriptures; that is blasphemy.
*Bad Angel.*    Go forward Faustus, in that famous art
    Wherein all nature's treasury is contained:
    Be thou on earth as Jove ᶜ is in the sky,
    Lord and commander of these elements.ᵈ     *Exeunt.*
*Faustus.*    How am I glutted with conceit ᵉ of this!
    Shall I make spirits fetch me what I please,
    Resolve me of all ambiguities,
    Perform what desperate ᶠ enterprise I will?             80

ʸ supernatural studies    ᶻ motionless poles of the cosmos' axis    ᵃ perhaps, "tire yourselves, my brains"    ᵇ bad angel    ᶜ God    ᵈ i.e., earth and
sky    ᵉ the thought    ᶠ difficult

I'll have them fly to India for gold,
Ransack the ocean for orient <sup>g</sup> pearl,
And search all corners of the new-found world <sup>h</sup>
For pleasant fruits and princely delicates.<sup>i</sup>
I'll have them read me strange philosophy
And tell the secrets of all foreign kings;
I'll have them wall all Germany with brass
And with swift Rhine circle fair Wittenberg;
I'll have them fill the public schools <sup>j</sup> with silk
Wherewith the students shall be bravely clad.                90
I'll levy soldiers with the coin they bring
And chase the Prince of Parma <sup>k</sup> from our land
And reign sole king of all our provinces;
Yea, stranger engines <sup>l</sup> for the brunt <sup>m</sup> of war
Than was the fiery keel at Antwerp's bridge <sup>n</sup>
I'll make my servile spirits to invent.

*Enter* Valdes *and* Cornelius.

Come German Valdes and Cornelius,
And make me blest with your sage conference.
Valdes, sweet Valdes, and Cornelius,
Know that your words have won me at the last        100
To practice magic and concealèd arts;
Yet not your words only, but mine own fantasy,<sup>o</sup>
That will receive no object,<sup>p</sup> for my head
But ruminates on necromantic skill.
Philosophy is odious and obscure,
Both law and physic are for petty wits,<sup>q</sup>
Divinity is basest of the three,
Unpleasant, harsh, contemptible, and vild;<sup>r</sup>
'Tis magic, magic, that hath ravished me.
Then, gentle friends, aid me in this attempt,        110
And I, that have with concise syllogisms
Graveled <sup>s</sup> the pastors of the German church,
And made the flowering pride <sup>t</sup> of Wittenberg
Swarm to my problems <sup>u</sup> as the infernal spirits
On sweet Musaeus <sup>v</sup> when he came to hell,
Will be as cunning as Agrippa <sup>w</sup> was,
Whose shadows <sup>x</sup> made all Europe honor him.
*Valdes.*    Faustus, these books, thy wit, and our experience

---

<sup>g</sup> precious   <sup>h</sup> i.e., America   <sup>i</sup> delicacies   <sup>j</sup> universities   <sup>k</sup> the Spanish
governor-general of the Netherlands   <sup>l</sup> machines   <sup>m</sup> assault   <sup>n</sup> a burning ship used to destroy a bridge   <sup>o</sup> imagination   <sup>p</sup> think of nothing
else   <sup>q</sup> minds   <sup>r</sup> vile   <sup>s</sup> confounded   <sup>t</sup> i.e., best students   <sup>u</sup> disputations
<sup>v</sup> legendary Greek poet   <sup>w</sup> contemporary German magician   <sup>x</sup> conjured
spirits

Shall make all nations to canonize us.
As Indian Moors [y] obey their Spanish lords, 120
So shall the spirits of every element [z]
Be always serviceable to us three:
Like lions shall they guard us when we please,
Like Almain rutters [a] with their horsemen's staves [b]
Or Lapland giants trotting by our sides;
Sometimes like women or unwedded maids,
Shadowing more beauty in their airy brows
Than in the white breasts of the queen of love.
From Venice shall they drag whole argosies,
And from America the golden fleece 130
That yearly stuffs old Philip's [c] treasury,
If learnèd Faustus will be resolute.

*Faustus.* Valdes, as resolute am I in this
As thou to live; therefore object [d] it not.

*Cornelius.* The miracles that magic will perform
Will make thee vow to study nothing else.
He that is grounded in astrology,
Enriched with tongues, well seen [e] in minerals,
Hath all the principles magic doth require;
Then doubt not Faustus, but to be renowmed 140
And more frequented for this mystery
Than heretofore the Delphian oracle.
The spirits tell me they can dry the sea
And fetch the treasure of all foreign wracks,
Yea, all the wealth that our forefathers hid
Within the massy entrails of the earth.
Then tell me Faustus, what shall we three want?

*Faustus.* Nothing Cornelius. Oh, this cheers my soul.
Come, show me some demonstrations magical,
That I may conjure in some lusty [f] grove 150
And have these joys in full possession.

*Valdes.* Then haste thee to some solitary grove,
And bear wise Bacon's [g] and Abanus' [h] works,
The Hebrew Psalter, and New Testament;
And whatsoever else is requisite
We will inform thee ere our conference cease.

*Cornelius.* Valdes, first let him know the words of art,
And then, all other ceremonies learned,
Faustus may try his cunning by himself.

*Valdes.* First I'll instruct thee in the rudiments, 160

---

[y] i.e., any dark-skinned people  [z] i.e., fire, air, earth, water  [a] German
cavalry soldiers  [b] spears  [c] Philip II of Spain  [d] oppose  [e] versed
[f] pleasant  [g] Roger Bacon (1244–1294), English philosopher  [h] perhaps
Pietro d'Abano, a thirteenth-century medical writer

And then wilt thou be perfecter than I.
*Faustus.*     Then come and dine with me, and after meat [1]
  We'll canvass every quiddity [j] thereof,
  For ere I sleep I'll try what I can do:
  This night I'll conjure though I die therefor.

                                    *Exeunt omnes.*


            [I. ii.] *Enter two scholars.*


*1 Scholar.*     I wonder what's become of Faustus, that was
  wont to make our schools ring with *sic probo*.[k]


*Enter* Wagner.


*2 Scholar.*     That shall we presently know; here comes his
  boy.
*1 Scholar.*     How now sirrah,[l] where's thy master?
*Wagner.*     God in heaven knows.
*2 Scholar.*     Why, dost not thou know then?
*Wagner.*     Yes, I know; but that follows not.
*1 Scholar.*     Go to sirrah, leave your jesting and tell us
  where he is.
*Wagner.*     That follows not by force of argument, which          10
  you, being licentiates,[m] should stand upon; therefore acknowledge your error and be attentive.
*2 Scholar.*     Then you will not tell us?
*Wagner.*     You are deceived, for I will tell you. Yet, if you
  were not dunces,[n] you would never ask me such a
  question. For is he not *corpus naturale?*[o] and is not that
  *mobile?* [p] Then wherefore should you ask me such a
  question? But that I am by nature phlegmatic, slow to
  wrath, and prone to lechery—to love, I would say—it          20
  were not for you to come within forty foot of the place
  of execution [q]—although I do not doubt but to see you
  both hanged the next sessions.[r] Thus having triumphed
  over you, I will set my countenance like a precisian [s]
  and begin to speak thus: Truly, my dear brethren,
  my master is within at dinner with Valdes and
  Cornelius, as this wine, if it could speak, would
  inform your worships: and so, the Lord bless you,

---

¹ food   ʲ essential particular   ᵏ "thus, I prove it"   ˡ form of address to
inferiors   ᵐ candidates for a higher degree   ⁿ hairsplitters   ᵒ physical
body capable of being moved   ᵖ movable   ۹ i.e., action (here, the dining
room)   ʳ court sessions   ˢ Puritan

preserve you, and keep you, my dear brethren.     *Exit.*

*1 Scholar.*   O Faustus, then I fear that which I have long
  suspected,                                                   30
  That thou art fallen into that damnèd art
  For which they two are infamous through the world.

*2 Scholar.*   Were he a stranger, not allied to me,
  The danger of his soul would make me mourn.
  But come, let us go and inform the Rector:
  It may be his grave counsel may reclaim him.

*1 Scholar.*   I fear me nothing will reclaim him now.

*2 Scholar.*   Yet let us see what we can do.     *Exeunt.*


          [*I. iii.*] ⟨*Thunder. Enter* Lucifer *and four devils*
          [*above*]: Faustus *to them with this speech.*⟩


(*Enter* Faustus *to conjure.*)


*Faustus.*   Now that the gloomy shadow of the night,
  Longing to view Orion's ᵗ drizzling looks,
  Leaps from th' antarctic world into the sky
  And dims the welkin ᵘ with her pitchy breath,
  Faustus, begin thine incantations,
  And try if devils will obey thy hest ᵛ
  Seeing thou hast prayed and sacrificed to them.
  Within this circle is Jehovah's name
  Forward and backward anagrammatized,
  The breviated ʷ names of holy saints,                        10
  Figures of every adjunct ˣ to the heavens,
  And characters of signs ʸ and erring stars,ᶻ
  By which the spirits are enforced to rise:
  Then fear not, Faustus, to be resolute
  And try the uttermost magic can perform.


*Thunder.*


  *Sint mihi dei Acherontis propitii! Valeat numen triplex
  Iehouae! Ignei, aerii, aquatici, [terreni] spiritus, saluete!
  Orientis princeps [Lucifer], Beelzebub inferni ardentis
  monarcha, et Demogorgon, propitiamus uos ut appareat
  et surgat Mephostophilis!*                                    20


ᵗ winter constellation, supposedly brings rain   ᵘ heavens   ᵛ behest
ʷ abbreviated   ˣ fixed star   ʸ i.e., of the zodiac   ᶻ comets

*Dragon [appears in the air].*

>  *Quid tu moraris? Per Lehouam, Gehennam, et con-*
>  *secratam aquam quam nunc spargo, signumque crucis*
>  *quod nunc facio, et per uota nostra, ipse nunc surgat*
>  *nobis dicatus Mephostophilis!* ª

*Enter a devil*

I charge thee to return and change thy shape,
Thou art too ugly to attend on me.
Go, and return an old Franciscan friar,
That holy shape becomes a devil best.          *Exit devil.*
I see there's virtue in my heavenly words.
Who would not be proficient in this art?                      30
How pliant is this Mephostophilis,
Full of obedience and humility!
Such is the force of magic and my spells.
Now Faustus, thou art conjurer laureate,
That canst command great Mephostophilis.
*Quin redis, Mephostophilis, fratris imagine!* ᵇ

*Enter* Mephostophilis.

*Mephostophilis.*   Now Faustus, what wouldst thou have
   me do?
*Faustus.*   I charge thee wait upon me whilst I live,
   To do whatever Faustus shall command,
   Be it to make the moon drop from her sphere          40
   Or the ocean to overwhelm the world.
*Mephostophilis.*   I am a servant to great Luciver
   And may not follow thee without his leave;
   No more than he commands must we perform.
*Faustus.*   Did not he charge thee to appear to me?
*Mephostophilis.*   No, I came hither of mine own accord.
*Faustus.*   Did not my conjuring speeches raise thee?
   Speak.
*Mephostophilis.*   That was the cause, but yet *per*
   *accidens:* ᶜ

---

ª "Be propitious to me, gods of Acheron! May the triple name of
Jehovah prevail! Spirits of fire, air, water, and earth, hail! Lucifer,
prince of the East; Beelzebub, monarch of burning hell; and Demogorgon, we propitiate you so that Mephostophilis may appear and rise!
  "Why do you delay? By Jehovah, by Gehenna, and by the holy
water which I now sprinkle, and by the sign of the cross which I now
make, and by our prayers, let Mephostophilis now arise, summoned
by us!"   ᵇ "Return, Mephostophilis, in the image of a friar!"   ᶜ incidentally

    For when we hear one rack <sup>d</sup> the name of God,
    Abjure the scriptures and his savior Christ,      50
    We fly in hope to get his glorious soul;
    Nor will we come unless he use such means
    Whereby he is in danger to be damned.
    Therefore the shortest cut for conjuring
    Is stoutly to abjure the Trinity
    And pray devoutly to the prince of hell.
*Faustus.*   So I have done, and hold this principle,
    There is no chief but only Beelzebub,
    To whom Faustus doth dedicate himself.
    This word "damnation" terrifies not me,      60
    For I confound hell in Elysium:
    My ghost <sup>e</sup> be with the old philosophers!
    But leaving these vain trifles of men's souls,
    Tell me, what is that Lucifer thy lord?
*Mephostophilis.*   Arch-regent and commander of all
    spirits.<sup>f</sup>
*Faustus.*   Was not that Lucifer an angel once?
*Mephostophilis.*   Yes Faustus, and most dearly loved of
    God.
*Faustus.*   How comes it then that he is prince of devils?
*Mephostophilis.*   Oh, by aspiring pride and insolence,
    For which God threw him from the face of heaven.      70
*Faustus.*   And what are you that live with Lucifer?
*Mephostophilis.*   Unhappy spirits that fell with Lucifer,
    Conspired against our God with Lucifer,
    And are for ever damned with Lucifer.
*Faustus.*   Where are you damned?
*Mephostophilis.*           In hell.
*Faustus.*   How comes it then that thou art out of hell?
*Mephostophilis.*   Why this is hell, nor am I out of it.
    Thinkst thou that I, who saw the face of God
    And tasted the eternal joys of heaven,
    Am not tormented with ten thousand hells      80
    In being deprived of everlasting bliss?
    O Faustus, leave these frivolous demands,
    Which strike a terror to my fainting soul.
*Faustus.*   What, is great Mephostophilis so passionate
    For being deprivèd of the joys of heaven?
    Learn thou of Faustus manly fortitude
    And scorn those joys thou never shalt possess.
    Go bear these tidings to great Lucifer:
    Seeing Faustus hath incurred eternal death

---

<sup>d</sup> torture, either by anagrams or oaths    <sup>e</sup> spirit    <sup>f</sup> i.e., devils

By desperate thoughts against Jove's deity,                    90
Say he surrenders up to him his soul
So he will spare him four and twenty years,
Letting him live in all voluptuousness,
Having thee ever to attend on me,
To give me whatsoever I shall ask,
To tell me whatsoever I demand,
To slay mine enemies and aid my friends
And always be obedient to my will.
Go, and return to mighty Lucifer,
And meet me in my study at midnight,                           100
And then resolve[g] me of thy master's mind.
*Mephostophilis.*    I will, Faustus.               *Exit.*
*Faustus.*    Had I as many souls as there be stars
I'd give them all for Mephostophilis.
By him I'll be great emperor of the world,
And make a bridge thorough[h] the moving air
To pass the ocean with a band of men;
I'll join the hills that bind the Afric shore
And make that country continent[i] to Spain,
And both contributary to my crown;                            110
The Emperor shall not live but by my leave
Nor any potentate of Germany.
Now that I have obtained what I desire
I'll live in speculation[j] of this art
Till Mephostophilis return again.                   *Exit.*


[I. iv.] *Enter* Wagner *and the* Clown[k] [Robin].


*Wagner.*    Come hither, sirrah boy.
*Clown.*    Boy! Oh, disgrace to my person! Zounds,[l] boy
    in your face! You have seen many boys with such pick-
    adevants,[m] I am sure.
*Wagner.*    Sirrah, hast thou no comings in?[n]
*Clown.*    Yes, and goings out[o] too, you may see sir.
*Wagner.*    Alas poor slave; see how poverty jests in his
    nakedness. The villain's out of service, and so hungry
    that I know he would give his soul to the devil for a
    shoulder of mutton, though it were blood-raw.          10
*Clown.*    Not so, neither; I had need to have it well
    roasted, and good sauce to it, if I pay so dear, I can tell
    you.

_____

[g] inform  [h] through  [i] joined  [j] study  [k] i.e., a comic actor  [l] God's
wounds  [m] pointed beards  [n] income  [o] (i) expenses (ii) holes in his
tattered clothing

*Wagner.* Sirrah, wilt thou be my man and wait on me? and I will make thee go like *Qui mihi discipulus.*ᵖ

*Clown.* What, in verse?

*Wagner.* No, slave, in beaten �q silk and staves-acre.ʳ

*Clown.* Staves-acre! that's good to kill vermin. Then, belike, if I serve you I shall be lousy.

*Wagner.* Why, so thou shalt be, whether thou dost it or    20
no; for sirrah, if thou dost not presently bind thyself to me for seven years, I'll turn all the lice about thee into familiars ˢ and make them tear thee in pieces.

*Clown.* Nay sir, you may save yourself a labor, for they are as familiar with me as if they paid for their meat and drink, I can tell you.

*Wagner.* Well sirrah, leave your jesting and take these guilders.ᵗ

*Clown.* Yes marry sir, and I thank you too.

*Wagner.* So, now thou art to be at an hour's warning    30
whensoever and wheresoever the devil shall fetch thee.

*Clown.* Here, take your guilders again,ᵘ I'll none of 'em.

*Wagner.* Not I, thou art pressed;ᵛ prepare thyself, for I will presently raise up two devils to carry thee away. Banio! Belcher!

*Clown.* Belcher! And Belcher come here I'll belch him. I am not afraid of a devil.

*Enter two devils, and the* Clown *runs up and down crying.*

*Wagner.* How now sir, will you serve me now?

*Clown.* Ay good Wagner, take away the devil then.

*Wagner.* Spirits, away! [*Exeunt.*] Now sirrah, follow me.    40

*Clown.* I will sir. But hark you master, will you teach me this conjuring occupation?

*Wagner.* Ay sirrah, I'll teach thee to turn thyself to a dog, or a cat, or a mouse, or a rat, or anything.

*Clown.* A dog, or a cat, or a mouse, or a rat! O brave Wagner!

*Wagner.* Villain, call me Master Wagner; and see that you walk attentively, and let your right eye be always diametrically fixed upon my left heel, that thou mayst *quasi uestigiis nostris insistere.*ʷ    50

*Clown.* Well sir, I warrant you.        *Exeunt.*

---

ᵖ "you who are my pupil"    q embroidered (with a pun on beating)
ʳ a powder for killing lice    ˢ attendant spirits    ᵗ Dutch coins    ᵘ back
ᵛ conscripted    ʷ "as if to walk in my footsteps"

[II. i.] Faustus *in his study*.

*Faustus*.   Now, Faustus, must thou needs be damned,
   canst not be saved!
  What boots ˣ it then to think of God or heaven?
  Away with such vain fancies, and despair;
  Despair in God and trust in Beelzebub.
  Now go not backward; no, be resolute:
  Why waverest? Something soundeth in mine ears,
  'Abjure this magic, turn to God again!'
  Ay, and Faustus will turn to God again.
  To God! He loves thee not:
  The god thou servest is thine own appetite,      10
  Wherein is fixed the love of Beelzebub:
  To him I'll build an altar and a church
  And offer lukewarm blood of new-born babes.

*Enter the two* Angels.

*Good Angel*.   Sweet Faustus, leave that execrable art.
*Faustus*.   Contrition, prayer, repentance, what of these?
*Good Angel*.   Oh, they are means to bring thee unto
   heaven.
*Bad Angel*.   Rather illusions, fruits of lunacy,
That make men foolish that do use them most.
*Good Angel*.   Sweet Faustus, think of heaven and heav-
   enly things.
*Bad Angel*.   No Faustus, think of honor and of wealth.  20
                               *Exeunt* Angels.
*Faustus*.   Wealth!
  Why, the signory of Emden ʸ shall be mine.
  When Mephostophilis shall stand by me
  What power can hurt me? Faustus, thou art safe:
  Cast no more doubts! Mephostophilis, come,
  And bring glad tidings from great Lucifer.
  Is't not midnight? Come Mephostophilis,
  *Veni*,ᶻ *veni, Mephostophilis!*

*Enter* Mephostophilis.

  Now tell me, what saith Lucifer thy lord?

ˣ avails   ʸ lordship of Emden, a wealthy seaport   ᶻ "Come"

*Mephostophilis.*   That I shall wait on Faustus whilst he
   lives,                                                           30
  So he will buy my service with his soul.
*Faustus.*   Already Faustus hath hazarded that for thee.
*Mephostophilis.*   But now thou must bequeath it sol-
   emnly
  And write a deed of gift with thine own blood,
  For that security craves Lucifer.
  If thou deny it I must back to hell.
*Faustus.*   Stay Mephostophilis; tell me what good
  Will my soul do thy lord?
*Mephostophilis.*               Enlarge his kingdom.
*Faustus.*   Is that the reason why he tempts us thus?
*Mephostophilis.*   *Solamen miseris socios habuisse dol-
   oris.*[a]                                                        40
*Faustus.*   Why, have you any pain that torture other? [b]
*Mephostophilis.*   As great as have the human souls of
   men.
  But tell me Faustus, shall I have thy soul?
  And I will be thy slave and wait on thee
  And give thee more than thou hast wit [c] to ask.
*Faustus.*   Ay Mephostophilis, I'll give it him.
*Mephostophilis.*   Then Faustus, stab thy arm courageous-
   ly,
  And bind thy soul, that at some certain day
  Great Lucifer may claim it as his own;
  And then be thou as great as Lucifer.                             50
*Faustus.*   Lo Mephostophilis, for love of thee
  I cut mine arm, and with my proper [d] blood
  Assure my soul to be great Lucifer's,
  Chief lord and regent of perpetual night.
  View here this blood that trickles from mine arm,
  And let it be propitious for my wish.
*Mephostophilis.*   But Faustus,
  Write it in manner of a deed of gift.
*Faustus.*   Ay so I do: but Mephostophilis,
  My blood congeals and I can write no more.                        60
*Mephostophilis.*   I'll fetch thee fire to dissolve it straight.


                                     *Exit.*
*Faustus.*   What might the staying of my blood portend?
  Is it unwilling I should write this bill?
  Why streams it not that I may write afresh?
  "Faustus gives to thee his soul": ah there it stayed.

---

[a] "Misery loves company"   [b] i.e., any other pains that torture   [c] knowledge   [d] own

Why shouldst thou not? is not thy soul thine own?
Then write again: "Faustus gives to thee his soul."

*Enter* Mephostophilis *with a chafer of fire.*

*Mephostophilis.*   See Faustus, here is fire; set it on.
*Faustus.*   So, now the blood begins to clear again:
   Now will I make an end immediately.                        70
*Mephostophilis* [*aside*].   What will not I do to obtain his
      soul!
*Faustus.*   *Consummatum est:*[e] this bill is ended,
   And Faustus hath bequeathed his soul to Lucifer.
   But what is this inscription on mine arm?
   *Homo fuge!* [f] Whither should I fly?
   If unto God, he'll throw me down to hell.—
   My senses are deceived, here's nothing writ.—
   O yes, I see it plain; even here is writ
   *Homo fuge!* Yet shall not Faustus fly.
*Mephostophilis.*   I'll fetch him somewhat[g] to delight his
      mind.                                           *Exit.*  80

*Enter devils giving crowns and rich apparel to* Faustus:
      *they dance and then depart.*

*Enter* Mephostophilis.

*Faustus.*   What means this show? speak Mephostophilis.
*Mephostophilis.*   Nothing Faustus, but to delight thy mind
   And let thee see what magic can perform.
*Faustus.*   But may I raise such spirits when I please?
*Mephostophilis.*   Ay Faustus, and do greater things than
      these.
*Faustus.*   Then, Mephostophilis, receive this scroll,
   A deed of gift of body and of soul:
   But yet conditionally that thou perform
   All covenant-articles between us both.
*Mephostophilis.*   Faustus, I swear by hell and Lucifer   90
   To effect all promises between us made.
*Faustus.*   Then hear me read it Mephostophilis.
   *On these conditions following:*
      *First, that Faustus may be a spirit in form and sub-*
   *stance;*
      *Secondly, that Mephostophilis shall be his servant and*
   *at his command;*
      *Thirdly, that Mephostophilis shall do for him and*
   *bring him whatsoever;*

*Fourthly, that he shall be in his chamber or house in-* 100
*visible;*
 *Lastly, that he shall appear to the said John Faustus*
*at all times in what form or shape soever he please:*
 *I, John Faustus of Wittenberg, doctor, by these pres-*
*ents do give both body and soul to Lucifer, prince of the*
*east, and his minister Mephostophilis, and furthermore*
*grant unto them that, four and twenty years being ex-*
*pired, the articles above written inviolate, full power to*
*fetch or carry the said John Faustus, body and soul,*
*flesh, blood, or goods, into their habitation wheresoever.* 110
        *By me John Faustus.*

*Mephostophilis.* Speak Faustus, do you deliver this as
  your deed?
*Faustus.* Ay, take it, and the devil give thee good of it.
*Mephostophilis.* Now Faustus, ask what thou wilt.
*Faustus.* First will I question with thee about hell.
 Tell me, where is the place that men call hell?
*Mephostophilis.* Under the heavens.
*Faustus.* Ay, so are all things else; but whereabouts?
*Mephostophilis.* Within the bowels of these elements,[h]
 Where we are tortured and remain for ever.    120
 Hell hath no limits, nor is circumscribed
 In one self place, but where we are is hell,
 And where hell is, there must we ever be:
 And to be short, when all the world dissolves
 And every creature shall be purified
 All places shall be hell that is not heaven.
*Faustus.* I think hell's a fable.
*Mephostophilis.* Ay, think so still, till experience change
  thy mind.
*Faustus.* Why, dost thou think that Faustus shall be
  damned?
Mephostophilis. Ay, of necessity, for here's the scroll  130
 In which thou hast given thy soul to Lucifer.
*Faustus.* Ay, and body too; but what of that?
 Thinkst thou that Faustus is so fond [1] to imagine
 That after this life there is any pain?
 No, these are trifles and mere old wives' tales.
*Mephostophilis.* But I am an instance to prove the con-
  trary,
 For I tell thee I am damned and now in hell.
*Faustus.* Nay, and this be hell, I'll willingly be damned:
 What, sleeping, eating, walking, and disputing!
 But leaving this, let me have a wife, the fairest maid in 140

[h] created things  [1] foolish

Germany, for I am wanton and lascivious and cannot
live without a wife.

*Mephostophilis.*    I prethee[j] Faustus, talk not of a wife.

*Faustus.*    Nay sweet Mephostophilis, fetch me one, for I
will have one.

*Mephostophilis.*    Well Faustus, thou shalt have a wife, sit
there till I come.                                    [*Exit.*]

*Enter with a devil dressed like a woman, with fireworks.*

*Faustus.*    What sight is this?

*Mephostophilis.*    Now Faustus, how dost thou like thy
wife?

*Faustus.*    Here's a hot whore indeed! No, I'll no wife. 150

*Mephostophilis.*    Marriage is but a ceremonial toy,[k]
And if thou lovest me, think no more of it.
I'll cull thee out the fairest courtesans
And bring them every morning to thy bed;
She whom thine eye shall like thy heart shall have,
Were she as chaste as was Penelope,[l]
As wise as Saba,[m] or as beautiful
As was bright Lucifer before his fall.
Hold; take this book, peruse it thoroughly:
The iterating of these lines brings gold;                     160
The framing of this circle on the ground
Brings thunder, whirlwinds, storm, and lightning;
Pronounce this thrice devoutly to thyself,
And men in harness shall appear to thee,
Ready to execute what thou commandst.

*Faustus.*    Thanks Mephostophilis; yet fain would I have a
book wherein I might behold all spells and incantations,
that I might raise up spirits when I please.

*Mephostophilis.*    Here they are in this book.

*There turn to them.*

*Faustus.*    Now would I have a book where I might see all 170
characters of planets of the heavens, that I might know
their motions and dispositions.[n]

*Mephostophilis.*    Here they are too.

*Turn to them.*

*Faustus.*    Nay, let me have one book more, and then I

---

[j] I pray thee   [k] trifling ceremony   [l] wife of Ulysses   [m] the Queen of
Sheba   [n] effects

have done, wherein I might see all plants, herbs, and
trees that grow upon the earth.
*Mephostophilis.*    Here they be.
*Faustus.*    Oh, thou art deceived.
*Mephostophilis.*    Tut, I warrant thee!

*Turn to them.*                                    *Exeunt.*

[*Here a comic scene is lost, in which the* Clown, Robin,
*after stealing one of* Faustus' *books of magic, leaves* Wagner's *service and becomes an ostler*° *at an inn.*]


          [II. ii.] *Enter* Faustus *in his study and* Mephostophilis.

*Faustus.*    When I behold the heavens, then I repent
     And curse thee, wicked Mephostophilis,
     Because thou hast deprived me of those joys.
*Mephostophilis.*    'Twas thine own seeking Faustus, thank
     thyself.
     But thinkst thou heaven is such a glorious thing?
     I tell thee, Faustus, it is not half so fair
     As thou or any man that breathes on earth.
*Faustus.*    How provst thou that?
*Mephostophilis.*    'Twas made for man; then he's more ex-
     cellent.
*Faustus.*    If heaven was made for man, 'twas made for    10
     me:
     I will renounce this magic and repent.

*Enter the two* Angels.

*Good Angel.*    Faustus, repent; yet God will pity thee.
*Bad Angel.*    Thou art a spirit; God cannot pity thee.
*Faustus.*    Who buzzeth in mine ears I am a spirit?
     Be I a devil, yet God may pity me;
     Yea, God will pity me if I repent.
*Bad Angel.*    Ay, but Faustus never shall repent.
                                        *Exeunt* Angels.
*Faustus.*    My heart is hardened, I cannot repent.
     Scarce can I name salvation, faith, or heaven,
     But fearful echoes thunder in mine ears            20
     "Faustus, thou art damned!" Then guns and knives,
     Swords, poison, halters, and envenomed steel
     Are laid before me to dispatch myself;

° stableman

And long ere this I should have done the deed
Had not sweet pleasure conquered deep despair.
Have not I made blind Homer sing to me
Of Alexander's love and Oenon's death? [p]
And hath not he,[q] that built the walls of Thebes
With ravishing sound of his melodious harp,
Made music with my Mephostophilis?                    30
Why should I die then, or basely despair?
I am resolved Faustus shall not repent.—
Come Mephostophilis, let us dispute again,
And reason of divine astrology.[r]
Speak, are there many spheres above the moon?
Are all celestial bodies but one globe [s]
As is the substance of this centric earth?

*Mephostophilis.*    As are the elements, such are the heavens,
Even from the moon unto the empyreal orb [t]
Mutually folded in each others' spheres,                 40
And jointly move upon one axle-tree,
Whose termine [u] is termed the world's wide pole;
Nor are the names of Saturn, Mars, or Jupiter
Feigned, but are erring stars.

*Faustus.*    But have they all one motion both *situ et tempore?* [v]

*Mephostophilis.*    All move from east to west in four and
twenty hours upon the poles of the world, but differ in
their motions upon the poles of the zodiac.

*Faustus.*    These slender questions Wagner can decide:
Hath Mephostophilis no greater skill?                    50
Who knows not the double motion of the planets?
that the first is finished in a natural day; the second thus:
Saturn in thirty years, Jupiter in twelve, Mars in four,
the sun, Venus, and Mercury in a year, the moon in
twenty-eight days. These are freshmen's suppositions.
But tell me, hath every sphere a dominion or *intelligentia?* [w]

*Mephostophilis.*    Ay.

*Faustus.*    How many heavens or spheres are there?

*Mephostophilis.*    Nine: the seven planets, the firmament,
and the empyreal heaven.

*Faustus.*    But is there not *coelum igneum* and *crystallinum?* [x]    60

---

[p] Paris [Alexander] deserted Oenone for Helen   [q] Amphion, by his
music, caused stones to form the walls of Thebes   [r] astronomy. (What
follows is a discussion of the Ptolemaic system)   [s] i.e., is the entire universe one ball   [t] empyrean   [u] end   [v] in the direction and the duration of
their revolutions   [w] governing spirit   [x] a sphere of fire and one of
crystal

*Mephostophilis.*   No Faustus, they be but fables.
*Faustus.*   Resolve me then in this one question: why are
   not conjunctions, oppositions, aspects, eclipses all at one
   time, but in some years we have more, in some less?
*Mephostophilis.*   *Per inaequalem motum respectu totius.*[y]
*Faustus.*   Well, I am answered. Now tell me, who made
   the world?
*Mephostophilis.*   I will not.
*Faustus.*   Sweet Mephostophilis, tell me.
*Mephostophilis.*   Move me not, Faustus.
*Faustus.*   Villain, have not I bound thee to tell me any
   thing?                                                                70
*Mephostophilis.*   Ay, that is not against our kingdom: this
   is. Thou art damned; think thou of hell.
*Faustus.*   Think, Faustus, upon God, that made the world.
*Mephostophilis.*   Remember this!                          *Exit.*
*Faustus.*   Ay, go accursèd spirit, to ugly hell!
   'Tis thou hast damned distressèd Faustus' soul.
   Is't not too late?

*Enter the two* Angels.

*Bad Angel.*   Too late.
*Good Angel.*   Never too late, if Faustus will repent.
*Bad Angel.*   If thou repent, devils will tear thee in pieces.   80
*Good Angel.*   Repent, and they shall never raze[z] thy
   skin.                                             *Exeunt* Angels.
*Faustus.*   O Christ, my savior, my savior! help to save
   distressèd Faustus' soul.

*Enter* Lucifer, Beelzebub, *and* Mephostophilis.

*Lucifer.*   Christ cannot save thy soul, for he is just;
   There's none but I have interest [a] in the same.
*Faustus.*   Oh, what art thou that lookst so terrible?
*Lucifer.*   I am Lucifer,
   And this is my companion prince in hell.
*Faustus.*   O Faustus, they are come to fetch thy soul.      90
*Beelzebub.*   We are come to tell thee thou dost injure us.
*Lucifer.*   Thou callst on Christ contrary to thy promise.
*Beelzebub.*   Thou shouldst not think on God.
*Lucifer.*   Think on the devil.
*Beelzebub.*   And his dam too.
*Faustus.*   Nor will I henceforth; pardon me in this,

---

   [y] "Because of unequal rates of motion in respect to the whole universe"
   [z] scratch    [a] legal title

And Faustus vows never to look to heaven,
Never to name God or to pray to him,
To burn his scriptures, slay his ministers,
And make my spirits pull his churches down.                    100

*Lucifer.*  So shalt thou show thyself an obedient servant,
and we will highly gratify thee for it.

*Beelzebub.*  Faustus, we are come from hell in person to
show thee some pastime. Sit down, and thou shalt behold
the Seven Deadly Sins appear to thee in their own proper
shapes and likeness.

*Faustus.*  That sight will be as pleasant to me as paradise
was to Adam the first day of his creation.

*Lucifer.*  Talk not of paradise or creation, but mark[b] the
show. Go Mephostophilis, fetch them in.                        110

*Enter the* Seven Deadly Sins [*led by a piper*].

*Beelzebub.*  Now Faustus, question them of their names
and dispositions.

*Faustus.*  That shall I soon. What art thou, the first?

*Pride.*  I am Pride. I disdain to have any parents. I am
like to Ovid's flea;[c] I can creep into every corner of a
wench: sometimes, like a periwig I sit upon her brow;
next, like a necklace I hang about her neck; then, like a
fan of feathers I kiss her lips; and then, turning myself
to a wrought smock,[d] do what I list.[e] But fie, what a
smell is here! I'll not speak another word, except the     120
ground be perfumed and covered with cloth of Arras.[f]

*Faustus.*  Thou art a proud knave indeed. What are thou,
the second?

*Covetousness.*  I am Covetousness, begotten of an old
churl[g] in a leather bag; and might I now obtain my
wish, this house, you and all, should turn to gold, that I
might lock you safe into my chest. O my sweet gold!

*Faustus.*  And what art thou, the third?

*Envy.*  I am Envy, begotten of a chimney-sweeper and
an oyster-wife. I cannot read, and therefore wish all     130
books burned. I am lean with seeing others eat. Oh, that
there would come a famine over all the world, that all
might die, and I live alone! then thou shouldst see how
fat I'd be. But must thou sit and I stand? Come down,
with a vengeance!

*Faustus.*  Out, envious wretch! But what art thou, the
fourth?

---

[b] observe   [c] a lascivious medieval poem, "Carmen de Pulice," incorrectly attributed to Ovid   [d] embroidered dress   [e] wish   [f] tapestry, from Arras, France   [g] miser

*Wrath.* I am Wrath. I had neither father nor mother; I leapt out of a lion's mouth when I was scarce an hour old, and ever since have run up and down the world with 140 these case of rapiers, wounding myself when I could get none to fight withal. I was born in hell; and look to it, for some ʰ of you shall be my father.

*Faustus.* And what art thou, the fifth?

*Gluttony.* I am Gluttony. My parents are all dead, and the devil a penny they have left me but a small pension, and that buys me thirty meals a day and ten bevers,ⁱ a small trifle to suffice nature. I come of a royal pedigree: my father was a gammon ʲ of bacon, and my mother was a hogshead of claret wine; my godfathers were these, 150 Peter Pickled-herring and Martin Martlemas-beef.ᵏ But my godmother, oh, she was a jolly gentlewoman and well beloved in every good town and city; her name was Mistress Margery March-beer.ˡ Now Faustus, thou hast heard all my progeny; wilt thou bid me to supper?

*Faustus.* Not I; thou wilt eat up all my victuals.

*Gluttony.* Then the devil choke thee.

*Faustus.* Choke thyself glutton! What art thou, the sixth?

*Sloth.* Heigh-ho! I am Sloth. I was begotten on a sunny bank, where I have lain ever since; and you have done 160 me great injury to bring me from thence: let me be carried thither again by Gluttony and Lechery. Heigh-ho! I'll not speak a word more for a king's ransom.

*Faustus.* And what are you, Mistress Minx, the seventh and last?

*Lechery.* Who, I sir? I am one that loves an inch of raw mutton better than an ellᵐ of fried stockfish,ⁿ and the first letter of my name begins with Lechery.

*Lucifer.* Away to hell, away! On, piper!

*Exeunt the* Seven Sins.

*Faustus.* Oh, how this sight doth delight my soul! 170

*Lucifer.* Tut Faustus, in hell is all manner of delight.

*Faustus.* Oh, might I see hell and return again safe, how happy were I then!

*Lucifer.* Faustus, thou shalt; at midnight I will send for thee. Meanwhile peruse this book and view it thoroughly, and thou shalt turn thyself into what shape thou wilt.

*Faustus.* Thanks mighty Lucifer: this will I keep as chary ° as my life.

*Lucifer.* Now Faustus, farewell.

ʰ someone ⁱ lunches ʲ side ᵏ beef salted at Matinmas (November 11)
ˡ a strong beer brewed in March ᵐ 45 inches ⁿ dried cod ° carefully

*Faustus.*     Farewell great Lucifer. Come Mephostophilis.
                                        *Exeunt omnes several ways.*


[II. iii.] *Enter the* Clown [Robin].


*Robin.*     What, Dick, look to the horses there till I come
     again. I have gotten one of Doctor Faustus' conjur-
     ing books, and now we'll have such knavery as't passes.

*Enter* Dick.

*Dick.*     What, Robin, you must come away and walk the
     horses.
*Robin.*     I walk the horses! I scorn't, 'faith: I have other
     matters in hand; let the horses walk themselves and they
     will. *A per se, a; t, h, e, the; o per se, o;*[p] *deny orgon,
     gorgon.*[q] Keep further from me, O thou illiterate and
     unlearnèd hostler.                                                10
*Dick.*     'Snails,[r] what hast thou got there? a book? Why,
     thou canst not tell ne'er a word on't.
*Robin.*     That thou shalt see presently. Keep out of the
     circle, I say, lest I send you into the ostry[s] with a venge-
     ance.
*Dick.*     That's like, 'faith! You had best leave your foolery,
     for an[t] my master come, he'll conjure you, 'faith.
*Robin.*     My master conjure me! I'll tell thee what; an my
     master come here, I'll clap as fair a pair of horns[u] on's
     head as e'er thou sawest in thy life.                           20
*Dick.*     Thou needst not do that, for my mistress hath
     done it.
*Robin.*     Ay, there be of us here have waded as deep into
     matters as other men, if they were disposed to talk.
*Dick.*     A plague take you! I thought you did not sneak up
     and down after her for nothing. But I prithee tell me in
     good sadness Robin, is that a conjuring book?
*Robin.*     Do but speak what thou't have me to do, and I'll
     do't. If thou't dance naked, put off thy clothes, and I'll
     conjure thee about presently. Or if thou't go but to the     30
     tavern with me, I'll give thee white wine, red wine, claret
     wine, sack, muscadine, malmesey, and whippincrust,[v]

---

[p] *A* by itself [spells] *a; t-h-e* spells "the," etc.     [q] corruption of Demogorgon, primordial god of classical mythology, but her (and in I. iii. 18)
with one of the rulers of the underworld     [r] God's nails     [s] inn     [t] if
[u] i.e., cuckold's horns     [v] various wines

hold-belly-hold,ʷ and we'll not pay one penny for it.

*Dick.*     O brave! prithee let's to it presently, for I am as dry
as a dog.

*Robin.*     Come then, let's away.                              *Exeunt.*


#### [III. Ch.] *Enter the* Chorus.

Learnèd Faustus,
To find the secrets of astronomy,
Graven in the book of Jove's high firmament,
Did mount him up to scale Olympus' top;
Where, sitting in a chariot burning bright
Drawn by the strength of yoky ˣ dragons' necks,
He views the clouds, the planets, and the stars,
The tropics, zones, and quarters of the sky,
From the bright circle of the hornèd moon
Even to the height of *primum mobile*; ʸ                          10
And whirling round with this circumference
Within the concave compass of the pole,
From east to west his dragons swiftly glide
And in eight days did bring him home again.
Not long he stayed within his quiet house
To rest his bones after his weary toil,
But new exploits do hale him out again.
And mounted then upon a dragon's back,
That with his wings did part the subtle air,
He now is gone to prove ᶻ cosmography,                            20
That measures coasts and kingdoms of the earth,
And as I guess will first arrive in Rome
To see the Pope and manner of his court
And take some part of holy Peter's feast,
The which this day is highly solemnized.                          *Exit.*


#### [III. i.] *Enter* Faustus *and* Mephostophilis.

*Faustus.*     Having now, my good Mephostophilis,
Passed with delight the stately town of Trier,ᵃ
Environed round with airy mountain tops,
With walls of flint, and deep-entrenchèd lakes,ᵇ
Not to be won by any conquering prince:

---

ʷ i.e., as much as you can drink   ˣ yoked   ʸ outermost heaven in
medieval astronomy   ᶻ verify   ᵃ in the valley of the Mosel River   ᵇ moats

 From Paris next, coasting the realm of France,
 We saw the river Main fall into Rhine,
 Whose banks are set with groves of fruitful vines:
 Then up to Naples, rich Campania,<sup>c</sup>
 With buildings fair and gorgeous to the eye,      10
 Whose streets straight forth and paved with finest brick
 Quarter the town in four equivalents.
 There saw we learnèd Maro's <sup>d</sup> golden tomb,
 The way <sup>e</sup> he cut, an English mile in length,
 Thorough a rock of stone in one night's space.
 From thence to Venice, Padua, and the rest,
 In midst of which a sumptuous temple stands,
 That threats the stars with her aspiring top,
 Whose frame is paved with sundry colored stones
 And roofed aloft with curious <sup>f</sup> work in gold.     20
 Thus hitherto hath Faustus spent his time.
 But tell me now, what resting-place is this?
 Hast thou, as erst <sup>g</sup> I did command,
 Conducted me within the walls of Rome?
*Mephostophilis.* I have, my Faustus, and for proof
  thereof
 This is the goodly palace of the Pope,
 And 'cause we are no common guests
 I choose his privy chamber for our use.
*Faustus.* I hope his Holiness will bid us welcome.
*Mephostophilis.* All's one, for we'll be bold with his
  venison.                 30
 But now my Faustus, that thou mayst perceive
 What Rome contains for to delight thine eyes,
 Know that this city stands upon seven hills
 That underprop the groundwork of the same:
 Just through the midst runs flowing Tiber's stream,
 With winding banks that cut it in two parts,
 Over the which four stately bridges lean,
 That make safe passage to each part of Rome.
 Upon the bridge called Ponte Angelo
 Erected is a castle passing strong,       40
 Where thou shalt see such store of ordinance
 As that the double cannons forged of brass
 Do match the number of the days contained
 Within the compass of one complete year;
 Beside the gates, and high pyramides <sup>h</sup>
 That Julius Caesar brought from Africa.
*Faustus.* Now, by the kingdoms of infernal rule,

---

<sup>c</sup> Naples is part of the Roman Campagna <sup>d</sup> Vergil <sup>e</sup> tunnel <sup>f</sup> intricate <sup>g</sup> before <sup>h</sup> obelisks

Of Styx, of Acheron, and the fiery lake
Of ever-burning Phlegethon,[1] I swear
That I do long to see the monuments                        50
And situation [j] of bright-splendent Rome.
Come therefore, let's away.
*Mephostophilis.*    Nay stay my Faustus; I know you'd see
    the Pope
And take some part of holy Peter's feast,
The which in state and high solemnity
This day is held through Rome and Italy
In honor of the Pope's triumphant victory.
*Faustus.*    Sweet Mephostophilis, thou pleasest me:
Whilst I am here on earth let me be cloyed
With all things that delight the heart of man.             60
My four and twenty years of liberty
I'll spend in pleasure and in dalliance,
That Faustus' name, whilst this bright frame doth stand,
May be admirèd through the furthest land.
*Mephostophilis.*    'Tis well said, Faustus, come then, stand
    by me
And thou shalt see them come immediately.
*Faustus.*    Nay stay, my gentle Mephostophilis,
And grant me my request, and then I go.
Thou knowst, within the compass of eight days             70
We viewed the face of heaven, of earth, and hell:
So high our dragons soared into the air
That looking down the earth appeared to me
No bigger than my hand in quantity:
There did we view the kingdoms of the world,
And what might please mine eye I there beheld:
Then in this show let me an actor be,
That this proud Pope may Faustus' cunning see.
*Mephostophilis.*    Let it be so my Faustus, but first stay
And view their triumphs [k] as they pass this way;
And then devise what best contents thy mind,              80
By cunning of thine art to cross the Pope
Or dash the pride of this solemnity,
To make his monks and abbots stand like apes
And point like antics [l] at his triple crown,
To beat the beads about the friars' pates
Or clap huge horns upon the cardinals' heads,
Or any villainy thou canst devise,
And I'll perform it, Faustus. Hark, they come!
This day shall make thee be admired [m] in Rome.

[1] three   rivers   of   Hades   [j] plan   [k] pageants   [l] grotesque   dancers
[m] wondered at

*Enter the cardinals and bishops, some bearing crosiers,*
   *some the pillars;* [n] *monks and friars singing their*
   *procession; then the* Pope *and* Raymond King of
   Hungary, *with* Bruno *led in chains.*

*Pope.*   Cast down our footstool.
*Raymond.*                     Saxon Bruno, stoop,                90
   Whilst on thy back his Holiness ascends
   Saint Peter's chair and state pontifical. [o]
*Bruno.*   Proud Lucifer, that state belongs to me:
   But thus I fall, to Peter not to thee.
*Pope.*   To me and Peter shalt thou groveling lie.
   And crouch before the papal dignity:
   Sound trumpets then, for thus Saint Peter's heir
   From Bruno's back ascends Saint Peter's chair.

*A flourish* [p] *while he ascends.*

   Thus as the gods creep on with feet of wool
   Long ere with iron hands they punish men,                    100
   So shall our sleeping vengeance now arise
   And smite with death thy hated enterprise.
   Lord Cardinals of France and Padua,
   Go forthwith to our holy consistory [q]
   And read amongst the statutes decretal [r]
   What, by the holy council held at Trent,
   The sacred synod hath decreed for him
   That doth assume the papal government
   Without election and a true consent.
   Away, and bring us word [again] with speed.                  110
*1 Cardinal.*   We go my lord.              *Exeunt cardinals.*
*Pope.*   Lord Raymond—

[*They talk apart.*]

*Faustus.*   Go haste thee gentle Mephostophilis,
   Follow the cardinals to the consistory,
   And as they turn their superstitious books,
   Strike them with sloth and drowsy idleness;
   And make them sleep so sound that in their shapes
   Thyself and I may parley with this Pope,
   This proud confronter of the Emperor,
   And in despite of all his holiness                           120
   Restore this Bruno to his liberty

   [n] silver staffs   [o] i.e., the papal throne   [p] fanfare   [q] meeting place of
the papal senate   [r] i.e., the papal decrees

And bear him to the states of Germany.
*Mephostophilis.*     Faustus, I go.
*Faustus.*                     Dispatch it soon:
  The Pope shall curse that Faustus came to Rome.
                    *Exeunt* Faustus *and* Mephostophilis.
*Bruno.*   Pope Adrian, let me have some right of law;
  I was elected by the Emperor.
*Pope.*   We will depose the Emperor for that deed
  And curse the people that submit to him;
  Both he and thou shalt stand excommunicate
  And interdict ˢ from church's privilege                    130
  And all society of holy men.
  He grows too proud in his authority,
  Lifting his lofty head above the clouds,
  And like a steeple overpeers the church;
  But we'll pull down his haughty insolence.
  And as Pope Alexander, our progenitor,
  Trod on the neck of German Frederick,
  Adding this golden sentence to our praise,
  That Peter's heirs should tread on emperors
  And walk upon the dreadful adder's back,                   140
  Treading the lion and the dragon down,
  And fearless spurn the killing basilisk; ᵗ
  So will we quell that haughty schismatic,
  And by authority apostolical
  Depose him from his regal government.
*Bruno.*   Pope Julius swore to princely Sigismond,
  For him and the succeeding popes of Rome,
  To hold the emperors their lawful lords.
*Pope.*   Pope Julius did abuse the church's rights,
  And therefore none of his decrees can stand.               150
  Is not all power on earth bestowed on us?
  And therefore though we would we cannot err.
  Behold this silver belt, whereto is fixed
  Seven golden keys fast sealed with seven seals
  In token of our sevenfold power from heaven,
  To bind or loose, lock fast, condemn, or judge,
  Resignᵘ or seal, or whatso pleaseth us.
  Then he and thou and all the world shall stoop,
  Or be assurèd of our dreadful curse
  To light as heavy as the pains of hell.                    160

*Enter* Faustus *and* Mephostophilis *like the cardinals.*

ˢ forbidden   ᵗ mythological beast that kills with its look   ᵘ unseal

*Mephostophilis.*    Now tell me Faustus, are we not fitted <sup>v</sup>
   well?
*Faustus.*    Yes Mephostophilis, and two such cardinals
   Ne'er served a holy pope as we shall do.
   But whilst they sleep within the consistory
   Let us salute his reverend Fatherhood.
*Raymond.*    Behold my lord, the cardinals are returned.
*Pope.*    Welcome grave fathers, answer presently,
   What have our holy council there decreed
   Concerning Bruno and the Emperor,
   In quittance <sup>w</sup> of their late conspiracy                    170
   Against our state and papal dignity?
*Faustus.*    Most sacred patron of the church of Rome,
   By full consent of all the [holy] synod
   Of priests and prelates it is thus decreed,
   That Bruno and the German Emperor
   Be held as lollards <sup>x</sup> and bold schismatics
   And proud disturbers of the church's peace.
   And if that Bruno by his own assent,
   Without enforcement of the German peers,
   Did seek to wear the triple diadem                              180
   And by your death to climb Saint Peter's chair,
   The statutes decretal have thus decreed,
   He shall be straight condemned of heresy
   And on a pile of fagots burnt to death.
*Pope.* It is enough. Here, take him to your charge
   And bear him straight to Ponte Angelo,
   And in the strongest tower enclose him fast.
   Tomorrow, sitting in our consistory
   With all our college of grave cardinals,
   We will determine of his life or death.                        190
   Here, take his triple crown along with you
   And leave it in the church's treasury.
   Make haste again, my good lord cardinals,
   And take our blessing apostolical.
*Mephostophilis.*    So, so; was never devil thus blessed
   before.
*Faustus.*    Away sweet Mephostophilis, be gone:
   The cardinals will be plagued for this anon.<sup>y</sup>
          *Exeunt* Faustus *and* Mephostophilis [*with* Bruno].

*Pope.*    Go presently and bring a banket <sup>z</sup> forth,
   That we may solemnize Saint Peter's feast
   And with Lord Raymond, King of Hungary,                        200
   Drink to our late and happy victory.          *Exeunt.*

   <sup>v</sup> outfitted    <sup>w</sup> requital    <sup>x</sup> i.e., heretics    <sup>y</sup> presently    <sup>z</sup> banquet

[III. ii.] *The banquet is brought in, and then enter*
   Faustus *and* Mephostophilis *in their own shapes*.

*Mephostophilis.*    Now Faustus, come prepare thyself for
   mirth:
  The sleepy cardinals are hard at hand
  To censure Bruno, that is posted hence,
  And on a proud-paced steed as swift as thought
  Flies o'er the Alps to fruitful Germany,
  There to salute the woeful Emperor.
*Faustus.*    The Pope will curse them for their sloth today
  That slept both Bruno and his crown away.
  But now, that Faustus may delight his mind
  And by their folly make some merriment,             10
  Sweet Mephostophilis, so charm me here
  That I may walk invisible to all
  And do whate'er I please unseen of any.
*Mephostophilis.*    Faustus, thou shalt; then kneel down
   presently;
   *Whilst on thy head I lay my hand*
   *And charm thee with this magic wand.*
   *First wear this girdle,*[a] *then appear*
   *Invisible to all are here:*
   *The planets seven, the gloomy air,*
   *Hell, and the Furies' forked*[b] *hair,*             20
   *Pluto's*[c] *blue fire, and Hecat's*[d] *tree*
   *With magic spells so compass thee*
   *That no eye may thy body see.*
  So Faustus, now for all their holiness,
  Do what thou wilt thou shalt not be discerned.
*Faustus.*    Thanks Mephostophilis: now friars, take heed
  Lest Faustus make your shaven crowns to bleed.
*Mephostophilis.*    Faustus, no more; see where the cardi-
   nals come.

*Sound a sennet.*[e] *Enter* Pope *and all the lords* [*with* King
   Raymond *and the* Archbishop of Rheims]. *Enter the*
   *cardinals with a book*.

*Pope.*    Welcome lord cardinals; come, sit down.
  Lord Raymond, take your seat. Friars, attend,        30

  [a] belt   [b] hair formed of snakes' tongues   [c] king of the underworld
[d] goddess of witchcraft   [e] trumpet fanfare

    And see that all things be in readiness
    As best beseems this solemn festival.
*1 Cardinal.*   First may it please your sacred Holiness
    To view the sentence of the reverend synod
    Concerning Bruno and the Emperor.
*Pope.*   What needs this question? Did I not tell you
    Tomorrow we would sit i' th' consistory
    And there determine of his punishment?
    You brought us word, even now, it was decreed
    That Bruno and the cursèd Emperor          40
    Were by the holy council both condemned
    For lothèd lollards and base schismatics:
    Then wherefore would you have me view that book?
*1 Cardinal.*   Your Grace mistakes; you gave us no such
    charge.
*Raymond.*   Deny it not; we all are witnesses
    That Bruno here was late delivered you,
    With his rich triple crown to be reserved
    And put into the church's treasury.
*Ambo*[f] *Cardinals.*   By holy Paul we saw them not.
*Pope.*   By Peter you shall die              50
    Unless you bring them forth immediately.
    Hale them to prison, lade their limbs with gyves!
    False prelates, for this hateful treachery
    Cursed by your souls to hellish misery.
                                  *[Exeunt cardinals]*.
*Faustus.*   So, they are safe. Now Faustus, to the feast:
    The Pope had never such a frolic[g] guest.
*Pope.*   Lord Archbishop of Rheims, sit down with us.
*Archbishop.*   I thank your Holiness.
*Faustus.*   Fall to,[h] the devil choke you an you spare![i]
*Pope.*   Who's that spoke? Friars, look about.—       60
    Lord Raymond, pray fall to: I am beholding
    To the Bishop of Milan for this so rare a present.
*Faustus.*   I thank you sir.

*[Snatches]*.

*Pope.*   How now! Who snatched the meat from me?
    Villains, why speak you not?
*Friar.*   Here's nobody, if it like[j] your Holiness.
*Pope.*   My good Lord Archbishop, here's a most dainty
    dish
    Was sent me from a cardinal in France.

    [f] a pair of    [g] frolicsome    [h] begin    [i] hold back    [j] please

*Faustus.* I'll have that too.

[*Snatches.*]

*Pope.* What lollards do attend oŭr Holiness          70
  That we receive such great indignity!
  Fetch me some wine.
*Faustus.* Ay, pray do, for Faustus is adry.
*Pope.* Lord Raymond, I drink unto your Grace.
*Faustus.* I pledge your Grace.

[*Snatches.*]

*Pope.* My wine gone too? Ye lubbers,ᵏ look about
  And find the man that doth this villainy,
  Or by my sanctitude you all shall die.—
  I pray, my lords, have patience at this troublesome
    banquet.
*Archbishop.* Please it your Holiness, I think it be some    80
  ghost crept out of purgatory, and now is come unto your
  Holiness for his pardon.
*Pope.* It may be so:
  Go then, command our priests to sing a dirge
  To lay the fury ¹ of this same troublesome ghost.
  Once again my lord, fall to.

*The* Pope *crosseth himself.*

*Faustus.* How now?
  Must every bit be spicèd with a cross?
  Well, use that trick no more I would advise you.

*Cross again.*

  Well, there's the second time; aware ᵐ the third:    90
  I give you fair warning.

*Cross again.*

  Nay then take that!

Faustus *hits him a box of the ear.*

*Pope.* Oh, I am slain! help me my lords;
  O come and help to bear my body hence.

  ᵏ a term of abuse  ¹ calm the importunity  ᵐ beware

Damned be this soul for ever for this deed.
                    *Exeunt the* Pope *and his train.*
*Mephostophilis.*   Now Faustus, what will you do now?
   for I can tell you you'll be cursed with bell, book, and
   candle.[n]
*Faustus.*   Bell, book, and candle; candle, book, and bell;
   Forward and backward, to curse Faustus to hell!

*Enter all the friars, with bell, book, and candle, to sing the
   dirge.*

*1 Friar.*   Come brethren, let's about our business with      100
   good devotion.

*Sing this.*

   Cursèd be he that stole away his Holiness' meat from the
                    table.
            Maledicat Dominus! [o]
   Cursèd be he that struck his Holiness a blow on the face.
            Maledicat Dominus!
   Cursèd be he that took Friar Sandelo a blow on the pate.
            Maledicat Dominus!
   Cursèd be he that disturbeth our holy dirge.
            Maledicat Dominus!                                  110
   Cursèd be he that took away his Holiness' wine.
            Maledicat Dominus! et omnes sancti! [p] Amen.

[Faustus *and* Mephostophilis] *Beat the friars and fling
   fireworks among them and so exeunt.*


   [III. iii.] *Enter* Clown [Robin] *and* Dick *with a cup.*

*Dick.*   Sirrah Robin, we were best look that your devil can
   answer [q] the stealing of this same cup, for the vintner's
   boy follows us at the hard heels.[r]
*Robin.*   'Tis no matter, let him come! An he follows us
   I'll so conjure him as he was never conjured in his life, I
   warrant him. Let me see the cup.

*Enter* Vintner.

   [n] here, sacred implements used to exorcise evil spirits   [o] "May God
damn him"   [p] "and all the saints"   [q] answer for   [r] i.e., closely

*Dick.* Here 'tis. Yonder he comes. Now Robin, now or
never show thy cunning.

*Vintner.* Oh, are you here? I am glad I have found you.
You are a couple of fine companions! Pray, where's the 10
cup you stole from the tavern?

*Robin.* How, how? we steal a cup! Take heed what you
say; we look not like cup-stealers, I can tell you.

*Vintner.* Never deny't, for I know you have it, and I'll
search you.

*Robin.* Search me? Ay, and spare not.—Hold the cup,
Dick!—Come come; search me, search me.

*Vintner.* Come on sirrah, let me search you now.

*Dick.* Ay, ay, do do.—Hold the cup, Robin.—I fear not
your searching. We scorn to steal your cups, I can tell 20
you.

*Vintner.* Never outface ⁸ me for the matter, for sure the
cup is between you two.

*Robin.* Nay there you lie; 'tis beyond us both.

*Vintner.* A plague take you! I thought 'twas your knavery
to take it away. Come, give it me again.

*Robin.* Ay, much! ᵗ when, can you tell? Dick, make me
a circle, and stand close at my back and stir not for thy
life. Vintner, you shall have your cup anon. Say nothing,ᵘ Dick. *O per se, o; Demogorgon, Belcher, and* 30
*Mephostophilis!*

*Enter* Mephostophilis.

*Mephostophilis.* Monarch of hell, under whose black sur-
vey ᵛ
Great potentates do kneel with awful fear,
Upon whose altars thousand souls do lie,
How am I vexèd by these villains' charms!
From Constantinople am I hither brought
Only for pleasure of these damnèd slaves.

[*Exit* Vintner.]

*Robin.* By lady ʷ sir, you have had a shrewd journey of
it: will it please you to take a shoulder of mutton to supper and a tester ˣ in your purse, and go back again? 40

*Dick.* Ay, I pray you heartily sir; for we called you but
in jest, I promise you.

*Mephostophilis.* To pure the rashness of this cursèd
deed,
First be thou turnèd to this ugly shape,

---

⁸ defy   ᵗ I don't think   ᵘ warning not to speak when spirits are about
ᵛ angry glance   ʷ by our lady (the Virgin)   ˣ sixpence

For apish <sup>y</sup> deeds transformèd to an ape.

*Robin.*   O brave! an ape! I pray sir, let me have the carrying of him about to show some tricks.

*Mephostophilis.*   And so thou shalt: be thou transformed
   to a dog and carry him upon thy back. Away, be gone!

*Robin.*   A dog! that's excellent. Let the maids look well to
   their porridge-pots, for I'll into the kitchen presently.   50
   Come Dick, come.                    *Exeunt the two* Clowns.

*Mephostophilis.*   Now with the flames of ever-burning
      fire
   I'll wing myself and forthwith fly amain <sup>z</sup>
   Unto my Faustus, to the Great Turk's court.        *Exit.*


### [IV. Ch.] *Enter* Chorus.


When Faustus had with pleasure ta'en the view
Of rarest things and royal courts of kings,
He stayed <sup>a</sup> his course, and so returnèd home;
Where such as bare <sup>b</sup> his absence but with grief,
I mean his friends and nearest companions,
Did gratulate <sup>c</sup> his safety with kind words;
And in their conference of what befell
Touching his journey through the world and air
They put forth questions of astrology,
Which Faustus answered with such learnèd skill        10
As they admired and wondered at his wit.
Now is his fame spread forth in every land:
Amongst the rest the Emperor is one,
Carolus the Fifth, at whose palace now
Faustus is feasted 'mongst his noblemen.
What there he did in trial of his art
I leave untold, your eyes shall see performed.        *Exit.*


### [IV. i.] *Enter* Martino *and* Frederick *at several doors.*


*Martino.*   What ho, officers, gentlemen!
   Hie <sup>d</sup> to the presence to attend the Emperor;
   Good Frederick, see the rooms be voided straight,
   His Majesty is coming to the hall;
   Go back, and see the state <sup>e</sup> in readiness.

*Frederick.*   But where is Bruno, our elected Pope,

---

  <sup>y</sup> foolish    <sup>z</sup> hastily    <sup>a</sup> checked    <sup>b</sup> bore    <sup>c</sup> congratulate    <sup>d</sup> hasten
<sup>e</sup> chair of state

  That on a fury's back came post from Rome?
  Will not his Grace consort <sup>f</sup> the Emperor?
*Martino*. O yes, and with him comes the German conjurer,
  The learnèd Faustus, fame of Wittenberg,    10
  The wonder of the world for magic art;
  And he intends to show great Carolus
  The race of all his stout progenitors,
  And bring in presence of his Majesty
  The royal shapes and warlike semblances
  Of Alexander and his beauteous paramour.
*Frederick*. Where is Benvolio?
*Martino*. Fast asleep, I warrant you:
  He took his rouse <sup>g</sup> with stoups <sup>h</sup> of Rhenish wine
  So kindly yesternight to Bruno's health    20
  That all this day the sluggard keeps his bed.
*Frederick*. See, see, his window's ope; we'll call to him.
*Martino*. What ho, Benvolio!

*Enter* Benvolio *above at a window, in his night-cap, but-*
  *toning.*

*Benvolio*. What a devil ail you two?
*Martino*. Speak softly sir, lest the devil hear you;
  For Faustus at the court is late arrived,
  And at his heels a thousand furies wait
  To accomplish whatsoever the doctor please.
*Benvolio*. What of this?
*Martino*. Come, leave thy chamber first, and thou shalt
   see    30
  This conjurer perform such rare exploits
  Before the Pope <sup>i</sup> and royal Emperor
  As never yet was seen in Germany.
*Benvolio*. Has not the Pope enough of conjuring yet?
  He was upon the devil's back late enough;
  And if he be so far in love with him
  I would he would post with him to Rome again.
*Frederick*. Speak, wilt thou come and see this sport?
*Benvolio*. Not I.
*Martino*. Wilt thou stand in thy window and see it then? 40
*Benvolio*. Ay, and I fall not asleep i' th' mean time.
*Martino*. The Emperor is at hand, who comes to see
  What wonders by black spells may compassed be.
*Benvolio*. Well, go you attend the Emperor. I am content
  for this once to thrust my head out at a window, for they

  <sup>f</sup> attend  <sup>g</sup> i.e., a drinking bout  <sup>h</sup> cups  <sup>i</sup> i.e., Bruno

say if a man be drunk overnight the devil cannot hurt
him in the morning. If that be true, I have a charm in
my head shall control him as well as the conjurer, I
warrant you.                          *Exit* [Martino *and* Frederick].


[IV. ii.] *A sennet.* Charles the German Emperor, Bruno,
    [the Duke of] Saxony, Faustus, Mephostophilis,
    Frederick, Martino, *and attendants.* [Benvolio *re-
    mains at his window.*]

*Emperor.*    Wonder of men, renowned magician,
    Thrice-learnèd Faustus, welcome to our court.
    This deed of thine, in setting Bruno free
    From his and our professèd enemy,
    Shall add more excellence unto thine art
    Than if by powerful necromantic spells
    Thou couldst command the world's obedience.
    For ever be beloved of Carolus;
    And if this Bruno thou hast late redeemed
    In peace possess the triple diadem                              10
    And sit in Peter's chair despite of chance,
    Thou shalt be famous through all Italy
    And honored of the German Emperor.
*Faustus.*    These gracious words, most royal Carolus,
    Shall make poor Faustus to his utmost power
    Both love and serve the German Emperor
    And lay his life at holy Bruno's feet.
    For proof whereof, if so your Grace be pleased,
    The doctor stands prepared by power of art
    To cast his magic charms, that shall pierce through          20
    The ebon ^j gates of ever-burning hell,
    And hale the stubborn furies from their caves
    To compass whatsoe'er your Grace commands.
*Benvolio.*    Blood! ^k he speaks terribly; but for all that I
    do not greatly believe him: he looks as like a conjurer
    as the Pope to a costermonger.^l
*Emperor.*    Then Faustus, as thou late didst promise us,
    We would behold that famous conqueror
    Great Alexander and his paramour
    In their true shapes and state majestical,                      30
    That we may wonder at their excellence.
*Faustus.*    Your Majesty shall see them presently.

    ^j ebony   ^k God's blood   ^l vegetable seller

Mephostophilis away,
And with a solemn noise of trumpets' sound
Present before this royal Emperor
Great Alexander and his beauteous paramour.

*Mephostophilis.*   Faustus, I will.                     [*Exit.*]

*Benvolio.*   Well master doctor, an your devils come not
away quickly, you shall have me asleep presently.
Zounds, I could eat myself for anger to think I have     40
been such an ass all this while to stand gaping after the
devil's governor, and can see nothing.

*Faustus.*   I'll make you feel something anon if my art fail
me not.—

My lord, I must forewarn your Majesty
That when my spirits present the royal shapes
Of Alexander and his paramour,
Your Grace demand no questions of the King,
But in dumb silence let them come and go.

*Emperor.*   Be it as Faustus please; we are content.

*Benvolio.*   Ay ay, and I am content too. And thou bring     50
Alexander and his paramour ᵐ before the Emperor, I'll
be Actaeon ⁿ and turn myself to a stag.

*Faustus.*   And I'll play Diana and send you the horns
presently.

*Sennet. Enter at one door the* Emperor Alexander, *at the
other* Darius: *they meet;* Darius *is thrown down;*
Alexander *kills him, takes off his crown, and offering
to go out, his* Paramour *meets him; he embraceth her
and sets* Darius' *crown upon her head, and coming
back both salute the* Emperor; *who leaving his state
offers to embrace them, which* Faustus *seeing suddenly stays him. Then trumpets cease and music sounds.*

My gracious lord, you do forget yourself;
These are but shadows, not substantial.

*Emperor.*   O pardon me, my thoughts are ravished so
With sight of this renownèd Emperor,
That in mine arms I would have compassed him.
But Faustus, since I may not speak to them           60
To satisfy my longing thoughts at full,
Let me this tell thee: I I have heard it said
That this fair lady, whilst she lived on earth,
Had on her neck a little wart or mole;
How may I prove that saying to be true?

ᵐ i.e., Thaïs   ⁿ turned by Diana into a stag for spying upon her while
she bathed

*Faustus.*    Your Majesty may boldly go and see.
*Emperor.*    Faustus, I see it plain;
   And in this sight thou better pleasest me
   Than if I gained another monarchy.
*Faustus.*    Away, be gone!                              *Exit show.*    70
   See, see, my gracious lord, what strange beast is yon,
   that thrusts his head out at the window!
*Emperor.*    O wondrous sight! See, Duke of Saxony, two
   spreading horns most strangely fastened upon the head
   of young Benvolio.
*Saxony.*    What, is he asleep, or dead?
*Faustus.*    He sleeps my lord, but dreams not of his horns.
*Emperor.*    This sport is excellent: we'll call and wake
   him. What ho, Benvolio!
*Benvolio.*    A plague upon you! let me sleep awhile.        80
*Emperor.*    I blame thee not to sleep, much, having such a
   head of thine own.
*Saxony.*    Look up Benvolio, 'tis the Emperor calls.
*Benvolio.*    The Emperor! where? O zounds, my head!
*Emperor.*    Nay, and thy horns hold 'tis no matter for thy
   head, for that's armed sufficiently.
*Faustus.*    Why, how now sir knight? what, hanged by the
   horns? This is most horrible: fie fie, pull in your head
   for shame! let not all the world wonder at you.
*Benvolio.*    Zounds doctor, is this your villainy?          90
*Faustus.*    Oh, say not so sir: the doctor has no skill,
   No art, no cunning to present these lords
   Or bring before this royal Emperor
   The mighty monarch, warlike Alexander.
   If Faustus do it, you are straight resolved
   In bold Actaeon's shape to turn a stag.
   And therefore my lord, so please your Majesty,
   I'll raise a kennel of hounds shall hunt him so
   As all his footmanship shall scarce prevail
   To keep his carcass from their bloody fangs.            100
   Ho, Belimote, Argiron, Asterote! °
*Benvolio.*    Hold, hold! Zounds, he'll raise up a kennel of
   devils I think, anon. Good my lord, entreat for me.
   'Sblood, I am never able to endure these torments.
*Emperor.*    Then good master doctor,
   Let me entreat you to remove his horns,
   He has done penance now sufficiently.
*Faustus.*    My gracious lord, not so much for injury done

° perhaps a corruption of Behemoth, Acheron, and Astarte

to me, as to delight your Majesty with some mirth, hath
Faustus justly requited this injurious knight; which 110
being all I desire, I am content to remove his horns.—
Mephostophilis, transform him.—And hereafter sir,
look you speak well of scholars.

*Benvolio* [*aside*].    Speak well of ye! 'Sblood, and scholars
be such cuckold-makers to clap horns of honest men's
heads o' this order, I'll ne'er trust smooth faces and
small ruffs more. But an I be not revenged for this,
would I might be turned to a gaping oyster and drink
nothing but salt water.

*Emperor.*    Come Faustus, while the Emperor lives,     120
   In recompense of this thy high desert,
   Thou shalt command the state of Germany
   And live beloved of mighty Carolus.     *Exeunt omnes.*


[IV. iii.] *Enter* Benvolio, Martino, Frederick, *and soldiers.*

*Martino.*    Nay sweet Benvolio, let us sway thy thoughts
   From this attempt against the conjurer.
*Benvolio.*    Away! you love me not to urge me thus.
   Shall I let slip so great an injury,
   When every servile groom jests at my wrongs
   And in their rustic gambols proudly say,
   'Benvolio's head was graced with horns today'?
   Oh, may these eyelids never close again
   Till with my sword I have that conjurer slain.
   If you will aid me in this enterprise,     10
   Then draw your weapons and be resolute:
   If not, depart: here will Benvolio die
   But ᵖ Faustus' death shall quit �q my infamy.
*Frederick.*    Nay, we will stay with thee, betide what may,
   And kill that doctor if he come this way.
*Benvolio.*    Then gentle Frederick, hie thee to the grove,
   And place our servants and our followers
   Close in an ambush there behind the trees.
   By this, I know, the conjurer is near:
   I saw him kneel and kiss the Emperor's hand     20
   And take his leave laden with rich rewards.
   Then soldiers, boldly fight: if Faustus die,
   Take you the wealth, leave us the victory.
*Frederick.*    Come soldiers, follow me unto the grove:

ᵖ unless    q requite

Who kills him shall have gold and endless love.
                         *Exit* Frederick *with the soldiers.*
*Benvolio.*   My head is lighter than it was by th' horns,
   But yet my heart's more ponderous than my head
   And pants until I see that conjurer dead.
*Martino.*   Where shall we place ourselves, Benvolio?
*Benvolio.*   Here will we stay to bide the first assault.       30
   Oh, were that damnèd hell-hound but in place
   Thou soon shouldst see me quit my foul disgrace.

*Enter* Frederick.

*Frederick.*   Close, close! the [hated] conjurer is at hand
   And all alone comes walking in his gown;
   Be ready then and strike the peasant down.
*Benvolio.*   Mine be that honor then: now sword strike
      home;
   For horns he gave I'll have his head anon.

*Enter* Faustus *with the false head.*

*Martino.*   See see, he comes.
*Benvolio.*                     No words; this blow ends
      all:
   Hell take his soul, his body thus must fall.
*Faustus.*   Oh!                                                 40
*Frederick.*   Groan you, master doctor?
*Benvolio.*   Break may his heart with groans: dear Fred-
      erick, see,
   Thus will I end his griefs immediately.
*Martino.*   Strike with a willing hand! His head is off.
*Benvolio.*   The devil's dead; the furies now may laugh.
*Frederick.*   Was this that stern aspect, that awful frown,
   Made the grim monarch of infernal spirits
   Tremble and quake at his commanding charms?
*Martino.*   Was this that damnèd head whose art conspired
   Benvolio's shame before the Emperor?                          50
*Benvolio.*   Ay, that's the head, and here the body lies
   Justly rewarded for his villainies.
*Frederick.*   Come let's devise how we may add more
      shame
   To the black scandal of his hated name.
*Benvolio.*   First, on his head, in quittance of my wrongs,
   I'll nail huge forkèd horns and let them hang
   Within the window where he yoked me first,
   That all the world may see my just revenge.
*Martino.*   What use shall we put his beard to?

*Benvolio.*   We'll sell it to a chimney-sweeper: it will wear   60
    out ten birchen brooms, I warrant you.
*Frederick.*   What shall his eyes do?
*Benvolio.*   We'll pull out his eyes, and they shall serve for
    buttons to his lips to keep his tongue from catching cold.
*Martino.*   An excellent policy. And now sirs, having di-
    vided him, what shall the body do?

[Faustus *rises.*]

*Benvolio.*   Zounds, the devil's alive again!
*Frederick.*   Give him his head for God's sake!
*Faustus.*   Nay keep it; Faustus will have heads and
    hands,
  Ay, all your hearts, to recompense this deed.         70
  Knew you not, traitors, I was limited
  For four and twenty years to breathe on earth?
  And had you cut my body with your swords,
  Or hewed this flesh and bones as small as sand,
  Yet in a minute had my spirit returned
  And I had breathed a man made free from harm.
  But wherefore do I dally my revenge?
  Asteroth, Belimoth, Mephostophilis!

*Enter* Mephostophilis *and other devils.*

  Go horse these traitors on your fiery backs
  And mount aloft with them as high as heaven,     80
  Thence pitch them headlong to the lowest hell.
  Yet stay, the world shall see their misery,
  And hell shall after plague their treachery.
  Go Belimoth, and take this caitiff[r] hence
  And hurl him in some lake of mud and dirt;
  Take thou this other, drag him through the woods
  Amongst the pricking thorns and sharpest briers,
  Whilst with my gentle Mephostophilis
  This traitor flies unto some steepy rock
  That rolling down may break the villain's bones     90
  As he intended to dismember me.
  Fly hence, dispatch my charge immediately.
*Frederick.*   Pity us gentle Faustus, save our lives!
*Faustus.*   Away!
*Frederick.*   He must needs go that the devil drives.
                   *Exeunt spirits with the knights.*

*Enter the ambushed soldiers.*

  [r] wretch

*1 Soldier.*   Come sirs, prepare yourselves in readiness,
   Make haste to help these noble gentlemen;
   I heard them parley with the conjurer.
*2 Soldier.*   See where he comes; dispatch, and kill the
      slave.
*Faustus.*   What's here? an ambush to betray my life!      100
   Then Faustus, try thy skill. Base peasants, stand!
   For lo, these trees remove at my command
   And stand as bulwarks 'twixt yourselves and me
   To shield me from your hated treachery:
   Yet to encounter this your weak attempt
   Behold an army comes incontinent.[a]

*Faustus strikes the door, and enter a devil playing on a*
   *drum, after him another bearing an ensign, and*
   *divers with weapons;* Mephostophilis *with fireworks:*
   *they set upon the soldiers and drive them out.*
                                             [*Exeunt*]

[IV. iv.] *Enter at several doors* Benvolio, Frederick, *and*
   Martino, *their heads and faces bloody, and besmeared*
   *with mud and dirt, all having horns on their heads.*

*Martino.*   What ho Benvolio!
*Benvolio.*   Here! What Frederick, ho!
*Frederick.*   O help me gentle friend. Where is Martino?
*Martino.*   Dear Frederick, here,
   Half smothered in a lake of mud and dirt,
   Through which the furies dragged me by the heels.
*Frederick.*   Martino, see! Benvolio's horns again.
*Martino.*   O misery! How now Benvolio?
*Benvolio.*   Defend me heaven, shall I be haunted still?[t]
*Martino.*   Nay fear not man, we have no power to kill.      10
*Benvolio.*   My friends transformèd thus! O hellish spite,
   Your heads are all set with horns.
*Frederick.*   You hit it right:
   It is your own you mean; feel on your head.
*Benvolio.*   Zounds, horns again!
*Martino.*   Nay chafe not man, we all are sped.[u]
*Benvolio.*   What devil attends this damned magician,
   That spite of spite our wrongs are doublèd?

   [a] immediately   [t] always   [u] i.e., unfortunate

*Frederick.*    What may we do that we may hide our
     shames?
*Benvolio.*     If we should follow him to work revenge,          20
     He'd join long asses' ears to these huge horns
     And make us laughing-stocks to all the world.
*Martino.*    What shall we then do, dear Benvolio?
*Benvolio.*    I have a castle joining near these woods,
     And thither we'll repair and live obscure
     Till time shall alter this our brutish shapes.
     Sith ᵛ black disgrace hath thus eclipsed our fame
     We'll rather die with grief than live with shame.

                                   *Exeunt omnes.*


     [IV. v.]  *Enter* Faustus *and the* Horse-corser.


*Horse-corser.*    I beseech your worship, accept of these
     forty dollars.
*Faustus.*    Friend, thou canst not buy so good a horse
     for so small a price. I have no great need to sell him, but
     if thou likest him for ten dollars ʷ more, take him, be-
     cause I see thou hast a good mind to him.
*Horse-corser.*    I beseech you sir, accept of this: I am a
     very poor man and have lost very much of late by horse-
     flesh, and this bargain will set me up again.
*Faustus.*    Well, I will not stand ˣ with thee; give me the    10
     money. Now sirrah, I must tell you that you may ride
     him o'er hedge and ditch and spare him not; but do you
     hear? in any case ride him not into the water.
*Horse-corser.*    How sir, not into the water! Why, will he
     not drink of all waters? ʸ
*Faustus.*    Yes, he will drink of all waters, but ride him not
     into the water; o'er hedge and ditch or where thou wilt,
     but not into the water. Go bid the hostler deliver him
     unto you, and remember what I say.
*Horse-corser.*    I warrant you sir. O joyful day! now am I    20
     a made man for ever.                          *Exit.*
*Faustus.*    What art thou, Faustus, but a man condemned
     to die?
     Thy fatal time draws to a final end;
     Despair doth drive distrust into my thoughts.
     Confound ᶻ these passions with a quiet sleep.
     Tush, Christ did call the thief upon the cross;

     ᵛ since   ʷ Dutch coins   ˣ haggle   ʸ i.e., go anywhere   ᶻ conquer

Then rest thee Faustus, quiet in conceit.[a]

*He sits to sleep in his chair.*

*Enter the* Horse-corser *wet.*

*Horse-corser.*   O what a cozening [b] doctor was this! I
  riding my horse into the water, thinking some hidden
  mystery had been in the horse, I had nothing under me    30
  but a little straw, and had much ado to escape drowning.
  Well, I'll go rouse him and make him give me my forty
  dollars again. Ho! sirrah doctor, you cozening scab!
  Master doctor, awake and rise, and give me my money
  again, for your horse is turned to a bottle [c] of hay.
  Master doctor— *He pulls off his leg.* Alas, I am undone!
  what shall I do? I have pulled off his leg.
*Faustus.*   O help, help! the villain hath murdered me.
*Horse-corser.*   Murder or not murder, now he has but one
  leg I'll outrun him, and cast this leg into some ditch or    40
  other.                                                     [*Exit.*]
*Faustus.*   Stop him, stop him, stop him!—Ha ha ha! Faustus hath his leg again, and the horse-corser a bundle of
  hay for his forty dollars.

*Enter* Wagner.

  How now Wagner? what news with thee?
*Wagner.*   If it please you, the Duke of Vanholt doth earnestly entreat your company, and hath sent some of his
  men to attend you with provision fit for your journey.
*Faustus.*   The Duke of Vanholt's an honorable gentleman, and one to whom I must be no niggard of my cun-    50
  ning. Come, away!                                *Exeunt.*

[IV. vi.] *Enter* Clown [Robin], Dick, Horse-corser, *and a*
  Carter.

*Carter.*   Come my masters, I'll bring you to the best beer
  in Europe.—What ho, Hostess!—Where be these
  whores?

*Enter* Hostess.

  [a] mind   [b] cheating   [c] bale

*Hostess.* How now? what lack you? What, my old guesse,[d] welcome.

*Robin.* Sirrah Dick, dost thou know why I stand so mute?

*Dick.* No Robin, why is't?

*Robin.* I am eighteen pence on the score:[e] but say nothing; see if she have forgotten me.

*Hostess.* Who's this that stands so solemnly by himself? What, my old guest!

*Robin.* Oh, hostess, how do you? I hope my score stands still.

*Hostess.* Ay, there's no doubt of that, for methinks you make no haste to wipe it out.

*Dick.* Why hostess, I say! fetch us some beer.

*Hostess.* You shall presently; look up into th' hall. There, ho!                                                *Exit.*

*Dick.* Come sirs, what shall we do now till mine hostess comes?

*Carter.* Marry sir, I'll tell you the bravest tale how a conjurer served me. You know Doctor Fauster?

*Horse-corser.* Ay, a plague take him! Here's some on's[f] have cause to know him. Did he conjure thee too?

*Carter.* I'll tell you how he served me. As I was going to Wittenberg t'other day with a load of hay, he met me and asked me what he should give me for as much hay as he could eat. Now sir, I thinking that a little would serve his turn, bade him take as much as he would for three farthings. So he presently gave me my money and fell to eating; and as I am a cursen[g] man, he never left eating till he had eat up all my load of hay.

*All.* O monstrous, eat a whole load of hay!

*Robin.* Yes, yes, that may be, for I have heard of one that has eat a load of logs.

*Horse-corser.* Now sirs, you shall hear how villainously he served me. I went to him yesterday to buy a horse of him, and he would by no means sell him under forty dollars. So sir, because I knew him to be such a horse as would run over hedge and ditch and never tire, I gave him his money. So, when I had my horse, Doctor Fauster bade me ride him night and day and spare him no time; "But," quoth he, "in any case ride him not into the water." Now sir, I thinking the horse had had some rare quality that he would not have me know of, what did I but rid him into a great river, and when I came just in the midst my horse vanished away and I sate straddling upon a bottle of hay.

---

[d] guests  [e] i.e., in debt  [f] of us  [g] Christian

*All.*   O brave doctor!

*Horse-corser.*   But you shall hear how bravely I served   50
    him for it. I went me home to his house, and there I
    found him asleep: I kept a hallowing and whooping in
    his ears, but all could not wake him. I seeing that, took
    him by the leg and never rested pulling till I had pulled
    me his leg quite off, and now 'tis at home in mine hostry.

*Dick.*   And has the doctor but one leg then? that's excel-
    lent, for one of his devils turned me into the likeness of
    an ape's face.

*Carter.*   Some more drink, hostess!

*Robin.*   Hark you, we'll into another room and drink   60
    awhile, and then we'll go seek out the doctor.

                                          *Exeunt omnes.*

[IV. vii.] *Enter the* Duke of Vanholt, *his* Duchess, Faus-
    tus, *and* Mephostophilis.

*Duke.*   Thanks master doctor, for these pleasant sights:
    nor know I how sufficiently to recompense your great
    deserts in erecting that enchanted castle in the air, the
    sight whereof so delighted me, as nothing in the world
    could please me more.

*Faustus.*   I do think myself, my good lord, highly recom-
    pensed in that it pleaseth your Grace to think but well of
    that which Faustus hath performed. But gracious lady,
    it may be that you have taken no pleasure in those
    sights; therefore I pray you tell me what is the thing you   10
    most desire to have: be it in the world it shall be yours.
    I have heard that great-bellied women do long for
    things are rare and dainty.

*Duchess.*   True master doctor, and since I find you so
    kind, I will make known unto you what my heart de-
    sires to have; and were it now summer, as it is January,
    a dead time of the winter, I would request no better
    meat than a dish of ripe grapes.

*Faustus.*   This is but a small matter.—Go Mephostoph-
    ilis, away!—                    *Exit* Mephostophilis.   20
    Madam, I will do more than this for your content.

*Enter* Mephostophilis *again with the grapes.*

    Here, now taste ye these; they should be good, for they
    come from a far country, I can tell you.

*Duke.*   This makes me wonder more than all the rest, that
  at this time of the year, when every tree is barren of his
  fruit, from whence you had these ripe grapes.

*Faustus.*   Please it your Grace, the year is divided into two
  circles over the whole world, so that when it is winter
  with us, in the contrary circle it is likewise summer with
  them, as in India, Saba,[h] and such countries that lie      30
  far east, where they have fruit twice a year. From
  whence, by means of a swift spirit that I have, I had these
  grapes brought as you see.

*Duchess.*   And trust me, they are the sweetest grapes that
  e'er I tasted.

*The* Clowns *bounce at the gate within.*

*Duke.*   What rude disturbers have we at the gate?
  Go pacify their fury, set it ope,
  And then demand of them what they would have.

*They knock again and call out to talk with* Faustus.

*A Servant.*   Why, how now masters, what a coil[1] is
  there! What is the reason you disturb the Duke?       40

*Dick.*   We have no reason for it, therefore a fig for him!

*Servant.*   Why saucy varlets![j] dare you be so bold?

*Horse-corser.*   I hope sir, we have wit enough to be more
  bold than welcome.

*Servant.*   It appears so: pray be bold elsewhere
  And trouble not the Duke.

*Duke.*                          What would they have?

*Servant.*   They all cry out to speak with Doctor Faustus.

*Carter.*   Ay, and we will speak with him.

*Duke.*   Will you sir? Commit the rascals.

*Dick.*   Commit with us! He were as good commit with his    50
  father as commit with us.

*Faustus.*   I do beseech your Grace, let them come in;
  They are good subject for a merriment.

*Duke.*   Do as thou wilt Faustus; I give thee leave.

*Faustus.*   I thank your Grace.

*Enter the* Clown [Robin], Dick, Carter, *and* Horse-corser.

                          Why, how now my good friends?
  'Faith, you are too outrageous; but come near,

---

[h] Sheba, country of southern Arabia   [1] tumult   [j] knaves

I have procured your pardons. Welcome all!

*Robin.*   Nay sir, we will be welcome for our money, and
we will pay for what we take. What ho! give's half a
dozen of beer here, and be hanged.                                    60

*Faustus.*   Nay, hark you, can you tell me where you are?

*Carter.*   Ay, marry can I; we are under heaven.

*Servant.*   Ay, but sir sauce-box, know you in what place?

*Horse-corser.*   Ay ay, the house is good enough to drink
in. Zounds, fill us some beer, or we'll break all the bar-
rels in the house and dash out all your brains with your
bottles.

*Faustus.*   Be not so furious; come, you shall have beer.
My lord, beseech you give me leave awhile;
I'll gage ᵏ my credit 'twill content your Grace.                      70

*Duke.*   With all my heart kind doctor, please thyself;
Our servants and our court's at thy command.

*Faustus.*   I humbly thank your Grace. Then fetch some
beer.

*Horse-corser.*   Ay marry, there spake a doctor indeed;
and 'faith I'll drink a health to thy wooden leg for that
word.

*Faustus.*   My wooden leg! what dost thou mean by that?

*Carter.*   Ha ha ha, dost hear him Dick? He has forgot his
leg.

*Horse-corser.*   Ay ay, he does not stand much upon that.     80

*Faustus.*   No 'faith, not much upon a wooden leg.

*Carter.*   Good lord, that flesh and blood should be so frail
with your worship! Do not you remember a horse-corser
you sold a horse to?

*Faustus.*   Yes, I remember I sold one a horse.

*Carter.*   And do you remember you bid he should not ride
him into the water?

*Faustus.*   Yes, I do very well remember that.

*Carter.*   And do you remember nothing of your leg?

*Faustus.*   No, in good sooth.                                       90

*Carter.*   Then I pray remember your curtesy.¹

*Faustus.*   I thank you sir.

*Carter.*   'Tis not so much worth. I pray you tell me one
thing.

*Faustus.*   What's that?

*Carter.*   Be both your legs bedfellows every night together?

*Faustus.*   Wouldst thou make a colossus of me, that thou
askest me such questions?

ᵏ stake    ¹ curtsy; also, a leg, i.e., a bow

*Carter.*   No, truly sir, I would make nothing of you, but I 100
would fain [m] know that.

*Enter* Hostess *with drink.*

*Faustus.*   Then I assure thee certainly they are.
*Carter.*   I thank you; I am fully satisfied.
*Faustus.*   But wherefore dost thou ask?
*Carter.*   For nothing sir; but methinks you should have a
wooden bedfellow of one of 'em.
*Horse-corser.*   Why, do you hear sir, did not I pull off one
of your legs when you were asleep?
*Faustus.*   But I have it again now I am awake: look you
here sir.     110
*All.*   O horrible! had the doctor three legs?
*Carter.*   Do you remember sir, how you cozened me and
eat up my load of—

Faustus *charms him dumb.*

*Dick.*   Do you remember how you made me wear an
ape's—
*Horse-corser.*   You whoreson conjuring scab, do you re-
member how you cozened me of a ho—
*Robin.*   Ha' you forgotten me? You think to carry it away
with your "hey-pass" and "re-pass": [n] do you remem-
ber the dog's fa—     *Exeunt* Clowns. 120
*Hostess.*   Who pays for the ale? Hear you master doctor,
now you have sent away my guesse, I pray who shall
pay me for my a—     *Exit* Hostess.
*Duchess.*   My lord,
We are much beholding to this learnèd man.
*Duke.*   So are we madam, which we will recompense
With all the love and kindness that we may:
His artful sport drives all sad thoughts away.

       *Exeunt.*

[V. i.] ⟨*Thunder and lightning. Enter devils with covered dishes:* Mephostophilis *leads them into* Faustus'
*study.*⟩ *Then enter* Wagner.

*Wagner.*   I think my master means to die shortly:
He has made his will and given me his wealth,

[m] gladly    [n] conjuring terms

His house, his goods, and store of golden plate,
Besides two thousand ducats ready coined.
And yet I wonder; for if death were nigh
He would not banquet and carouse and swill
Amongst the students as even now he doth,
Who are at supper with such belly-cheer
As Wagner ne'er beheld in all his life.
See where they come: belike the feast is ended.                    10
                                                     *Exit.*


*Enter* Faustus, Mephostophilis, *and two or three scholars.*

{*1 Scholar.*  Master Doctor Faustus, since our conference about fair ladies, which was the beautifulst in
all the world, we have determined with ourselves that
Helen of Greece was the admirablest lady that ever
lived. Therefore master doctor, if you will do us that
favor, as to let us see that peerless dame of Greece,
whom all the world admires for majesty, we should
think ourselves much beholding unto you. }
*Faustus.*    Gentlemen,
    For that I know your friendship is unfeigned,               20
    And Faustus' custom is not to deny
    The just requests of those that wish him well,
    You shall behold that peerless dame of Greece
    No otherways for pomp and majesty
    Than when Sir Paris crossed the seas for her
    And brought the spoils to rich Dardania.°
    Be silent then, for danger is in words.


*Music sounds.* Mephostophilis *brings in* Helen: *she passeth
        over the stage.*

*2 Scholar.*    Too simple is my wit to tell her praise
    Whom all the world admires for majesty.
*3 Scholar.*    No marvel though the angry Greeks pursued    30
    With ten years' war the rapeᵖ of such a queen.
    Whose heavenly beauty passeth all compare.
*1 Scholar.*    Since we have seen the pride of nature's work
    And only paragon of excellence,
    Let us depart, and for this blessèd sight
    Happy and blest be Faustus evermore.
*Faustus.*    Gentlemen farewell; the same I wish to you.
                                              *Exeunt scholars.*


° Troy    ᵖ abduction

*Enter an* Old Man.

*Old Man.*    O gentle Faustus, leave this damnèd art,
   This magic, that will charm thy soul to hell
   And quite bereave thee of salvation.         40
   Though thou hast now offended like a man,
   Do not persever in it like a devil.
   Yet, yet, thou hast an amiable[q] soul
   If sin by custom grow not into nature;
   Then, Faustus, will repentance come too late,
   Then thou art banished from the sight of heaven:
   No mortal can express the pains of hell.
   It may be this my exhortation
   Seems harsh and all unpleasant; let it not,
   For gentle son, I speak it not in wrath       50
   Or envy of thee, but in tender love
   And pity of thy future misery;
   And so have hope that this my kind rebuke,
   Checking thy body, may amend thy soul.
*Faustus.*    Where art thou Faustus? wretch, what hast
    thou done?
   Damned art thou Faustus, damned; despair and die!

Mephostophilis *gives him a dagger.*

   Hell claims his right, and with a roaring voice
   Says "Faustus, come; thine hour is almost come";
   And Faustus now will come to do thee right.
*Old Man.*    O stay, good Faustus, stay thy desperate steps!  60
   I see an angel hovers o'er thy head,
   And with a vial full of precious grace
   Offers to pour the same into thy soul:
   Then call for mercy and avoid despair.
*Faustus.*    Ah my sweet friend, I feel thy words
   To comfort my distressèd soul:
   Leave me awhile to ponder on my sins.
*Old Man.*    Faustus, I leave thee, but with grief of heart,
   Fearing the enemy of thy hapless soul.    *Exit.*
*Faustus.*    Accursèd Faustus! where is mercy now?  70
   I do repent, and yet I do despair:
   Hell strives with grace for conquest in my breast.
   What shall I do to shun the snares of death?
*Mephostophilis.*    Thou traitor Faustus, I arrest thy soul
   For disobedience to my sovereign lord:

[q] i.e., worthy of love

    Revolt,[r] or I'll in piecemeal tear thy flesh.
*Faustus.*   I do repent I e'er offended him.
    Sweet Mephostophilis, entreat thy lord
    To pardon my unjust presumption,
    And with my blood again I will confirm        80
    The former vow I made to Lucifer.
*Mephostophilis.*   Do it then, Faustus, with unfeignèd
    heart,
    Lest greater dangers do attend thy drift.[s]
*Faustus.*   Torment, sweet friend, that base and agèd
    man
    That durst dissuade me from thy Lucifer,
    With greatest torments that our hell affords.
*Mephostophilis.*   His faith is great, I cannot touch his
    soul;
    But what I may afflict his body with
    I will attempt, which is but little worth.
*Faustus.* One thing, good servant, let me crave of thee    90
    To glut the longing of my heart's desire;
    That I may have unto my paramour
    That heavenly Helen which I saw of late,
    Whose sweet embracings may extinguish clear
    Those thoughts that do dissuade me from my vow,
    And keep the oath I made to Lucifer.
*Mephostophilis.*   This or what else my Faustus shall de-
    sire
    Shall be performed in twinkling of an eye.

*Enter* Helen *again, passing over between two* Cupids.

*Faustus.* Was this the face that launched a thousand ships
    And burnt the topless towers of Ilium?[t]    100
    Sweet Helen, make me immortal with a kiss.
    Her lips suck forth my soul: see where it flies!
    Come Helen, come, give me my soul again.
    Here will I dwell, for heaven is in these lips
    And all is dross that is not Helena.

*Enter* Old Man.

    I will be Paris, and for love of thee
    Instead of Troy shall Wittenberg be sacked,
    And I will combat with weak Menelaus [u]
    And wear thy colors on my plumèd crest,

    [r] deny   [s] delay   [t] Troy   [u] Helen's husband

Yea, I will wound Achilles ᵛ in the heel　　　110
And then return to Helen for a kiss.
Oh, thou art fairer than the evening's air
Clad in the beauty of a thousand stars,
Brighter art thou than flaming Jupiter
When he appeared to hapless Semele,ʷ
More lovely than the monarch of the skyˣ
In wanton Arethusa'sʸ azured arms,
And none but thou shalt be my paramour.　　*Exeunt.*

*Old Man.* Accursèd Faustus, miserable man,
That from thy soul excludst the grace of heaven　　　120
And fliest the throne of his tribunal seat!

*Enter the devils.*

Satan begins to siftᶻ me with his pride:
As in this furnace God shall try my faith,
My faith, vile hell, shall triumph over thee.
Ambitious fiends, see how the heavens smile
At your repulse and laughs your stateᵃ to scorn!
Hence hell! for hence I fly unto my God.　　*Exeunt.*

[V. ii.] ⟨*Thunder. Enter* Lucifer, Beelzebub, *and* Mepho-
　　stophilis [*above*].

*Lucifer.*　　Thus from infernal Dis ᵇ do we ascend
To view the subjects of our monarchy,
Those souls which sin seals the black sons of hell.
'Mong which as chief, Faustus, we come to thee,
Bringing with us lasting damnation
To wait upon thy soul; the time is come
Which makes it forfeit.
*Mephostophilis.*　　　　　　And this gloomy night
Here in this room will wretched Faustus be.
*Beelzebub.*　　And here we'll stay
To mark him how he doth demean himself.　　　10
*Mephostophilis.*　　How should he but with desperate
　　lunacy?
Fond worldling, now his heart-blood dries with grief,
His conscience kills it, and his laboring brain
Begets a world of idle fantasies
To overreach the devil, but all in vain:

---

ᵛ greatest of the Greek warriors　ʷ a mortal, beloved of Jupiter and
destroyed by his brightness　ˣ i.e., the sun　ʸ a fountain　ᶻ test　ᵃ power
ᵇ the lower regions of hell

His store of pleasures must be sauced with pain.
He and his servant Wagner are at hand,
Both come from drawing Faustus' latest will.
See where they come!

*Enter* Faustus *and* Wagner.

*Faustus.* Say Wagner, thou hast perused my will;                    20
  How dost thou like it?
*Wagner.*                        Sir, so wondrous well
  As in all humble duty I do yield
My life and lasting service for your love.

*Enter the scholars.*

*Faustus.*    Gramercies ᵉ Wagner.—Welcome gentlemen.
*1 Scholar.*    Now worthy Faustus, methinks your looks are
    changed.⟩

(*Enter* Faustus *with the scholars.*)

*Faustus.*    Ah Gentlemen!
*2 Scholar.*    What ails Faustus?
*Faustus.*    Ah my sweet chamber-fellow, had I lived with
    thee, then had I lived still, but now must die eternally.
    Look sirs! comes he not, comes he not?                           30
*1 Scholar.*    O my dear Faustus, what imports this fear?
*2 Scholar.*    Is all our pleasure turned to melancholy?
*3 Scholar.*    He is not well with being over-solitary.
*2 Scholar.*    If it be so, we'll have physicians, and Faustus
    shall be cured.
*3 Scholar.*    'Tis but a surfeit sir, fear nothing.
*Faustus.*    A surfeit of deadly sin, that hath damned both
    body and soul.
*2 Scholar.*    Yet Faustus, look up to heaven and remem-
    ber God's mercy is infinite.                                     40
*Faustus.*    But Faustus' offense can ne'er be pardoned:
    the serpent that tempted Eve may be saved, but not
    Faustus. Ah gentlemen, hear me with patience and
    tremble not at my speeches. Though my heart pants and
    quivers to remember that I have been a student here
    these thirty years, oh, would I had never seen Witten-
    berg, never read book! and what wonders I have done

ᵉ many thanks

all Germany can witness, yea all the world, for which
Faustus hath lost both Germany and the world, yea
heaven itself—heaven, the seat of God, the throne of the    50
blessèd, the kingdom of joy—and must remain in hell
for ever. Hell, ah hell for ever! Sweet friends, what shall
become of Faustus, being in hell for ever?

*2 Scholar.*  Yet Faustus, call on God.

*Faustus.*  On God, whom Faustus hath abjured? On God,
whom Faustus hath blasphemed? Ah my God, I would
weep, but the devil draws in my tears. Gush forth
blood instead of tears, yea life and soul! Oh, he stays my
tongue: I would lift up my hands, but see, they hold 'em,
they hold 'em.

*All.*  Who, Faustus?

*Faustus.*  Why, Lucifer and Mephostophilis. Ah gentle-    60
men, I gave them my soul for my cunning.

*All.*  God forbid!

*Faustus.*  God forbade it indeed, but Faustus hath done
it. For the vain pleasure of four and twenty years hath
Faustus lost eternal joy and felicity. I writ them a bill
with mine own blood: the date is expired, this is the
time, and he will fetch me.

*1 Scholar.*  Why did not Faustus tell us of this before, that    70
divines might have prayed for thee?

*Faustus.*  Oft have I thought to have done so; but the
devil threatened to tear me in pieces if I named God, to
fetch me body and soul if I once gave ear to divinity; and
now 'tis too late. Gentlemen, away, lest you perish with
me!

*2 Scholar.*  Oh, what may we do to save Faustus?

*Faustus.*  Talk not of me, but save yourselves and depart.

*3 Scholar.*  God will strengthen me; I will stay with
Faustus.    80

*1 Scholar.*  Tempt not God sweet friend; but let us into
the next room and there pray for him.

*Faustus.*  Ay, pray for me, pray for me; and what noise
soever ye hear, come not unto me, for nothing can
rescue me.

*2 Scholar.*  Pray thou, and we will pray, that God may
have mercy upon thee.

*Faustus.*  Gentlemen farewell. If I live till morning I'll
visit you; if not, Faustus is gone to hell.    90

*All.*  Faustus, farewell.                    *Exeunt scholars.*

⟨*Mephostophilis.*  Ay, Faustus, now hast thou no hope
of heaven;

        Therefore despair, think only upon hell,
        For that must be thy mansion, there to dwell.
*Faustus.*   O thou bewitching fiend, 'twas thy temptation
        Hath robbed me of eternal happiness.
*Mephostophilis.*   I do confess it Faustus, and rejoice.
        'Twas I, that when thou wert i' the way to heaven,
        Dammed up thy passage; when thou tookst the book
        To view the scriptures, then I turned the leaves
        And led thine eye.                                          100
        What, weepst thou? 'tis too late, despair, farewell:
        Fools that will laugh on earth must weep in hell.    *Exit.*


*Enter the* Good Angel *and the* Bad Angel *at several doors.*


*Good Angel.*   Ah Faustus, if thou hadst given ear to me
        Innumerable joys had followed thee;
        But thou didst love the world.
*Bad Angel.*                            Gave ear to me,
        And now must taste hell's pains perpetually.
*Good Angel.* Oh, what will all thy riches, pleasures,
            pomps
        Avail thee now?
*Bad Angel.*   Nothing but vex thee more
        To want in hell, that had on earth such store.


*Music while the throne* [d] *descends.*


*Good Angel.*   Oh, thou hast lost celestial happiness,    110
        Pleasures unspeakable, bliss without end.
        Hadst thou affected [e] sweet divinity
        Hell or the devil had had no power on thee:
        Hadst thou kept on that way, Faustus behold
        In what resplendent glory thou hadst sit
        In yonder throne, like those bright shining saints,
        And triumphed over hell; that hast thou lost.
        And now, poor soul, must thy good angel leave thee;
        The jaws of hell are open to receive thee.        *Exit.*


*Hell is discovered.*


*Bad Angel.*   Now Faustus, let thine eyes with horror
            stare                                                   120
        Into that vast perpetual torture-house.
        There are the furies, tossing damnèd souls
        On burning forks; their bodies boil in lead:

        [d] symbol of heaven   [e] been devoted to

There are live quarters broiling on the coals,
That ne'er can die: this ever-burning chair
Is for o'er-tortured souls to rest them in:
These that are fed with sops of flaming fire
Were gluttons and loved only delicates
And laughed to see the poor starve at their gates.
But yet all these are nothing; thou shalt see                    130
  Ten thousand tortures that more horrid be.
*Faustus.*    Oh, I have seen enough to torture me.
*Bad Angel.*    Nay, thou must feel them, taste the smart of
  all:
  He that loves pleasure must for pleasure fall.
  And so I leave thee Faustus, till anon;
  Then wilt thou tumble in confusion.                    *Exit.*⟩


*The clock strikes eleven.*


*Faustus.*    Ah Faustus,
  Now hast thou but one bare hour to live,
  And then thou must be damned perpetually.
  Stand still, you ever-moving spheres of heaven,                    140
  That time may cease and midnight never come;
  Fair nature's eye,[f] rise, rise again and make
  Perpetual day; or let this hour but be
  A year, a month, a week, a natural day,[g]
  That Faustus may repent and save his soul.
  *O lente lente currite noctis equi!* [h]
  The stars move still, time runs, the clock will strike,
  The devil will come, and Faustus must be damned.
  Oh, I'll leap up to my God! Who pulls me down?
  See see where Christ's blood streams in the firmament!                    150
  One drop would save my soul, half a drop. Ah my
      Christ!—
  Rend not my heart for naming of my Christ;
  Yet will I call on him: oh, spare me Lucifer!—
  Where is it now? 'Tis gone: and see where God
  Stretcheth out his arm and bends his ireful brows.
  Mountains and hills, come, come and fall on me
  And hide me from the heavy wrath of God!
  No, no:
  Then will I headlong run into the earth.
  Earth gape! O no, it will not harbor me.                    160
  You stars that reigned at my nativity,
  Whose influence hath allotted death and hell,

[f] i.e., the sun    [g] sunrise to sunset    [h] "Run slowly, slowly, horses of
the night" (Ovid, *Amores*, I, 13)

Now draw up Faustus like a foggy mist
Into the entrails of yon laboring clouds,
That when they vomit forth into the air,
My limbs may issue from their smoky mouths,
So that my soul may but ascend to heaven.

*The watch strikes.*

Ah, half the hour is passed: 'twill all be passed anon.
O God,
If thou wilt not have mercy on my soul,                    170
Yet for Christ's sake, whose blood hath ransomed me,
Impose some end to my incessant pain;
Let Faustus live in hell a thousand years,
A hundred thousand, and at last be saved!
Oh, no end is limited to damnèd souls.
Why wert thou not a creature wanting[1] soul?
Or why is this immortal that thou hast?
Ah, Pythagoras' metempsycosis,[J] were that true
This soul should fly from me and I be changed
Unto some brutish beast: all beasts are happy,          180
For when they die
Their souls are soon dissolved in elements;
But mine must live still to be plagued in hell.
Cursed be the parents that engendered me!
No Faustus, curse thyself, curse Lucifer
That hath deprived thee of the joys of heaven.

*The clock striketh twelve.*

It strikes, it strikes! Now body, turn to air,
Or Lucifer will bear thee quick to hell!

*Thunder and lightning.*

O soul, be changed to little water-drops
And fall into the ocean, ne'er be found.                    190

*Enter devils.*

My God, my God! Look not so fierce on me!
Adders and serpents, let me breathe awhile!
Ugly hell, gape not! Come not Lucifer;
I'll burn my books!—Ah, Mephostophilis!
                                        *Exeunt with him.*

[1] lacking   [J] theory held by Pythagoras, a Greek philosopher, that
souls transmigrated from one body to another

⟨ [V. iii.] *Enter the scholars.*

*1 Scholar.*    Come gentlemen, let us go visit Faustus,
  For such a dreadful night was never seen
  Since first the world's creation did begin,
  Such fearful shrieks and cries were never heard.
  Pray heaven the doctor have escaped the danger.
*2 Scholar.*    Oh, help us heaven! see, here are Faustus'
      limbs
  All torn asunder by the hand of death.
*3 Scholar.*    The devils whom Faustus served have torn
      him thus;
  For 'twixt the hours of twelve and one, methought
  I heard him shriek and call aloud for help,                    10
  At which self time the house seemed all on fire
  With dreadful horror of these damnèd fiends.
*2 Scholar.*    Well gentlemen, though Faustus' end be
      such
  As every Christian heart laments to think on,
  Yet for[k] he was a scholar once admired
  For wondrous knowledge in our German schools,
  We'll give his mangled limbs due burial;
  And all the students, clothed in mourning black,
      Shall wait upon his heavy funeral.        *Exeunt.*⟩


[Epilogue.] *Enter* Chorus.

Cut is the branch that might have grown full straight,
And burnèd is Apollo's [1] laurel bough
That sometime[m] grew within this learnèd man.
Faustus is gone: regard his hellish fall,
Whose fiendful fortune may exhort the wise
Only to wonder at unlawful things,
Whose deepness doth entice such forward wits
To practice more than heavenly power permits.
                  *Finis.*

[k] because   [1] god of learning   [m] formerly

# William Shakespeare:

## *MACBETH*

"The fiend is at mine elbow, and tempts me, saying to me . . ., 'Use your legs, take the start, run away.' My conscience says 'No. Take heed. . . .' 'Budge,' says the fiend. 'Budge not,' says my conscience. 'Conscience,' say I, 'you counsel well.' 'Fiend,' say I, 'you counsel well.'" These lines are not a parody of Macbeth's hesitation to murder Duncan, his king, but they easily could be. They are from a comic scene in *The Merchant of Venice*, in which a clown debates with himself whether to flee from Shylock's service. The Fiend and Conscience are, like the Good and Evil Angels in *Doctor Faustus*, derived directly from the old morality plays (see p. 14), which Shakespeare probably saw in his youth and which helped shape *Macbeth*. *Macbeth* is based on history, or what was alleged to be history, and it has echoes of the Roman tragedian Seneca (compare Seneca's "What Tanais will wash me . . . ? Not the great father himself, with all his ocean, will cleanse such sin," with Shakespeare's "Will all great Neptune's ocean wash this blood/ Clean from my hand? No; this my hand will rather/ The multitudinous seas incarnadine"); but despite the historical source and despite Shakespeare's undoubted acquaintance with Seneca, the underlying form is the morality play.

At one side of Macbeth stands Duncan, offering him all that an honorable man can lawfully desire: "Welcome hither:/ I have begun to plant thee, and will labor/ To make thee full of growing." Duncan is "the Lord's anointed temple," and Macbeth himself says that Duncan's "virtues will plead like angels." At Macbeth's other side stands Lady Macbeth: "Hie thee hither,/ That I may pour my spirits in thine ear"; "Look like the innocent flower,/ But be the serpent under 't." The Weïrd Sisters are of a less certain nature; they are called witches, but they seem to be embodiments of Macbeth's own half-thought evil plans, beguiling him to do what he is already in-

clined to do. Coleridge's characterization of them is as good
as any: "They are . . . the lawless of human nature."

When Macbeth yields to his murderous impulses and to the
promptings of Lady Macbeth, he commits a crime that he himself recognizes is triply heinous. Duncan is Macbeth's kinsman,
lord, guest. Besides, Duncan is unquestionably virtuous. In
Shakespeare's source, Holinshed's *Chronicles*, Duncan was an
ineffectual king, under whose reign lawlessness thrived. Macbeth and Banquo rebelled against him, for the public good, it
seems. But Shakespeare's Macbeth has no such excuse, and
he never deludes himself into thinking his evil actions are good.
He knowingly commits the blackest deeds. The result is a
kingdom of instability, inversion, terror. "Fair is foul, and foul
is fair"; the clock says it is day, "And yet dark night strangles
the traveling lamp"; the honest Macduff must desert his wife;
Macbeth pretends to be good so that he may do evil, and Malcolm pretends to be evil so that he may do good.

Macbeth, one can almost say, is not the king, but a man disguised as a king. James I, before whom the play was probably
performed in 1606, would have found impeccable Shakespeare's picture of a kingdom distempered by regicide. A
usurper could hardly bring to a kingdom the health that James
believed a king must bring. "It is the king's part, as the proper
physician of his politic-body, to purge it of all those diseases
by medicinals meet for the same." Macbeth, on the contrary,
has infected the realm:

> If thou couldst, doctor, cast
> The water of my land, find her disease
> And purge it to a sound and pristine health,
> I would applaud thee to the very echo.

The wry contrarieties, or reversals, or ironies, of *Macbeth*,
though especially prominent, are not unusual; they are the
stuff of tragedy. Near the end of *Hamlet*, Horatio speaks of the
tragic happenings as (in part) "purposes mistook/ Fall'n on
the inventors' heads." Consider, as examples, these ironies.
First, Duncan, having been betrayed by the Thane of Cawdor,
says to his loyal subjects:

> There's no art
> To find the mind's construction in the face:
> He was a gentleman on whom I built
> An absolute trust.

At this moment Macbeth enters, and Duncan courteously
greets another man whose mind's construction cannot be read

in the face. Second, when Duncan's corpse is discovered, Macbeth, feigning horror, asserts he has nothing to live for now that his king is dead:

> Had I but died an hour before this chance,
> I had lived a blessèd time; for from this instant
> There's nothing serious in mortality.

He presumably does not mean what he says, yet what he says contains a truth: Macbeth's bliss is now gone. Third, Macbeth hypocritically urges Banquo to "fail not our feast." Banquo promises to attend, and again words have a meaning of which the speaker was not aware, for the ghost of the murdered Banquo will indeed attend the feast. One could give dozens of additional examples, but the most pervasive irony is that Macbeth, in reaching for the crown that he esteemed "the ornament of life," finds that he has annihilated life—not Duncan's only, but his own. Power has become impotence. In a recognition scene near the end of the play, he sees clearly that his doings have had effects opposed to those he desired:

> I have lived long enough. My way of life
> Is fall'n into the sear, the yellow leaf,
> And that which should accompany old age,
> As honor, love, obedience, troops of friends,
> I must not look to have.

Macbeth's insight appears not only in the fifth act. He is remarkably gifted with awareness even in the first, and it is partly this gift that distinguishes him from Lady Macbeth. His mind conjures up the visions of Duncan's virtues pleading like angels and of pity blowing the horrid deed in every eye. In the second act, when Macbeth is distressed by his inability to say "Amen" in the presence of the drugged grooms, Lady Macbeth seeks to brush his fears aside: "Consider it not so deeply." When he pursues the problem, she replies: "These deeds must not be thought/ After these ways; so, it will make us mad." Macbeth, looking at his bloody hands, says that the ocean cannot wash them; Lady Macbeth insists that "a little water clears us of this deed." His suggestive mind causes him to envision the murder when the first prediction of the Witches (that he will be Thane of Cawdor) proves true:

> Why do I yield to that suggestion
> Whose horrid image doth unfix my hair
> And make my seated heart knock at my ribs,
> Against the use of nature?

This potent imagination is manifested in rich utterance. When Macbeth learns of Lady Macbeth's death, he has a speech that, however perverse, is unforgettable; when Macduff learns of the death of his wife and children he is speechless. We like and honor Macduff; we are spellbound by Macbeth. There are other qualities, too, that prevent Macbeth from being a paltry knave. There is, notably, his valor. Early in the play, before the audience sees him, he is "brave Macbeth—well he deserves that name," "valor's minion," "valiant cousin! worthy gentleman," an eagle, a lion, "Bellona's bridegroom," and "noble Macbeth." Such epithets are not mere mouth-honor; by his exploits he merits them. But his valor and armor of the first act give way to heartlessness and the usurped robes of the king. His villainy forces the audience to condemn him; perhaps he is most loathsome when he cringes before Banquo's ghost and (taking refuge in the fact that he did not strike Banquo with his own hand) cries, "Thou canst not say I did it," or when he determines to destroy Macduff's helpless family. When we see him through Angus' eyes, he is not a magnificent villain but a contemptible one:

> Now does he feel his title
> Hang loose about him, like a giant's robe
> Upon a dwarfish thief.

Even when in the last act he rearms, he is clearly not what he was. His valor is characterized as madness or as (at best) "valiant fury"; he arms, prematurely it seems, in V. iii, but he is so distressed by the doctor's inability to minister to Lady Macbeth that he orders himself to be unarmed. Later, when he exits to arm, he is both weary and reckless. He himself says he is tied to a stake and must fight "bearlike." But shortly before he dies he reveals a touch of conscience that reminds us he is not a mere beast. The murder of Macduff's family has apparently weighed on him; confronted with Macduff he says, "Of all men else I have avoided thee./ But get thee back! My soul is too much charged/ With blood of thine already." Who would have thought the tyrant to have had so much conscience in him?

## Biographical Note

William Shakespeare (1564–1616) was born in Stratford, the son of a glover who in 1568 was elected High Bailiff (i.e., mayor) of Stratford. As the son of a solid citizen, Shakespeare almost surely attended the school at

Stratford, where he would have learned enough Latin to enter a university. At an uncertain date (1588 is a good guess) he went to London; by 1592 he was notable enough as an actor and/or dramatist to be attacked in a pamphlet by a discontented dramatist. In 1594 he became a charter member of the company that later built and jointly owned the Globe Theater. In 1603, King James, a few weeks after his coronation, issued Royal Letters Patent to Shakespeare and his fellow actors, making them the King's Company. *Macbeth* may have been written in 1606 for James, who was regarded as a descendant of Banquo. Shakespeare prospered as actor-author-entrepreneur, and about 1611 he retired to Stratford. In addition to writing England's greatest plays, he wrote her greatest sonnets.

# MACBETH

❧

## Characters

DUNCAN, *king of Scotland*

MALCOLM,
DONALBAIN, } *his sons*

MACBETH,
BANQUO,
MACDUFF,
LENNOX,
ROSS,
MENTEITH,
ANGUS,
CAITHNESS, } *noblemen of Scotland*

FLEANCE, *son to* BANQUO

SIWARD, *Earl of Northumberland*

YOUNG SIWARD, *his son*

SEYTON, *an officer attending on* MACBETH
BOY, *son to* MACDUFF
An English Doctor
A Scottish Doctor
A Captain
A Porter
An Old Man
Three Murderers
LADY MACBETH
LADY MACDUFF
Gentlewoman attending on LADY MACBETH
HECATE
Three Witches (the Weïrd Sisters)
Apparitions
Lords, Officers, Soldiers, Attendants, and Messengers

# ACT I

*Scene I* [*Scotland. A deserted place.*]

*Thunder and lightning. Enter three* Witches.

*First Witch.*   When shall we three meet again?
  In thunder, lightning, or in rain?
*Second Witch.*   When the hurlyburly's done,
  When the battle's lost and won.
*Third Witch.*   That will be ere the set of sun.
*First Witch.*   Where the place?
*Second Witch.*                    Upon the heath.
*Third Witch.*   There to meet with Macbeth.
*First Witch.*   I come, Graymalkin.[a]
*Second Witch.*   Paddock [b] calls.
*Third Witch.*   Anon! [c]
*All.*   Fair is foul, and foul is fair.
  Hover through the fog and filthy air.          *Exeunt.*   10


*Scene II* [*A camp.*]

*Alarum*[d] *within. Enter* King [Duncan], Malcolm, Donal-
     bain, Lennox, *with* Attendants, *meeting a bleeding*
     Captain.

*King.*   What bloody man is that? He can report,
  As seemeth by his plight, of the revolt
  The newest state.
*Malcolm.*                    This is the sergeant [e]
  Who like a good and hardy soldier fought
  'Gainst my captivity. Hail, brave friend!
  Say to the king the knowledge of the broil [f]
  As thou didst leave it.
*Captain.*                    Doubtful it stood,
  As two spent swimmers, that do cling together
  And choke their art.[g] The merciless Macdonwald—
  Worthy to be a rebel, for to that                    10
  The multiplying villainies of nature

---

  [a] a gray cat (the witch's familiar spirit)   [b] a toad   [c] at once   [d] alarm
(signal)   [e] i.e., captain   [f] battle   [g] i.e., impede each other

*168*

Do swarm upon him—from the Western Isles [h]
Of kerns and gallowglasses [i] is supplied;
And Fortune, on his damnèd quarrel [j] smiling,
Showed [k] like a rebel's whore. But all's too weak:
For brave Macbeth—well he deserves that name—
Disdaining Fortune, with his brandished steel,
Which smoked with bloody execution,
Like valor's minion [l] carved out his passage
Till he faced the slave;                                      20
Which ne'er shook hands, nor bade farewell to him,
Till he unseamed him from the nave to th' chops, [m]
And fixed his head upon our battlements.

*King.*    O valiant cousin! worthy gentleman!

*Captain.*    As whence the sun 'gins his reflection [n]
Shipwracking storms and direful thunders break,
So from that spring whence comfort seemed to come
Discomfort [o] swells. Mark, king of Scotland, mark:
No sooner justice had, with valor armed,
Compelled these skipping kerns to trust their heels,        30
But the Norweyan lord, surveying vantage, [p]
With furbished arms and new supplies of men,
Began a fresh assault.

*King.*                          Dismayed not this
Our captains, Macbeth and Banquo?

*Captain.*                          Yes;
As sparrows eagles, or the hare the lion.
If I say sooth, [q] I must report they were
As cannons overcharged with double cracks; [r]
So they
Doubly redoubled strokes upon the foe.
Except they meant to bathe in reeking wounds,               40
Or memorize [s] another Golgotha,
I cannot tell—
But I am faint; my gashes cry for help.

*King.*    So well thy words become thee as thy wounds;
They smack of honor both. Go get him surgeons.

                                   [*Exit* Captain, *attended*].
Who comes here?

*Enter* Ross *and* Angus.

*Malcolm.*                The worthy Thane [t] of Ross.

*Lennox.*    What a haste looks through his eyes! So should
      he look

[h] Hebrides   [i] Irish light-armed footsoldiers and Irish trained armored
soldiers   [j] cause   [k] appeared   [l] darling   [m] navel to the jaws   [n] shining
[o] discouragement   [p] seeing an opportunity   [q] truth   [r] explosives   [s] make
memorable   [t] a Scottish lord

That seems to ᵘ speak things strange.

*Ross.*                                        God save the king!

*King.*     Whence camest thou, worthy Thane?

*Ross.*                                 From Fife, great king;
   Where the Norweyan banners flout the sky                    50
   And fan our people cold.
   Norway himself with terrible numbers,
   Assisted by that most disloyal traitor
   The Thane of Cawdor, began a dismal ᵛ conflict;
   Till that Bellona's ʷ bridegroom, lapped in proof,ˣ
   Confronted him with self-comparisons,ʸ
   Point against point, rebellious arm 'gainst arm,
   Curbing his lavish ᶻ spirit: and, to conclude,
   The victory fell on us.

*King.*                                   Great happiness!

*Ross.*     That now
   Sweno, the Norways' king, craves composition; ᵃ              60
   Nor would we deign him burial of his men
   Till he disbursèd, at Saint Colme's Inch.ᵇ
   Ten thousand dollars ᶜ to our general use.

*King.*     No more that Thane of Cawdor shall deceive
   Our bosom interest.ᵈ Go pronounce his present death,
   And with his former title greet Macbeth.

*Ross.*     I'll see it done.

*King.*     What he hath lost, noble Macbeth hath won.

                              *Exeunt.*


### Scene III [*A heath.*]

*Thunder. Enter the three* Witches.


*First Witch.*     Where hast thou been, sister?

*Second Witch.*     Killing swine.

*Third Witch.*     Sister, where thou?

*First Witch.*     A sailor's wife had chestnuts in her lap,
   And mounched, and mounched, and mounched. "Give
     me," quoth I:
   "Aroint thee,ᵉ witch!" the rump-fed ronyonᶠ cries.
   Her husband's to Aleppo gone, master o' th' *Tiger;*
   But in a sieve I'll thither sail,
   And, like a rat without a tail,
   I'll do, I'll do, and I'll do.                                        10

---

ᵘ seems about to   ᵛ ominous   ʷ goddess of war   ˣ wrapped in proven
armor   ʸ equal powers   ᶻ wild   ᵃ terms of surrender   ᵇ island   ᶜ Spanish
coins   ᵈ heart's trust   ᵉ begone   ᶠ fat-rumped scabby creature

*Second Witch.*    I'll give thee a wind.
*First Witch.*    Th'art kind.
*Third Witch.*    And I another.
*First Witch.*    I myself have all the other;
　　And the very ports they blow,
　　All the quarters that they know
　　I' th' shipman's card. ᵍ
　　I'll drain him dry as hay:
　　Sleep shall neither night nor day
　　Hang upon his penthouse lid; ʰ                    20
　　He shall live a man forbid: ¹
　　Weary sev'nights nine times nine
　　Shall he dwindle, peak,ʲ and pine:
　　Though his bark cannot be lost,
　　Yet it shall be tempest-tost.
　　Look what I have.
*Second Witch.*    Show me, show me.
*First Witch.*    Here I have a pilot's thumb,
　　Wracked as homeward he did come.

*Drum within.*

*Third Witch.*    A drum, a drum!                    30
　　Macbeth doth come.
*All.*    The weïrd ᵏ sisters, hand in hand,
　　Posters ¹ of the sea and land,
　　Thus do go about, about:
　　Thrice to thine, and thrice to mine,
　　And thrice again, to make up nine.
　　Peace! The charm's wound up.

*Enter* Macbeth *and* Banquo.

*Macbeth.*    So foul and fair a day I have not seen.
*Banquo.*    How far is't called to Forres? What are these
　　So withered, and so wild in their attire,                    40
　　That look not like th' inhabitants o' the earth,
　　And yet are on't? Live you; or are you aught
　　That man may question? ᵐ You seem to understand me,
　　By each at once her choppy ⁿ finger laying
　　Upon her skinny lips. You should be women,

---

ᵍ compass card   ʰ eyelid   ¹ accursed   ʲ waste away   ᵏ weird (from
Old English *wyrd*: fate) is variously spelled "weyard" and "weyward" in
the original text. It has been argued that the weïrd sisters are witches or
devils or the Fates, but each of these interpretations is debatable.   ¹ swift
travelers   ᵐ converse with   ⁿ chapped

And yet your beards forbid me to interpret
That you are so.

*Macbeth.*            Speak, if you can. What are you?

*First Witch.*    All hail, Macbeth! Hail to thee, Thane of
        Glamis!

*Second Witch.*    All hail, Macbeth! Hail to thee, Thane of
        Cawdor!

*Third Witch.*    All hail, Macbeth, thou shalt be King here-
        after!                                                                    50

*Banquo.*    Good sir, why do you start, and seem to fear
    Things that do sound so fair? I' the name of truth,
    Are ye fantastical,° or that indeed
    Which outwardly ye show? My noble partner
    You greet with present grace ᵖ and great prediction
    Of noble having and of royal hope,
    That he seems rapt withal. To me you speak not.
    If you can look into the seeds of time,
    And say which grain will grow and which will not,
    Speak to me, who neither beg nor fear                            60
    Your favors nor your hate.

*First Witch.*    Hail!

*Second Witch.*    Hail!

*Third Witch.*    Hail!

*First Witch.*    Lesser than Macbeth, and greater.

*Second Witch.*    Not so happy,ʳ yet much happier.

*Third Witch.*    Thou shalt get ˢ kings, though thou be
        none.
    So all hail, Macbeth and Banquo!

*First Witch.*    Banquo and Macbeth, all hail!

*Macbeth.*    Stay, you imperfect ᵗ speakers, tell me more:        70
    By Sinel's ᵘ death I know I am Thane of Glamis;
    But how of Cawdor? the Thane of Cawdor lives,
    A prosperous gentleman; and to be king
    Stands not within the prospect of belief,
    No more than to be Cawdor. Say from whence
    You owe ᵛ this strange intelligence? Or why
    Upon this blasted heath you stop our way
    With such prophetic greeting? Speak, I charge you.
                                                        *Witches vanish.*

*Banquo.*    The earth hath bubbles as the water has,
    And these are of them. Whither are they vanished?            80

*Macbeth.*    Into the air, and what seemed corporal ʷ melted
    As breath into the wind. Would they had stayed!

*Banquo.*    Were such things here as we do speak about?

---

° imaginary    ᵖ honor    ʳ fortunate    ˢ beget    ᵗ incomplete    ᵘ Macbeth's
father    ᵛ own    ʷ corporeal

    Or have we eaten on the insane <sup>x</sup> root
    That takes the reason prisoner?
*Macbeth.*     Your children shall be kings.
*Banquo.*                  You shall be King.
*Macbeth.*    And Thane of Cawdor too: went it not so?
*Banquo.*    To th' selfsame tune and words. Who's here?

*Enter* Ross *and* Angus.

*Ross.*    The King hath happily received, Macbeth,
    The news of thy success: and when he reads <sup>y</sup>          90
    Thy personal venture in the rebels' fight,
    His wonders <sup>z</sup> and his praises do contend
    Which should be thine or his: silenced with that,
    In viewing o'er the rest o' th' selfsame day,
    He finds thee in the stout Norweyan ranks,
    Nothing afeard of what thyself didst make,
    Strange images of death. As thick as tale <sup>a</sup>
    Came post with post,<sup>b</sup> and every one did bear
    Thy praises in his kindgom's great defense,
    And poured them down before him.
*Angus.*                 We are sent       100
    To give thee, from our royal master, thanks;
    Only to herald thee into his sight,
    Not pay thee.
*Ross.*    And for an earnest <sup>c</sup> of a greater honor,
    He bade me, from him, call thee Thane of Cawdor:
    In which addition,<sup>d</sup> hail, most worthy Thane!
    For it is thine.
*Banquo.*     What, can the devil speak true?
*Macbeth.*    The Thane of Cawdor lives: why do you dress
    me
    In borrowed robes?
*Angus.*            Who was the Thane lives yet,
    But under heavy judgment bears that life        110
    Which he deserves to lose. Whether he was combined
    With those of Norway, or did line <sup>e</sup> the rebel
    With hidden help and vantage,<sup>f</sup> or that with both
    He labored in his country's wrack, I know not;
    But treasons capital, confessed and proved,
    Have overthrown him.
*Macbeth.* [*Aside.*]      Glamis, and Thane of Cawdor:

---

<sup>x</sup> madness-inducing    <sup>y</sup> considers    <sup>z</sup> admiration    <sup>a</sup> as fast as they can be
counted    <sup>b</sup> messenger after messenger    <sup>c</sup> pledge    <sup>d</sup> title    <sup>e</sup> support    <sup>f</sup> opportunity

The greatest is behind.ᵍ [*To* Ross *and* Angus.] Thanks
    for your pains.
[*Aside to* Banquo.] Do you not hope your children shall be
    kings,
When those that gave the Thane of Cawdor to me
Promised no less to them?
*Banquo.* [*Aside to* Macbeth.]    That, trusted home,ʰ       120
    Might yet enkindle you unto the crown,
Besides the Thane of Cawdor. But 'tis strange:
And oftentimes, to win us to our harm,
The instruments of darkness tell us truths,
Win us with honest trifles, to betray 's
In deepest consequence.
    Cousins,ⁱ a word, I pray you.
*Macbeth.* [*Aside.*]            Two truths are told,
    As happy prologues to the swelling act ʲ
Of the imperial theme.—I thank you, gentlemen.
[*Aside.*]    This supernatural soliciting ᵏ       130
Cannot be ill, cannot be good. If ill,
Why hath it given me earnest of success,
Commencing in a truth? I am Thane of Cawdor.
If good, why do I yield to that suggestion
Whose horrid image doth unfix my hair
And make my seatedˡ heart knock at my ribs,
Against the use ᵐ of nature? Present fears
Are less than horrible imaginings:
My thought, whose murder yet is but fantastical,
Shakes so my single ⁿ state of man that function ᵒ    140
Is smothered in surmise, and nothing is
But what is not.
*Banquo.*        Look, how our partner's rapt.
*Macbeth.* [*Aside.*]    If chance will have me king, why,
    chance may crown me
Without my stir.
*Banquo.*        New honors come upon him,
    Like our strange ᵖ garments, cleave not to their mold
But with the aid of use.
*Macbeth.* [*Aside.*]        Come what come may,
    Time and the hour runs through the roughest day.
*Banquo.* Worthy Macbeth, we stay upon your leisure.
*Macbeth.*    Give me your favor: my dull brain was
    wrought
With things forgotten. Kind gentlemen, your pains    150
Are registered where every day I turn

ᵍ to come  ʰ fully  ⁱ i.e., fellow lords  ʲ stately drama  ᵏ prompting
ˡ firmly fixed  ᵐ custom  ⁿ weak  ᵒ normal action  ᵖ new  �q pardon

    The leaf to read them. Let us toward the King.
    [*Aside to* Banquo.] Think upon what hath chanced, and
       at more time,
    The interim having weighed it, let us speak
    Our free hearts ʳ each to other.
*Banquo.*                                    Very gladly.
*Macbeth.*    Till then, enough. Come, friends.      *Exeunt.*


### Scene IV  [*Forres. The palace.*]

*Flourish.*ˢ *Enter* King [Duncan], Lennox,  Malcolm,
    Donalbain, *and* Attendants.
*King.*    Is execution done on Cawdor? Are not
    Those in commission ᵗ yet returned?
*Malcolm.*                                    My liege,
    They are not yet come back. But I have spoke
    With one that saw him die, who did report
    That very frankly he confessed his treasons,
    Implored your Highness' pardon and set forth
    A deep repentance. Nothing in his life
    Became him like the leaving it; he died
    As one that had been studied ᵘ in his death          10
    To throw away the dearest thing he owedᵛ
    As 'twere a carelessʷ trifle.
*King.*                                    There's no art
    To find the mind's construction in the face:
    He was a gentleman on whom I built
    An absolute trust.

*Enter* Macbeth, Banquo, Ross, *and* Angus.

            O worthiest cousin!
    The sin of my ingratitude even now
    Was heavy on me: thou art so far before,ˣ
    That swiftest wing of recompense is slow
    To overtake thee. Would thou hadst less deserved,
    That the proportion ʸ both of thanks and payment
    Might have been mine! Only I have left to say,          20
    More is thy due than more than all can pay.
*Macbeth.*    The service and the loyalty I owe,
    In doing it, pays itself. Your Highness' part
    Is to receive our duties; and our duties

ʳ our thoughts freely   ˢ fanfare   ᵗ commissioned with the duty   ᵘ rehearsed   ᵛ owned   ʷ not cared for   ˣ more deserving   ʸ preponderance

Are to your throne and state children and servants;
Which do but what they should, by doing everything
Safe ᶻ toward your love and honor.

*King.*                              Welcome hither:
I have begun to plant ª thee, and will labor
To make thee full of growing. Noble Banquo,
That hast no less deserved, nor must be known                    30
No less to have done so: let me infold thee
And hold thee to my heart.

*Banquo.*                          There if I grow,
The harvest is your own.

*King.*                          My plenteous joys,
Wanton ᵇ in fullness, seek to hide themselves
In drops of sorrow. Sons, kinsmen, thanes,
And you whose places are the nearest, know,
We will establish our estate ᶜ upon
Our eldest, Malcolm, whom we name hereafter
The Prince of Cumberland: which honor must
Not unaccompanied invest him only,                               40
But signs of nobleness, like stars, shall shine
On all deservers. From hence to Inverness,
And bind us further to you.

*Macbeth.*    The rest ᵈ is labor which is not used for you:
I'll be myself the harbinger, and make joyful
The hearing of my wife with your approach;
So humbly take my leave.

*King.*                       My worthy Cawdor!

*Macbeth.* [*Aside.*]   The Prince of Cumberland! That is a
     step
On which I must fall down, or else o'erleap,
For in my way it lies. Stars, hide your fires;                   50
Let not light see my black and deep desires:
The eye wink at the hand; ᵉ yet let that be
Which the eye fears, when it is done, to see.        *Exit.*

*King.*   True, worthy Banquo; he is full so valiant,
And in his commendations I am fed;
It is a banquet to me. Let's after him,
Whose care is gone before to bid us welcome:
It is a peerless kinsman.              *Flourish. Exeunt.*

---

ᶻ appropriate   ª establish   ᵇ unrestrained   ᶜ title   ᵈ repose   ᵉ be blind
to what the hand does

## Scene V [*Inverness*. Macbeth's *castle*.]

*Enter* Macbeth's Wife, *alone, with a letter.*

*Lady Macbeth.* [*Reading.*]    "They met me in the day of
    success; and I have learned by the perfect'st report, they
    have more in them than mortal knowledge. When I
    burned in desire to question them further, they made
    themselves air, into which they vanished. Whiles I
    stood rapt in the wonder of it, came missives [f] from the
    King, who all-hailed me 'Thane of Cawdor'; by which
    title, before, these weïrd sisters saluted me, and referred
    me to the coming on of time, with 'Hail, king that shalt
    be!' This have I thought good to deliver thee, my dear-    10
    est partner of greatness, that thou mightst not lose the
    dues of rejoicing, by being ignorant of what greatness
    is promised thee. Lay it to thy heart, and farewell."

Glamis thou art, and Cawdor, and shalt be
What thou art promised. Yet do I fear thy nature;
It is too full o' the milk of human kindness[g]
To catch the nearest way. Thou wouldst be great;
Art not without ambition, but without
The illness [h] should attend it: what thou wouldst highly,
That wouldst thou holily; [i] wouldst not play false,    20
And yet wouldst wrongly win; thou 'ldst have, great
    Glamis,
That which cries "Thus thou must do" if thou have it;
And that which rather thou dost fear to do
Than wishest should be undone.[j] Hie[k] thee hither,
That I may pour my spirits [l] in thine ear,
And chastise with the valor of my tongue
All that impedes thee from the golden round,[m]
Which fate and metaphysical [n] aid doth seem
To have thee crowned withal.

*Enter* Messenger.

                                What is your tidings?
*Messenger.*    The King comes here tonight.
*Lady Macbeth.*                          Thou'rt mad to say it.    30
    Is not thy master with him? Who, were't so,
    Would have informed for preparation.

---

[f] messengers   [g] nature   [h] wickedness   [i] honorably   [j] not done   [k] hurry   [l] resolution   [m] crown   [n] supernatural

*Messenger*.   So please you, it is true: our Thane is coming.
    One of my fellows had the speed of ° him,
    Who, almost dead for ᵖ breath, had scarcely more
    Than would make up his message.
*Lady Macbeth*.                   Give him tending;
    He brings great news.             *Exit* Messenger.
                  The raven himself is hoarse
    That croaks the fatal entrance of Duncan
    Under my battlements. Come, you spirits
    That tend on mortal �q thoughts, unsex me here,    40
    And fill me, from the crown to the toe, top-full
    Of direst cruelty! Make thick my blood,
    Stop up th' access and passage to remorse,ʳ
    That no compunctious ˢ visitings of nature ᵗ
    Shake my fell ᵘ purpose, nor keep peace between
    The effect ᵛ and it! Come to my woman's breasts,
    And take my milk for ʷ gall, you murd'ring ministers,ˣ
    Wherever in your sightless ʸ substances
    You wait on ᶻ nature's mischief! Come, thick night,
    And pall thee in the dunnest ᵃ smoke of hell,    50
    That my keen knife see not the wound it makes,
    Nor heaven peep through the blanket of the dark,
    To cry "Hold, hold!"

*Enter* Macbeth.

                  Great Glamis! Worthy Cawdor!
    Greater than both, by the all-hail hereafter!
    Thy letters have transported me beyond
    This ignorant ᵇ present, and I feel now
    The future in the instant.
*Macbeth*.             My dearest love,
    Duncan comes here tonight.
*Lady Macbeth*.          And when goes hence?
*Macbeth*.   Tomorrow, as he purposes.
*Lady Macbeth*.           O, never
    Shall sun that morrow see!    60
    Your face, my Thane, is as a book where men
    May read strange matters. To beguile the time,ᶜ
    Look like the time; bear welcome in your eye,
    Your hand, your tongue: look like the innocent flower,
    But be the serpent under 't. He that's coming
    Must be provided for: and you shall put

---

° outdistanced   ᵖ for want of   q deadly   ʳ pity   ˢ remorseful   ᵗ natural
feelings   ᵘ fierce   ᵛ fulfillment   ʷ in exchange for   ˣ agents   ʸ invisible
ᶻ assist   ᵃ darkest   ᵇ unknowing   ᶜ world

This night's great business into my dispatch; [d]
Which shall to all our nights and days to come
Give solely sovereign sway and masterdom.
Macbeth.    We will speak further.
Lady Macbeth.                        Only look up clear; [e]           70
To alter favor [f] is to fear:
Leave all the rest to me.                     *Exeunt.*


Scene VI [*Before* Macbeth's *castle.*]

*Hautboys*[g] *and torches. Enter* King [Duncan], Malcolm,
   Donalbain, Banquo, Lennox, Macduff, Ross, Angus,
   *and* Attendants.

*King.*    This castle hath a pleasant seat; [h] the air
   Nimbly and sweetly recommends itself
   Unto our gentle [i] senses.
*Banquo.*                     This guest of summer,
   The temple-haunting martlet,[j] does approve[k]
   By his loved mansionry [l] that the heaven's breath
   Smells wooingly here: no jutty,[m] frieze,
   Buttress, nor coign of vantage,[n] but this bird
   Hath made his pendant bed and procreant cradle:
   Where they most breed and haunt, I have observed
   The air is delicate.

*Enter* Lady [Macbeth].

*King.*                     See, see, our honored hostess!        10
   The love that follows us sometime [o] is our trouble,
   Which still we thank as[p] love. Herein I teach you
   How you shall bid God 'ield [q] us for your pains,
   And thank us for your trouble.
*Lady Macbeth.*                     All our service
   In every point twice done, and then done double,
   Were poor and single [r] business to contend
   Against [s] those honors deep and broad wherewith
   Your majesty loads our house: for those of old,
   And the late dignities heaped up to [t] them,
   We rest your hermits.[u]
*King.*                     Where's the Thane of Cawdor?        20

[d] prompt management   [e] look cheerful   [f] countenance   [g] oboes   [h] site
[i] soothed   [j] the sparrow nesting in church spires   [k] prove   [l] i.e., nest-building   [m] projection   [n] convenient corner   [o] sometimes   [p] i.e., because it is   [q] yield (reward)   [r] weak   [s] offset   [t] in addition to   [u] beadsmen

We coursed [v] him at the heels, and had a purpose
To be his purveyor: [w] but he rides well,
And his great love, sharp as his spur, hath holp [x] him
To his home before us. Fair and noble hostess,
We are your guest tonight.
*Lady Macbeth.*                Your servants ever
Have theirs, [y] themselves, and what is theirs, [z] in compt, [a]
To make their audit at your Highness' pleasure,
Still [b] to return your own.
*King.*                        Give me your hand.
Conduct me to mine host: we love him highly,
And shall continue our graces [c] towards him.                    30
By your leave, hostess.                        *Exeunt.*


### Scene VII [Macbeth's *castle*.]

*Hautboys. Torches. Enter a* Sewer, [d] *and divers* Servants
*with dishes and service over the stage. Then enter*
Macbeth.


*Macbeth.*   If it were done [e] when 'tis done, than 'twere
well
It were done quickly. If th' assassination
Could trammel up [f] the consequence, and catch,
With his surcease, [g] success; [h] that but this blow
Might be the be-all and the end-all—here,
But [i] here, upon this bank and shoal of time,
We 'ld jump [j] the life to come. But in these cases
We still have judgment [k] here; that we but teach
Bloody instructions, which being taught return
To plague th' inventor. This even-handed justice          10
Commends [l] th' ingredients of our poisoned chalice
To our own lips. He's here in double trust:
First, as I am his kinsman and his subject,
Strong both against the deed; then, as his host,
Who should against his murderer shut the door,
Not bear the knife myself. Besides, this Duncan
Hath borne his faculties [m] so meek, hath been

---

[v] pursued     [w] agent sent ahead to make provision for his master
[x] helped     [y] i.e., their servants     [z] i.e., their possessions     [a] in trust
[b] always     [c] favors     [d] chief waiter     [e] i.e., done with     [f] entangle as in a net
[g] Duncan's end (or perhaps, the assassination's completion)     [h] what follows     [i] only     [j] risk     [k] receive sentence     [l] delivers     [m] powers

So clear ⁿ in his great office, that his virtues
Will plead like angels trumpet-tongued against
The deep damnation of his taking-off:                           20
And pity, like a naked new-born babe,
Striding the blast, or heaven's cherubin horsed
Upon the sightless couriers ° of the air,
Shall blow the horrid deed in every eye,
That tears shall drown the wind. I have no spur
To prick the sides of my intent, but only
Vaulting ambition, which o'erleaps itself
And falls on the other—

*Enter* Lady [Macbeth].

                              How now! What news?
*Lady Macbeth.*    He has almost supped. Why have you
    left the chamber?
*Macbeth.*    Hath he asked for me?
*Lady Macbeth.*                        Know you not he has?      30
*Macbeth.*    We will proceed no further in this business:
    He hath honored me of late; and I have bought ᵖ
    Golden opinions from all sorts of people,
    Which would ᑫ be worn now in their newest gloss,
    Not cast aside so soon.
*Lady Macbeth.*                    Was the hope drunk
    Wherein you dressed yourself? Hath it slept since?
    And wakes it now, to look so green and pale
    At what it did so freely? From this time
    Such I account thy love. Art thou afeared
    To be the same in thine own act and valor                   40
    As thou art in desire? Would'st thou have that
    Which thou esteem'st the ornament of life,
    And live a coward in thine own esteem,
    Letting "I dare not" wait upon "I would,"
    Like the poor cat i' th' adage? ʳ
*Macbeth.*                        Prithee, peace!
    I dare do all that may become a man;
    Who dares do more is none.
*Lady Macbeth.*                    What beast was 't then
    That made you break ˢ this enterprise to me?
    When you durst do it, then you were a man;
    And, to be more than what you were, you would               50
    Be so much more the man. Nor time nor place

---

ⁿ blameless   ° invisible coursers (i.e., the winds)   ᵖ acquired   ᑫ i.e.,
should   ʳ "The cat would eat fish and would not wet her feet."   ˢ broach

Did then adhere,[t] and yet you would make both:
They have made themselves, and that their[u] fitness now
Does unmake[v] you. I have given suck, and know
How tender 'tis to love the babe that milks me:
I would, while it was smiling in my face,
Have plucked my nipple from his boneless gums,
And dashed the brains out, had I so sworn as you
Have done to this.

*Macbeth.*          If we should fail?

*Lady Macbeth.*                    We fail?
But[w] screw your courage to the sticking place,[x]          60
And we'll not fail. When Duncan is asleep—
Whereto the rather shall his day's hard journey
Soundly invite him—his two chamberlains
Will I with wine and wassail[y] so convince,[z]
That memory, the warder of the brain,
Shall be a fume, and the receipt[a] of reason
A limbec[b] only. When in swinish sleep
Their drenched natures lie as in a death,
What cannot you and I perform upon
Th' unguarded Duncan? What not put upon          70
His spongy[c] officers, who shall bear the guilt
Of our great quell?[d]

*Macbeth.*          Bring forth men-children only;
For thy undaunted mettle[e] should compose
Nothing but males. Will it not be received,
When we have marked with blood those sleepy two
Of his own chamber, and used their very daggers,
That they have done 't?

*Lady Macbeth.*          Who dares receive it other,[f]
As we shall make our griefs and clamor roar
Upon his death?

*Macbeth.*          I am settled, and bend up
Each corporal agent[g] to this terrible feat.          80
Away, and mock the time[h] with fairest show:
False face must hide what the false heart doth know.
                                   *Exeunt.*

---

[t] suit   [u] their very   [v] unnerve   [w] only   [x] the notch of the crossbow on
which the cord is tightened for shooting   [y] carousing   [z] overpower   [a] re-
ceptacle   [b] alembic   [c] drunken   [d] killing   [e] substance   [f] otherwise
[g] bodily faculty   [h] deceive the world

# ACT II

*Scene I* [*Inverness. Court of* Macbeth's *castle.*]

*Enter* Banquo *and* Fleance, *with a torch before him.*

*Banquo.*    How goes the night, boy?
*Fleance.*    The moon is down; I have not heard the clock.
*Banquo.*    And she goes down at twelve.
*Fleance.*                                    I take 't, 'tis later, sir.
*Banquo.*    Hold, take my sword. There's husbandry [1] in
    heaven,
    Their candles are all out. Take thee that too.
    A heavy summons [j] lies like lead upon me,
    And yet I would not sleep. Merciful powers,
    Restrain in me the cursèd thoughts that nature
    Gives way to in repose!

*Enter* Macbeth, *and a* Servant *with a torch.*

                              Give me my sword.
    Who's there?                                                      10
*Macbeth.*    A friend.
*Banquo.*    What, sir, not yet at rest? The King's a-bed:
    He hath been in unusual pleasure, and
    Sent forth great largess to your offices.[k]
    This diamond he greets your wife withal,
    By the name of most kind hostess, and shut up [l]
    In measureless content.
*Macbeth.*                    Being unprepared,
    Our will became the servant to defect,[m]
    Which else should free have wrought.
*Banquo.*                                    All's well.
    I dreamt last night of the three weïrd sisters.                  20
    To you they have showed some truth.
*Macbeth.*                                    I think not of them.
    Yet, when we can entreat an hour to serve,
    We would spend it in some words upon that business,
    If you would grant the time.
*Banquo.*                    At your kind'st leisure.

---

[1] economy    [j] i.e., to sleep    [k] gifts to your servants' quarters    [l] concluded    [m] deficient means

*Macbeth.*     If you shall cleave to my consent, when 'tis[n]
  It shall make honor for you.
*Banquo.*                     So I lose none
  In seeking to augment it, but still keep
  My bosom franchised[o] and allegiance clear,
  I shall be counseled.
*Macbeth.*          Good repose the while!
*Banquo.*   Thanks, sir: the like to you!                    30
                *Exeunt* Banquo [*and* Fleance].
*Macbeth.*     Go bid thy mistress, when my drink is ready,
  She strike upon the bell. Get thee to bed. *Exit* [Servant].
  Is this a dagger which I see before me,
  The handle toward my hand? Come, let me clutch thee!
  I have thee not, and yet I see thee still.
  Art thou not, fatal [p] vision, sensible [q]
  To feeling as to sight? Or art thou but
  A dagger of the mind, a false creation,
  Proceeding from the heat-oppressèd brain?
  I see thee yet, in form as palpable                    40
  As this which now I draw.
  Thou marshal'st me the way that I was going;
  And such an instrument I was to use.
  Mine eyes are made the fools o' th' other senses,
  Or else worth all the rest. I see thee still;
  And on thy blade and dudgeon [r] gouts [s] of blood,
  Which was not so before. There's no such thing:
  It is the bloody business which informs [t]
  Thus to mine eyes. Now o'er the one half-world
  Nature seems dead, and wicked dreams abuse [u]              50
  The curtained sleep. Witchcraft celebrates
  Pale Hecate's offerings; [v] and withered murder,
  Alarumed by his sentinel, the wolf,
  Whose howl's his watch, thus with his stealthy pace,
  With Tarquin's [w] ravishing strides, towards his design
  Moves like a ghost. Thou sure and firm-set earth,
  Hear not my steps, which way they walk, for fear
  Thy very stones prate of my whereabout,
  And take the present horror from the time,
  Which now suits with it. Whiles I threat, he lives:        60
  Words to the heat of deeds too cold breath gives.
                      *A bell rings.*
  I go, and it is done: the bell invites me.

[n] i.e., if you join my cause, when the time comes   [o] free of blame
[p] prophetic   [q] perceptible   [r] wooden hilt   [s] drops   [t] takes shape   [u] deceive   [v] offerings to Hecate (goddess of witchcraft)   [w] Roman tyrant who ravished Lucrece

Hear it not, Duncan, for it is a knell
That summons thee to heaven, or to hell.        *Exit.*

### Scene II [*The same.*]

*Enter* Lady [Macbeth].

*Lady Macbeth.*   That which hath made them drunk hath
   made me bold;
   What hath quenched them hath given me fire. Hark! Peace!
   It was the owl that shrieked, the fatal bellman,ˣ
   Which gives the stern'st good-night.ʸ He is about it.
   The doors are open, and the surfeited grooms
   Do mock their charge with snores. I have drugged their
      possets,ᶻ
   That death and nature do contend about them,
   Whether they live or die.
*Macbeth.* [*Within.*]        Who's there? What, ho!
*Lady Macbeth.*   Alack, I am afraid they have awaked
   And 'tis not done! Th' attempt, and not the deed,        10
   Confoundsᵃ us. Hark! I laid their daggers ready;
   He could not miss 'em. Had he not resembled
   My father as he slept, I had done 't.

*Enter* Macbeth.

                              My husband!
*Macbeth.*   I have done the deed. Didst thou not hear a
   noise?
*Lady Macbeth.*   I heard the owl scream and the crickets
   cry.
   Did not you speak?
*Macbeth.*            When?
*Lady Macbeth.*            Now.
*Macbeth.*                  As I descended?
*Lady Macbeth.*   Aye.
*Macbeth.*   Hark!
   Who lies i' th' second chamber?
*Lady Macbeth.*            Donalbain.
*Macbeth.*   This is a sorry sight. [*Looking at his hands.*]        20
*Lady Macbeth.*   A foolish thought, to say a sorry sight.
*Macbeth.*   There's one did laugh in 's sleep, and one cried
   "Murder!"
   That they did wake each other. I stood and heard them.

---

ˣ night watchman   ʸ i.e., of death   ᶻ bedtime punch   ᵃ ruins

But they did say their prayers, and addressed them
    Again to sleep.
*Lady Macbeth.*    There are two [b] lodged together.
*Macbeth.*    One cried "God bless us!" and "Amen!" the
    other,
As [c] they had seen me with these hangman's hands.
List'ning their fear, I could not say "Amen!"
When they did say "God bless us!"
*Lady Macbeth.*    Consider it not so deeply.
*Macbeth.*    But wherefore could not I pronounce "Amen"?   30
I had most need of blessing, and "Amen"
    Stuck in my throat.
*Lady Macbeth.*         These deeds must not be thought
After these ways; so, it will make us mad.
*Macbeth.*    Methought I heard a voice cry "Sleep no more!
Macbeth does murder sleep"—the innocent sleep,
Sleep that knits up [d] the raveled sleave [e] of care,
The death of each day's life, sore labor's bath,
Balm of hurt minds, great nature's second course, [f]
Chief nourisher in life's feast—
*Lady Macbeth.*         What do you mean?
*Macbeth.*    Still it cried "Sleep no more!" to all the house:   40
"Glamis hath murdered sleep, and therefore Cawdor
Shall sleep no more: Macbeth shall sleep no more."
*Lady Macbeth.*    Who was it that thus cried? Why, worthy
    Thane,
You do unbend [g] your noble strength, to think
So brainsickly of things. Go get some water,
And wash this filthy witness from your hand.
Why did you bring these daggers from the place?
They must lie there: go carry them, and smear
The sleepy grooms with blood.
*Macbeth.*         I'll go no more:
I am afraid to think what I have done;   50
Look on 't again I dare not.
*Lady Macbeth.*         Infirm of purpose!
Give me the daggers: the sleeping and the dead
Are but as pictures: 'tis the eye of childhood
That fears a painted devil. [h] If he do bleed,
I'll gild [i] the faces of the grooms withal,
For it must seem their guilt.     *Exit. Knock within.*
*Macbeth.*         Whence is that knocking?

---

[b] i.e., Malcolm and Donalbain   [c] as if   [d] smoothes out   [e] tangled
skein   [f] i.e., sleep is second to food   [g] relax   [h] i.e., picture of the devil
[i] paint

How is 't with me, when every noise appals me?
What hands are here? Ha! They pluck out mine eyes!
Will all great Neptune's ocean wash this blood
Clean from my hand? No; this my hand will rather          60
The multitudinous seas incarnadine,[j]
Making the green one red.

*Enter* Lady [Macbeth].

*Lady Macbeth.*    My hands are of your color, but I shame
To wear a heart so white. (*Knock.*) I hear a knocking
At the south entry. Retire we to our chamber.
A little water clears us of this deed:
How easy it is then! Your constancy
Hath left you unattended.[k] (*Knock.*) Hark! More
    knocking.
Get on your nightgown,[l] lest occasion call us
And show us to be watchers.[m] Be not lost               70
So poorly [n] in your thoughts.
*Macbeth.*    To know my deed, 'twere best not know my-
    self.                                    *Knock.*
Wake Duncan with thy knocking! I would thou couldst!
                                              *Exeunt.*

## Scene III  [*The same.*]

*Enter a* Porter. *Knocking within.*

*Porter.*    Here's a knocking indeed! If a man were porter
of hell-gate, he should have old [o] turning the key.
(*Knock.*) Knock, knock, knock! Who's there, i' th'
name of Belzebub? Here's a farmer,[p] that hanged
himself on th' expectation of plenty.[q] Come in time!
Have napkins enow [r] about you; here you'll sweat for
't. (*Knock.*) Knock, knock! Who's there, in th' other
devil's name? Faith, here's an equivocator, that could
swear in both the scales against either scale; who committed treason enough for God's sake, yet could not     10
equivocate to heaven: [s] O, come in, equivocator.
(*Knock.*) Knock, knock, knock! Who's there? Faith,
here's an English tailor come hither, for stealing out
of a French hose.[t] Come in, tailor; here you may

[j] redden  [k] abandoned  [l] dressing gown  [m] i.e., up late  [n] dejectedly
[o] plenty of  [p] i.e., who has hoarded grain  [q] forecast of a plentiful crop
[r] enough handkerchiefs  [s] perhaps an allusion to a contemporary Jesuit
who defended his equivocation and treason on religious grounds  [t] tight-
fitting breeches

roast your goose.ᵘ (*Knock.*) Knock, knock. Never
at quiet! What are you? But this place is too cold for
hell. I'll devil-porter it no further. I had thought to
have let in some of all professions that go the primrose
way to the everlasting bonfire. (*Knock.*) Anon, anon!
[*Opens the gate.*] I pray you, remember the porter.     20

*Enter* Macduff *and* Lennox.

*Macduff.*   Was it so late, friend, ere you went to bed,
          That you do lie so late?
*Porter.*   Faith, sir, we were carousing till the second
cock:ᵛ and drink, sir, is a great provoker of three
things.
*Macduff.*   What three things does drink especially provoke?
*Porter.*   Marry, sir, nose-painting, sleep, and urine.
Lechery, sir, it provokes and unprovokes; it provokes
the desire, but it takes away the performance. There-   30
fore much drink may be said to be an equivocator with
lechery; it makes him and it mars him; it sets him on
and it takes him off; it persuades him and disheartens
him; makes him stand to and not stand to; in conclusion, equivocates him in a sleep, and giving him the
lie,ʷ leaves him.
*Macduff.*   I believe drink gave thee the lie last night.
*Porter.*   That it did, sir, i' the very throat on me: but I
requited him for his lie, and, I think, being too strong for
him, though he took up ˣ my legs sometime, yet I made   40
a shift to castʸ him.
*Macduff.*   Is thy master stirring?

*Enter* Macbeth.

   Our knocking has awaked him; here he comes.
*Lennox.*   Good morrow, noble sir.
*Macbeth.*                         Good morrow, both.
*Macduff.*   Is the king stirring, worthy Thane?
*Macbeth.*                              Not yet.
*Macduff.*   He did command me to call timely ᶻ on him:
          I had almost slippedᵃ the hour.
*Macbeth.*                         I'll bring you to him.
*Macduff.*   I know this is a joyful trouble to you;
          But yet 'tis one.

   ᵘ pressing-iron   ᵛ 3 A.M.   ʷ (i) laying him low (ii) calling him a liar
ˣ tripped   ʸ contrived to (i) throw (ii) vomit   ᶻ early   ᵃ let slip

*Macbeth*.     The labor we delight in physics pain.[b]          50
   This is the door.
*Macduff*.                    I'll make so bold to call,
   For 'tis my limited [c] service.                    *Exit* Macduff
*Lennox*.    Goes the king hence today?
*Macbeth*.                              He does; he did appoint so.
*Lennox*.    The night has been unruly: where we lay,
   Our chimneys were blown down, and, as they say,
   Lamentings heard i' th' air, strange screams of death,
   And prophesying with accents terrible
   Of dire combustion [d] and confused events
   New hatched to th' woeful time. The obscure bird [e]
   Clamored the livelong night. Some say, the earth          60
   Was feverous and did shake.
*Macbeth*.                         'Twas a rough night.
*Lennox*.    My young remembrance cannot parallel
   A fellow to it.

*Enter* Macduff.

*Macduff*.    O horror, horror, horror! Tongue nor heart
   Cannot conceive nor name thee!
*Macbeth* and *Lennox*.    What's the matter?
*Macduff*.    Confusion now hath made his masterpiece.
   Most sacrilegious murder hath broke ope
   The Lord's anointed temple, and stole thence
   The life o' th' building.
*Macbeth*.                    What is 't you say? The life?
*Lennox*.    Mean you his Majesty?          70
*Macduff*.    Approach the chamber, and destroy your
       sight
   With a new Gorgon: [f] do not bid me speak;
   See, and then speak yourselves.
                              *Exeunt* Macbeth *and* Lennox.
                              Awake, awake!
   Ring the alarum bell. Murder and treason!
   Banquo and Donalbain! Malcolm! Awake!
   Shake off this downy sleep, death's counterfeit,
   And look on death itself! Up, up, and see
   The great doom's [g] image! Malcolm! Banquo!
   As from your graves rise up, and walk like sprites,[h]
   To countenance [i] this horror. Ring the bell!          80

*Bell rings*.

[b] cures trouble   [c] appointed   [d] tumult   [e] i.e., the owl   [f] mythological
female who turned to stone those who beheld her   [g] judgment Day's
[h] spirits   [i] (i) suit (ii) face

*Enter* Lady [Macbeth].

*Lady Macbeth.*    What's the business,
    That such a hideous trumpet calls to parley
    The sleepers of the house? Speak, speak!
*Macduff.*                                    O gentle lady,
    'Tis not for you to hear what I can speak:
    The repetition, in a woman's ear,
    Would murder as it fell.

*Enter* Banquo.

              O Banquo, Banquo!
    Our royal master's murdered.
*Lady Macbeth.*                    Woe, alas!
    What, in our house?
*Banquo.*                    Too cruel anywhere.
    Dear Duff, I prithee, contradict thyself,
    And say it is not so.                                    90

*Enter* Macbeth, Lennox, *and* Ross.

*Macbeth.*    Had I but died an hour before this chance,
    I had lived a blessèd time; for from this instant
    There's nothing serious in mortality: [j]
    All is but toys: [k] renown and grace is dead;
    The wine of life is drawn, and the mere lees
    Is left this vault[l] to brag of.

*Enter* Malcolm *and* Donalbain.

*Donalbain.*    What is amiss?
*Macbeth.*                    You are, and do not know 't:
    The spring, the head, the fountain of your blood
    Is stopped; the very source of it is stopped.
*Macduff.*    Your royal father's murdered.
*Malcolm.*                                    O, by whom?        100
*Lennox.*    Those of his chamber, as it seemed, had done 't.
    Their hands and faces were all badged [m] with blood;
    So were their daggers, which unwiped we found
    Upon their pillows:
    They stared, and were distracted; no man's life
    Was to be trusted with them.
*Macbeth.*    O, yet I do repent me of my fury,

[j] mortal life    [k] trifles    [l] (i) wine cellar (ii) earth    [m] marked

    That I did kill them.
*Macduff.*                Wherefore did you so?
*Macbeth.*    Who can be wise, amazed, temp'rate and
    furious,
    Loyal and neutral, in a moment? No man:
    The expedition[n] of my violent love          110
    Outrun the pauser, reason. Here lay Duncan,
    His silver skin laced with his golden blood,
    And his gashed stabs looked like a breach in nature
    For ruin's wasteful entrance; there, the murderers,
    Steeped in the colors of their trade, their daggers
    Unmannerly[o] breeched[p] with gore. Who could refrain,
    That had a heart to love, and in that heart
    Courage to make 's love known?
*Lady Macbeth.*                        Help me hence, ho!
*Macduff.*    Look to the lady.
*Malcolm.*    [*Aside to* Donalbain.]   Why do we hold
    our tongues,
    That most may claim this argument for ours? [q]    120
*Donalbain.* [*Aside to* Malcolm.]   What should be spoken
    here, where our fate,
    Hid in an auger-hole,[r] may rush, and seize us?
    Let 's away;
    Our tears are not yet brewed.
*Malcolm.* [*Aside to* Donalbain.]   Nor our strong sorrow
    Upon the foot of [s] motion.
*Banquo.*                    Look to the lady:
                [*Lady Macbeth is carried out.*]
    And when we have our naked frailties hid,[t]
    That suffer in exposure, let us meet,
    And question this most bloody piece of work,
    To know it further. Fears and scruples [u] shake us:
    In the great hand of God I stand, and thence    130
    Against the undivulged pretense [v] I fight
    Of treasonous malice.
*Macduff.*                And so do I.
*All.*                        So all.
*Macbeth.*    Let 's briefly [w] put on manly readiness,
    And meet i' th' hall together.
*All.*                        Well contented.
          *Exeunt* [*all but* Malcolm *and* Donalbain].
*Malcolm.*    What will you do? Let's not consort with them.

---

[n] speed   [o] indecently   [p] sheathed (as with breeches)   [q] subject for our concern   [r] i.e., a tiny hole   [s] yet in   [t] bodies clothed   [u] doubts   [v] design   [w] quickly

To show an unfelt sorrow is an office
Which the false man does easy. I'll to England.
*Donalbain.*     To Ireland, I; our separated fortune
　Shall keep us both the safer: where we are
　There's daggers in men's smiles; the near ˣ in blood,          140
　The nearer bloody.
*Malcolm.*                  This murderous shaft that's shot
　Hath not yet lighted, and our safest way
　Is to avoid the aim. Therefore to horse;
　And let us not be dainty of ʸ leave-taking,
　But shift ᶻ away: there's warrant ᵃ in that theft
　Which steals itself when there's no mercy left.     *Exeunt.*


Scene IV  [*Outside* Macbeth's *castle.*]

*Enter* Ross *with an* Old Man.

*Old Man.*     Threescore and ten I can remember well:
　Within the volume of which time I have seen
　Hours dreadful and things strange, but this sore night
　Hath trifled former knowings.ᵇ
*Ross.*                              Ha, good father,
　Thou seest the heavens, as troubled with man's act,
　Threaten his bloody stage: by th' clock 'tis day,
　And yet dark night strangles the traveling lamp.ᶜ
　Is't night's predominance,ᵈ or the day's shame,
　That darkness does the face of earth entomb,
　When living light should kiss it?
*Old Man.*                          'Tis unnatural,          10
　Even like the deed that's done. On Tuesday last
　A falcon, tow'ring ᵉ in her pride of place ᶠ
　Was by a mousing ᵍ owl hawked at ʰ and killed.
*Ross.*     And Duncan's horses—a thing most strange and
　　certain—
　Beauteous and swift, the minions of their race,
　Turned wild in nature, broke their stalls, flung out,
　Contending 'gainst obedience, as they would make
　War with mankind.
*Old Man.*                  'Tis said they eatⁱ each other.
*Ross.*     They did so, to the amazement of mine eyes,
　That looked upon 't.

---

ˣ nearer  ʸ fussy about  ᶻ steal  ᵃ justification  ᵇ made trifles of former
experiences  ᶜ i.e., the sun  ᵈ astrological ascendancy  ᵉ circling upward
ᶠ highest point of flight  ᵍ i.e., normally hunting mice  ʰ pounced on
ⁱ ate

*Enter* Macduff.

                    Here comes the good Macduff.          20
  How goes the world, sir, now?
*Macduff*.                    Why, see you not?
*Ross*.    Is 't known who did this more than bloody deed?
*Macduff*.    Those that Macbeth hath slain.
*Ross*.                              Alas, the day!
  What good could they pretend? [j]
*Macduff*.                    They were suborned: [k]
  Malcolm and Donalbain, the King's two sons,
  Are stol'n away and fled, which puts upon them
  Suspicion of the deed.
*Ross*.                    'Gainst nature still.
  Thriftless [l] ambition, that wilt raven [m] up
  Thine own life's means! Then 'tis most like
  The sovereignty will fall upon Macbeth.                30
*Macduff*.    He is already named, and gone to Scone
  To be invested.
*Ross*.            Where is Duncan's body?
*Macduff*.    Carried to Colmekill,
  The sacred storehouse of his predecessors
  And guardian of their bones.
*Ross*.                    Will you to Scone?
*Macduff*.    No, cousin, I'll to Fife.
*Ross*.                              Well, I will thither.
*Macduff*.    Well, may you see things well done there: adieu!
  Lest our old robes sit easier than our new!
*Ross*.    Farewell, father.
*Old Man*.    God's benison [n] go with you, and with those    40
  That would make good of bad and friends of foes!
                              *Exeunt omnes.*


# ACT III

### Scene I [Forres. The palace].

*Enter* Banquo.

*Banquo*.    Thou hast it now: King, Cawdor, Glamis, all,
  As the weïrd women promised, and I fear

[j] expect   [k] induced to commit a crime   [l] wasteful   [m] greedily swallow
[n] blessing

Thou play'dst most foully for 't: yet it was said
It should not stand ° in thy posterity,
But that myself should be the root and father
Of many kings. If there come truth from them—
As upon thee, Macbeth, their speeches shine ᴾ—
Why, by the verities on thee made good,
May they not be my oracles as well
And set me up in hope? But hush, no more.        10

*Sennet*ꟴ *sounded. Enter* Macbeth, *as king,* Lady [Macbeth],
    Lennox, Ross, Lords, *and* Attendants.

*Macbeth.*   Here's our chief guest.
*Lady Macbeth.*                          If he had been forgotten,
  It had been as a gap in our great feast,
  And all-thing ʳ unbecoming.
*Macbeth.*   Tonight we hold a solemn ˢ supper, sir,
  And I'll request your presence.
*Banquo.*                          Let your highness
  Command upon me, to the which my duties
  Are with a most indissoluble tie
  For ever knit.
*Macbeth.*   Ride you this afternoon?
*Banquo.*   Aye, my good lord.
*Macbeth.*   We should have else desired your good advice,   20
  Which still hath been both grave and prosperous,ᵗ
  In this day's council; but we'll take tomorrow.
  Is 't far you ride?
*Banquo.*   As far, my lord, as will fill up the time
  'Twixt this supper: go not my horse the better,ᵘ
  I must become a borrower of the night
  For a dark hour or twain.
*Macbeth.*                          Fail not our feast.
*Banquo.*   My lord, I will not.
*Macbeth.*   We hear our bloody cousins are bestowed
  In England and in Ireland, not confessing        30
  Their cruel parricide, filling their hearers
  With strange invention: but of that tomorrow,
  When therewithal we shall have cause of state
  Craving us jointly. Hie you to horse: adieu,
  Till you return at night. Goes Fleance with you?
*Banquo.*   Aye, my good lord: our time does call upon 's.
*Macbeth.*   I wish your horses swift and sure of foot,
  And so I do commend you to their backs.

° continue   ᴾ are brightly verified   ꟴ trumpet salute   ʳ wholly   ˢ formal   ᵗ profitable   ᵘ unless my horse goes faster than expected

Farewell.                                    *Exit* Banquo.
Let every man be master of his time                        40
Till seven at night. To make society
The sweeter welcome, we will keep ourself
Till supper-time alone. While <sup>v</sup> then, God be with you!
                              *Exeunt* Lords [*and others*].
Sirrah,<sup>w</sup> a word with you: attend those men
Our pleasure?
*Attendant.*   They are, my lord, without the palace gate.
*Macbeth.*   Bring them before us.          *Exit* Servant.
To be thus is nothing, but <sup>x</sup> to be safely thus:
Our fears in Banquo stick deep; <sup>y</sup>
And in his royalty of nature reigns that                   50
Which would be feared: 'tis much he dares,
And, to that dauntless temper of his mind,
He hath a wisdom that doth guide his valor
To act in safety. There is none but he
Whose being I do fear: and under him
My genius <sup>z</sup> is rebuked,<sup>a</sup> as it is said
Mark Antony's was by Caesar. He chid the sisters,
When first they put the name of King upon me,
And bade them speak to him; then prophet-like
They hailed him father to a line of kings:                 60
Upon my head they placed a fruitless crown
And put a barren scepter in my gripe,<sup>b</sup>
Thence to be wrenched with an unlineal hand,
No son of mine succeeding. If 't be so,
For Banquo's issue <sup>c</sup> have I filed <sup>d</sup> my mind;
For them the gracious Duncan have I murdered;
Put rancors in the vessel of my peace
Only for them, and mine eternal jewel <sup>e</sup>
Given to the common enemy of man,<sup>f</sup>
To make them kings—the seed of Banquo kings!              70
Rather than so, come, Fate, into the list,<sup>g</sup>
And champion <sup>h</sup> me to th' utterance! <sup>i</sup> Who's there?

*Enter* Servant *and two* Murderers.

Now go to the door, and stay there till we call.
                                   *Exit* Servant.
Was it not yesterday we spoke together?
*Murderers.*   It was, so please your Highness.

---

<sup>v</sup> until   <sup>w</sup> form of address to inferiors   <sup>x</sup> unless   <sup>y</sup> are deeply rooted
<sup>z</sup> attendant   spirit   <sup>a</sup> cowed   <sup>b</sup> grasp   <sup>c</sup> offspring   <sup>d</sup> defiled   <sup>e</sup> i.e.,   soul
<sup>f</sup> i.e., Satan   <sup>g</sup> lists (of battle)   <sup>h</sup> fight in single combat   <sup>i</sup> uttermost (i.e.,
death)

*Macbeth.*　　　　　　　　　　　　　　　Well then, now
　Have you consider'd of my speeches? Know
　That it was he in the times past which held you
　So under fortune,[j] which you thought had been
　Our innocent self: this I made good [k] to you
　In our last conference; passed in probation[l] with you,　　80
　How you were borne in hand,[m] how crossed, the instru-
　　ments,
　Who wrought with them, and all things else that might
　To half a soul and to a notion [n] crazed
　Say "Thus did Banquo."
*First Murderer.*　　　　　　You made it known to us.
*Macbeth.*　I did so; and went further, which is now
　Our point of second meeting. Do you find
　Your patience so predominant in your nature,
　That you can let this go? Are you so gospeled,[o]
　To pray for this good man and for his issue,
　Whose heavy hand hath bowed you to the grave　　90
　And beggared yours for ever?
*First Murderer.*　　　　　　We are men, my liege.
*Macbeth.*　Aye, in the catalogue ye go for men;
　As hounds and greyhounds, mongrels, spaniels, curs,
　Shoughs,[p] water-rugs,[q] and demi-wolves, are clept [r]
　All by the name of dogs: the valued file [s]
　Distinguishes the swift, the slow, the subtle,
　The housekeeper,[t] the hunter, every one
　According to the gift which bounteous nature
　Hath in him closed,[u] whereby he does receive
　Particular addition,[v] from the bill [w]　　　　　100
　That writes them all alike: and so of men.
　Now if you have a station in the file,
　Not i' the worst rank of manhood, say 't,
　And I will put that business in your bosoms [x]
　Whose execution takes your enemy off,
　Grapples you to the heart and love of us,
　Who wear our health but sickly in his life,
　Which in his death were perfect.
*Second Murderer.*　　　　　I am one, my liege,
　Whom the vile blows and buffets of the world
　Have so incensed that I am reckless what　　　110
　I do to spite the world.
*First Murderer.*　　　　And I another

---

[j] prevented your advancement　[k] proved　[l] reviewed the proof　[m] deceived　[n] mind　[o] steeped in the Gospel　[p] shag-haired dogs　[q] long-haired water dogs　[r] called　[s] list recording the values　[t] watchdog　[u] enclosed　[v] distinction　[w] list　[x] trust

So weary with disasters, tugged with <sup>y</sup> fortune,
That I would set my life on any chance,
To mend it or be rid on 't.

*Macbeth.*                         Both of you
Know Banquo was your enemy.

*Murderers.*                                True, my lord.

*Macbeth.*     So is he mine, and in such bloody distance <sup>z</sup>
That every minute of his being thrusts
Against my nearest of life: <sup>a</sup> and though I could
With barefaced power sweep him from my sight
And bid my will avouch <sup>b</sup> it, yet I must not,                   120
For certain friends that are both his and mine,
Whose loves I may not drop, but wail <sup>c</sup> his fall
Who I myself struck down: and thence it is
That I to your assistance do make love,
Masking the business from the common eye
For sundry weighty reasons.

*Second Murderer.*                   We shall, my lord,
Perform what you command us.

*First Murderer.*                      Though our lives—

*Macbeth.*    Your spirits shine through you. Within this
    hour at most
I will advise you where to plant yourselves,
Acquaint you with the perfect spy o' th' time,<sup>d</sup>                  130
The moment on 't; <sup>e</sup> for 't must be done tonight,
And something <sup>f</sup> from the palace; always thought <sup>g</sup>
That I require a clearness: <sup>h</sup> and with him—
To leave no rubs <sup>i</sup> nor botches in the work—
Fleance his son, that keeps him company,
Whose absence is no less material to me
Than is his father's, must embrace the fate
Of that dark hour. Resolve yourselves <sup>j</sup> apart:
I'll come to you anon.

*Murderers.*                  We are resolved, my lord.

*Macbeth.*    I'll call upon you straight: abide within.          140
It is concluded: Banquo thy soul's flight,
If it find heaven, must find it out tonight.          *Exeunt.*


### Scene II  [*The same.*]

*Enter* Macbeth's Lady *and a* Servant.

<sup>y</sup> about by   <sup>z</sup> enmity   <sup>a</sup> most vital parts   <sup>b</sup> justify   <sup>c</sup> i.e., I must wail
<sup>d</sup> i.e., the exact indication   <sup>e</sup> for it   <sup>f</sup> i.e., some distance   <sup>g</sup> i.e., borne in
mind   <sup>h</sup> freedom from suspicion   <sup>i</sup> defects   <sup>j</sup> make up your minds

*Lady Macbeth.*    Is Banquo gone from court?
*Servant.*    Aye, madam, but returns again tonight.
*Lady Macbeth.*    Say to the King, I would attend his leisure
     For a few words.
*Servant.*              Madam, I will.                    *Exit.*
*Lady Macbeth.*                    Naught 's had, all 's spent,
     Where our desire is got without content.
     'Tis safer to be that which we destroy
     Than by destruction dwell in doubtful joy.

*Enter* Macbeth.

     How now, my lord! Why do you keep alone,
     Of sorriest fancies your companions making;
     Using those thoughts which should indeed have died          10
     With them they think on? Things without all remedy
     Should be without regard: what's done is done.
*Macbeth.*    We have scorched ᵏ the snake, not killed it:
     She 'll close ¹ and be herself, whilst our poor malice ᵐ
     Remains in danger of her former tooth.
     But let the frame of things disjoint,ⁿ both the worlds °
          suffer,
     Ere we will eat our meal in fear, and sleep
     In the affliction of these terrible dreams
     That shake us nightly: better be with the dead,
     Whom we, to gain our peace, have sent to peace,          20
     Than on the torture of the mind to lie
     In restless ecstasy.ᵖ Duncan is in his grave;
     After life's fitful fever he sleeps well;
     Treason has done his worst: nor steel, nor poison,
     Malice domestic,�q foreign levy, nothing,
     Can touch him further.
*Lady Macbeth.*          Come on;
     Gentle my lord, seek o'er your rugged looks;
     Be bright and jovial among your guests tonight.
*Macbeth.*    So shall I, love; and so, I pray, be you:
     Let your remembrance apply to Banquo;          30
     Present him eminence,ʳ both with eye and tongue:
     Unsafe the while, that ˢ we
     Must lave ᵗ our honors in these flattering streams,
     And make our faces vizards ᵘ to our hearts,
     Disguising what they are.
*Lady Macbeth.*          You must leave this.

     ᵏ slashed   ¹ heal   ᵐ opposition   ⁿ order of the universe collapse
     ° i.e., heaven and earth   ᵖ frenzy   q civil war   ʳ pay him deference
     ˢ because   ᵗ wash   ᵘ masks

*Macbeth.*   O, full of scorpions is my mind, dear wife!
  Thou knowest that Banquo, and his Fleance, lives.
*Lady Macbeth.*   But in them nature's copy's not eterne. [v]
*Macbeth.*   There's comfort yet; they are assailable;
  Then be thou jocund: ere the bat hath flown          40
  His cloister'd flight: ere to black Hecate's summons
  The shard-borne [w] beetle with his drowsy hums
  Hath rung night's yawning peal, there shall be done
  A deed of dreadful note.
*Lady Macbeth.*                   What's to be done?
*Macbeth.*   Be innocent of the knowledge, dearest chuck,[x]
  Till thou applaud the deed. Come, seeling [y] night,
  Scarf up [z] the tender eye of pitiful day,
  And with thy bloody and invisible hand
  Cancel and tear to pieces that great bond [a]
  Which keeps me pale! Light thickens, and the crow    50
  Makes wing to th' rooky [b] wood:
  Good things of day begin to droop and drowse,
  Whiles night's black agents to their preys do rouse.
  Thou marvelest at my words: but hold thee still;
  Things bad begun make strong themselves by ill:
  So, prithee, go with me.                   *Exeunt.*


## Scene III  [*Near the palace.*]

*Enter three* Murderers.


*First Murderer.*   But who did bid thee join with us?
*Third Murderer.*                            Macbeth.
*Second Murderer.*   He needs not our mistrust; since he de-
    livers [c]
  Our offices, and what we have to do,
  To the direction just.[d]
*First Murderer.*      Then stand with us.
  The west yet glimmers with some streaks of day:
  Now spurs the lated traveler apace
  To gain the timely inn,[e] and near approaches
  The subject of our watch.
*Third Murderer.*            Hark! I hear horses.
*Banquo. (Within.)*   Give us a light there, ho!

[v] i.e., their lease of life is not eternal   [w] borne on scaly wings   [x] chick
[y] sewing up the eyelids (from falconry)   [z] blindfold   [a] i.e., between Banquo and his fate   [b] full of rooks   [c] reports   [d] exactly as instructed (by
Macbeth)   [e] i.e., to reach the inn in good time

*Second Murderer.*                 Then 'tis he: the rest
    That are within the note of expectation [f]          10
    Already are i' th' court.
*First Murderer.*              His horses go about.[g]
*Third Murderer.*    Almost a mile: but he does usually—
    So all men do—from hence to the palace gate
    Make it their walk.


*Enter* Banquo *and* Fleance, *with a torch.*


*Second Murderer.*    A light, a light!
*Third Murderer.*                   'Tis he.
*First Murderer.*    Stand to 't.
*Banquo.*    It will be rain tonight.
*First Murderer.*              Let it come down!


[*They set upon* Banquo.]


*Banquo.*    O, treachery! Fly, good Fleance, fly, fly, fly!
    Thou mayst revenge. O slave!    [*Dies.* Fleance *escapes.*]
*Third Murderer.*    Who did strike out the light?
*First Murderer.*                   Was 't not the way?
*Third Murderer.*    There's but one down; the son is fled.          20
*Second Murderer.*    We have lost best half of our affair.
*First Murderer.*    Well, let's away and say how much is
    done.                              *Exeunt.*


### Scene IV [*The palace.*]


*Banquet prepared. Enter* Macbeth, Lady [Macbeth],
    Ross, Lennox, Lords, *and* Attendants.


*Macbeth.*    You know your own degrees; [h] sit down:
    At first and last [i] a hearty welcome.
*Lords.*                      Thanks to your majesty.
*Macbeth.*    Ourself will mingle with society [j]
    And play the humble host.
    Our hostess keeps her state,[k] but in best time
    We will require [l] her welcome.
*Lady Macbeth.*    Pronounce it for me, sir, to all our friends,
    For my heart speaks they are welcome.


*Enter* First Murderer.


[f] on the invitation list   [g] take a roundabout way   [h] ranks   [i] once for
all   [j] the company   [k] i.e., remains on her throne   [l] request

*Macbeth.*    See, they encounter [m] thee with their hearts'
     thanks.
   Both sides [n] are even: here I'll sit i' th' midst.        10
   Be large in mirth; anon we'll drink a measure [o]
   The table round. [*Goes to* Murderer.]
   There's blood upon thy face.
*Murderer.*    'Tis Banquo's then.
*Macbeth.*    'Tis better thee without than he within.
   Is he dispatch'd?
*Murderer.*    My lord, his throat is cut; that I did for him.
*Macbeth.*    Thou art the best o' the cut-throats.
   Yet he's good that did the like for Fleance.
   If thou didst it, thou art the nonpareil.
*Murderer.*              Most royal sir, Fleance is 'scaped.      20
*Macbeth.* [*Aside.*]    Then comes my fit again: I had else
     been perfect,[p]
   Whole as the marble, founded [q] as the rock,
   As broad and general [r] as the casing air:
   But now I am cabined, cribbed,[t] confined, bound in
   To saucy [u] doubts and fears.—But Banquo's safe?
*Murderer.*    Aye, my good lord: safe in a ditch he bides,
   With twenty trenchèd [v] gashes on his head,
   The least a death to nature.[w]
*Macbeth.*              Thanks for that.
   [*Aside.*] There the grown serpent lies; the worm [x]
     that's fled
   Hath nature that in time will venom breed,        30
   No teeth for th' present. Get thee gone: tomorrow
   We'll hear ourselves [y] again.      *Exit* Murderer.
*Lady Macbeth.*          My royal lord,
   You do not give the cheer: [z] the feast is sold [a]
   That is not often vouched,[b] while 'tis a-making,
   'Tis given with welcome: to feed [c] were best at home;
   From thence [d] the sauce to meat [e] is ceremony;
   Meeting were bare without it.


*Enter the* Ghost *of* Banquo, *and sits in* Macbeth's *place.*


*Macbeth*              Sweet remembrancer![f]
   Now good digestion wait on appetite,
   And health on both!
*Lennox.*           May 't please your Highness sit.

---

[m] greet   [n] i.e., of the table   [o] goblet   [p] sound of health   [q] solid   [r] free
and unconfined     [u] insolent    [v] deep-cut   [w] life   [x] serpent   [y] confer
[z] kindly   [a] i.e., is like one sold   [b] sworn (i.e., ceremoniously commended)
[c] i.e., mere eating   [d] i.e., away from home   [e] food   [f] prompter

*Macbeth.*          Here had we now our country's honor[g]
    roofed,[h]                                                          40
    Were the graced person of our Banquo present;
    Who may I rather challenge [i] for unkindness
    Than pity for mischance!
*Ross.*                            His absence, sir,
    Lays blame upon his promise. Please 't your Highness
    To grace us with your royal company?
*Macbeth.*     The table's full.
*Lennox.*                          Here is a place reserved, sir.
*Macbeth.*     Where?
*Lennox.*     Here, my good lord. What is 't that moves your
    Highness?
*Macbeth.*     Which of you have done this?
*Lords.*                                  What, my good lord?
*Macbeth.*     Thou canst not say I did it: never shake        50
    Thy gory locks at me.
*Ross.*     Gentlemen, rise; his Highness is not well.
*Lady Macbeth.*     Sit, worthy friends: my lord is often thus,
    And hath been from his youth: pray you, keep seat;
    The fit is momentary; upon a thought [j]
    He will again be well: if much you note him,
    You shall offend him and extend his passion: [k]
    Feed, and regard him not. Are you a man?
*Macbeth.*     Aye, and a bold one, that dare look on that
    Which might appal the devil.
*Lady Macbeth.*                      O proper stuff!              60
    This is the very painting of your fear:
    This is the air-drawn [l] dagger which, you said,
    Led you to Duncan. O, these flaws [m] and starts
    (Impostors [n] to true fear) would well become
    A woman's story at a winter's fire,
    Authorized by her grandam. Shame itself!
    Why do you make such faces? When all 's done,
    You look but on a stool.
*Macbeth.*                        Prithee, see there!
    Behold! Look! Lo! How say you?
    Why, what care I? If thou canst nod, speak too.              70
    If charnel-houses [o] and our graves must send
    Those that we bury back, our monuments [p]
    Shall be the maws[q] of kites.            [*Exit* Ghost.]
*Lady Macbeth.*              What, quite unmanned in folly?
*Macbeth.*     If I stand here, I saw him.

---

[g] nobility   [h] under one roof   [i] reprove   [j] in a moment   [k] seizure
[l] made of air   [m] outbursts   [n] compared to   [o] graveyard vaults for storing
bones   [p] tombs   [q] gullets

*Lady Macbeth.*　　　　　　　　Fie, for shame!
*Macbeth.*　　Blood hath been shed ere now, i' th' olden time,
　　Ere humane statute purged the gentle weal; ʳ
　　Aye, and since too, murders have been performed
　　Too terrible for the ear: the time has been,
　　That, when the brains were out, the man would die,
　　And there an end; but now they rise again,　　　　　　80
　　With twenty mortal murders ˢ on their crowns,ᵗ
　　And push us from our stools: this is more strange
　　Than such a murder is.
*Lady Macbeth.*　　　　　　　My worthy lord,
　　Your noble friends do lack you.
*Macbeth.*　　　　　　　　　　I do forget.
　　Do not muse at me, my most worthy friends;
　　I have a strange infirmity, which is nothing
　　To those that know me. Come, love and health to all;
　　Then I'll sit down. Give me some wine, fill full.

*Enter Ghost.*

　　I drink to the general joy o' the whole table,
　　And to our dear friend Banquo, whom we miss;　　　90
　　Would he were here! To all, and him, we thirst,ᵘ
　　And all to all.ᵛ
*Lords.*　　　　Our duties, and the pledge.
*Macbeth.*　　Avaunt!ʷ And quit my sight! Let the earth hide
　　thee!
　　Thy bones are marrowless, thy blood is cold;
　　Thou hast no speculation ˣ in those eyes
　　Which thou dost glare with.
*Lady Macbeth.*　　　　　　Think of this, good peers,
　　But as a thing of custom: 'tis no other;
　　Only it spoils the pleasure of the time.
*Macbeth.*　　What man dare, I dare:
　　Approach thou like the rugged Russian bear,　　　　100
　　The armed rhinoceros, or th' Hyrcan ʸ tiger;
　　Take any shape but that, and my firm nerves ᶻ
　　Shall never tremble. Or be alive again,
　　And dare me to the desert ª with thy sword;
　　If trembling I inhabitᵇ then, protestᶜ me
　　The baby of a girl.ᵈ Hence, horrible shadow!
　　Unreal mockery, hence.　　　　　　　[*Exit Ghost.*]
　　　　　　　　Why, so: being gone,

ʳ i.e., purged the state (of savagery) and made it gentle　ˢ i.e., wounds
ᵗ heads　ᵘ are eager to drink　ᵛ all drink to all　ʷ begone　ˣ understanding vision　ʸ of Hyrcania, near the Caspian Sea　ᶻ sinews　ª i.e., any
solitary place　ᵇ i.e., if I tremble　ᶜ proclaim　ᵈ a baby girl

I am a man again. Pray you, sit still.

*Lady Macbeth.*   You have displaced the mirth, broke the
    good meeting,
  With most admired disorder.[e]

*Macbeth.*                    Can such things be,                    110
  And overcome [f] us like a summer's cloud,
  Without our special wonder? You make me strange [g]
  Even to the disposition [h] that I owe,[i]
  When now I think you can behold such sights,
  And keep the natural ruby of your cheeks,
  When mine is blanch'd with fear.

*Ross.*                         What sights, my lord?

*Lady Macbeth.*   I pray you, speak not; he grows worse and
    worse;
  Question enrages him: at once, good night.
  Stand [j] not upon the order of your going,
  But go at once.

*Lennox.*         Good night; and better health                    120
  Attend his majesty!

*Lady Macbeth.*       A kind good night to all!

                                            *Exeunt* Lords.

*Macbeth.*   It will have blood, they say: blood will have
    blood.
  Stones have been known to move and trees to speak;
  Augures [k] and understood relations [l] have
  By maggot-pies and choughs [m] and rooks brought forth
  The secretest man of blood. What is the night?[n]

*Lady Macbeth.*   Almost at odds with morning, which is
    which.

*Macbeth.*   How sayest thou, that Macduff denies his person
  At our great bidding?

*Lady Macbeth.*        Did you send to him, sir?

*Macbeth.*   I hear it by the way,[o] but I will send.              130
  There's not a one of them but in his house
  I keep a servant fee'd.[p] I will tomorrow,
  And betimes [q] I will, to the weïrd sisters:
  More shall they speak, for now I am bent to know,
  By the worst means, the worst, for mine own good.
  All causes [r] shall give way. I am in blood
  Stepped in so far that, should I wade no more,
  Returning were as tedious as go o'er:
  Strange things I have in head that will to hand,
  Which must be acted ere they may be scanned.[s]              140

---

  [e] amazing lack of self-control   [f] come over   [g] unfamiliar   [h] nature
[i] own   [j] insist   [k] auguries   [l] intelligible utterances   [m] magpies and jack-
daws   [n] time   [o] casually   [p] in my pay   [q] early   [r] everything   [s] considered closely

*Lady Macbeth.*    You lack the season ᵗ of all natures, sleep.
*Macbeth.*    Come, we'll to sleep. My strange and self-
    abuse ᵘ
  Is the initiate ᵛ fear that wants hard use.ʷ
  We are yet but young in deed.                    *Exeunt.*


### Scene V [*A heath.*]


*Thunder. Enter the three* Witches, *meeting* Hecate.


*First Witch.*    Why, how now, Hecate! You look angerly.
*Hecate.*    Have I not reason, beldams ˣ as you are,
    Saucy and over-bold? How did you dare
    To trade and traffic with Macbeth
    In riddles and affairs of death;
    And I, the mistress of your charms,
    The close ʸ contriver of all harms,
    Was never called to bear my part,
    Or show the glory of our art?
    And, which is worse, all you have done          10
    Hath been but for a wayward son,
    Spiteful and wrathful, who, as others do,
    Loves for his own ends, not for you.
    But make amends now: get you gone,
    And at the pit of Acheron ᶻ
    Meet me i' th' morning: thither he
    Will come to know his destiny:
    Your vessels and your spells provide,
    Your charms and everything beside.
    I am for th' air; this night I'll spend           20
    Unto a dismal and a fatal end:
    Great business must be wrought ere noon:
    Upon the corner of the moon
    There hangs a vap'rous drop profound; ᵃ
    I'll catch it ere it comes to ground:
    And that distill'd by magic sleights
    Shall raise such artificial sprites
    As by the strength of their illusion
    Shall draw him on to his confusion:
    He shall spurn fate, scorn death, and bear        30
    His hopes 'bove wisdom, grace and fear:
    And you all know security ᵇ
    Is mortals' chiefest enemy.

---

ᵗ preservative    ᵘ beginner's    ʷ lacks hardening practice    ˣ hags    ʸ secret    ᶻ a river of Hades    ᵃ heavy    ᵇ overconfidence

*Music, and a song.*

Hark! I am called; my little spirit, see,
Sits in a foggy cloud, and stays for me.          [*Exit.*]

*Sing within, "Come away, come away," &c.*

*First Witch.*    Come, let's make haste; she'll soon be back
   again.                                    *Exeunt.*

### Scene VI [*Forres. The palace.*]

*Enter* Lennox *and another* Lord.

*Lennox.*    My former speeches ᶜ have but hit ᵈ your
      thoughts,
   Which can interpret ᵉ farther: only I say
   Things have been strangely borne.ᶠ The gracious Duncan
   Was pitied of Macbeth: marry, he was dead!
   And the right-valiant Banquo walked too late;
   Whom, you may say, if 't please you, Fleance killed,
   For Fleance fled. Men must not walk too late.
   Who cannot want the thought,ᵍ how monstrous
   It was for Malcolm and for Donalbain
   To kill their gracious father? Damned fact! ʰ                    10
   How it did grieve Macbeth! Did he not straight,
   In pious rage, the two delinquents tear,
   That were the slaves of drink and thralls of sleep?
   Was not that nobly done? Aye, and wisely too;
   For 'twould have angered any heart alive
   To hear the men deny 't. So that, I say,
   He has borne all things well: and I do think
   That, had he Duncan's sons under his key—
   As, an 't ⁱ please heaven, he shall not—they should find
   What 'twere to kill a father; so should Fleance.                20
   But, peace! For from broad ʲ words, and 'cause he failed
   His presence at the tyrant's feast, I hear,
   Macduff lives in disgrace: sir, can you tell
   Where he bestows himself?
*Lord.*                        The son of Duncan,
   From whom this tyrant holds the due of birth,ᵏ
   Lives in the English court, and is received
   Of the most pious Edwardˡ with such grace
   That the malevolence of fortune nothing

---

ᶜ i.e., what I have just spoken    ᵈ coincided with    ᵉ draw conclusions
ᶠ managed    ᵍ can fail to think    ʰ damned evil deed    ⁱ if it    ʲ frank
ᵏ birthright    ˡ Edward the Confessor

Takes from his high respect. Thither Macduff
Is gone to pray the holy King, upon his aid [m]          30
To wake Northumberland [n] and warlike Siward:
That by the help of these, with Him above
To ratify the work, we may again
Give to our tables meat, sleep to our nights,
Free from our feasts and banquets bloody knives,
Do faithful homage and receive free [o] honors:
All which we pine for now: and this report
Hath so exasperate the king that he
Prepares for some attempt of war.
*Lennox.*                         Sent he to Macduff?
*Lord.*    He did: and :with an abs:olute [p] "Sir, not I,"   40
The cloudy [q] messenger turns me his back,
And hums, as who would say "You'll rue the time
That clogs [r] me with this answer."
*Lennox.*                     And that well might
Advise him to a caution, [s] t' hold what distance
His wisdom can provide. Some holy angel
Fly to the court of England and unfold
His message ere he come, that a swift blessing
May soon return to this our suffering country
Under a hand accursed!
*Lord.*                     I'll send my prayers with him.
                                          *Exeunt.*


# ACT IV

### *Scene I* [*A desolate place.*]

*Thunder. Enter the three* Witches.

*First Witch.*    Thrice the brinded [t] cat hath mewed.
*Second Witch.*    Thrice and once the hedge-pig [u] whined.
*Third Witch.*    Harpier [v] cries " 'Tis time, 'tis time."
*First Witch.*    Round about the cauldron go:
   In the poisoned entrails throw.
   Toad, that under cold stone
   Days and nights has thirty-one

---

[m] i.e., on Malcolm's behalf   [n] the English county   [o] i.e., not subject to
a tyrant   [p] curt   [q] sullen   [r] burdens   [s] precaution   [t] brindled   [u] hedg-
hog   [v] familiar spirit of the Third Witch

Sweltered <sup>w</sup> venom sleeping got,<sup>x</sup>
Boil thou first i' th' charmèd pot.

*All.*    Double, double, toil and trouble;                                     10
Fire burn, and cauldron bubble.

*Second Witch.*    Fillet of a fenny <sup>y</sup> snake,
In the cauldron boil and bake;
Eye of newt, and toe of frog,
Wool of bat, and tongue of dog,
Adder's fork <sup>z</sup> and blindworm's <sup>a</sup> sting,
Lizard's leg, and howlet's <sup>b</sup> wing,
For a charm of pow'rful trouble,
Like a hell-broth boil and bubble.

*All.*    Double, double, toil and trouble;                                     20
Fire burn, and cauldron bubble.

*Third Witch.*    Scale of dragon, tooth of wolf,
Witch's mummy,<sup>c</sup> maw and gulf <sup>d</sup>
Of the ravined <sup>e</sup> salt-sea shark,
Root of hemlock digged i' th' dark,
Liver of blaspheming Jew,
Gall of goat, and slips of yew
Slivered in the moon's eclipse,
Nose of Turk, and Tartar's lips,
Finger of birth-strangled babe                                                  30
Ditch-delivered by a drab,<sup>f</sup>
Make the gruel thick and slab.<sup>g</sup>
Add thereto a tiger's chaudron,<sup>h</sup>
For th' ingredients of our cauldron.

*All.*    Double, double toil and trouble;
Fire burn and cauldron bubble.

*Second Witch.*    Cool it with a baboon's blood,
Then the charm is firm and good.


*Enter* Hecate, *and the other three* Witches.


*Hecate.*    O, well done! I commend your pains;
And every one shall share i' th' gains:                                         40
And now about the cauldron sing,
Like elves and fairies in a ring,
Enchanting all that you put in.


*Music and a song: "Black spirits," etc.* [Hecate *retires.*]


*Second Witch.*    By the pricking of my thumbs,

<sup>w</sup> exuded    <sup>x</sup> produced while sleeping    <sup>y</sup> swamp    <sup>z</sup> forked tongue    <sup>a</sup> a
snakelike lizard, supposedly poisonous      <sup>b</sup> owlet's    <sup>c</sup> mummified flesh
<sup>d</sup> gullet    <sup>e</sup> (i) ravenous (ii) glutted    <sup>f</sup> harlot    <sup>g</sup> sticky    <sup>h</sup> entrails

Something wicked this way comes:
Open, locks,
Whoever knocks!

*Enter* Macbeth.

*Macbeth.*   How now, you secret, black, and midnight
    hags!
  What is 't you do?
*All.*                 A deed without a name.
*Macbeth.*   I conjure you, by that which you profess,     50
  Howe'er you come to know it, answer me:
  Though you untie the winds and let them fight
  Against the churches! Though the yesty [1] waves
  Confound and swallow navigation up;
  Though bladed corn be lodged [j] and trees blown down;
  Though castles topple on their warders' heads;
  Though palaces and pyramids do slope
  Their heads to their foundations; though the treasure
  Of nature's germens [k] tumble all together,
  Even till destruction sicken; [l] answer me         60
  To what I ask you.
*First Witch.*   Speak.
*Second Witch.*       Demand.
*Third Witch.*                We'll answer.
*First Witch.*   Say if thou 'dst rather hear it from our
    mouths,
  Or from our masters.
*Macbeth.*             Call 'em, let me see 'em.
*First Witch.*   Pour in sow's blood, that hath eaten
  Her nine farrow; grease that's sweaten
  From the murderer's gibbet throw
  Into the flame.
*All.*             Come, high or low;
  Thyself and office deftly show!

*Thunder.* First Apparition: *an Armed Head.*

*Macbeth.*   Tell me, thou unknown power—
*First Witch.*                He knows thy thought:   70
  Hear his speech, but say thou nought.
*First Apparition.*   Macbeth! Macbeth! Macbeth! Beware
    Macduff;
  Beware the Thane of Fife. Dismiss me: enough.

¹ frothy    ʲ though ripe grain be beaten flat    ᵏ seeds    ¹ i.e., through
surfeit

                                              *He descends.*
*Macbeth.*   Whate'er thou art, for thy good caution thanks;
   Thou hast harped ᵐ my fear aright: but one word more—
*First Witch.*   He will not be commanded: here's another,
   More potent than the first.


*Thunder.* Second Apparition:  *a Bloody Child.*


*Second Apparition.*   Macbeth! Macbeth! Macbeth!
*Macbeth.*   Had I three ears, I 'ld hear thee.
*Second Apparition.*   Be bloody, bold and resolute; laugh
      to scorn
   The power of man, for none of woman born             80
   Shall harm Macbeth.                        *Descends.*
*Macbeth.*   Then live, Macduff: what need I fear of thee?
   But yet I'll make assurance double sure,
   And take a bond ⁿ of fate: thou shalt not live;
   That I may bell pale-hearted fear it lies,
   And sleep in spite of thunder.


*Thunder.* Third Apparition: *a Child Crowned, with a tree
   in his hand.*


                              What is this,
   That rises like the issue of a king,
   And wears upon his baby-brow the round
   And top of sovereignty?
*All.*                         Listen, but speak not to 't.
*Third Apparition.*   Be lion-mettled, proud, and take no    90
      care
   Who chafes, who frets, or where conspirers are:
   Macbeth shall never vanquished be until
   Great Birnam Wood to high Dunsinane Hill
   Shall come against him.                     *Descends.*
*Macbeth.*                    That will never be:
   Who can impress ° the forest, bid the tree
   Unfix his earth-bound root? Sweet bodements! ᵖ Good!
   Rebellious dead rise never till the wood
   Of Birnam rise, and our high-placed Macbeth
   Shall live the lease of nature,�q pay his breath
   To time and mortal custom.ʳ Yet my heart          100
   Throbs to know one thing: tell me, if you art
   Can tell so much: shall Banquo's issue ever
   Reign in this kingdom?


   ᵐ struck  the  chord  of  ⁿ get  a  guarantee  ° conscript  ᵖ omens
 q natural life span   ʳ natural death

*All.*                    Seek to know no more.
*Macbeth.*   I will be satisfied: deny me this,
  And an eternal curse fall on you! Let me know:
  Why sinks that cauldron? And what noise ⁱ is this?
                                                    *Hautboys.*

*First Witch.*   Show!
*Second Witch.*   Show!
*Third Witch.*   Show!
*All.*   Show his eyes, and grieve his heart;          110
  Come like shadows, so depart!


*A show of eight Kings, and* Banquo, *last* [King] *with a
    glass*ᵗ *in his hand.*


*Macbeth.*    Thou art too like the spirit of Banquo: down!
  Thy crown does sear mine eyeballs. And thy hair,
  Thou other gold-bound brow, is like the first.
  A third is like the former. Filthy hags!
  Why do you show me this? A fourth? Start,ᵘ eyes!
  What, will the line stretch out to the crack of doom?
  Another yet? A seventh? I'll see no more:
  And yet the eighth appears, who bears a glass
  Which shows me many more; and some I see          120
  That twofold balls and treble sceptres ᵛ carry:
  Horrible sight! Now I see 'tis true;
  For the blood-boltered ʷ Banquo smiles upon me,
  And points at them for his. What? Is this so?
*First Witch.*   Aye, sir, all this is so. But why
  Stands Macbeth thus amazedly?
  Come, sisters, cheer we up his sprites,
  And show the best of our delights.
  I'll charm the air to give a sound,
  While you perform your antic round,ˣ               130
  That this great king may kindly say
  Our duties did his welcome pay.
                      *Music. The* Witches *dance, and vanish.*
*Macbeth.*   Where are they? Gone? Let this pernicious
      hour
  Stand aye accursèd in the calendar!
  Come in, without there!


*Enter* Lennox.


*Lennox.*                  What's your Grace's will?


ⁱ music   ᵗ mirror   ᵘ bulge   ᵛ emblems of English coronation   ʷ blood-
matted   ˣ grotesque round dance

*Macbeth.*    Saw you the weïrd sisters?
*Lennox.*                                    No, my lord.
*Macbeth.*    Came they not by you?
*Lennox.*                                    No indeed, my lord.
*Macbeth.*    Infected be the air whereon they ride,
   And damned all those that trust them! I did hear
   The galloping of horse. Who was 't came by?        140
   Macduff is fled to England.
*Lennox.*    'Tis two or three, my lord, that bring you word
*Macbeth.*                    Fled to England!
*Lennox.*    Aye, my good lord.
*Macbeth.* [*Aside.*]    Time, thou anticipat'st my dread
      exploits.
   The flighty ʸ purpose never is o'ertook
   Unless the deed go with it. From this moment
   The very firstlings ᶻ of my heart shall be
   The firstlings of my hand. And even now,
   To crown my thoughts with acts, be it thought and done:
   The castle of Macduff I will surprise;              150
   Seize upon Fife; give to the edge o' th' sword
   His wife, his babes, and all unfortunate souls
   That trace him in his line. No boasting like a fool;
   This deed I'll do before this purpose cool.
   But no more sights!—Where are these gentlemen?
   Come bring me where they are.            *Exeunt.*


### Scene II [*Fife*. Macduff's *castle*.]

*Enter* Macduff's Wife, *her* Son, *and* Ross.

*Lady Macduff.*    What had he done, to make him fly the
      land?
*Ross.*    You must have patience,ᵃ madam.
*Lady Macduff.*                            He had none:
   His flight was madness. When our actions do not,
   Our fears do make us traitors.
*Ross.*                        You know not
   Whether it was his wisdom or his fear.
*Lady Macduff.*    Wisdom! To leave his wife, to leave his
      babes,
   His mansion and his titles ᵇ in a place
   From whence himself does fly? He loves us not;

   ʸ fleeting    ᶻ first-born    ᵃ self-control    ᵇ possessions

He wants <sup>c</sup> the natural touch: for the poor wren,
The most diminutive of birds, will fight,                          10
Her young ones in her nest, against the owl.
All is the fear and nothing is the love;
As little is the wisdom, where the flight
So runs against all reason.

*Ross.*                        My dearest coz,<sup>d</sup>
I pray you, school <sup>e</sup> yourself. But, for your husband,
He is noble, wise, judicious, and best knows
The fits <sup>f</sup> o' th' season. I dare not speak much further:
But cruel are the times, when we are traitors
And do not know ourselves; <sup>g</sup> when we hold <sup>h</sup> rumor
From <sup>i</sup> what we fear, yet know not what we fear,             20
But float upon a wild and violent sea
Each way and move. I take my leave of you:
Shall not be long but I'll be here again.
Things at the worst will cease, or else climb upward
To what they were before. My pretty cousin,
Blessing upon you!

*Lady Macduff.*    Fathered he is, and yet he's fatherless.

*Ross.*    I am so much a fool, should I stay longer,
It <sup>j</sup> would be my disgrace and your discomfort:
I take my leave at once.                        *Exit* Ross.

*Lady Macduff.*            Sirrah, your father's dead:          30
And what will you do now? How will you live?

*Son.*    As birds do, mother.

*Lady Macduff.*            What, with worms and flies?

*Son.*    With what I get, I mean; and so do they.

*Lady Macduff.*    Poor bird! Thou'dst never fear the net nor
   lime,<sup>k</sup>
The pitfall nor the gin.<sup>l</sup>

*Son.*    Why should I, mother? Poor birds they are not set
   for.
My father is not dead, for all your saying.

*Lady Macduff.*    Yes, he is dead. How wilt thou do for a
   father?

*Son.*    Nay, how will you do for a husband?

*Lady Macduff.*    Why, I can buy me twenty at any market.     40

*Son.*    Then you'll buy 'em to sell <sup>m</sup> again.

*Lady Macduff.*    Thou speakest with all thy wit, and yet, i'
   faith,
With wit enough for thee.

*Son.*    Was my father a traitor, mother?

*Lady Macduff.*    Aye, that he was.

----

<sup>e</sup> lacks  <sup>d</sup> cousin  <sup>e</sup> control  <sup>f</sup> disorders  <sup>g</sup> i.e., do not know ourselves
to be so  <sup>h</sup> believe  <sup>i</sup> because of  <sup>j</sup> i.e., his weeping  <sup>k</sup> birdlime  <sup>l</sup> trap
<sup>m</sup> betray

*Son.* What is a traitor?

*Lady Macduff.* Why, one that swears and lies.

*Son.* And be all traitors that do so?

*Lady Macduff.* Every one that does so is a traitor, and
    must be hanged.        50

*Son.* And must they all be hanged that swear and lie?

*Lady Macduff.* Every one.

*Son.* Who must hang them?

*Lady Macduff.* Why, the honest men.

*Son.* Then the liars and swearers are fools; for there are
    liars and swearers enow [n] to beat the honest men and
    hang up them.

*Lady Macduff.* Now, God help thee, poor monkey! But
    how wilt thou do for a father.

*Son.* If he were dead, you 'ld weep for him. If you would    60
    not, it were a good sign that I should quickly have a
    new father.

*Lady Macduff.* Poor prattler, how thou talkest!

*Enter a* Messenger.

*Messenger.* Bless you, fair dame! I am not to you known,
    Though in [o] your state of honor I am perfect. [p]
    I doubt [q] some danger does approach you nearly:
    If you will take a homely [r] man's advice,
    Be not found here. Hence, with your little ones!
    To fright you thus, methinks I am too savage;
    To do worse to you were fell cruelty,
    Which is too nigh your person. Heaven preserve you!    70
    I dare abide no longer.        *Exit* Messenger.

*Lady Macduff.*        Whither should I fly?
    I have done no harm. But I remember now
    I am in this earthly world, where to do harm
    Is often laudable, to do good sometime
    Accounted dangerous folly. Why then, alas,
    Do I put up that womanly defense,
    To say I have done no harm?— What are these faces?

*Enter* Murderers.

*First Murderer.* Where is your husband?

*Lady Macduff.* I hope in no place so unsanctified    80
    Where such as thou mayst find him.

*First Murderer.*              He's a traitor.

---

[n] enough   [o] of   [p] i.e., perfectly informed   [q] fear   [r] humble

*Son.*   Thou liest, thou shag-eared ⁵ villain!
*First Murderer.*               What, you egg!
                           [*Stabbing him.*]
   Young fry ᵗ of treachery!
*Son.*          He has killed me, mother:
   Run away, I pray you!          [*Dies.*]
         *Exit* [Lady Macduff] *crying "Murder!"*
            [*Exeunt* Murderers, *following her.*]


     *Scene III* [*England. Before the* King's *palace.*]

*Enter* Malcolm *and* Macduff.

*Malcolm.*   Let us seek out some desolate shade, and there
   Weep our sad bosoms empty.
*Macduff.*           Let us rather
   Hold fast the mortal ᵘ sword, and like good men
   Bestride ᵛ our down-fallen birthdom: ʷ each new morn
   New widows howl, new orphans cry, new sorrows
   Strike heaven on the face, that it resounds
   As if it felt with Scotland and yelled out
   Like ˣ syllable of dolor.ʸ
*Malcolm.*         What I believe, I'll wail;
   What know, believe; and what I can redress,
   As I shall find the time to friend,ᶻ I will.        10
   What you have spoke, it may be so perchance.
   This tyrant, whose sole ᵃ name blisters our tongues,
   Was once thought honest: you have loved him well;
   He hath not touched you yet. I am young; but
      something
   You may discern ᵇ of him through me; and wisdom
   To offer up a weak, poor, innocent lamb
   T' appease an angry god.
*Macduff.*   I am not treacherous.
*Malcolm.*         But Macbeth is.
   A good and virtuous nature may recoil ᶜ
   In ᵈ an imperial charge.ᵉ But I shall crave your pardon;  20
   That which you are, my thoughts cannot transpose: ᶠ
   Angels are bright still, though the brightest ᵍ fell:
   Though all things foul would wear the brows of grace,
   Yet grace must still look so.
*Macduff.*        I have lost my hopes.

---

⁵ shaggy-haired  ᵗ spawn  ᵘ deadly  ᵛ in defense of  ʷ native land
ˣ similar  ʸ pain  ᶻ propitious  ᵃ very  ᵇ learn  ᶜ fall away  ᵈ i.e., under
pressure  ᶠ change  ᵍ i.e., Lucifer

*Malcolm.*    Perchance even there where I did find my
        doubts.
    Why in that rawness [h] left you wife and child,
    Those precious motives, those strong knots of love,
    Without leave-taking?[i] I pray you,
    Let not my jealousies[i] be your dishonors,
    But mine own safeties. You may be rightly just,                30
    Whatever I shall think.
*Macduff.*                    Bleed, bleed, poor country!
    Great tyranny, lay thou thy basis sure,
    For goodness dare not check thee: wear thou thy
        wrongs;
    The title is affeered.[j] Fare thee well, lord:
    I would not be the villain that thou think'st
    For the whole space that's in the tyrant's grasp
    And the rich East to boot.
*Malcolm.*                    Be not offended:
    I speak not as in absolute fear of you.
    I think our country sinks beneath the yoke;
    It weeps, it bleeds, and each new day a gash                   40
    Is added to her wounds: I think withal [k]
    There would be hands uplifted in my right;
    And here from gracious England [l] have I offer
    Of goodly thousands. But for [m] all this,
    When I shall tread upon the tyrant's head,
    Or wear it on my sword, yet my poor country
    Shall have more vices than it had before,
    More suffer and more sundry ways than ever,
    By him that shall succeed.
*Macduff.*                    What should he be?
*Malcolm.*    It is myself I mean: in whom I know               50
    All the particulars[n] of vice so grafted
    That, when they shall be opened,[o] black Macbeth
    Will seem as pure as snow, and the poor state
    Esteem him as a lamb, being compared
    With my confineless harms.[p]
*Macduff.*                    Not in the legions
    Of horrid hell can come a devil more damned
    In evils to top Macbeth.
*Malcolm.*                    I grant him bloody,
    Luxurious,[q] avaricious, false, deceitful,
    Sudden,[r] malicious, smacking of every sin
    That has a name: but there's no bottom, none,                 60
    In my voluptuousness. Your wives, your daughters,

[h] unprotected  state    [i] suspicious    [j] confirmed    [k] furthermore    [l] i.e.,
the  English  king    [m] despite    [n] varieties    [o] disclosed    [p] unlimited  vices
[q] lecherous    [r] violent

Your matrons, and your maids, could not fill up
The cistern of my lust, and my desire
All continent ⁱ impediments would o'erbear,
That did oppose my will. Better Macbeth
Than such an one to reign.
*Macduff.*                          Boundless intemperance
In nature is a tyranny; it hath been
The untimely emptying of the happy throne,
And fall of many kings. But fear not yet
To take upon you what is yours. You may                   70
Convey ᵗ your pleasures in a spacious plenty,
And yet seem cold,ᵘ the time ᵛ you may so hoodwink:
We have willing dames enough; there cannot be
That vulture in you, to devour so many
As will to greatness dedicate themselves,
Finding it so inclined.
*Malcolm.*                      With this there grows
In my most ill-composed affection ʷ such
A stanchlessˣ avarice that, were I King,
I should cut off the nobles for their lands,
Desire his ʸ jewels, and this other's house,                   80
And my more-having would be as a sauce,
To make me hunger more, that I should forge
Quarrels unjust against the good and loyal,
Destroying them for wealth.
*Macduff.*                            This avarice
Sticks deeper, grows with more pernicious root
Than summer-seeming ᶻ lust, and it hath been
The sword ᵃ of our slain kings. Yet do not fear.
Scotland hath foisons ᵇ to fill up your will
Of your mere own.ᶜ All these are portable,ᵈ
With other graces weighed.                   90
*Malcolm.*    But I have none: the king-becoming graces,
As justice, verity, temp'rance, stableness,
Bounty, perseverance, mercy, lowliness,
Devotion, patience, courage, fortitude,
I have no relish for ᵉ them, but abound
In the division ᶠof each several crime,
Acting in many ways. Nay, had I pow'r, I should
Pour the sweet milk of concord into hell,
Uproar ᵍ the universal peace, confound
All unity on earth.

---

ⁱ restraining  ᵗ secretly gratify  ᵘ chaste  ᵛ world  ʷ disordered disposition  ˣ insatiable  ʸ i.e., one man's  ᶻ i.e., transitory  ᵃ i.e., the
cause of death  ᵇ abundance  ᶜ i.e., what is completely your own
ᵈ bearable  ᵉ trace of  ᶠ subdivisions  ᵍ disturb

*Macduff.*                    O Scotland, Scotland!
*Malcolm.*    If such a one be fit to govern, speak:
  I am as I have spoken.
*Macduff.*                    Fit to govern!
  No, not to live! O nation miserable,
  With an untitled tyrant bloody-sceptered,
  When shalt thou see thy wholesome days again,
  Since that the truest issue of thy throne
  By his own interdiction [h] stands accused,
  And does blaspheme his breed? Thy royal father
  Was a most sainted king: the queen that bore thee,
  Oftener upon her knees than on her feet,
  Died [i] every day she lived. Fare thee well!          110
  These evils thou repeat'st upon thyself
  Have banish'd me from Scotland. O my breast,
  Thy hope ends here!
*Malcolm.*                    Macduff, this noble passion,
  Child of integrity, hath from my soul
  Wiped the black scruples, reconciled my thoughts
  To thy good truth and honor. Devilish Macbeth
  By many of these trains [j] hath sought to win me
  Into his power; and modest [k] wisdom plucks [l] me
  From over-credulous haste; but God above          120
  Deal between thee and me! For even now
  I put myself to thy direction, and
  Unspeak mine own detraction; here abjure
  The taints and blames I laid upon myself,
  For [m] strangers to my nature. I am yet
  Unknown to woman, never was forsworn,
  Scarcely have coveted what was mine own,
  At no time broke my faith, would not betray
  The devil to his fellow, and delight
  No less in truth than life: my first false speaking          130
  Was this upon myself. What I am truly,
  Is thine and my poor country's to command:
  Whither indeed, before thy here-approach,
  Old Siward, with ten thousand warlike men,
  Already at a point,[n] was setting forth.
  Now we'll together, and the chance of goodness [a]
  Be like our warranted quarrel! [b] Why are you silent?
*Macduff.*    Such welcome and unwelcome things at once
  'Tis hard to reconcile.

*Enter a* Doctor.

  [h] statement of unfitness    [i] prepared for death    [j] plots    [k] cautious
  [l] holds back    [m] as    [n] in readiness    [a] success    [b] just cause

*Malcolm.*   Well, more anon. Comes the King forth, I
    pray you?                                              140
*Doctor.*   Aye, sir; there are a crew of wretched souls
    That stay <sup>c</sup> his cure. Their malady convinces <sup>d</sup>
    The great assay<sup>e</sup> of art;<sup>f</sup> but at his touch,
    Such sanctity hath heaven given his hand,
    They presently <sup>g</sup> amend.
*Malcolm.*                    I thank you, doctor.
                                        *Exit* [Doctor.]
*Macduff.*   What's the disease he means?
*Malcolm.*                         'Tis called the evil: <sup>h</sup>
    A most miraculous work in this good King;
    Which often, since my here-remain in England,
    I have seen him do. How he solicits heaven,
    Himself best knows: but strangely-visited <sup>i</sup> people,   150
    All swol'n and ulcerous, pitiful to the eye,
    The mere <sup>j</sup> despair of surgery, he cures,
    Hanging a golden stamp <sup>k</sup> about their necks,
    Put on with holy prayers; and 'tis spoken,
    To the succeeding royalty he leaves
    The healing benediction. With this strange virtue
    He hath a heavenly gift of prophecy,
    And sundry blessings hang about his throne
    That speak him full of grace.

*Enter* Ross.

*Macduff.*                    See, who comes here?
*Malcolm.*   My countryman; but yet I know him not.   160
*Macduff.*   My ever gentle cousin, welcome hither.
*Malcolm.*   I know him now. Good God, betimes<sup>l</sup> remove
    The means that makes us strangers!
*Ross.*                         Sir, amen.
*Macduff.*   Stands Scotland where it did?
*Ross.*                         Alas, poor country!
    Almost afraid to know itself! It cannot
    Be call'd our mother but our grave, where nothing,
    But who knows nothing, is once <sup>m</sup> seen to smile;
    Where sighs and groans, and shrieks that rend the air,
    Are made, not marked; <sup>n</sup> where violent sorrow seems
    A modern ecstasy.<sup>o</sup> The dead man's knell   170
    Is there scarce asked for who, and good men's lives
    Expire before the flowers in their caps,

<sup>e</sup> await  <sup>d</sup> overcomes  <sup>e</sup> greatest efforts  <sup>f</sup> i.e., medical science  <sup>g</sup> immediately  <sup>h</sup> "the king's evil" (scrofula)  <sup>i</sup> unusually afflicted  <sup>j</sup> complete  <sup>k</sup> coin  <sup>l</sup> quickly  <sup>m</sup> ever  <sup>n</sup> noticed  <sup>o</sup> ordinary emotion

Dying or ere ᵖ they sicken.
*Macduff.*                         O, relation �q
Too nice,ʳ and yet too true!
*Malcolm.*                      What's the newest grief?
*Ross.*     That of an hour's age doth hiss the speaker; ˢ
Each minute teems a new one.
*Macduff.*                         How does my wife?
*Ross.*   Why, well.
*Macduff.*           And all my children?
*Ross.*                               Well too.
*Macduff.*   The tyrant has not batter'd at their peace?
*Ross.*   No; they were well at peace when I did leave 'em.
*Macduff.*   Be not a niggard of your speech: how goes 't?    180
*Ross.*   When I came hither to transport the tidings,
Which I have heavily ᵗ borne, there ran a rumor
Of many worthy fellows that were out; ᵘ
Which was to my belief witnessed ᵛ the rather,
For that I saw the tyrant's power ʷ afoot.
Now is the time of help. Your eye in Scotland
Would create soldiers, make our women fight,
To doff their dire distresses.
*Malcolm.*                      Be 't their comfort
We are coming thither. Gracious England hath
Lent us good Siward and ten thousand men;    190
An older and a better soldier none
That Christendom gives out.
*Ross.*                         Would I could answer
This comfort with the like! But I have words
That would be howled out in the desert air,
Where hearing should not latch ˣ them.
*Macduff.*                      What concern they?
The general cause? Or is it a fee-grief ʸ
Due ᶻ to some single breast?
*Ross.*                         No mind that's honest
But in it shares some woe, though the main part
Pertains to you alone.
*Macduff.*           If it be mine,
Keep it not from me, quickly let me have it.    200
*Ross.*   Let not your ears despise my tongue for ever,
Which shall possess them with the heaviest sound
That ever yet they heard.
*Macduff.*                      Humh! I guess at it.

ᵖ dying before  q recital  ʳ precise  ˢ i.e., cause the speaker to be hissed
for giving stale information  ᵗ sadly  ᵘ up in arms  ᵛ attested  ʷ army
ˣ catch  ʸ private grief  ᶻ belonging

*Ross.*     Your castle is surprised; your wife and babes
Savagely slaughtered. To relate the manner,
Were, on the quarry [a] of these murdered deer,
To add the death of you.
*Malcolm.*             Merciful heaven!
What, man! Ne'er pull your hat upon your brows.
Give sorrow words. The grief that does not speak
Whispers [b] the o'erfraught heart and bids it break.      210
*Macduff.*     My children too?
*Ross.*            Wife, children, servants, all
That could be found.
*Macduff.*         And I must be from thence!
My wife killed too?
*Ross.*        I have said.
*Malcolm.*            Be comforted:
Let's make us med'cines of our great revenge,
To cure this deadly grief.
*Macduff.*     He has no children. All my pretty ones?
Did you say all? O hell-kite! All?
What, all my pretty chickens and their dam
At one fell swoop?
*Malcolm.*     Dispute [c] it like a man.
*Macduff.*            I shall do so;      220
But I must also feel it as a man:
I cannot but remember such things were,
That were most precious to me. Did heaven look on,
And would not take their part? Sinful Macduff,
They were all struck for thee! Naught [d] that I am,
Not for their own demerits but for mine,
Fell slaughter on their souls. Heaven rest them now!
*Malcolm.*     Be this the whetstone of your sword. Let grief
Convert to anger; blunt not the heart, enrage it.
*Macduff.*     O, I could play the woman with mine eyes,      230
And braggart with my tongue! But, gentle heavens,
Cut short all intermission; [e] front to front
Bring thou this fiend of Scotland and myself;
Within my sword's length set him; if he 'scape,
Heaven forgive him too!
*Malcolm.*            This tune goes manly.
Come, go we to the King. Our power is ready;
Our lack is nothing but our leave. [f] Macbeth
Is ripe for shaking, and the powers above
Put on their instruments. [g] Receive what cheer you
     may;
The night is long that never finds the day      *Exeunt* 240

---

[a] heap of game    [b] whispers to    [c] i.e., avenge    [d] wicked    [e] delay    [f] i.e., we have only to take our leave    [g] set their agents to work

# ACT V

## Scene I [*Dunsinane*. Macbeth's *castle*.]

*Enter a* Doctor of Physic *and a* Waiting Gentlewoman.

*Doctor.* I have two nights watched with you, but can
perceive no truth in your report. When was it she last
walked?

*Gentlewoman.* Since his majesty went into the field, I
have seen her rise from her bed, throw her nightgown
upon her, unlock her closet,[h] take forth paper, fold it,
write upon 't, read it, afterwards seal it, and again return
to bed; yet all this while in a most fast sleep.

*Doctor.* A great perturbation in nature, to receive at once
the benefit of sleep and do the effects of watching![i]   10
In this slumb'ry agitation,[j] besides her walking and
other actual performances, what, at any time, have you
heard her say?

*Gentlewoman.* That, sir, which I will not report after
her.

*Doctor.* You may to me, and 'tis most meet[k] you should.

*Gentlewoman.* Neither to you nor any one, having no
witness to confirm my speech.

*Enter* Lady [Macbeth], *with a taper.*

Lo you, here she comes! This is her very guise,[l] and,
upon my life, fast asleep. Observe her; stand close.[m]   20

*Doctor.* How came she by that light?

*Gentlewoman.* Why, it stood by her. She has light by her
continually. 'Tis her command.

*Doctor.* You see, her eyes are open.

*Gentlewoman.* Aye, but their sense[n] are shut.

*Doctor.* What is it she does now? Look, how she rubs
her hands.

*Gentlewoman.* It is an accustomed action with her, to
seem thus washing her hands: I have known her continue in this a quarter of an hour.   30

*Lady Macbeth.* Yet here's a spot.

[h] chest   [i] act as if awake   [j] activity   [k] fitting   [l] habit   [m] concealed
[n] senses of perception

*Doctor.* Hark! She speaks: I will set down what comes from her, to satisfy my remembrance the more strongly.

*Lady Macbeth.* Out, damned spot! Out, I say! One: two: why, then 'tis time to do 't. Hell is murky. Fie, my lord, fie! A soldier, and afeard? What need we fear who knows it, when none can call our pow'r to accompt? ° Yet who would have thought the old man to have had so much blood in him?

*Doctor.* Do you mark that?                                          40

*Lady Macbeth.* The Thane of Fife had a wife. Where is she now? What, will these hands ne'er be clean? No more o' that, my lord, no more o' that. You mar all with this starting. ᴾ

*Doctor.* Go to, go to. You have known what you should not.

*Gentlewoman.* She has spoke what she should not, I am sure of that. Heaven knows what she has known.

*Lady Macbeth.* Here's the smell of the blood still: all the perfumes of Arabia will not sweeten this little hand.   50 Oh, oh, oh!

*Doctor.* What a sigh is there! The heart is sorely charged.�q

*Gentlewoman.* I would not have such a heart in my bosom for the dignity of the whole body.

*Doctor.* Well, well, well—

*Gentlewoman.* Pray God it be, sir.

*Doctor.* This disease is beyond my practice.ʳ Yet I have known those which have walked in their sleep who have died holily in their beds.                                          60

*Lady Macbeth.* Wash your hands, put on your night-gown, look not so pale. I tell you yet again, Banquo's buried. He cannot come out on 's grave.

*Doctor.* Even so?

*Lady Macbeth.* To bed, to bed; there's knocking at the gate: come, come, come, come, give me your hand! What's done cannot be undone. To bed, to bed, to bed!

                                                              *Exit.*

*Doctor.* Will she go now to bed?

*Gentlewoman.* Directly.

*Doctor.* Foul whisperings are abroad: unnatural deeds   70
   Do breed unnatural troubles. Infected minds
To their deaf pillows will discharge their secrets.
More needs she the divine than the physician.

---

° account   ᴾ startled movements   q burdened   ʳ professional skill

God, God forgive us all! Look after her;
Remove from her the means of all annoyance,[a]
And still [t] keep eyes upon her. So good night:
My mind she has mated [u] and amazed my sight:
I think, but dare not speak.

*Gentlewoman.*                    Good night, good doctor.

*Exeunt.*


Scene II [*The country near Dunsinane.*]

*Drum and Colors. Enter* Menteith, Caithness, Angus, Len-
    nox, Soldiers.

*Menteith.*   The English pow'r is near, led on by Malcolm,
    His uncle Siward and the good Macduff:
    Revenges burn in them; for their dear causes
    Would to the bleeding [v] and the grim alarm [w]
    Excite the mortified man.[x]
*Angus.*                         Near Birnam Wood
    Shall we well meet them; that way are they coming.
*Caithness.*   Who knows if Donalbain be with his brother?
*Lennox.*   For certain, sir, he is not. I have a file
    Of all the gentry: there is Siward's son,
    And many unrough [y] youths, that even now          10
    Protest [z] their first of manhood.
*Menteith.*                    What does the tyrant?
*Caithness.*   Great Dunsinane he strongly fortifies:
    Some say he's mad; others, that lesser hate him,
    Do call it valiant fury; but, for certain,
    He cannot buckle his distempered cause
    Within the belt of rule.[a]
*Angus.*                    Now does he feel
    His secret murders sticking on his hands;
    Now minutely [b] revolts upbraid his faith-breach;
    Those he commands move only in command,
    Nothing in love. Now does he feel his title          20
    Hang loose about him, like a giant's robe
    Upon a dwarfish thief.
*Menteith.*                    Who then shall blame
    His pestered [c] senses to recoil and start,
    When all that is within him does condemn
    Itself for being there?
*Caithness.*                    Well, march we on,

[a] self-injury  [t] always  [u] bewildered  [v] bloody  [w] attack  [x] arouse the
deadened  man  [y] beardless  [z] assert  [a] reason  [b] every  minute  [c] tor-
mented

To give obedience where 'tis truly owed.
Meet we the med'cine [d] of the sickly weal, [e]
And with him pour we, in our country's purge,
Each drop of us.
*Lennox.*          Or so much as it needs
To dew [f] the sovereign [g] flower and drown the weeds.          30
Make we our march towards Birnam.

                    *Exeunt marching.*


## Scene III [*Dunsinane. Macbeth's* castle.]

*Enter* Macbeth, Doctor, *and* Attendants.

*Macbeth.*    Bring me no more reports; let them fly all.
Till Birnam Wood remove to Dunsinane
I cannot taint [h] with fear. What's the boy Malcolm?
Was he not born of woman? The spirits that know
All mortal consequences [i] have pronounced me thus:
"Fear not, Macbeth; no man that's born of woman
Shall e'er have power upon thee." Then fly, false thanes,
And mingle with the English epicures. [j]
The mind I sway [k] by and the heart I bear
Shall never sag with doubt nor shake with fear.          10

*Enter* Servant.

The devil damn thee black, thou cream-faced loon! [l]
Where got'st thou that goose look?
*Servant.*    There is ten thousand—
*Macbeth.*                    Geese, villain?
*Servant.*                        Soldiers, sir.
*Macbeth.*    Go prick thy face and over-red [m] thy fear,
Thou lily-liver'd boy. What soldiers, patch! [n]
Death of my soul! Those linen cheeks of thine
Are counselors to fear. What soldiers, whey-face?
*Servant.*    The English force, so please you.
*Macbeth.*    Take thy face hence.          [*Exit* Servant.]
                    Seyton!—I am sick at heart          20
When I behold—Seyton, I say!—This push
Will cheer me ever, or disseat [o] me now.

[d] physician (i.e., Malcolm)    [e] commonwealth    [f] water    [g] (i) remedial
(ii) royal (i.e., Malcolm)    [h] become tainted    [i] future human events
[j] i.e., the English lived in greater ease than the Scots    [k] direct myself
[l] lout    [m] cover with red    [n] fool    [o] unseat

I have lived long enough. My way of life
Is fallen into the sear,[p] the yellow leaf,
And that which should accompany old age,
As honor, love, obedience, troops of friends,
I must not look to have; but, in their stead,
Curses, not loud but deep, mouth-honor, breath,
Which the poor heart would fain deny,[q] and dare not.
Seyton!

*Enter* Seyton.

*Seyton.*   What's your gracious pleasure?
*Macbeth.*                    What news more?   30
*Seyton.*   All is confirmed, my lord, which was reported.
*Macbeth.*   I'll fight, till from my bones my flesh be hacked.
Give me my armor.
*Seyton.*              'Tis not needed yet.
*Macbeth.*   I'll put it on.
Send out moe[r] horses, skirr[s] the country round;
Hang those that talk of fear. Give me mine armor.
How does your patient, doctor?
*Doctor.*                    Not so sick, my lord,
As she is troubled with thick-coming fancies,
That keep her from her rest.
*Macbeth.*                    Cure her of that.
Canst thou not minister to a mind diseased,          40
Pluck from the memory a rooted sorrow,
Raze out[t] the written[u] troubles of the brain,
And with some sweet oblivious[v] antidote
Cleanse the stuffed[w] bosom of that perilous stuff
Which weighs upon the heart?
*Doctor.*                    Therein the patient
Must minister to himself.
*Macbeth.*   Throw physic to the dogs, I'll none of it.
Come, put mine armor on. Give me my staff.
Seyton, send out. Doctor, the thanes fly from me.
Come, sir, dispatch. If thou couldst, doctor, cast          50
The water[x] of my land, find her disease
And purge it to a sound and pristine health,
I would applaud thee to the very echo,
That should applaud again.[y] Pull 't[z] off, I say.—
What rhubarb, senna,[a] or what purgative drug,
Would scour these English hence? Hear'st thou of them?
*Doctor.*   Aye, my good lord; your royal preparation

---

[p] withered   state   [q] withhold   [r] more   [s] scour   [t] erase   [u] i.e., permanent   [v] causing forgetfulness   [w] clogged up   [x] analyze the urine   [y] back
[z] i.e., the armor   [a] a purgative

Makes us hear something.
Macbeth.　　　　　　　　Bring it <sup>b</sup> after me.
　I will not be afraid of death and bane<sup>c</sup>
　Till Birnam Forest come to Dunsinane.　　　　　　　60
Doctor. [*Aside.*]　Were I from Dunsinane away and clear,
　Profit again should hardly draw me here.　　　*Exeunt.*


## Scene IV [*Country near Birnam Wood.*]

*Drum and Colors. Enter* Malcolm, Siward, Siward's Son,
　Macduff, Menteith, Caithness, Angus, *and* Soldiers,
　*marching.*

Malcolm.　　Cousins, I hope the days are near at hand
　That chambers <sup>d</sup> will be safe.
Menteith.　　　　　　　We doubt it nothing.<sup>e</sup>
Siward.　What wood is this before us?
Menteith.　　　　　　　The Wood of Birnam.
Malcolm.　　Let every soldier hew him down a bough,
　And bear 't before him: thereby shall we shadow <sup>f</sup>
　The numbers of our host, and make discovery <sup>g</sup>
　Err in report of us.
Soldiers.　　　　It shall be done.
Siward.　　We learn no other but <sup>h</sup> the confident tyrant
　Keeps still in Dunsinane, and will endure
　Our setting down before 't.<sup>i</sup>
Malcolm.　　　　　　　'Tis his main hope:　　　　10
　For where there is advantage to be given,<sup>j</sup>
　Both more and less <sup>k</sup> have given him the revolt,
　And none serve with him but constrainèd things
　Whose hearts are absent too.
Macduff.　　　　　　　Let our just censures<sup>l</sup>
　Attend the true event,<sup>m</sup> and put we on
　Industrious soldiership.
Siward.　　　　　　　The time approaches,
　That will with due decision make us know
　What we shall say we have and what we owe.<sup>n</sup>
　Thoughts speculative their unsure hopes relate,
　But certain issue <sup>o</sup> strokes must arbitrate: <sup>p</sup>　　　20
　Towards which advance the war.<sup>q</sup>
　　　　　　　　　　*Exeunt, marching.*

<sup>b</sup> i.e., the rest of the armor　<sup>c</sup> destruction　<sup>d</sup> when bedchambers　<sup>e</sup> not
at all　<sup>f</sup> disguise　<sup>g</sup> i.e., reconnaissance　<sup>h</sup> nothing but that　<sup>i</sup> besieging
it　<sup>j</sup> opportunity offered　<sup>k</sup> high and low　<sup>l</sup> judgments　<sup>m</sup> await the actual outcome　<sup>n</sup> own　<sup>o</sup> outcome　<sup>p</sup> decide　<sup>q</sup> army

### Scene V [*Dunsinane*. Macbeth's *castle*.]

*Enter* Macbeth, Seyton, *and* Soldiers, *with Drum and Colors.*

*Macbeth.*    Hang out our banners on the outward walls;
    The cry is still <sup>r</sup> "They come!" Our castle's strength
    Will laugh a siege to scorn. Here let them lie
    Till famine and the ague eat them up:
    Were they not forced <sup>s</sup> with those that should be ours,
    We might have met them dareful, beard to beard,
    And beat them backward home.
*A cry within of women.*

                           What is that noise?
*Seyton.*    It is the cry of women, my good lord.    [*Exit.*]
*Macbeth.*    I have almost forgot the taste of fears:
    The time has been, my senses would have cooled                    10
    To hear a night-shriek, and my fell <sup>t</sup> of hair
    Would at a dismal treatise <sup>u</sup> rouse and stir
    As life were in 't. I have supped full with horrors.
    Direness, familiar to my slaughterous thoughts,
    Cannot once start <sup>v</sup> me.

[*Enter* Seyton.]

                     Wherefore was that cry?
*Seyton.*    The Queen, my lord, is dead.
*Macbeth.*    She should have died hereafter;
    There would have been a time for such a word.<sup>w</sup>
    Tomorrow, and tomorrow, and tomorrow,
    Creeps in this petty pace from day to day,                    20
    To the last syllable of recorded time;
    And all our yesterdays have lighted fools
    The way to dusty death. Out, out, brief candle!
    Life's but a walking shadow, a poor player
    That struts and frets his hour upon the stage
    And then is heard no more: it is a tale
    Told by an idiot, full of sound and fury,
    Signifying nothing.

*Enter a* Messenger.

    Thou comest to use thy tongue; thy story quickly!

---

<sup>r</sup> always    <sup>s</sup> reinforced    <sup>t</sup> pelt    <sup>u</sup> story    <sup>v</sup> startle    <sup>w</sup> i.e., announcement of her death

*Messenger.*   Gracious my lord,      30
  I should report that which I say I saw,
  But know not how to do't.
*Macbeth.*              Well, say, sir.
*Messenger.*   As I did stand my watch upon the hill,
  I looked toward Birnam, and anon, methought,
  The wood began to move.
*Macbeth.*              Liar and slave!
*Messenger.*   Let me endure your wrath, if't be not so:
  Within this three mile may you see it coming;
  I say, a moving grove.
*Macbeth.*          If thou speakest false,
  Upon the next tree shalt thou hang alive,
  Till famine cling [x] thee. If thy speech be sooth,[y]      40
  I care not if thou dost for me as much.
  I pull [z] in resolution, and begin
  To doubt [a] the equivocation [b] of the fiend,
  That lies like truth: "Fear not, till Birnam Wood
  Do come to Dunsinane!" and now a wood
  Comes toward Dunsinane. Arm, arm, and out!
  If this which he avouches [c] does appear,
  There is nor flying hence nor tarrying here.
  I 'gin to be aweary of the sun,
  And wish th' estate [d] o' th' world were now undone.     50
  Ring the alarum-bell! Blow, wind! Come, wrack! [e]
  At least we'll die with harness [f] on our back.
                             *Exeunt.*


*Scene VI* [*Dunsinane. Before the castle.*]

*Drum and Colors. Enter* Malcolm, Siward, Macduff, *and
  their Army, with boughs.*

*Malcolm.*   Now near enough; your leavy screens throw
  down,
  And show like those you are. You, worthy uncle,
  Shall, with my cousin, your right noble son,
  Lead our first battle: [g] worthy Macduff and we
  Shall take upon 's what else remains to do,
  According to our order.[h]
*Siward.*              Fare you well.
  Do we but find the tyrant's power [i] tonight,

[x] shrivel  [y] truth  [z] rein  [a] suspect  [b] ambiguity  [c] assures  [d] order
[e] ruin  [f] armor  [g] battalion  [h] plan  [i] forces

Let us be beaten if we cannot fight.
*Macduff.*     Make all our trumpets speak; give them all
    breath,
  Those clamorous harbingers of blood and death.       10
                     *Exeunt. Alarums continued.*


*Scene VII* [*Another part of the field.*]

*Enter* Macbeth.

*Macbeth.*     They have tied me to a stake; I cannot fly,
  But bear-like I must fight the course.[J] What's he
  That was not born of woman? Such a one
  Am I to fear, or none.

*Enter young* Siward.

*Young Siward.*     What is thy name?
*Macbeth.*                 Thou 'lt be afraid to hear it.
*Young Siward.*     No; though thou call'st thyself a hotter
  name
  Than any is in hell.
*Macbeth.*          My name's Macbeth.
*Young Siward.*     The devil himself could not pronounce
  a title
  More hateful to mine ear.
*Macbeth.*          No, nor more fearful.
*Young Siward.*     Thou liest, abhorrèd tyrant. With my    10
  sword
  I'll prove the lie thou speak'st.

*Fight, and young* Siward *slain.*

*Macbeth.*             Thou wast born of woman.
  But swords I smile at, weapons laugh to scorn,
  Brandish'd by man that's of a woman born.
                           *Exit.*

*Alarums. Enter* Macduff.

*Macduff.*     That way the noise is. Tyrant, show thy face!
  If thou beest slain and with no stroke of mine,
  My wife and children's ghosts will haunt me still.

[J] attack (by dogs, in bearbaiting)

I cannot strike at wretched kerns,[k] whose arms
Are hired to bear their staves.[l] Either thou, Macbeth,
Or else my sword, with an unbattered edge,
I sheathe again undeeded.[m] There thou shouldst be;    20
By this great clatter, one of greatest note
Seems bruited.[n] Let me find him, Fortune,
And more I beg not.                    *Exit. Alarums.*

*Enter* Malcolm *and* Siward.

*Siward.*    This way, my lord. The castle's gently rendered:[o]
The tyrant's people on both sides do fight;
The noble thanes do bravely in the war;
The day almost itself professes yours,
And little is to do.
*Malcolm.*                We have met with foes
That strike beside us.[p]
*Siward.*            Enter, sir, the castle.  *Exeunt. Alarum.*


Scene VIII [*Another part of the field.*]

*Enter* Macbeth.

*Macbeth.*    Why should I play the Roman fool, and die
On mine own sword? Whiles I see lives,[q] the gashes
Do better upon them.

*Enter* Macduff.

*Macduff.*                Turn, hell-hound, turn!
*Macbeth.*    Of all men else I have avoided thee.
But get thee back! My soul is too much charged[r]
With blood of thine already.
*Macduff.*                I have no words:
My voice is in my sword, thou bloodier villain
Than terms can give thee out!

*Fight. Alarum.*

*Macbeth.*                    Thou losest labor:
As easy mayst thou the intrenchant[s] air
With thy keen sword impress[t] as make me bleed:    10
Let fall thy blade on vulnerable crests;
I bear a charmèd life, which must not yield

[k] lowly footsoldiers  [l] spears  [m] having performed no deeds  [n] reported  [o] surrendered  [p] i.e., miss us on purpose (or perhaps, fight on our side)  [q] i.e., living enemies  [r] burdened  [s] incapable of being cut  [t] mark

To one of woman born.
*Macduff.*                    Despair[u] thy charm,
And let the angel [v] whom thou still [w] hast served
Tell thee, Macduff was from his mother's womb
Untimely ripp'd.
*Macbeth.*   Accursèd be that tongue that tells me so,
For it hath cowed my better part of man! [x]
And be these juggling fiends no more believed,
That palter [y] with us in a double sense;                    20
That keep the word of promise to our ear,
And break it to our hope. I'll not fight with thee.
*Macduff.*   Then yield thee, coward,
And live to be the show and gaze [z] o' th' time:
We'll have thee, as our rarer monsters [a] are,
Painted upon a pole,[b] and underwrit,
"Here may you see the tyrant."
*Macbeth.*                    I will not yield,
To kiss the ground before young Malcolm's feet,
And to be baited with the rabble's curse.
Though Birnam Wood be come to Dunsinane,                    30
And thou opposed, being of no woman born,
Yet I will try the last. Before my body
I throw my warlike shield. Lay on, Macduff;
And damned be him that first cries "Hold enough!"
            *Exeunt, fighting. Alarums. [Re-]enter fighting, and*
                                        Macbeth *slain.*[c]

*Retreat and Flourish. Enter, with Drum and Colors,*
      Malcolm, Siward, Ross, Thanes, *and* Soldiers.

*Malcolm.*   I would the friends we miss were safe arrived.
*Siward.*   Some must go off: [d] and yet, by these I see,
So great a day as this is cheaply bought.
*Malcolm.*   Macduff is missing, and your noble son.
*Ross.*   Your son, my lord, has paid a soldier's debt:
He only lived but till he was a man;                    40
The which no sooner had his prowess confirmed
In the unshrinking station [e] where he fought,
But like a man he died.
*Siward.*                    Then he is dead?
*Ross.*   Aye, and brought off the field. Your cause of
      sorrow

---

[u] despair of   [v] demon   [w] always   [x] i.e., manliness   [y] quibble
[z] sight   [a] freaks   [b] i.e., a painted likeness suspended on a pole before a
showman's booth   [c] The stage business is vague here; probably Macduff
exists, dragging Macbeth's corpse   [d] die   [e] the place which he did not
desert

Must not be measured by his worth, for then
It hath no end.

*Siward.*          Had he his hurts before?

*Ross.*   Aye, on the front.

*Siward.*          Why then, God's soldier be he!
Had I as many sons as I have hairs,
I would not wish them to a fairer death:
And so his knell is knolled.

*Malcolm.*               He's worth more sorrow,     50
And that I'll spend for him.

*Siward.*               He's worth no more:
They say he parted ᶠ well and paid his score: ᵍ
And so God be with him! Here comes newer comfort.

*Enter* Macduff, *with* Macbeth's *head.*

*Macduff.*   Hail, King! For so thou art. Behold, where
     stands
Th' usurper's cursèd head. The time is free.
I see thee compassed ʰ with thy kingdom's pearl,ⁱ
That speak my salutation in their minds;
Whose voices I desire aloud with mine:
Hail, King of Scotland!

*All.*               Hail, King of Scotland!

                         *Flourish.*

*Malcolm.*   We shall not spend a large expense of time     60
Before we reckon with your several loves,
And make us even with ʲ you. My Thanes and kinsmen,
Henceforth be Earls, the first that ever Scotland
In such an honor named. What's more to do,
Which would be planted newly ᵏ with the time,
As calling home our exiled friends abroad
That fled the snares of watchful tyranny,
Producing forth the cruel ministers
Of this dead butcher and his fiend-like queen,
Who, as 'tis thought, by self and violent ˡ hands
Took off her life; this, and what needful else
That calls upon us, by the grace of Grace
We will perform in measure, time and place.ᵐ
So thanks to all at once and to each one,
Whom we invite to see us crowned at Scone.

                    *Flourish. Exeunt omnes.*

ᶠ departed   ᵍ account   ʰ surrounded   ⁱ i.e., the nobles   ʲ i.e., reward
ᵏ established anew   ˡ her own violent   ᵐ with decorum, at the proper
time and place

# Ben Jonson:

## *VOLPONE*

In the nineteenth century *Volpone* was perhaps England's least pleasing dramatic masterpiece. Things were different earlier. *Volpone* when first written (*c.* 1606) was popular with both the general public at the Globe Theater and the academic audience of Oxford and Cambridge. Its popularity continued until the Puritans closed the theaters in 1642. With the reopening of the theaters in 1660, *Volpone* again became a favorite. In 1665, for example, Samuel Pepys found it "a most excellent play; the best I think I ever saw, and well acted." It was frequently performed in the eighteenth century too, until 1785, when it disappeared from the English stage until 1921. During its absence it was given notable praise but the praise was mixed with censure. William Hazlitt's distaste for it is alluded to in James Agate's essay (p. 444); additional examples will be helpful. Here is Samuel Taylor Coleridge, writing early in the nineteenth century:

> This admirable, indeed, but yet more wonderful than admirable, play is from the fertility and vigor of invention, character, language, and sentiment the strongest proof how impossible it is to keep up any pleasurable interest in a tale in which there is no goodness of heart in any of the prominent characters. After the third act, this play becomes not a dead, but a painful, weight on the feelings. . . . Bonario and Celia should have been made in some way or other principals in the plot—which they might be, and the objects of interest, without being made characters. . . . If it were practicable to lessen the paramountcy of Volpone, a most delightful comedy might be produced, Celia being the ward or niece instead of the wife of Corvino, and Bonario her lover.

Second, here is John Addington Symonds, writing of *Volpone* near the end of the century:

It is a sinister and remorseless analysis of avarice in its
corrosive influence on human character. . . . The spectacle,
alas! is too grisly.

In 1921, after seeing a revival of the play, William Butler Yeats
succeeded in lessening in his mind what Coleridge had called
"the paramountcy of Volpone," and in magnifying the roles of
Bonario and Celia:

> *Volpone* was even finer than I expected. I could think of
> nothing else for hours after I left the theater. The great
> surprise to me was the pathos of the two young people,
> united not in love but in innocence, and going in the end
> their separate way.

What has happened, apparently, is that an understanding of
Ben Jonson's kind of comedy disappeared late in the eighteenth
century and has only been slowly returning.

Most Elizabethan comedies fall into one of two classes, which
can be named Shakespearean and Jonsonian (for their most
notable practitioners), or romantic and satiric. In Shakespearean comedy we are in a noble home in Illyria or under the
greenwood tree in the Forest of Arden. If we are in Venice, it
is a Venice which (despite the presence of a detestable money-
lender) is richly ceremonious:

> Your mind is tossing on the ocean,
> There, where your argosies with portly sail,
> Like signiors and rich burghers of the flood,
> Or as it were, the pageants of the sea,
> Do overpeer the petty traffickers,
> That curtsy to them, do them reverence,
> As they fly by them with their woven wings.

In the fifth act of *The Merchant of Venice*, we leave Venice behind and dwell in Belmont:

> How sweet the moonlight sleeps upon this bank!
> Here will we sit, and let the sounds of music
> Creep in our ears. Soft stillness and the night
> Become the touches of sweet harmony.

Shakespearean comedies on the whole present an ideal world, a
golden world that is more or less the world of our reveries. Although these comedies ultimately derive some of their mishaps
from the classical comedy of Plautus and Terence, they seem
chiefly indebted to the improbable world of medieval romance,

with its pageantry and its entranced lovers. There is some satire, but it is subordinated to romance. Things end happily; as Puck promises in *A Midsummer Night's Dream*, "Jack shall have Jill;/ Nought shall go ill." The "otherworldliness" of romantic comedy delighted the Elizabethans and the nineteenth century, and delights the twentieth, but its fairy-tale surface did not greatly appeal to the later seventeenth and the eighteenth centuries. Samuel Pepys in 1663 found *Twelfth Night* "a silly play"; but he liked Jonsonian comedy. In this second sort of comedy we are allegedly in a world we recognize as the real world. The Venice of *Volpone* is the corrupt Venice that Englishmen saw as the real Venice, and Jonson peppers his play with Italian words and realistic details. In the real Venice courtesans were abundant and unmolested so long as they paid a tax; in Jonson's Venice they are often mentioned, but in Shakespeare's Venice they have no place. The point of Jonsonian comedy, as Jonson insisted, is that it holds the mirror up to nature, showing man his folly so that he may reform. It is satiric and claims that its satire is therapeutic. George Bernard Shaw puts himself in this tradition when he says in the preface to his *Complete Plays*, "My business as a classic writer of comedies is 'to chasten morals with ridicule'; and if I sometimes make you feel like a fool, remember that I have by the same action cured your folly." The end of a Shakespearean comedy brings universal joy; the end of a Jonsonian comedy brings public exposure of folly.

In an early play, *Every Man Out of His Humor*, Jonson discusses the two sorts of comedy and is clearly contemptuous of the romantic sort. The first speaker is almost describing *Twelfth Night*; the second speaker, who corrects the bad taste of the first, is describing the work Jonson set out to do.

> *Mitis.* The argument of his comedy might have been of some other nature, as of a duke to be in love with a countess, and that countess to be in love with the duke's son, and the son to love the lady's waiting-maid; some such cross wooing, with a clown to their servingman, better than to be thus near, and familiarly allied to the time.
>
> *Cordatus.* You say well, but I would fain hear one of these autumn-judgments define once, *Quid sit comoedia* [What is comedy]? if he cannot, let him content himself with Cicero's definition, till he have strength to propose to himself a better, who would have a comedy to be *imitatio vitae, speculum consuetudinis, imago veritatis* [an imitation of life, a mirror of custom, an image of truth]; a thing throughout pleasant, and ridiculous, and accommodated to the correction of manners.

As the allusion to Cicero suggests, Jonson had classical precedent for his practice. The Dedication of *Volpone* reminds his readers that he is following "ancient forms," and he frets that the severity of the punishments meted out at the end may be thought an error but in fact are justified by the classical conception which held that "the office of a comic poet [is] to imitate justice, and instruct to life." His prologue, in a similar vein, promises "rhyme, not empty of reason."

Yet one cannot help feeling that *Volpone* is darker than any Greek or Roman comedy, and that we are kept from tragedy only by the mirth that is continually evoked. In *Every Man in His Humor* Jonson had instructed the comic poet to "sport with human follies, not with crimes." In *Volpone,* as the defensive Dedication suggests, Jonson has moved into the realm of crime, thought in Elizabethan theory (see p. 402) to be the material of tragedy. The tragic hero was commonly said to be undone by *hybris* (a Greek word usually translated as "overweening pride"), which leads him to a criminal action. In Milton's *Samson Agonistes,* for example, the protagonist admits his pride and his guilt:

> Then, swoll'n with pride, into the snare I fell
> Of fair fallacious looks, venereal trains,
> Softened with pleasure and voluptuous life.

Volpone's *hybris* is no less evident than his criminality. In V.i, he agrees with Mosca that their most recent exploit "is our masterpiece;/ We cannot think to go beyond this." But soon Volpone itches for further sport and manufactures yet another scheme, one that undoes him. Like a tragic hero, he subsequently has his "recognition scene":

> To make a snare for mine own neck! and run
> My head into it wilfully, with laughter!
> When I had newly 'scaped, was free and clear!
> Out of mere wantonness! O, the dull devil
> Was in this brain of mine when I devised it.

Still, to say that a play resembles a tragedy is not to say that it is a tragedy. The "rare, ingenious knavery" gives the audience as well as Volpone "a rare meal of laughter." The public exposure of Volpone's dupes bothers us no more than the exposure of Sir Politic Wouldbe when he is stripped of the tortoise shell in which he attempts to hide; the punishment of Volpone is more disconcerting, but the forgiveness of folly and vice that usually colors the last act of a romantic comedy is impossible here. Volpone is too monstrous to be allowed a sudden con-

version. Still, talk of the "tragic" ending neglects the important
fact that the fox, not the court, has the last word. Detaching
himself from the Venetian court, Volpone speaks the epilogue,
and submits himself to a higher court, the audience. What can
you do—having been so entertained by this fox—but "fare
jovially, and clap your hands"?

## Biographical Note

Ben Jonson (1572?–1637) was the stepson of a brick-
layer, but he was well educated at Westminster School,
where he was taught by the illustrious William Camden.
He did not go to a university (Oxford and Cambridge later
gave him honorary degrees), and for a while he followed
his stepfather's trade. He then became an actor and playwright, leading a somewhat quarrelsome life. He killed a
fellow actor in a duel (but escaped with only a brand on
his thumb and the confiscation of his goods), claimed to
have beaten a playwright, and wrote some highly satirical
plays. He is notable not only as a writer of plays but of
masques (dramatic entertainments, for courtiers, stress-
ing spectacle and dance) and of impressive lyrics.

# *Volpone, or The Fox*

*To the most noble and most equal sisters, the two famous universities,*[a] *for their love and acceptance shown to his poem in the presentation, Ben Jonson, the grateful acknowledger, dedicates both it and himself.*

Never, most equal sisters, had any man a wit so presently [b] excellent as that it could raise itself, but there must come both matter, occasion, commenders, and favorers to it. If this be true, and that the fortune of all writers doth daily prove it, it behoves the careful to provide well toward these accidents, and, having acquired them, to preserve that part of reputation most tenderly wherein the benefit of a friend is also defended. Hence it is that I now render myself grateful and am studious to justify the bounty of your act, to which, though your mere authority were satisfying, yet, it being an age wherein poetry and the professors [c] of it hear so ill [d] on all sides, there will a reason be looked for in the subject. It is certain, nor can it with any forehead [e] be opposed, that the too much license of poetasters in this time hath much deformed their mistress, that every day their manifold and manifest ignorance doth stick unnatural reproaches upon her. But for their petulancy it were an act of the greatest injustice either to let the learned suffer, or so divine a skill, which indeed should not be attempted with unclean hands, to fall under the least contempt. For, if men will impartially and not asquint look toward the offices and function of a poet, they will easily conclude to themselves the impossibility of any man's being the good poet without first being a good man. He that is said to be able to inform [f] young men to all good disciplines, inflame grown men to all great virtues, keep old men in their best and supreme state, or, as they decline to childhood, recover them to their first strength; that comes forth the interpreter and arbiter of nature, a teacher of things divine no less than human, a master in manners, and can alone, or with a few, effect the business of mankind—this, I take him, is no subject for pride and ignorance to exercise their railing rhetoric upon. But it will here be hastily answered that the

writers of these days are other things; that not only their manners but their natures are inverted, and nothing remaining
with them of the dignity of poet but the abused name, which
every scribe usurps; that now, especially in dramatic or, as
they term it, stage poetry, nothing but ribaldry, profanation,
blasphemy, all license of offense to God and man is practiced.
I dare not deny a great part of this, and am sorry I dare not,
because in some men's abortive features (and would they had
never boasted the light) it is overtrue; but that all are embarked
in this bold adventure for hell is a most uncharitable thought
and, uttered, a more malicious slander. For my particular [g] I
can, and from a most clear conscience, affirm that I have ever
trembled to think toward the least profaneness, have loathed
the use of such foul and unwashed bawdry as is now made the
food of the scene; [h] and, howsoever I cannot escape from
some the imputation of sharpness but that they will say I have
taken a pride or lust to be bitter, and not my youngest infant
but hath come into the world with all his teeth, I would ask of
these supercilious politics [i] what nation, society, or general
order or state I have provoked?—what public person?—whether
I have not in all these preserved their dignity, as mine own person, safe? My works are read, allowed [j] (I speak of those that
are entirely mine); look into them. What broad reproofs have
I used? Where have I been particular, where personal, except
to a mimic, cheater, bawd, or buffoon—creatures for their in-
solencies worthy to be taxed? [k] Yet to which of these so point-
ingly as he might not either ingenuously have confessed or
wisely dissembled his disease? But it is not rumor can make
men guilty, much less entitle me to other men's crimes. I know
that nothing can be so innocently writ or carried [l] but may be
made obnoxious to construction; [m] marry, whilst I bear mine
innocence about me I fear it not. Application [n] is now grown
a trade with many; and there are that profess to have a key for
the deciphering of everything. But let wise and noble persons
take heed how they be too credulous or give leave to these in-
vading interpreters to be overfamiliar with their fames, [o] who
cunningly and often utter their own virulent malice under other
men's simplest meanings. As for those that will (by faults which
charity hath raked [p] up or common honesty concealed) make
themselves a name with the multitude, or, to draw their rude
and beastly claps, care not whose living faces they intrench [q]
with their petulant styles, may they do it without a rival, for

---

[a] i.e., Oxford and Cambridge   [b] instantly   [c] i.e., poets themselves
[d] have such a poor reputation   [e] shame   [f] shape   [g] myself   [h] stage
[i] intriguers   [j] licensed   [k] rebuked   [l] managed   [m] by interpretation   [n] i.e.,
personal application   [o] reputations   [q] engrave

me! I choose rather to live graved [r] in obscurity than share with them in so preposterous a fame. Nor can I blame the wishes of those severe and wiser patriots,[s] who, providing [t] the hurts these licentious spirits may do in a state, desire rather to see fools and devils and those antique relics of barbarism retrieved, with all other ridiculous and exploded follies, than behold the wounds of private men, of princes and nations, for, as Horace makes Trebatius speak among these,

*Sibi quisque timet, quanquam est intactus, et odit.*[u]

And men may justly impute such rages, if continued, to the writer as his sports. The increase of which lust in liberty, together with the present trade of the stage in all their misc'line interludes,[v] what learned or liberal soul doth not already abhor, where nothing but the filth of the time is uttered, and that with such impropriety of phrase, such plenty of solecisms, such dearth of sense, so bold prolepses,[w] so racked metaphors, with brothelry able to violate the ear of a pagan, and blasphemy to turn the blood of a Christian to water? I cannot but be serious in a cause of this nature, wherein my fame and the reputations of divers honest and learned are the question, when a name so full of authority, antiquity, and all great mark is through their insolence become the lowest scorn of the age, and those men subject to the petulancy of every vernaculous [x] orator, that were wont to be the care of kings and happiest monarchs. This it is that hath not only rapt me to present indignation, but made me studious heretofore, and, by all my actions, to stand off from them, which may most appear in this my latest work, which you, most learned arbitresses, have seen, judged, and to my crown approved, wherein I have labored for their instruction and amendment, to reduce [y] not only the ancient forms but manners of the scene, the easiness, the propriety, the innocence, and, last, the doctrine, which is the principal end of poesy, to inform men in the best reason of living. And, though my catastrophe [z] may, in the strict rigor of comic law, meet with censure, as turning back to my promise, I desire the learned and charitable critic to have so much faith in me to think it was done of industry,[a] for with what ease I could have varied it nearer his scale (but that I fear to boast my own faculty) I could here insert. But my special aim being to put the snaffle in their mouths that cry out, "We never punish vice in

---

[r] buried  [s] fellow countrymen  [t] foreseeing  [u] "Everyone fears for himself and is angry, although he is untouched"  [v] variety entertainment  [w] anachronisms  [x] scurrilous  [y] bring back  [z] ending  [a] intentionally

our interludes," etc., I took the more liberty, though not without some lines of example, drawn even in the ancients themselves, the goings out [b] of whose comedies are not always
joyful, but ofttimes the bawds, the servants, the rivals, yea, and
the masters are mulcted—and fitly, it being the office of a comic
poet to imitate justice and instruct to life as well as purity of
language, or stir up gentle affections,[c] to which I shall take the
occasion elsewhere to speak.

For the present, most reverenced sisters, as I have cared to be
thankful for your affections past, and here made the understanding acquainted with some ground of your favors, let me
not despair their continuance to the maturing of some worthier
fruits, wherein, if my muses be true to me, I shall raise the despised head of poetry again, and, stripping her out of those rotten and base rags wherewith the times have adulterated her
form, restore her to her primitive habit, feature, and majesty,
and render her worthy to be embraced and kissed of all the
great and master spirits of our world. As for the vile and sloth-
ful, who never affected an act worthy of celebration, or are so
inward [d] with their own vicious natures as they worthily fear
her and think it a high point of policy to keep her in contempt
with their declamatory and windy invectives, she shall out of
just rage incite her servants (who are *"genus irritabile"* [e]) to
spout ink in their faces, that shall eat farder [f] than their marrow, into their fames; and not Cinnamus the barber,[g] with his
art, shall be able to take out the brands; but they shall live and
be read till the wretches die, as things worst deserving of themselves in chief and then of all mankind.

[b] conclusions    [c] feelings    [d] familiar    [e] "the excitable race [of poets]"
(Horace)    [f] farther    [g] barbers were also surgeons

# *VOLPONE*

❧

## CHARACTERS

VOLPONE [*the Fox*], *a magnifico*

MOSCA [*the Fly*], *his parasite* [h]

VOLTORE [*the Vulture*], *an advocate*

CORBACCIO [*the Raven*], *an old gentleman*

CORVINO [*the Crow*], *a merchant*

AVOCATORI, *four magistrates*

NOTARIO, *the register*

NANO, *a dwarf*

CASTRONE, *an eunuch*

[SIR] POLITIC WOULDBE, *a knight*

GREGE [*or* MOB]

PEREGRINE, *a gent[leman] traveler*

BONARIO, *a young gentleman*

[LADY] WOULDBE, *the knight's wife.*

CELIA, *the merchant's wife*

COMMENDADORI, *officers*

MERCATORI, *three merchants*

ANDROGYNO, *a hermaphrodite*

SERVITORE, *a servant;* WOMEN [SERVANTS]

*The Scene: Venice*

## THE ARGUMENT [1]

V OLPONE, childless, rich, feigns sick, despairs,
O ffers his state to hopes of several heirs,
L ies languishing. His parasite receives
P resents of all, assures, deludes, then weaves
O ther cross-plots, which ope themselves, are told.
N ew tricks for safety are sought; they thrive; when, bold,
E ach tempts th' other again, and all are sold.[j]

[h] a hanger-on   [1] summary   [j] duped

# PROLOGUE

Now luck yet send us, and a little wit
    Will serve to make our play hit;
According to the palates of the season,
    Here is rhyme not empty of reason.
This we were bid to credit from our poet,
    Whose true scope, if you would know it,
In all his poems still [k] hath been this measure,
    To mix profit with your pleasure;
And not as some, whose throats their envy failing,
    Cry hoarsely, all he writes is railing;        10
And when his plays come forth, think they can flout them
    With saying he was a year about them.
To these there needs no lie but this his creature,[l]
    Which was two months since no feature;
And though he dares give them five lives to mend it,
    'Tis known, five weeks fully penned it,
From his own hand, without a coadjutor,[m]
    Novice, journeyman, or tutor.
Yet thus much I can give you as a token
    Of his play's worth: no eggs are broken,        20
Nor quaking custards [n] with fierce teeth affrighted,
    Wherewith your rout [o] are so delighted;
Nor hales he in a gull,[p] old ends [q] reciting,
    To stop gaps in his loose writing;
With such a deal of monstrous and forced action,
    As might make Bedlam a faction.[r]
Nor made he his play for jests stol'n from each table,[s]
    But makes jests to fit [t] his fable;
And so presents quick [u] comedy, refined
    As best critics have designed;        30
The laws of time, place, persons he observeth;
    From no needful rule he swerveth.
All gall and copperas [v] from his ink he draineth;
    Only a little salt remaineth,
Wherewith he'll rub your cheeks till, red with laughter,
    They shall look fresh a week after.

[k] always  [l] i.e., the play  [m] co-author  [n] During city feasts a foc
jumped into a huge custard set on the Lord Mayor's table  [o] mo
[p] dupe  [q] scraps of old sayings  [r] make the inmates of Bethlehem,
London insane asylum, your supporters  [s] i.e., plagiarized  [t] related t
[u] lively  [v] vitriol

# ACT I

[*Enter* Volpone *and* Mosca.]

*Volpone.*     Good morning to the day; and next, my gold!—
    Open the shrine, that I may see my saint. [Mosca *draws a
        curtain and reveals a heap of gold*.]
    Hail the world's soul, and mine! More glad than is
    The teeming earth to see the longed-for sun
    Peep through the horns of the celestial Ram,[w]
    Am I, to view thy splendor darkening his;
    That lying here, amongst my other hoards,
    Show'st like a flame by night, or like the day
    Struck out of chaos, when all darkness fled
    Unto the center.[x] O thou son of Sol,[y]                    10
    But brighter than thy father, let me kiss,
    With adoration, thee, and every relic
    Of sacred treasure in this blessèd room.
    Well did wise poets, by thy glorious name,
    Title that age [z] which they would have the best;
    Thou being the best of things, and far transcending
    All style of joy, in children, parents, friends,
    Or any other waking dream on earth.
    Thy looks when they to Venus did ascribe,[a]
    They should have giv'n her twenty thousand Cupids;        20
    Such are thy beauties and our loves! Dear saint,
    Riches, the dumb god, that giv'st all men tongues,
    That canst do nought, and yet mak'st men do all things.
    The price of souls! Even hell, with thee to boot,
    Is made worth heaven. Thou art virtue, fame,
    Honor, and all things else. Who can get thee,
    He shall be noble, valiant, honest, wise—
*Mosca.*     And what he will, sir. Riches are in fortune
    A greater good than wisdom is in nature.
*Volpone.*     True, my belovèd Mosca. Yet I glory           30
    More in the cunning purchase [b] of my wealth
    Than in the glad possession, since I gain

---

[w] in the zodiac, the sign of Aries   [x] i.e., of the earth   [y] the sun
the Golden Age   [a] Venus was called "golden"   [b] acquisition

No common way. I use no trade, no venture; [c]
I wound no earth with plowshares, fat no beasts
To feed the shambles; [d] have no mills for iron,
Oil, corn, or men, to grind 'em into powder;
I blow no subtle glass, expose no ships
To threat'nings of the furrow-facèd sea;
I turn no moneys in the public bank,
Nor usure private—

*Mosca.*                    No sir, nor devour                    40
Soft prodigals. You shall ha' some will swallow
A melting heir as glibly as your Dutch
Will pills of butter, and ne'er purge for 't;
Tear forth the fathers of poor families
Out of their beds, and coffin them alive
In some kind, clasping prison, where their bones
May be forthcoming when the flesh is rotten.
But your sweet nature doth abhor these courses;
You loath the widow's or the orphan's tears
Should wash your pavements, or their piteous cries    50
Ring in your roofs, and beat the air for vengeance.

*Volpone.*    Right, Mosca, I do loath it.

*Mosca.*                              And, besides, sir,
You are not like the thresher that doth stand
With a huge flail, watching a heap of corn, [e]
And, hungry, dares not taste the smallest grain,
But feeds on mallows and such bitter herbs;
Nor like the merchant who hath filled his vaults
With Romagnía, [f] and rich Candian [g] wines,
Yet drinks the lees of Lombard's vinegar.             60
You will not lie in straw, whilst moths and worms
Feed on your sumptuous hangings and soft beds.
You know the use of riches, and dare give now
From that bright heap, to me, your poor observer, [h]
Or to your dwarf, or your hermaphrodite,
Your eunuch, or what other household trifle [i]
Your pleasure allows maint'nance—

*Volpone.*                          Hold thee, Mosca,
Take of my hand; thou strik'st on truth in all,
And they are envious term thee parasite.
Call forth my dwarf, my eunuch, and my fool,
And let 'em make me sport! [*Exit* Mosca.] What should
    I do                                              70
But cocker up my genius, [j] and live free
To all delights my fortune calls me to?

[c] speculation  [d] slaughterhouse  [e] grain  [f] a sweet wine  [g] Greek or
Cretan  [h] attendant  [i] pet  [j] pamper my spirit

I have no wife, no parent, child, ally,
To give my substance to; but whom I make
Must be my heir, and this makes men observe ᵏ me.
This draws new clients daily to my house,
Women and men of every sex and age,
That bring me presents, send me plate, coin, jewels,
With hope that when I die—which they expect
Each greedy minute—it shall then return                      80
Tenfold upon them; whilst some, covetous
Above the rest, seek to engross ˡ me whole,
And counter-work the one unto the other,
Contend in gifts, as they would seem, in love.
All which I suffer,ᵐ playing with their hopes,
And am content to coin 'em into profit,
And look upon their kindness, and take more,
And look on that; still bearing them in hand,ⁿ
Letting the cherry knock against their lips,
And draw it by their mouths, and back again.                 90
                                                    How now!

[Re-enter Mosca with Nano, Androgyno, and Castrone.]

Nano.   "Now, room for fresh gamesters, who do will you
        to know,
    They do bring you neither play nor university show;
    And therefore do entreat you that whatsoever they re-
        hearse
    May not fare a whit the worse for the false pace of the
        verse.º
If you wonder at this, you will wonder more ere we pass,
For know, here is enclosed the soul of Pythagoras,ᵖ
That juggler divine, as hereafter shall follow:
Which soul, fast and loose, sir, came first from Apollo,
And was breathed into Aethalides, Mercurius' son,
Where it had the gift to remember all that ever was done. 100
From thence it fled forth, and made quick transmigration
To goldy-locked Euphorbus, who was killed in good
    fashion
At the siege of old Troy, by the cuckold of Sparta.�q
Hermotimus was next—I find it in my charta ʳ—
To whom it did pass, where no sooner it was missing,
But with one Pyrrhus of Delos it learned to go a-fishing;
And thence did it enter the Sophist of Greece.

ᵏ pay court to  ˡ monopolize  ᵐ allow  ⁿ deluding them  º loose four-
stressed line of the old morality plays  ᵖ Greek philosopher whose soul's
various reincarnations are named in the following lines  q Menelaus,
Helen's husband  ʳ list

From Pythagore, she went into a beautiful piece,
Hight [s] Aspasia the Meretrix; [t] and the next toss of her
Was again of a whore she became a philosopher,                    110
Crates the Cynic, as itself doth relate it.
Since, kings, knights, and beggars, knaves, lords, and
    fools gat it,
Besides ox and ass, camel, mule, goat, and brock,[u]
In all which it hath spoke, as in the cobbler's cock.[v]
But I come not here to discourse of that matter,
Or his one, two, or three, or his great oath, 'By Quater!'
His musics, his trigon, his golden thigh,
Or his telling how elements shift.[w] But I
Would ask how of late thou hast suffered translation,[x]
And shifted thy coat in these days of reformation?" [y]          120
*Androgyno.*  "Like one of the reformèd,[z] a fool as you
    see,
    Counting all old doctrine [a] heresy."
*Nano.*  "But not on thine own forbid meats has thou
    ventured?"
*Androgyno.*  "On fish, when first a Carthusian [b] I entered."
*Nano.*  "Why, then thy dogmatical silence[c] hath left
    thee?"
*Androgyno.*  "Of that an obstreperous lawyer bereft me."
*Nano.*  "O wonderful change! When Sir Lawyer forsook
    thee,
    For Pythagore's sake, what body then took thee?"
*Androgyno.*  "A good dull moyle." [d]
*Nano.*            "And how! By that means
    Thou wert brought to allow of the eating of beans?"      130
*Androgyno.*  "Yes."
*Nano.*  "But from the moyle into whom didst thou pass?"
*Androgyno.*  "Into a very strange beast, by some writers
    called an ass;
    By others a precise, pure, illuminate brother,[e]
    Of those devour flesh, and sometimes one another;
    And will drop you forth a libel, or a sanctified lie,
    Betwixt every spoonful of a nativity-pie." [f]
*Nano.*  "Now quit thee, 'fore heaven, of that profane
    nation,[g]

[s] called   [t] harlot   [u] badger   [v] this interlude is based on a dialogue in
which a cobbler's rooster, containing the soul of Pythagoras, tells the
cobbler of its previous transmigrations   [w] lines 116–118 refer to various
Pythagorian doctrines and traditions   [x] transformation   [y] i.e., since the
Reformation   [z] a Protestant   [a] orthodox Roman Catholic   [b] member of
a Catholic order with severe rules of fasting   [c] Pythagoras enjoined his
followers to five years of silence   [d] mule   [e] a Puritan   [f] Christmas pie
[g] sect

And gently report thy next transmigration."
*Androgyno.*    "To the same that I am."
*Nano.*                  "A creature of delight,
   And, what is more than a fool, an hermaphrodite!     140
   Now, pray thee, sweet soul, in all thy variation,
   Which body wouldst thou choose to take up thy station?"
*Androgyno.*    "Troth,[h] this I am in; even here would I
     tarry."
*Nano.*    " 'Cause here the delight of each sex thou canst
     vary?"
*Androgyno.*    "Alas, those pleasures be stale and forsaken.
   No, 'tis your fool wherewith I am so taken,
   The only one creature that I can call blessèd;
   For all other forms I have proved most distressèd."
*Nano.*    "Spoke true as thou wert in Pythagoras still.
   This learnèd opinion we celebrate will,            150
   Fellow eunuch, as behoves us, with all our wit and art,
   To dignify that whereof ourselves are so great and spe-
     cial a part."
*Volpone.*    Now, very, very pretty! Mosca, this
   Was thy invention?
*Mosca.*              If it please my patron,
   Not else.
*Volpone.*    It doth, good Mosca.
*Mosca.*                Then it was, sir.

SONG.

"Fools, they are the only nation
   Worth men's envy or admiration,
   Free from care or sorrow taking,
   Selves and others merry making.
   All they speak or do is sterling.            160
   Your fool he is your great man's darling,
   And your ladies' sport and pleasure;
   Tongue and bauble are his treasure.
   E'en his face begetteth laughter,
   And he speaks truth free from slaughter.[1]
   He's the grace of every feast,
   And sometimes the chiefest guest;
   Hath his trencher [j] and his stool,
   When wit waits upon the fool.            170
     O, who would not be
       He, he, he?"

[h] in truth    [1] without punishment    [j] wooden plate

*One knocks without.*

*Volpone.*   Who's that? Away! Look, Mosca.
                                        [*Exeunt* Nano *and* Castrone.]
*Mosca.*                              Fool, begone!
                                        [*Exit* Androgyno.]
   'Tis Signor Voltore, the advocate;
   I know him by his knock.
*Volpone.*                    Fetch me my gown,
   My furs, and nightcaps; say my couch is changing; ᵏ
   And let him entertain himself awhile
   Without i' th' gallery. [*Exit* Mosca.] Now, now my
      clients
   Begin their visitation! Vulture, kite,
   Raven, and gorcrow,¹ all my birds of prey,
   That think me turning carcass, now they come.                    180

   I am not for 'em yet. [*Re-enter* Mosca.] How now! The
      news?
*Mosca.*   A piece of plate, sir.
*Volpone.*                    Of what bigness?
*Mosca.*                                    Huge,
   Massy, and antique, with your name inscribed
   And arms engraven.
*Volpone.*         Good! And not a fox
   Stretched on the earth, with fine delusive sleights,
   Mocking a gaping crow? Ha, Mosca?
*Mosca.*                          Sharp, sir.
*Volpone.*   Give me my furs. Why dost thou laugh so,
      man?
*Mosca.*   I cannot choose, sir, when I apprehend
   What thoughts he has, without, now as he walks:
   That this might be the last gift he should give;               190
   That this would fetch you; if you died today,
   And gave him all, what he should be tomorrow;
   What large return would come of all his ventures;
   How he should worshiped be, and reverenced;
   Ride with his furs and foot-cloths, waited on
   By herds of fools and clients; have clear way
   Made for his moyle, as lettered ᵐ as himself;
   Be called the great and learnèd advocate;
   And then concludes there's nought impossible.
*Volpone.*   Yes, to be learnèd, Mosca.
*Mosca.*                          O no, rich                       200
   Implies it. Hood an ass with reverend purple,

ᵏ bed is being changed   ¹ carrion crow   ᵐ literate

So you can hide his two ambitious [n] ears,
And he shall pass for a cathedral doctor.
*Volpone.*    My caps, my caps, good Mosca. Fetch him in.
*Mosca.*    Stay, sir, your ointment for your eyes.
*Volpone.*                              That's true;
Dispatch, dispatch. I long to have possession
Of my new present.
*Mosca.*              That and thousands more
I hope to see you lord of.
*Volpone.*              Thanks, kind Mosca.
*Mosca.*    And that, when I am lost in blended dust,
And hundred such as I am, in succession—                     210
*Volpone.*    Nay, that were too much, Mosca.
*Mosca.*                              You shall live
Still to delude these harpies.
*Volpone.*                    Loving Mosca!
'Tis well; my pillow now, and let him enter.
                                        [*Exit* Mosca.]
Now, my feigned cough, my phthisic, and my gout,
My apoplexy, palsy, and catarrhs,
Help, with your forcèd functions, this my posture,
Wherein this three year I have milked their hopes.
He comes; I hear him—Uh! [*Coughing.*] uh! uh! uh! O!


[*Re-enter* Mosca *with* Voltore.]


*Mosca.*    You still are what you were, sir. Only you,          220
Of all the rest, are he, commands his love;
And you do wisely to preserve it thus
With early visitation, and kind notes
Of your good meaning to him, which, I know,
Cannot but come most grateful. Patron! Sir!
Here's Signor Voltore is come—
*Volpone.* [*Faintly.*]              What say you?
*Mosca.*    Sir, Signor Voltore is come this morning
To visit you.
*Volpone.*    I thank him.
*Mosca.*              And hath brought
A piece of antique plate, bought of St. Mark,[o]
With which he here presents you.
*Volpone.*                    He is welcome.
Pray him to come more often.
*Mosca.*                    Yes.
*Voltore.*                    What says he?                     230

[n] rising    [o] in St. Mark's Place

*Mosca.*   He thanks you, and desires you see him often.
*Volpone.*   Mosca.
*Mosca.*                    My patron!
*Volpone.*                            Bring him near; where is he?
   I long to feel his hand.
*Mosca.*                    The plate is here, sir.
*Voltore.*   How fare you, sir?
*Volpone.*                    I thank you, Signor Voltore.
   Where is the plate? Mine eyes are bad.
*Voltore.*                              I'm sorry.
   To see you still thus weak.
*Mosca.* [*Aside.*]            That he is not weaker.
*Volpone.*   You are too munificent.
*Voltore.*                         No, sir, would to heaven
   I could as well give health to you, as that plate.
*Volpone.*   You give, sir, what you can. I thank you. Your       240
   love
   Hath taste in this, and shall not be unanswered.
   I pray you see me often.
*Voltore.*                    Yes, I shall, sir.
*Volpone.*   Be not far from me.
*Mosca.*                    Do you observe that, sir?
*Volpone.*   Hearken unto me still. It will concern you.
*Mosca.*   You are a happy man, sir; know your good.
*Volpone.*   I cannot now last long—
*Mosca.*                    You are his heir, sir.
*Voltore.*   Am I?
*Volpone.*   I feel me going. Uh! uh! uh! uh!
   I am sailing to my port. Uh! uh! uh! uh!
   And I am glad I am so near my haven.
*Mosca.*   Alas, kind gentleman! Well, we must all go—
*Voltore.*   But, Mosca—
*Mosca.*                    Age will conquer.
*Voltore.*                              Pray thee hear, me.  250
   Am I inscribed his heir for certain?
*Mosca.*                              Are you!
   I do beseech you, sir, you will vouchsafe
   To write me i' your family.ᴾ All my hopes
   Depend upon your worship. I am lost,
   Except the rising sun do shine on me.
*Voltore.*   It shall both shine and warm thee, Mosca.
*Mosca.*                                        Sir,
   I am a man that have not done your love
   All the worst offices: here I wear your keys,

ᴾ make me a servant in your household

See all your coffers and your caskets locked,
Keep the poor inventory of your jewels,                  260
Your plate, and moneys; am your steward, sir,
Husband your goods here.
*Voltore.*                     But am I sole heir?
*Mosca.*     Without a partner, sir, confirmed this morning;
The wax is warm yet, and the ink scarce dry
Upon the parchment.
*Voltore.*              Happy, happy me!
By what good chance, sweet Mosca?
*Mosca.*                      Your desert, sir;
I know no second cause.
*Voltore.*               Thy modesty
Is loath to know it; well, we shall requite it.
*Mosca.*     He ever liked your course,�q sir; that first took
    him.                                               270
I oft have heard him say how he admired
Men of your large ʳ profession, that could speak
To every cause, and things mere  contraries,
Till they were hoarse again, yet all be law;
That, with most quick agility, could turn
And re-turn, make knots and undo them,
Give forkèd ᵗ counsel, take provoking ᵘ gold
On either hand, and put it up. These men,
He knew, would thrive with their humility.
And, for his part, he thought he should be blest
To have his heir of such a suffering spirit,            280
So wise, so grave, of so perplexed ᵛ a tongue,
And loud withal, that would not wag, nor scarce
Lie still, without a fee; when every word
Your worship but lets fall, is a *cecchine.*ʷ

*Another knocks.*

Who's that? One knocks; I would not have you seen,
    sir.
And yet—pretend you came and went in haste;
I'll fashion an excuse. And, gentle sir,
When you do come to swim in golden lard,
Up to the arms in honey, that your chin
Is borne up stiff with fatness of the flood,           290
Think on your vassal; but remember me.
I ha' not been your worst of clients.
*Voltore.*                     Mosca—

�q pursuit, i.e., the law  ʳ generous  ˢ exact  ᵗ ambiguous  ᵘ bribing
ᵛ contradictory  ʷ Venetian gold coin

*Mosca.*   When will you have your inventory brought, sir?
   Or see a copy of the will? Anon! [x]
   I'll bring 'em to you, sir. Away, begone,
   Put business i' your face.                    [*Exit* Voltore.]
*Volpone.*   [*Springing up.*] Excellent, Mosca!
   Come hither, let me kiss thee.
*Mosca.*                             Keep you still, sir.
   Here is Corbaccio.
*Volpone.*              Set the plate away.
   The vulture's gone, and the old raven's come.
*Mosca.*   Betake you to your silence, and your sleep.        300
   Stand there and multiply. [*Adding the plate to the rest.*]
      Now shall we see
   A wretch who is indeed more impotent
   Than this can feign to be, yet hopes to hop
   Over his grave.

[*Enter* Corbaccio.]

                         Signor Corbaccio!
   You're very welcome, sir.
*Corbaccio.*                   How does your patron?
*Mosca.*   Troth, as he did, sir; no amends.
*Corbaccio.*                         What! Mends he?
*Mosca.*   No, sir, he is rather worse.
*Corbaccio.*                   That's well. Where is he?
*Mosca.*   Upon his couch, sir, newly fall'n asleep.
*Corbaccio.*   Does he sleep well?
*Mosca.*                     No wink, sir, all this night
   Nor yesterday, but slumbers. [y]
*Corbaccio.*                   Good! He should take        310
   Some counsel of physicians: I have brought him
   An opiate here, from mine own doctor.
*Mosca.*   He will not hear of drugs.
*Corbaccio.*                   Why? I myself
   Stood by while 't was made, saw all th' ingredients;
   And know it cannot but most gently work.
   My life for his, 'tis but to make him sleep.
*Volpone.* [*Aside.*]   Aye, his last sleep, if he would take
      it.
*Mosca.*                                      Sir,
   He has no faith in physic. [z]
*Corbaccio.*                   Say you? Say you?
*Mosca.*   He has no faith in physic; he does think        320

   [x] presently    [y] dozes    [z] medicine

Most of your doctors are the greater danger,
And worse disease, t' escape. I often have
Heard him protest that your physician
Should never be his heir.
*Corbaccio.*                    Not I his heir?
*Mosca.*    Not your physician, sir.
*Corbaccio.*                              O no, no, no.
I do not mean it.
*Mosca.*            No, sir, nor their fees
He cannot brook; he says they flay a man
Before they kill him.
*Corbaccio.*            Right, I do conceive you.
*Mosca.*    And then, they do it by [a] experiment;
For which the law not only doth absolve 'em,
But gives them great reward; and he is loath                    330
To hire his death so.
*Corbaccio.*            It is true, they kill
With as much license as a judge.
*Mosca.*                              Nay, more;
For he but kills, sir, where the law condemns,
And these can kill him too.
*Corbaccio.*                    Aye, or me,
Or any man. How does his apoplex?
Is that strong on him still?
*Mosca.*                    Most violent.
His speech is broken and his eyes are set,
His face drawn longer than 'twas wont—
*Corbaccio.*                              How? How?
Stronger than he was wont?
*Mosca.*                    No, sir; his face
Drawn longer than 'twas wont.
*Corbaccio.*            O, good.                              340
*Mosca.*                              His mouth
Is ever gaping, and his eyelids hang.
*Corbaccio.*                    Good.
*Mosca.*    A freezing numbness stiffens all his joints,
And makes the color of his flesh like lead.
*Corbaccio.*                              'Tis good.
*Mosca.*    His pulse beats slow and dull.
*Corbaccio.*                    Good symptoms still.
*Mosca.*    And from his brain—
*Corbaccio.*            Ha? How? Not from his brain?
*Mosca.*    Yes, sir, and from his brain—
*Corbaccio.*                    I conceive you; good.

[a] as

*Mosca.*    Flows a cold sweat, with a continual rheum,
    Forth [b] the resolved [c] corners of his eyes.
*Corbaccio.*    Is't possible? Yet I am better, ha!
    How does he with the swimming of his head?                    350
*Mosca.*    O, sir, 'tis past the scotomy; [d] he now
    Hath lost his feeling, and hath left to snort.
    You hardly can perceive him, that he breathes.
*Corbaccio.*    Excellent, excellent! Sure I shall outlast him!
    This makes me young again a score of years.
*Mosca.*    I was a-coming for you, sir.
*Corbaccio.*                              Has he made his will?
    What has he giv'n me?
*Mosca.*                      No, sir.
*Corbaccio.*                              Nothing? Ha?
*Mosca.*    He has not made his will, sir.
*Corbaccio.*                              Oh, oh, oh.
    What then did Voltore, the lawyer, here?
*Mosca.*    He smelt a carcass, sir, when he but heard      360
    My master was about his testament;
    As I did urge him to it, for your good—
*Corbaccio.*    He came unto him, did he? I thought so.
*Mosca.*    Yes, and presented him this piece of plate.
*Corbaccio.*    To be his heir?
*Mosca.*                      I do not know, sir.
*Corbaccio.*                              True,
    I know it too.
*Mosca.* [*Aside.*]    By your own scale, sir.
*Corbaccio.*                              Well,
    I shall prevent [e] him yet. See, Mosca, look,
    Here I have brought a bag of bright *cecchines,*
    Will quite weigh down his plate.
*Mosca.*                      Yea, marry, [f] sir,
    This is true physic, this your sacred medicine!         370
    No talk of opiates to this great elixir!
*Corbaccio.*    'Tis *aurum palpabile,* if not *potabile.* [g]
*Mosca.*    It shall be ministered to him in his bowl.
*Corbaccio.*    Aye, do, do, do.
*Mosca.*                      Most blessèd cordial!
    This will recover him.
*Corbaccio.*        Yes, do, do, do.
*Mosca.*    I think it were not best, sir.
*Corbaccio.*                      What?
*Mosca.*                              To recover him.
*Corbaccio.*    O no, no, no, by no means.

    [b] from   [c] watery   [d] dizziness   [e] anticipate   [f] indeed   [g] gold that can
be felt, if not drunk (as a medicine)

*Mosca.*                                    Why, sir, this
   Will work some strange effect, if he but feel it.
*Corbaccio.*   'Tis true, therefore forbear; I'll take my ven-
   ture; [h]
   Give me 't again.
*Mosca.*                   At no hand,[i] pardon me;                    380
   You shall not do yourself that wrong, sir. I
   Will so advise you, you shall have it all.
*Corbaccio.*   How?
*Mosca.*   All, sir, 'tis your right, your own; no man
   Can claim a part. 'Tis yours without a rival,
   Decreed by destiny.
*Corbaccio.*                  How, how, good Mosca?
*Mosca.*   I'll tell you, sir. This fit he shall recover—
*Corbaccio.*   I do conceive you.
*Mosca.*                      And on first advantage
   Of his gained sense, will I re-importune him
   Unto the making of his testament;
   And show him this. [*Pointing to the bag of coins.*]
*Corbaccio.*          Good, good.                              390
*Mosca.*                      'Tis better yet,
   If you will hear, sir.
*Corbaccio.*           Yes, with all my heart.
*Mosca.*   Now would I counsel you, make home with
     speed;
   There, frame a will, whereto you shall inscribe
   My master your sole heir.
*Corbaccio.*               And disinherit
   My son?
*Mosca.*   O, sir, the better; for that color [j]
   Shall make it much more taking.[k]
*Corbaccio.*                      O, but color?
*Mosca.*   This will, sir, you shall send it unto me.
   Now, when I come to enforce,[l] as I will do,
   Your cares, your watchings,[m] and your many prayers,       400
   Your more than many gifts, your this day's present;
   And last, produce your will, where, without thought
   Or least regard unto your proper issue,[n]
   A son so brave [o] and highly meriting,
   The stream of your diverted love hath thrown you
   Upon my master, and made him your heir;
   He cannot be so stupid, or stone-dead,
   But out of conscience and mere gratitude—
*Corbaccio.*   He must pronounce me his?

[h] investment, i.e., the gold   [i] by no means   [j] appearance   [k] pleasing
[l] urge   [m] vigils   [n] own child   [o] fine

*Mosca.*                                       'Tis true.
*Corbaccio.*                                        This plot
  Did I think on before.
*Mosca.*                    I do believe it.
*Corbaccio.*    Do you not believe it?
*Mosca.*                                       Yes, sir.
*Corbaccio.*                               Mine own project. 410
*Mosca.*    Which, when he hath done, sir—
*Corbaccio.*                         Published me his heir?
*Mosca.*    And you so certain to survive him—
*Corbaccio.*                                        Aye.
*Mosca.*    Being so lusty a man—
*Corbaccio.*                        'Tis true.
*Mosca.*                                       Yes, sir—
*Corbaccio.*    I thought on that, too. See, how he should
  be
  The very organ to express my thoughts!
*Mosca.*    You have not only done yourself a good—
*Corbaccio.*    But multiplied it on my son!
*Mosca.*                                       'Tis right, sir.
*Corbaccio.*    Still ᵖ my invention.
*Mosca.*                              'Las, sir! Heaven knows,
  It hath been all my study, all my care—
  I e'en grow gray withal—how to work things—        420
*Corbaccio.*    I do conceive, sweet Mosca.
*Mosca.*                                      You are he
  For whom I labor here.
*Corbaccio.*                 Aye, do, do, do!
  I'll straight about it.
*Mosca.* [*Aside.*]    Rook go with you,ʳ raven!
*Corbaccio.*    I know thee honest.
*Mosca.* [*Aside.*]                  You do lie, sir!
*Corbaccio.*                                        And—
*Mosca.* [*Aside.*]    Your knowledge is no better than your
  ears, sir.
*Corbaccio.*    I do not doubt to be a father to thee.
*Mosca.* [*Aside.*]    Nor I to gull ˢ my brother of his
  blessing.
*Corbaccio.*    I may ha' my youth restored to me, why not?
*Mosca.* [*Aside*].    Your worship is a precious ass!
*Corbaccio.*                            What say'st thou?
*Mosca.*    I do desire your worship to make haste, sir.    430
*Corbaccio.*    'Tis done, 'tis done; I go.        [*Exit.*]
*Volpone.* [*Leaping from his couch.*]    O, I shall burst!

  ᵖ always   ʳ may you be rooked   ˢ cheat

Let out my sides, let out my sides—

*Mosca.*                                    Contain
  Your flux <sup>t</sup> of laughter, sir. You know this hope
  Is such a bait, it covers any hook.

*Volpone.*    O, but thy working and thy placing it!
  I cannot hold; good rascal, let me kiss thee!
  I never knew thee in so rare a humor.

*Mosca.*    Alas, sir, I but do as I am taught;
  Follow your grave instructions; give 'em words; <sup>u</sup>
  Pour oil into their ears,<sup>v</sup> and send them hence.          440

*Volpone.*    'Tis true, 'tis true. What a rare punishment
  Is avarice to itself!

*Mosca.*                    Aye, with our help, sir.

*Volpone.*    So many cares, so many maladies,
  So many fears attending on old age,
  Yea, death so often called on, as <sup>w</sup> no wish
  Can be more frequent with 'em, their limbs faint,
  Their senses dull, their seeing, hearing, going,<sup>x</sup>
  All dead before them; yea, their very teeth,
  Their instruments of eating, failing them;
  Yet this is reckoned life! Nay, here was one,          450
  Is now gone home, that wishes to live longer!
  Feels not his gout, nor palsy; feigns himself
  Younger by scores of years, flatters his age
  With confident belying it, hopes he may
  With charms, like Aeson,<sup>y</sup> have his youth restored;
  And with these thoughts so battens,<sup>z</sup> as if fate
  Would be as easily cheated on as he,
  And all turns air! (*Another knocks.*) Who's that there,
    now? A third?

*Mosca.*    Close, to your couch again. I hear his voice.
  It is Corvino, our spruce merchant.

*Volpone.* [*Lies down as before.*]    Dead.          460

*Mosca.*    Another bout, sir, with your eyes. Who's there?

[*Enter* Corvino.]

  Signor Corvino! Come most wished for! O,
  How happy were you, if you knew it, now!

*Corvino.*    Why? What? Wherein?

*Mosca.*                    The tardy hour is come, sir.

*Corvino.*    He is not dead?

*Mosca.*                    Not dead, sir, but as good;
  He knows no man.

---

<sup>t</sup> outburst   <sup>u</sup> deceive them   <sup>v</sup> cheat them plausibly   <sup>w</sup> that   <sup>x</sup> walking
<sup>y</sup> Jason's father whose youth was restored by Medea's magic   <sup>z</sup> fattens

*Corvino.*              How shall I do, then?
*Mosca.*                                Why, sir?
*Corvino.*   I have brought him here a pearl.
*Mosca.*                                Perhaps he has
   So much remembrance left as to know you, sir;
   He still calls on you; nothing but your name
   Is in his mouth. Is your pearl orient,[a] sir?            470
*Corvino.*   Venice was never owner of the like.
*Volpone.* [*Faintly.*]   Signor Corvino.
*Mosca.*                        Hark.
*Volpone.*                                Signor Corvino.
*Mosca.*   He calls you; step and give it him. He's here, sir,
   And he has brought you a rich pearl.
*Corvino.*                        How do you, sir?
   Tell him it doubles the twelfth carat.
*Mosca.*                                Sir,
   He cannot understand; his hearing's gone;
   And yet it comforts him to see you—
*Corvino.*                        Say
   I have a diamond for him, too.
*Mosca.*                        Best show't, sir,
   Put it into his hand; 'tis only there
   He apprehends. He has his feeling yet.            480
   See how he grasps it!
*Corvino.*          'Las, good gentleman!
   How pitiful the sight is!
*Mosca.*                    Tut, forget, sir.
   The weeping of an heir should still be laughter
   Under a visor.[b]
*Corvino.*   Why, am I his heir?
*Mosca.*   Sir, I am sworn, I may not show the will
   Till he be dead; but here has been Corbaccio,
   Here has been Voltore, here were others too,
   I cannot number 'em, they were so many,
   All gaping here for legacies; but I,
   Taking the vantage of his naming you,            490
   "Signor Corvino," "Signor Corvino," took
   Paper and pen and ink, and there I asked him
   Whom he would have his heir? "Corvino!" Who
   Should be executor? "Corvino!" And
   To any question he was silent to,
   I still interpreted the nods he made,
   Through weakness, for consent; and sent home th'
      others,

---

[a] precious   [b] mask

Nothing bequeathed them but to cry and curse.

*Corvino.* O my dear Mosca! (*They embrace.*) Does he not
    perceive us?

*Mosca.* No more than a blind harper. He knows no man,   500
    No face of friend nor name of any servant,
    Who 'twas that fed him last or gave him drink;
    Not those he hath begotten or brought up
    Can he remember.

*Corvino.*          Has he children?

*Mosca.*                   Bastards,
    Some dozen or more that he begot on beggars,
    Gypsies, and Jews, and black-moors, when he was
        drunk.
    Knew you not that, sir? 'Tis the common fable.
    The dwarf, the fool, the eunuch, are all his;
    He's the true father of his family,
    In all save me—but he has giv'n 'em nothing.     510

*Corvino.* That's well, that's well! Art sure he does not
    hear us?

*Mosca.* Sure, sir? Why, look you, credit your own sense.

[*Shouts in* Volpone's *ear.*]

    The pox <sup>c</sup> approach, and add to your diseases,
    If it would send you hence the sooner, sir.
    For your incontinence it hath deserved it
    Throughly <sup>d</sup> and throughly, and the plague to boot!—
    You may come near, sir.— Would you would once close
    Those filthy eyes of yours, that flow with slime,
    Like two frog-pits; and those same hanging cheeks,
    Covered with hide instead of skin—nay, help, sir—   520
    That look like frozen dish-clouts <sup>e</sup> set on end.

*Corvino.* Or like an old smoked wall, on which the rain
    Ran down in streaks.

*Mosca.*          Excellent, sir! Speak out;
    You may be louder yet. A culverin <sup>f</sup>
    Dischargèd in his ear would hardly bore it.

*Corvino.* His nose is like a common sewer, still running.

*Mosca.* 'Tis good! And what his mouth?

*Corvino.*               A very draught.

*Mosca.* O, stop it up—

*Corvino.*       By no means.

*Mosca.*                Pray you let me.
    Faith, I could stifle him rarely with a pillow,
    As well as any woman that should keep <sup>g</sup> him.   530

<sup>c</sup> syphilis   <sup>d</sup> thoroughly   <sup>e</sup> dishclothes   <sup>f</sup> small cannon   <sup>g</sup> nurse

*Corvino.*   Do as you will, but I'll be gone.
*Mosca.*                                        Be so;
  It is your presence makes him last so long.
*Corvino.*   I pray you use no violence.
*Mosca.*                            No, sir? Why?
  Why should you be thus scrupulous, pray you, sir?
*Corvino.*   Nay, at your discretion.
*Mosca.*                        Well, good sir, begone.
*Corvino.*   I will not trouble him now to take my pearl.
*Mosca.*   Pooh! Nor your diamond. What a needless care
  Is this afflicts you? Is not all here yours?
  Am not I here, whom you have made your creature,
  That owe my being to you?
*Corvino.*                    Grateful Mosca!                    540
  Thou art my friend, my fellow, my companion,
  My partner, and shalt share in all my fortunes.
*Mosca.*   Excepting one.
*Corvino.*                What's that?
*Mosca.*                            Your gallant wife, sir.
                                      [*Exit* Corvino.]

  Now is he gone. We had no other means
  To shoot him hence, but this.
*Volpone.*                My divine Mosca!
  Thou hast today out-gone thyself. (*Another knocks.*)
      Who's there?
  I will be troubled with no more. Prepare
  Me music, dances, banquets, all delights;
  The Turk is not more sensual in his pleasures
  Than will Volpone. [*Exit* Mosca.] Let me see, a pearl!    550
  A diamond! Plate! *Cecchines!* Good morning's purchase.
  Why, this is better than rob churches yet!
  Or fat,[h] by eating once a month a man—[*Re-enter*
      Mosca.]
  Who is 't?
*Mosca.*   The beauteous Lady Wouldbe, sir,
  Wife to the English knight, Sir Politic Wouldbe—
  This is the style, sir, is directed me—
  Hath sent to know how you have slept tonight,
  And if you would be visited?
*Volpone.*                    Not now.
  Some three hours hence—
*Mosca.*                    I told the squire[1] so much.
*Volpone.*   When I am high with mirth and wine, then,
      then.                                                    560

---

[h] fatten   [1] messenger

'Fore heaven, I wonder at the desperate valor
Of the bold English, that they dare let loose
Their wives to all encounters!
*Mosca.*                              Sir, this knight
Had not his name for nothing; he is politic,[j]
And knows, howe'er his wife affect strange airs,
She hath not yet the face [k] to be dishonest.[l]
But had she Signor Corvino's wife's face—
*Volpone.*   Has she so rare a face?
*Mosca.*                              O, sir, the wonder,
The blazing star of Italy! A wench
O' the first year! A beauty ripe as harvest!                570
Whose skin is whiter than a swan all over!
Than silver, snow, or lilies! A soft lip,
Would tempt you to eternity of kissing!
And flesh that melteth in the touch to blood!
Bright as your gold, and lovely as your gold!
*Volpone.*   Why had not I known this before?
*Mosca.*                              Alas, sir,
Myself but yesterday discovered it.
*Volpone.*   How might I see her?
*Mosca.*                              O, not possible.
She's kept as warily as is your gold;
Never does come abroad, never takes air                     580
But at a window. All her looks are sweet
As the first grapes or cherries, and are watched
As near as they are.
*Volpone.*            I must see her!
*Mosca.*                              Sir,
There is a guard of ten spies thick upon her—
All his whole household—each of which is set
Upon his fellow, and have all their charge,[m]
When he goes out, when he comes in, examined.
*Volpone.*   I will go see her, though but at her window.
*Mosca.*   In some disguise, then.
*Volpone.*                          That is true. I must
Maintain mine own shape still the same. We'll think.     590
                                        [*Exeunt.*]

---

[j] shrewd   [k] (i) looks (ii) audacity   [l] unfaithful   [m] orders

# ACT II

## *Scene I*

[*Before* Corvino's *house*]

[*Enter* Sir Politic Wouldbe *and* Peregrine.]

*Sir Politic.*    Sir, to a wise man, all the world's his soil.[n]
It is not Italy, nor France, nor Europe,
That must bound me, if my fates call me forth.
Yet I protest, it is no salt [o] desire
Of seeing countries, shifting a religion,
Nor any disaffection to the state
Where I was bred, and unto which I owe
My dearest plots, hath brought me out; much less
That idle, antique, stale, gray-headed project
Of knowing men's minds and manners, with Ulysses;            10
But a peculiar humor of my wife's,
Laid for this height [p] of Venice, to observe,
To quote,[q] to learn the language, and so forth—
I hope you travel, sir, with license? [r]
*Peregrine.*                                Yes.
*Sir Politic.*    I dare the safelier converse [s]—How long,
    sir,
  Since you left England?
*Peregrine.*                        Seven weeks.
*Sir Politic.*                                So lately!
  You ha' not been with my Lord Ambassador?
*Peregrine.*    Now yet, sir.
*Sir Politic.*                        Pray you, what news, sir, vents[t]
    our climate?
  I heard last night a most strange thing reported
  By some of my Lord's followers, and I long            20
  To hear how 'twill be seconded!
*Peregrine.*                        What was't, sir?
*Sir Politic.* Marry, sir, of a raven that should build
  In a ship royal of the King's.
*Peregrine.* [*Aside.*]                This fellow,
  Does he gull me, trow,[u] or is gulled?—Your name, sir?

---

[n] native land  [o] inordinate  [p] latitude  [q] take notes  [r] official permission (necessary for knights leaving England)    [s] i.e., the more cautious subject  [t] circulates  [u] I wonder

*Sir Politic.*    My name is Politic Wouldbe.
*Peregrine.* [*Aside.*]            O, that speaks him.—
   A knight, sir?
*Sir Politic.*    A poor knight, sir.
*Peregrine.*            Your lady
   Lies <sup>v</sup> here in Venice, for intelligence <sup>w</sup>
   Of tires <sup>x</sup> and fashions and behavior
   Among the courtesans? The fine Lady Wouldbe?
*Sir Politic.*    Yes, sir, the spider and the bee oft-times      30
   Suck from one flower.
*Peregrine.*            Good Sir Politic,
   I cry you mercy.<sup>y</sup> I have heard much of you.
   'Tis true, sir, of your raven.
*Sir Politic.*            On your knowledge?
*Peregrine.*    Yes, and your lion's whelping in the Tower.<sup>z</sup>
*Sir Politic.*    Another whelp?
*Peregrine.*            Another, sir.
*Sir Politic.*            Now, heaven!
   What prodigies <sup>a</sup> be these? The fires at Berwick! <sup>b</sup>
   And the new star! These things concurring, strange
   And full of omen! Saw you those meteors?
*Peregrine.*    I did, sir.
*Sir Politic.*        Fearful! Pray you, sir, confirm
   me,
   Were there three porpoises seen above the bridge,      40
   As they give out?
*Peregrine.*        Six, and a sturgeon, sir.
*Sir Politic.*    I am astonished!
*Peregrine.*            Nay, sir, be not so;
   I'll tell you a greater prodigy than these—
*Sir Politic.*    What should these things portend?
*Peregrine.*            The very day—
   Let me be sure—that I put forth from London,
   There was a whale discovered in the river,
   As high <sup>c</sup> as Woolwich, that had waited there,
   Few know how many months, for the subversion
   Of the Stode <sup>d</sup> fleet.
*Sir Politic.*        Is't possible? Believe it,
   'Twas either sent from Spain, or the Archduke's! <sup>e</sup>      50
   Spinola's <sup>f</sup> whale, upon my life, my credit!

---

<sup>v</sup> stays    <sup>w</sup> information    <sup>x</sup> dress    <sup>y</sup> I beg your pardon    <sup>z</sup> Tower of London    <sup>a</sup> omens    <sup>b</sup> apparitions were reported warring near the Scottish border    <sup>c</sup> far    <sup>d</sup> German seaport    <sup>e</sup> Spanish Governor of the Netherlands    <sup>f</sup> Spanish general of the Netherlands, believed to have "invented a whale that would have drowned London by snuffing up the Thames and spouting it upon the City"

    Will they not leave [g] these projects? Worthy sir,
    Some other news.
*Peregrine.*              Faith, Stone the fool is dead,
    And they do lack a tavern-fool extremely.
*Sir Politic.*   Is Mas' [h] Stone dead?
*Peregrine.*                    He's dead, sir; why, I hope
    You thought him not immortal? [*Aside.*] O, this
        knight,
    Were he well known, would be a precious thing
    To fit our English stage. He that should write
    But such a fellow, should be thought to feign
    Extremely, if not maliciously.
*Sir Politic.*                    Stone dead!                    60
*Peregrine.*   Dead. Lord, how deeply, sir, you apprehend [i]
        it!
    He was no kinsman to you?
*Sir Politic.*                    That I know of.
    Well, that same fellow was an unknown fool.
*Peregrine.*   And yet you knew him, it seems?
*Sir Politic.*                    I did so. Sir,
    I knew him one of the most dangerous heads
    Living within the state, and so I held him.
*Peregrine.*   Indeed, sir?
*Sir Politic.*                    While he lived, in action.
    He has received weekly intelligence,
    Upon my knowledge, out of the Low Countries,
    For all parts of the world, in cabbages;                    70
    And those dispensed again t'ambassadors,
    In oranges, muskmelons, apricots,
    Lemons, pomecitrons, and suchlike; sometimes
    In Colchester oysters, and your Selsey cockles.
*Peregrine.*   You make me wonder!
*Sir Politic.*                    Sir, upon my knowledge.
    Nay, I have observed him, at your public ordinary, [j]
    Take his advertisement [k] from a traveler—
    A concealed [l] statesman—in a trencher of meat;
    And instantly, before the meal was done,
    Convey an answer in a toothpick.
*Peregrine.*                    Strange!                    80
    How could this be, sir?
*Sir Politic.*              Why, the meat was cut
    So like his character, [m] and so laid, as he
    Must easily read the cipher.
*Peregrine.*                    I have heard

   [g] give up   [h] Master   [i] feel   [j] tavern meal   [k] information   [l] disguised
[m] code

    He could not read, sir.
*Sir Politic.*            So 'twas given out,
    In policy,[n] by those that did employ him.
    But he could read, and had your languages,
    And to 't,[o] as sound a noddle[p]——
*Peregrine.*             I have heard, sir,
    That your baboons were spies, and that they were
    A kind of subtle nation near to China.
*Sir Politic.*    Ay, ay, your *Mamaluchi*.[q] Faith, they had      90
    Their hand in a French plot or two; but they
    Were so extremely given to women, as
    They made discovery of[r] all. Yet I
    Had my advices [s] here, on Wednesday last,
    From one of their own coat,[t] they were returned,
    Made their relations,[u] as the fashion is,
    And now stand fair for fresh employment.
*Peregrine.* [*Aside.*]               Heart!
    This Sir Poll will be ignorant of nothing.——
    It seems, sir, you know all.
*Sir Politic.*            Not all, sir, but
    I have some general notions. I do love        100
    To note and to observe. Though I live out,
    Free from the active torrent, yet I'd mark
    The currents and the passages of things
    For mine own private use; and know the ebbs
    And flows of state.
*Peregrine.*        Believe it, sir, I hold
    Myself in no small tie [v] unto my fortunes,
    For casting me thus luckily upon you,
    Whose knowledge, if your bounty equal it,
    May do me great assistance, in instruction
    For my behavior and my bearing, which        110
    Is yet so rude and raw——
*Sir Politic.*           Why? Came you forth
    Empty of rules for travel?
*Peregrine.*          Faith, I had
    Some common ones, from out that vulgar grammar,
    Which he that cried [w] Italian to me, taught me.
*Sir Politic.*    Why, this it is that spoils all our brave
        bloods: [x]
    Trusting our hopeful gentry unto pedants,
    Fellows of outside, and mere bark. You seem
    To be a gentleman of ingenuous [y] race——

---

[n] for reasons of state    [o] more    [p] head    [q] Mamaluke (former slaves who gained power in Egypt)    [r] revealed    [s] dispatches    [t] kind    [u] reports    [v] much obligated    [w] spoke    [x] fine young gentlemen    [y] noble

I not profess[z] it, but my fate hath been                          120
To be where I have been consulted with,
In this high kind,[a] touching some great men's sons,
Persons of blood and honor—

[*Enter* Mosca *and* Nano *disguised, followed by* Grege.]

*Peregrine.*                     Who be these, sir?
*Mosca.*   Under that window, there 't must be. The same.
*Sir Politic.*   Fellows to mount a bank![b] Did your instruc-
   tor
   In the dear tongues never discourse to you
   Of the Italian mountebanks?
*Peregrine.*                     Yes, sir.
*Sir Politic.*                             Why,
   Here shall you see one.
*Peregrine.*                  They are quacksalvers,[c]
   Fellows that live by venting[d] oils and drugs.
*Sir Politic.*   Was that the character he gave you of them?
*Peregrine.*   As I remember.
*Sir Politic.*                  Pity his ignorance.          130
   They are the only knowing men of Europe!
   Great general scholars, excellent physicians,
   Most admired statesmen, professed favorites,
   And cabinet counselors to the greatest princes!
   The only languaged men of all the world!
*Peregrine.*   And, I have heard, they are most lewd[e] im-
      postors,
   Made all of terms and shreds;[f] no less beliers
   Of great men's favors, than their own vile med'cines;
   Which they will utter, upon monstrous oaths,
   Selling that drug for twopence, ere they part,          140
   Which they have valued at twelve crowns before.
*Sir Politic.*   Sir, calumnies are answered best with si-
      lence.
   Yourself shall judge. Who is it mounts, my friends?
*Mosca.*   Scoto[g] of Mantua, sir.
*Sir Politic.*                  Is't he? Nay, then
   I'll proudly promise, sir, you shall behold
   Another man than has been fancied to you.
   I wonder yet that he should mount his bank
   Here in this nook, that has been wont t' appear
   In face of the Piazza. Here he comes.

[*Enter* Volpone *disguised as a mountebank.*]

   [z] boast   [a] matter   [b] bench   [c] quacks   [d] selling   [e] ignorant   [f] jargon
and quotations   [g] famous Italian juggler

*Volpone.* [*To* Nano.]    Mount, zany.[h]
*Grege.*          Follow, follow, follow, follow, follow.    150
*Sir Politic.* See how people follow him! He's a man
   May write ten thousand crowns in bank here. Note,
   Mark but his gesture. I do use to observe
   The state [i] he keeps in getting up.
*Peregrine.*                'Tis worth it, sir.
*Volpone.* "Most noble gentlemen, and my worthy pa-
   trons: It may seem strange that I, your Scoto Man-
   tuano, who was ever wont to fix my bank in face of the
   public Piazza, near the shelter of the portico to the
   *Procuratía,*[j] should now, after eight months' absence
   from this illustrious city of Venice, humbly retire my- 160
   self into an obscure nook of the Piazza."
*Sir Politic.* Did not I now object the same?
*Peregrine.*             Peace, sir.
*Volpone.* "Let me tell you: I am not—as your Lombard
   proverb saith—cold on my feet,[k] or content to part with
   my commodities at a cheaper rate than I accustomed;
   look not for it. Nor that the calumnious reports of that
   impudent detractor and shame to our profession—
   Alessandro Buttone,[l] I mean—who gave out in public,
   I was condemned a *sforzato*[m] to the galleys, for poison-
   ing the Cardinal Bembo's—[n] cook, hath at all at- 170
   tached,[o] much less dejected me. No, no, worthy gentlemen, to tell you true, I cannot endure to see the rabble
   of these ground *ciarlatani,*[p] that spread their cloaks on
   the pavement as if they meant to do feats of activity,[q]
   and then come in lamely, with their moldy tales out of
   Boccaccio, like stale Tabarine,[r] the fabulist; [s] some of
   them discoursing their travels, and of their tedious captivity in the Turk's galleys, when indeed—were the
   truth known—they were the Christian's galleys, where
   very temperately they eat [t] bread and drunk water, as a 180
   wholesome penance, enjoined them by their confessors,
   for base pilferies."
*Sir Politic.* Note but his bearing, and contempt of these.
*Volpone.* "These turdy-facy-nasty-paty-lousy-fartical
   rogues, with one poor groatsworth of unprepared an-
   timony, finely wrapped up in several [u] *scartoccios,*[v] are

[h] lesser clown who mimics gestures of another clown   [i] ceremony [j] residence of officials of St. Mark's   [k] reduced to poverty   [l] another mountebank   [m] prisoner   [n] the dash marks a pause for the actor to insinuate, without saying, "whore," etc.   [o] incriminated   [p] common imposters   [q] acrobatics   [r] a zany   [s] storyteller   [t] ate   [u] separate   [v] paper containers

able very well to kill their twenty a week, and play. Yet
these meager, starved spirits, who have half stopped
the organs of their minds with earthly oppilations,[w]
want [x] not their favorers among your shriveled, salad-   190
eating artisans, who are overjoyed that they may have
their half-pe'rth [y] of physic; though it purge 'em into
another world, 't makes no matter."

*Sir Politic.*   Excellent! Ha' you heard better language, sir?

*Volpone.*   "Well, let 'em go. And, gentlemen, honorable
gentlemen, know that for this time our bank, being thus
removed from the clamors of the *canaglia,*[z] shall be
the scene of pleasure and delight; for I have nothing to
sell, little or nothing to sell."

*Sir Politic.*   I told you, sir, his end.

*Peregrine.*                    You did so, sir.          200

*Volpone.*   "I protest, I and my six servants are not able to
make of this precious liquor so fast as it is fetched away
from my lodging by gentlemen of your city, strangers
of the *Terra Firma,*[a] worshipful merchants, ay, and
senators too, who, ever since my arrival, have detained
me to their uses, by their splendidous liberalities. And
worthily; for what avails your rich man to have his
magazines [b] stuffed with *moscadelli,*[c] or of the purest
grape, when his physicians prescribe him, on pain of
death, to drink nothing but water cocted [d] with aniseeds?  210
O health! Health! The blessing of the rich! The riches
of the poor! Who can buy thee at too dear a rate,
since there is no enjoying this world without thee? Be
not then so sparing of your purses, honorable gentlemen, as to abridge the natural course of life—"

*Peregrine.*   You see his end?

*Sir Politic.*                    Aye, is't not good?

*Volpone.*   "For when a humid flux, or catarrh, by the
mutability of air, falls from your head into an arm, or
shoulder, or any other part; take you a ducat, or your
*cecchine* of gold, and apply to the place affected; see  220
what good effect it can work. No, no, 'tis this blessed
*unguento,* this rare extraction, that hath only power to
disperse all malignant humors,[e] that proceed either of
hot, cold, moist, or windy causes—"

*Peregrine.*   I would he had put in dry, too.

*Sir Politic.*                    Pray you observe.

*Volpone.*   "To fortify the most indigest and crude[f] stom-

---

[w] obstructions   [x] lack   [y] halfpenny worth   [z] rabble   [a] mainland possessions of the Venetian State   [b] storehouses   [c] muscatel   [d] boiled
[e] body fluids   [f] queasy

ach, ay, were it of one that, through extreme weakness,
vomited blood, applying only a warm napkin to the
place, after the unction [g] and fricace; [h] for the *ver-*
*tigine* [i] in the head, putting but a drop into your nos- 230
trils, likewise behind the ears, a most sovereign and
approved remedy; the *mal caduco*,[j] cramps, convul-
sions, paralyses, epilepsies, *tremor cordia*,[k] retired
nerves,[l] ill vapors of the spleen, stoppings [m] of the liver,
the stone,[n] the strangury,[o] *hernia ventosa*,[p] *iliaca passio;*[q]
stops a *dysenteria* immediately; easeth the torsion [r] of
the small guts; and cures *melancholia hypocondriaca,*
being taken and applied, according to my printed receipt. (*Pointing to his bill and his glass.*) For this is the
physician, this the medicine, this counsels, this cures; 240
this gives the direction, this works the effect; and, in
sum, both together may be termed an abstract of the
theoric and practic in the Aesculapian art. 'Twill cost
you eight crowns. And, Zan Fritada, pray thee sing a
verse extempore in honor of it."

*Sir Politic.*    How do you like him, sir?
*Peregrine.*                           Most strangely, I!
*Sir Politic.*    Is not his language rare?
*Peregrine.*                           But [s] alchemy,
I never heard the like; or Broughton's books.[t]


### SONG.


"Had old Hippocrates or Galen,[u]
That to their books put med'cines all in,             250
But known this secret, they had never—
Of which they will be guilty ever—
Been murderers of so much paper,
Or wasted many a hurtless taper.
No Indian drug had e'er been famèd,
Tobacco, sassafras not namèd;
Ne [v] yet of guacum [w] one small stick, sir,
Nor Raymund Lully's great elixir.[x]
Ne had been known the Danish Gonswart,[y]          260
Or Paracelsus,[z] with his long-sword."

---

[g] ointment  [h] massage  [i] dizziness  [j] epilepsy  [k] heart trouble  [l] shrunk-
en sinews  [m] obstructions  [n] kidney stone  [o] painful urination  [p] tumor
[q] intestinal cramp  [r] convulsion  [s] except for  [t] a scholar  [u] physicians
of antiquity  [v] nor  [w] medicinal bark  [x] medieval alchemist credited with
discovering the elixir of life  [y] unidentified  [z] German alchemist who hid
his remedies in the hilt of his sword

*Peregrine.*   All this yet will not do; eight crowns is high.
*Volpone.*   "No more. Gentlemen, if I had but time to discourse to you the miraculous effects of this my oil, sur-
named *oglio del Scoto;* with the countless catalogue of
those I have cured of th' aforesaid and many more diseases; the patents and privileges of all the princes and
commonwealths of Christendom; or but the depositions
of those that appeared on my part, before the signory of
the *Sanità*[a] and most learned college of physicians;
where I was authorized, upon notice taken of the ad-   270
mirable virtues of my medicaments, and mine own excel-
lency in matter of rare and unknown secrets, not only to
disperse them publicly in this famous city, but in all the
territories that happily joy under the government of the
most pious and magnificent states of Italy. But may
some other gallant fellow say, 'O, there be divers [b] that
make profession to have as good and as experimented
receipts [c] as yours.' Indeed, very many have assayed,
like apes, in imitation of that which is really and essentially in me, to make of this oil; bestowed great cost   280
in furnaces, stills, alembics, continual fires, and preparation of the ingredients,—as indeed there goes to it
six hundred several simples,[d] besides some quantity of
human fat, for the conglutination, which we buy of the
anatomists—but when these practitioners come to the
last decoction: blow, blow, puff, puff, and all flies in
*fumo.*[e] Ha, ha, ha! Poor wretches! I rather pity their
folly and indiscretion than their loss of time and
money; for those may be recovered by industry, but to
be a fool born is a disease incurable. For myself, I al-   290
ways from my youth have endeavored to get the rarest
secrets, and book them, either in exchange or for money.
I spared nor cost nor labor, where anything was worthy
to be learned. And gentlemen, honorable gentlemen, I
will undertake, by virtue of chemical art, out of the
honorable hat that covers your head, to extract the four
elements: that is to say, the fire, air, water, and earth,
and return you your felt without burn or stain. For
whilst others have been at the balloo,[f] I have been at
my book; and am now past the craggy paths of study,   300
and come to the flowery plains of honor and reputation."
*Sir Politic.*   I do assure you, sir, that is his aim.
*Volpone.*   "But to our price—"

[a] Venetian health board   [b] many   [c] tested formulas   [d] herbs   [e] smoke
[f] a game of ball

*Peregrine.*                    And that withal, Sir Poll.
*Volpone.*    "You all know, honorable gentlemen, I never
valued this *ampulla,* or vial, at less than eight crowns;
but for this time, I am content to be deprived of it for
six. Six crowns is the price, and less, in courtesy, I know
you cannot offer me. Take it or leave it, howsoever, both
it and I am at your service. I ask you not as the value of 310
the thing, for then I should demand of you a thousand
crowns; so the Cardinals Montalto, Farnese, the Great
Duke of Tuscany, my gossip,ᵍ with divers other princes,
have given me, but I despise money. Only to show my
affection to you, honorable gentlemen, and your illustrious state here, I have neglected the messages of these
princes, mine own offices; ʰ framed my journey hither
only to present you with the fruits of my travels. Tune
your voices once more to the touch of your instruments,
and give the honorable assembly some delightful recrea- 320
tion."
*Peregrine.*    What monstrous and most painful circum-
    stance
  Is here, to get some three or four *gazets,*¹
Some threepence i' the whole! For that 'twill come to.

SONG.

  "You that would last long, list to my song,
    Make no more coil,ʲ but buy of this oil.
  Would you be ever fair and young?
  Stout of teeth and strong of tongue?
  Tart ᵏ of palate? Quick of ear?
  Sharp of sight? Of nostril clear?                        330
  Moist of hand and light of foot?
  Or I will come nearer to't—
  Would you live free from all diseases?
  Do the act your mistress pleases,
  Yet fright all aches from your bones?
  Here's a med'cine for the nones." ¹

*Volpone.*    "Well, I am in a humor at this time to make
  a present of the small quantity my coffer contains; to the
  rich, in courtesy, and to the poor, for God's sake. Wherefore now mark: I asked you six crowns, and six crowns, 340
  at other times, you have paid me. You shall not give me
  six crowns, nor five, nor four, nor three, nor two, nor

ᵍ godfather   ʰ duties   ¹ small coins   ʲ fuss   ᵏ sharp   ¹ for the occasion

one; nor half a ducat; no, nor a *muccinigo*.[m] Six—pence
it will cost you, or six hundred pound—expect no lower
price, for by the banner of my front, I will not bate a
*bagatine;* [m] that I will have, only, a pledge of your
loves, to carry something from amongst you, to show I
am not contemned by you. Therefore now, toss your
handkerchiefs, cheerfully, cheerfully; and be advertised
that the first heroic spirit that deigns to grace me 350
with a handkerchief, I will give it a little remembrance
of something beside, shall please it better than if I had
presented it with a double pistolet." [n]

*Peregrine.*    Will you be that heroic spark,[o] Sir Poll?

*Celia, at the window, throws down her handkerchief.*

O, see, the window has prevented[p] you!

*Volpone.*    "Lady, I kiss your bounty; and for this timely
grace you have done your poor Scoto of Mantua, I will
return you, over and above my oil, a secret of that high
and inestimable nature, shall make you forever enamored on that minute wherein your eye first descended 360
on so mean, yet not altogether to be despised, an object. Here is a powder concealed in this paper, of which,
if I should speak to the worth, nine thousand volumes
were but as one page, that page as a line, that line as a
word; so short is this pilgrimage of man, which some
call life, to the expressing of it. Would I reflect on the
price? Why, the whole world were but as an empire, that
empire as a province, that province as a bank, that bank
as a private purse, to the purchase of it. I will only tell
you: it is the powder that made Venus a goddess—given 370
her by Apollo—that kept her perpetually young, cleared
her wrinkles, firmed her gums, filled her skin, colored
her hair; from her derived [q] to Helen, and at the sack
of Troy unfortunately lost; till now, in this our age, it
was as happily recovered by a studious antiquary, out
of some ruins of Asia; who sent a moiety [r] of it to the
court of France—but much sophisticated [s]—wherewith
the ladies there now color their hair. The rest, at this
present, remains with me; extracted to a quintessence,
so that, wherever it but touches, in youth it perpetually 380
preserves, in age restores the complexion; seats your
teeth, did they dance like virginal jacks,[t] firm as a wall;
makes them white as ivory, that were black as—"

[m] small coin    [n] gold piece    [o] young gentleman    [p] anticipated    [q] given
[r] part    [s] adulterated    [t] keys

[*Enter* Corvino.]

*Corvino.*     Spite o' the devil, and my shame! Come down,
     here,
    Come down! No house but mine to make your scene? <sup>u</sup>
    Signor Flaminio, will you down, sir? Down?
    What, is my wife your *Franciscina,*<sup>v</sup> sir?
    No windows on the whole Piazza here,
    To make your properties, but mine? But mine?

*He beats away* Volpone, Mosca, Nano, *and* Grege.

    Heart! Ere tomorrow I shall be new christened,        390
    And called the *Pantalone di Bisognosi*<sup>w</sup>
    About the town.
*Peregrine.*     What should this mean, Sir Poll?
*Sir Politic.*     Some trick of state, believe it. I will home.
*Peregrine.*     It may be some design on you.
*Sir Politic.*                 I know not.
    I'll stand upon my guard.
*Peregrine.*             It is your best, sir.
*Sir Politic.*     This three weeks, all my advices, all my let-
     ters,
    They have been intercepted.
*Peregrine.*              Indeed, sir?
    Best have a care.
*Sir Politic.*      Nay, so I will.
*Peregrine.*             This knight,
    I may not lose him, for my mirth, till night.     [*Exeunt.*]

## Scene II

### [*Somewhere in Venice.*]

[*Enter* Volpone *and* Mosca.]

*Volpone.*     O, I am wounded!
*Mosca.*             Where, sir?
*Volpone.*                Not without;
    Those blows were nothing. I could bear them ever.
    But angry Cupid, bolting from her eyes,
    Hath shot himself into me like a flame;
    Where now he flings about his burning heat,

<sup>u</sup> stage   <sup>v</sup> flirtatious maid of the *commedia dell' arte*   <sup>w</sup> jealous old
husband and cuckold of the *commedia dell' arte*

As in a furnace an ambitious fire,
Whose vent is stopped. The fight is all within me.
I cannot live, except thou help me, Mosca.
My liver ˣ melts, and I, without the hope
Of some soft air from her refreshing breath,                    10
Am but a heap of cinders.

*Mosca.*                              'Las, good sir,
Would you had never seen her!

*Volpone.*                              Nay, would thou
Hadst never told me of her!

*Mosca.*                              Sir, 'tis true;
I do confess I was unfortunate,
And you unhappy; but I'm bound in conscience,
No less than duty, to effect my best
To your release of torment, and I will, sir.

*Volpone.*   Dear Mosca, shall I hope?

*Mosca.*                              Sir, more than dear,
I will not bid you to despair of aught
Within a human compass.

*Volpone.*                        O, there spoke                    20
My better angel. Mosca, take my keys,
Gold, plate, and jewels—all's at thy devotion.ʸ
Employ them how thou wilt; nay, coin me, too—
So thou in this but crown my longings, Mosca.

*Mosca.*   Use but your patience.

*Volpone.*                              So I have.

*Mosca.*                              I doubt not
To bring success to your desires.

*Volpone.*                        Nay, then,
I not repent me of my late disguise.

*Mosca.*   If you can horn ᶻ him, sir, you need not.

*Volpone.*                              True.
Besides, I never meant him for my heir.
Is not the color o' my beard and eyebrows                    30
To make me known?

*Mosca.*                        No jot.

*Volpone.*                        I did it well.

*Mosca.*   So well, would I could follow you in mine,
With half the happiness! And yet I would
Escape your epilogue.ᵃ

*Volpone.*                        But were they gulled
With a belief that I was Scoto?

*Mosca.*                              Sir,
Scoto himself could hardly have distinguished!

---

ˣ supposedly the seat of passion   ʸ disposal   ᶻ cuckold   ᵃ i.e., beating

I have not time to flatter you now, we'll part;
And as I prosper, so applaud my art.    [*Exeunt.*]


### Scene III

[Corvino's *house.*]

[*Enter* Corvino *dragging in* Celia.]

*Corvino.*    Death of mine honor, with the city's fool!
A juggling, tooth-drawing, prating mountebank!
And at a public window! Where, whilst he,
With his strained action, and his dole of faces,<sup>b</sup>
To his drug-lecture draws your itching ears,
A crew of old, unmarried, noted lechers
Stood leering up like satyrs; and you smile
Most graciously, and fan your favors forth,
To give your hot spectators satisfaction!
What, was your mountebank their call? Their whistle?    10
Or were you enamored on his copper rings?
His saffron jewel with the toad-stone <sup>c</sup> in't?
Or his embroidered suit, with the cope-stitch,<sup>d</sup>
Made of a hearse-cloth? Or his old tilt<sup>e</sup>-feather?
Or his starched beard? Well, you shall have him, yes!
He shall come home, and minister unto you
The fricace for the mother.<sup>f</sup> Or, let me see,
I think you'd rather mount; <sup>g</sup> would you not mount?
Why, if you'll mount, you may; yes, truly, you may!
And so you may be seen, down to th' foot.    20
Get you a cittern,<sup>h</sup> Lady Vanity,<sup>i</sup>
And be a dealer <sup>j</sup> with the virtuous man;
Make one. I'll but protest myself a cuckold,
And save your dowry. I am a Dutchman, I!
For if you thought me an Italian,
You would be damned ere you did this, you whore!
Thou'dst tremble to imagine that the murder
Of father, mother, brother, all thy race,
Should follow, as the subject of my justice!
*Celia.*    Good sir, have patience.
*Corvino.*                    What couldst thou propose    30
Less to thyself than, in this heat of wrath,

<sup>b</sup> collection of grimaces  <sup>c</sup> a charm  <sup>d</sup> vestment embroidery  <sup>e</sup> jousting
<sup>f</sup> hysteria  <sup>g</sup> go on the stage  <sup>h</sup> zither  <sup>i</sup> character in morality plays
<sup>j</sup> prostitute

And stung with my dishonor, I should strike
This steel into thee, with as many stabs
As thou wert gazed upon with goatish [k] eyes?
*Celia.*    Alas, sir, be appeased! I could not think
My being at the window, should more now
Move your impatience than at other times.
*Corvino.*    No? Not to seek and entertain a parley
With a known knave, before a multitude?
You were an actor, with your handkerchief,                      40
Which he most sweetly kissed in the receipt,
And might, no doubt, return it with a letter,
And 'point the place where you might meet—your
      sister's,
Your mother's, or your aunt's might serve the turn.
*Celia.*    Why, dear sir, when do I make these excuses,
Or ever stir abroad, but to the church?
And that so seldom—
*Corvino.*                    Well, it shall be less;
And thy restraint before was liberty
To what I now decree. And therefore mark me:
First, I will have this bawdy light dammed up;                  50
And till't be done, some two or three yards off,
I'll chalk a line, o'er which if thou but chance
To set thy desp'rate foot, more hell, more horror,
More wild remorseless rage shall seize on thee
Than on a conjuror that had heedless left
His circle's safety ere his devil was laid.[1]
Then, here's a lock which I will hang upon thee;
And, now I think on't, I will keep thee backwards;
Thy lodging shall be backwards, thy walks backwards,
Thy prospect—all be backwards, and no pleasure                 60
That thou shalt know, but backwards. Nay, since you
      force
My honest nature, know it is your own
Being too open, makes me use you thus;
Since you will not contain your subtle nostrils
In a sweet room, but they must snuff the air
Of rank and sweaty passengers.[m] (*Knock within.*)
      One knocks.
Away, and be not seen, pain of thy life;
Not look toward the window; if thou dost—
Nay, stay, hear this—let me not prosper, whore,
But I will make thee an anatomy,[n]                            70

[k] lustful   [1] i.e., left the protection of his charmed circle before the devil
he had raised was exorcized   [m] passers-by   [n] use you as a cadaver for
demonstration

Dissect thee mine own self, and read a lecture
Upon thee to the city, and in public.
Away!                                         [*Exit* Celia.]

[*Enter* Servitore.]

          Who's there?
*Servitore.*          'Tis Signor Mosca, sir.
*Corvino.*    Let him come in. [*Exit* Servitore.] His master's
    dead! there's yet
    Some good to help the bad.

[*Enter* Mosca.]

                          My Mosca, welcome!
    I guess your news.
*Mosca.*               I fear you cannot, sir.
*Corvino.*    Is't not his death?
*Mosca.*                     Rather the contrary.
*Corvino.*    Not his recovery?
*Mosca.*                     Yes, sir.
*Corvino.*                          I am cursed.
    I am bewitched, my crosses meet to vex me.
    How? How? How? How?
*Mosca.*                     Why, sir, with Scoto's oil!      80
    Corbaccio and Voltore brought of it
    Whilst I was busy in an inner room—
*Corvino.*    Death! That damned mountebank! But for the
    law
    Now, I could kill the rascal; 't cannot be
    His oil should have that virtue.° Ha' not I
    Known him, a common rogue, come fiddling in
    To th' *ostería*,ᵖ with a tumbling whore,
    And, when he has done all his forced tricks, been glad
    Of a poor spoonful of dead wine, with flies in't?
    It cannot be. All his ingredients                        90
    Are a sheep's gall, a roasted bitch's marrow,
    Some few sod ᑫ earwigs, pounded caterpillars,
    A little capon's grease, and fasting spittle.ʳ
    I know 'em to a dram.
*Mosca.*               I know not, sir,
    But some on't there they poured into his ears,
    Some in his nostrils, and recovered him,
    Applying but the fricace!

---

° power    ᵖ inn    ᑫ boiled    ʳ saliva from one who fasts

*Corvino.*                    Pox o' that fricace!
*Mosca.*    And since, to seem the more officious,
    And flatt'ring of his health, there they have had,
    At èxtreme fees, the college of physicians                    100
    Consulting on him, how they might restore him;
    Where one would have a cataplasm [a] of spices,
    Another a flayed ape clapped to his breast,
    A third would ha' it a dog, a fourth an oil,
    With wild cats' skins; at last, they all resolved
    That, to preserve him, was no other means
    But some young woman must be straight sought out,
    Lusty and full of juice, to sleep by him.
    And to this service, most unhappily,
    And most unwillingly, am I now employed;                    110
    Which here I thought to pre-acquaint you with,
    For your advice, since it concerns you most,
    Because I would not do that thing might cross
    Your ends, on whom I have my whole dependence, sir.
    Yet, if I do it not, they may delate [t]
    My slackness to my patron, work me out
    Of his opinion; and there all your hopes,
    Ventures, or whatsoever, are all frustrate.
    I do but tell you, sir. Besides, they are all
    Now striving who shall first present him. Therefore—    120
    I could entreat you, briefly, conclude somewhat;
    Prevent 'em if you can.
*Corvino.*                    Death to my hopes,
    This is my villainous fortune! Best to hire
    Some common courtesan.
*Mosca.*                            Aye, I thought on that, sir;
    But they are all so subtle, full of art;
    And age again doting and flexible,
    So as—I cannot tell—we may perchance
    Light on a quean [u] may cheat us all.
*Corvino.*                            'Tis true.
*Mosca.*    No, no. It must be one that has no tricks, sir,
    Some simple thing, a creature made unto it; [v]                    130
    Some wench you may command. Ha' you no
        kinswoman?
    God's so'—Think, think, think, think, think, think,
        think, sir.
    One o' the doctors offered there his daughter.
*Corvino.*    How!
*Mosca.*                Yes, Signor Lupo, the physician.

    [a] poultice    [t] accuse    [u] whore    [v] i.e., coached

*Corvino.*    His daughter!

*Mosca.*                And a virgin, sir. Why, alas,
   He knows the state of's body, what it is;
   That nought can warm his blood, sir, but a fever;
   Nor any incantation raise his spirit—
   A long forgetfulness hath seized that part.
   Besides, sir, who shall know it? Some one or two—    140

*Corvino.*    I pray thee give me leave. [*Walks aside.*] If any
     man
   But I had had this luck—The thing in'tself,
   I know, is nothing—Wherefore should not I
   As well command my blood and my affections
   As this dull doctor? In the point of honor,
   The cases are all one, of wife and daughter.

*Mosca.* [*Aside.*]    —I hear him coming.<sup>w</sup>

*Corvino.*                She shall do't. 'Tis done.
   'Slight! If this doctor, who is not engaged,
   Unless 't be for his counsel, which is nothing,
   Offer his daughter, what should I, that am    150
   So deeply in? I will prevent him. Wretch!
   Covetous wretch!—Mosca, I have determined.

*Mosca.*    How, sir?

*Corvino.*         We'll make all sure. The party you wot <sup>x</sup>
     of
   Shall be mine own wife, Mosca.

*Mosca.*             Sir, the thing,
   But that I would not seem to counsel you,
   I should have motioned <sup>y</sup> to you at the first;
   And, make your count,<sup>z</sup> you have cut all their throats.
   Why, 'tis directly taking a possession!
   And in his next fit, we may let him go.
   'Tis but to pull the pillow from his head,    160
   And he is throttled; 't had been done before,
   But for your scrupulous doubts.

*Corvino.*           Aye, a plague on't,
   My conscience fools my wit! Well, I'll be brief,
   And so be thou, lest they should be before us.
   Go home, prepare him, tell him with what zeal
   And willingness I do it. Swear it was
   On the first hearing—as thou mayst do, truly—
   Mine own free motion.

*Mosca.*        Sir, I warrant you,
   I'll so possess him with it, that the rest
   Of his starved clients shall be banished all,    170

<sup>w</sup> yielding    <sup>x</sup> know    <sup>y</sup> proposed    <sup>z</sup> be sure

And only you received. But come not, sir,
Until I send, for I have something else
To ripen for your good; you must not know't.
Corvino.   But do not you forget to send now.
Mosca.                                          Fear not.
                                                    [*Exit.*]

Corvino.   Where are you, wife? My Celia! Wife!

[*Re-enter* Celia.]

                                        What, blubbering?
Come, dry those tears. I think thou thought'st me in
   earnest!
Ha! By this light, I talked so but to try thee.
Methinks the lightness of the occasion
Should ha' confirmed thee. Come, I am not jealous.
Celia.   No?
Corvino.   Faith I am not, I, nor never was;          180
It is a poor, unprofitable humor.
Do not I know, if women have a will,
They'll do 'gainst all the watches [a] o' the world?
And that the fiercest spies are tamed with gold?
Tut, I am confident in thee, thou shalt see't;
And see, I'll give thee cause, too, to believe it.
Come kiss me. Go, and make thee ready straight
In all thy best attire, thy choicest jewels,
Put 'em all on, and, with 'em, thy best looks.
We are invited to a solemn feast          190
At old Volpone's, where it shall appear
How far I am free from jealousy or fear.          [*Exeunt.*]

# ACT III

## Scene I

[*A street.*]

[*Enter* Mosca.]

Mosca.   I fear I shall begin to grow in love
With my dear self, and my most prosp'rous parts,[b]

---

[a] guards   [b] talents

They do so spring and burgeon. I can feel
A whimsy i' my blood; I know not how,
Success hath made me wanton. I could skip
Out of my skin now, like a subtle snake,
I am so limber. O! Your parasite
Is a most precious thing, dropped from above,
Not bred 'mongst clods and clodpolls here on earth.
I muse the mystery [c] was not made a science,                          10
It is so liberally professed! [d] Almost
All the wise world is little else, in nature,
But parasites or sub-parasites. And yet
I mean not those that have your bare town-art,
To know who's fit to feed 'em; have no house,
No family, no care, and therefore mold
Tales for men's ears, to bait that sense; or get
Kitchen-invention, [e] and some stale receipts
To please the belly and the groin; nor those,
With their court-dog tricks, that can fawn and fleer, [f]               20
Make their revènue out of legs and faces, [g]
Echo my lord, and lick away a moth; [h]
But your fine, elegant rascal, that can rise
And stoop, almost together, like an arrow;
Shoot through the air as nimbly as a star;
Turn short as doth a swallow; and be here,
And there, and here, and yonder, all at once;
Present to any humor all occasion, [i]
And change a visor [j] swifter than a thought!
This is the creature had the art born with him;                         30
Toils not to learn it, but doth practice it
Out of most excellent nature; [k] and such sparks
Are the true parasites, others but their zanies.

[*Enter* Bonario.]

Who's this? Bonario, old Corbaccio's son?
The person I was bound to seek. Fair sir,
  You are happ'ly met.
*Bonario.*                    That cannot be by thee.
*Mosca.*    Why, sir?
*Bonario.*                Nay, pray thee know thy way, and
    leave me.
I would be loath to interchange discourse
With such a mate [l] as thou art.

[c] craft   [d] generally practiced   [e] culinary skill   [f] smile hypocritically
[g] advancement by bows and smirks   [h] i.e., from the lord's clothing   [i] i.e.,
please any whim   [j] expression   [k] natural talent   [l] fellow

*Mosca.*                 Courteous sir,
   Scorn not my poverty.
*Bonario.*           Not I, by heaven!
   But thou shalt give me leave to hate thy baseness.       40
*Mosca.*    Baseness?
*Bonario.*          Aye, answer me, is not thy sloth
   Sufficient argument? Thy flattery?
   Thy means of feeding?
*Mosca.*          Heaven be good to me!
   These imputations are too common, sir,
   And eas'ly stuck on virtue when she's poor;
   You are unequal $^m$ to me, and howe'er
   Your sentence may be righteous, yet you are not,
   That, ere you know me, thus proceed in censure.
   St. Mark bear witness 'gainst you, 'tis inhuman!       50
*Bonario.* [*Aside.*]    What! Does he weep! The sign is soft
     and good.
   I do repent me that I was so harsh.
*Mosca.*    'Tis true that, swayed by strong necessity,
   I am enforced to eat my careful $^n$ bread
   With too much obsequy.$^o$ 'Tis true, beside,
   That I am fain $^p$ to spin mine own poor raiment
   Out of my mere observance,$^q$ being not born
   To a free fortune. But that I have done
   Base offices, in rending friends asunder,
   Dividing families, betraying counsels,       60
   Whispering false lies, or mining $^r$ men with praises,
   Trained $^s$ their credulity with perjuries,
   Corrupted chastity, or am in love
   With mine own tender ease; but would not rather
   Prove $^t$ the most rugged and laborious course
   That might redeem my present estimation,$^u$
   Let me here perish, in all hope of goodness!
*Bonario.* [*Aside.*]    This cannot be a personated $^v$
     passion.—
   I was to blame, so to mistake thy nature.
   Pray thee forgive me, and speak out thy business.       70
*Mosca.*    Sir, it concerns you; and though I may seem
   At first to make a main $^w$ offense in manners,
   And in my gratitude unto my master,
   Yet for the pure love which I bear all right,
   And hatred of the wrong, I must reveal it.
   This very hour your father is in purpose
   To disinherit you—

---

$^m$ unjust    $^n$ full of care    $^o$ obsequiousness    $^p$ inclined    $^q$ service    $^r$ undermining    $^s$ trapped    $^t$ try    $^u$ reputation    $^v$ pretended    $^w$ great

*Bonario.*                How!
*Mosca.*                        And thrust you forth,
  As a mere stranger to his blood; 'tis true, sir.
  The work no way engageth me, but as
  I claim an interest in the general state                    80
  Of goodness and true virtue, which I hear
  T' abound in you; and for which mere respect,[x]
  Without a second aim, sir, I have done it.
*Bonario.*    This tale hath lost thee much of the late trust
  Thou hadst with me; it is impossible.
  I know not how to lend it any thought,
  My father should be so unnatural.
*Mosca.*    It is a confidence that well becomes
  Your piety; [y] and formed, no doubt, it is
  From your own simple innocence; which makes             90
  Your wrong more monstrous and abhorred. But, sir,
  I now will tell you more: this very minute
  It is, or will be, doing; and if you
  Shall be but pleased to go with me, I'll bring you—
  I dare not say where you shall see—but where
  Your ear shall be a witness of the deed;
  Hear yourself written bastard, and professed
  The common issue of the earth.[z]
*Bonario.*                    I'm 'mazed!
*Mosca.*    Sir, if I do it not, draw your just sword,
  And score your vengeance on my front [a] and face;       100
  Mark me your villain. You have too much wrong,
  And I do suffer for you, sir. My heart
  Weeps blood in anguish—
*Bonario.*                    Lead. I follow thee.
                                      [*Exeunt.*]


## Scene II

### [Volpone's *house*.]

[*Enter* Volpone.]

*Volpone.*    Mosca stays long, methinks.—Bring forth
    your sports,
  And help to make the wretched time more sweet.

[*Enter* Nano, Androgyno, *and* Castrone.]

[x] i.e., only for his reason    [y] filial affection    [z] i.e., of unknown parentage    [a] forehead

*Nano.*    "Dwarf, fool, and eunuch, well met here we be.
   A question it were now, whether [b] of us three,
   Being all the known delicates [c] of a rich man,
   In pleasing him, claim the precedency can?"
*Castrone.*    "I claim for myself."
*Androgyno.*                          "And so doth the fool."
*Nano.*    " 'Tis foolish indeed. Let me set you both to
        school:
   First, for your dwarf, he's little and witty,
   And everything, as it is little, is pretty;                          10
   Else why do men say to a creature of my shape,
   So soon as they see him, 'It's a pretty little ape'?
   And why a pretty ape, but for pleasing imitation
   Of greater men's action, in a ridiculous fashion?
   Beside, this feat [d] body of mine doth not crave
   Half the meat, drink, and cloth one of your bulks will
        have.
   Admit your fool's face be the mother of laughter,
   Yet, for his brain, it must always come after;
   And though that do feed him, it's a pitiful case,
   His body is beholden to such a bad face."                          20


*One knocks.*


*Volpone.*    Who's there? My couch! Away! Look!
        Nano, see! [*Exeunt* Androgyno *and* Castrone.]
   Give me my caps first—go, inquire. [*Exit Nano.*]
        Now, Cupid
   Send [e] it be Mosca, and with fair return!


[*Re-enter* Nano.]


*Nano.*    It is the beauteous Madam—
*Volpone.*                          Wouldbe—is it?
*Nano.*    The same.
*Volpone.*                Now torment on me! Squire her in;
   For she will enter, or dwell here forever.
   Nay, quickly, that my fit were past. [*Exit Nano.*] I fear
   A second hell, too, that my loathing this [f]
   Will quite expel my appetite to the other. [g]
   Would she were taking now her tedious leave.
   Lord, how it threats me, what I am to suffer!                          30


[*Re-enter* Nano *with* Lady Wouldbe.]


   [b] which   [c] pets   [d] dainty   [e] grant that   [f] i.e., Lady Wouldbe   [g] i.e.,
Celia

*Lady Wouldbe.*    I thank you, good sir. Pray you signify
  Unto your patron I am here.    This band [h]
  Shows not my neck enough.    I trouble you, sir;
  Let me request you bid one of my women
  Come hither to me. In good faith, I am dressed
  Most favorably today! It is no matter;
  'Tis well enough.

[*Enter* 1st Woman.]

             Look, see these petulant things!
  How they have done this!
*Volpone.* [*Aside.*]     —I do feel the fever
  Ent'ring in at mine ears. O for a charm              40
  To fright it hence!
*Lady Wouldbe.*    Come nearer. Is this curl
  In his right place, or this? Why is this higher
  Than all the rest? You ha' not washed your eyes yet!
  Or do they not stand even i' your head?
  Where is your fellow? Call her.    [*Exit* 1st Woman.]
*Nano.*    —Now, St. Mark
  Deliver us! Anon she'll beat her women,
  Because her nose is red.

[*Re-enter* 1st Woman *with* 2nd Woman.]

*Lady Wouldbe.*          I pray you, view
  This tire,[i] forsooth; are all things apt, or no?
*1st Woman.*    One hair a little here sticks out, forsooth.
*Lady Wouldbe.*    Does't so, forsooth? And where was
    your dear sight,                                         50
  When it did so, forsooth? What now! Bird-eyed?
  And you, too? Pray you, both approach and mend it.
  Now, by that light, I muse [j] you're not ashamed!
  I, that have preached these things so oft unto you,
  Read you the principles, argued all the grounds,
  Disputed every fitness, every grace,
  Called you to counsel of so frequent dressings—
*Nano.* [*Aside.*]    —More carefully than of your fame
  or honor.
*Lady Wouldbe.*    Made you acquainted what an ample
  dowry
  The knowledge of these things would be unto you,       60
  Able alone to get you noble husbands

[h] ruff  [i] coiffure  [j] wonder

At your return; and you thus to neglect it!
Besides, you seeing what a curious [k] nation
Th' Italians are, what will they say of me?
"The English lady cannot dress herself."
Here's a fine imputation to our country!
Well, go your ways, and stay i' the next room.
This fucus [1] was too coarse, too; it's no matter.
Good sir, you'll give 'em entertainment?

                              [*Exit* Nano *with* Women.]

*Volpone.*    —The storm comes toward me.
*Lady Wouldbe.*                        How does my Volp!    70
*Volpone.*    Troubled with noise, I cannot sleep; I dreamt
  That a strange fury entered now my house,
  And with the dreadful tempest of her breath
  Did cleave my roof asunder.
*Lady Wouldbe.*          Believe me, and I
  Had the most fearful dream, could I remember't—
*Volpone.* [*Aside.*]    —Out on my fate! I ha' giv'n her
    the occasion
  How to torment me: she will tell me hers.
*Lady Wouldbe.*    Methought the golden mediocrity,
  Polite and delicate—
*Volpone.*                O, if you do love me,
  No more. I sweat and suffer at the mention    80
  Of any dream. Feel how I tremble yet.
*Lady Wouldbe.*    Alas, good soul! The passion of the
  heart.[m]
  Seed-pearl [n] were good now, boiled with syrup of
    apples,
  Tincture of gold, and coral, citron pills,
  Your elecampane root, myrobalanes—
*Volpone.* [*Aside.*]    Aye me, I have ta'en a
  grasshopper by the wing!
*Lady Wouldbe.*    Burnt silk and amber; you have musca-
  del
  Good i' the house—
*Volpone.*                You will not drink, and part?
*Lady Wouldbe.*    No, fear not that. I doubt we shall not
  get
  Some English saffron—half a dram would serve—    90
  Your sixteen cloves, a little musk, dried mints,
  Bugloss, and barley-meal—
*Volpone.* [*Aside.*]                She's in again!
  Before, I feigned diseases; now I have one.

---

[k] careful    [1] rouge    [m] heartburn    [n] Lady Wouldbe here offers numerous
remedies

*Lady Wouldbe.*    And these applied with a right scarlet
cloth.

*Volpone.* [*Aside.*]    Another flood of words! A very
torrent!

*Lady Wouldbe.*    Shall I, sir, make you a poultice?

*Volpone.*                                          No, no, no!
I'm very well; you need prescribe no more.

*Lady Wouldbe.*    I have a little studied physic; but now
I'm all for music, save, i' the forenoons,
An hour or two for painting. I would have                100
A lady, indeed, t' have all, letters and arts,
Be able to discourse, to write, to paint;
But principal—as Plato holds—your music—
And so does wise Pythagoras, I take it—
Is your true rapture; when there is consent °
In face, in voice, and clothes; and is, indeed,
Our sex's chiefest ornament.

*Volpone.*                          The poet
As old in time as Plato, and as knowing,
Says that your highest female grace is silence.

*Lady Wouldbe.*    Which o' your poets? Petrarch, or
Tasso, or Dante?                                          110
Guarini? Ariosto? Aretine?
Cieco di Hadria? I have read them all.

*Volpone.* [*Aside.*]    Is everything a cause to my destruction?

*Lady Wouldbe.*    I think I ha' two or three of 'em about
me.

*Volpone.* [*Aside.*]    —The sun, the sea, will sooner
both stand still
Than her eternal tongue! Nothing can 'scape it.

*Lady Wouldbe.*    Here's *Pastor Fido* ᵖ—

*Volpone.* [*Aside.*]              Profess obstinate silence,
That's now my safest.

*Lady Wouldbe.*          All our English writers,
I mean such as are happy ᑫ in th' Italian,
Will deign to steal out of this author mainly,            120
Almost as much as from Montagnié.ʳ
He has so modern and facile a vein,
Fitting the time, and catching the court ear.
Your Petrarch is more passionate, yet he,
In days of sonnetting, trusted 'em with much.
Dante is hard, and few can understand him.
But, for a desperate ˢ wit, there's Aretine!

° harmony  ᵖ *The Faithful Shepherd*, a pastoral play, by Guarini
ᑫ fluent  ʳ Montaigne  ˢ outrageous

Only his pictures are a little obscene—
You mark me not.
*Volpone.*          Alas, my mind's perturbed.
*Lady Wouldbe.*   Why, in such cases we must cure our-
     selves,                                                    130
   Make use of our philosophy—
*Volpone.*                          O 'y me!
*Lady Wouldbe.*   And as we find our passions do rebel,
   Encounter 'em with reason, or divert 'em,
   By giving scope unto some other humor
   Of lesser danger; as, in politic bodies,
   There's nothing more doth overwhelm the judgment
   And clouds the understanding, than too much
   Settling and fixing and, as 'twere, subsiding
   Upon one object. For the incorporating
   Of these same outward things into that part        140
   Of which we call mental, leaves some certain faeces [t]
   That stop the organs, and, as Plato says,
   Assassinates our knowledge.
*Volpone.* [*Aside.*]          Now, the spirit
   Of patience help me!
*Lady Wouldbe.*       Come, in faith, I must
   Visit you more a-days, and make you well;
   Laugh and be lusty!
*Volpone.* [*Aside.*]   My good angel save me!
*Lady Wouldbe.*   There was but one sole man in all the
     world
   With whom I e'er could sympathize; and he
   Would lie you [u] often three, four hours together
   To hear me speak; and be sometime so rapt,        150
   As he would answer me quite from the purpose,
   Like you, and you are like him, just. I'll discourse,
   An't be but only, sir, to bring you asleep,
   How we did spend our time and loves together,
   For some six years.
*Volpone.*          O, O, O, O, O, O!
*Lady Wouldbe.*   For we were *coaetanei,*[v] and brought
     up—
*Volpone.*   Some power, some fate, some fortune rescue
   me!

[*Enter* Mosca.]

*Mosca.*   God save you, madam!

   [t] dregs   [u] lie   [v] of equal age

*Lady Wouldbe.*                    Good sir.
*Volpone.*                              Mosca! Welcome,
  Welcome to my redemption.
*Mosca.*                    Why, sir?
*Volpone.*                              O,
  Rid me of this my torture, quickly, there,          160
  My madam with the everlasting voice!
  The bells, in time of pestilence, ne'er made
  Like noise, or were in that perpetual motion;
  The cock-pit ᵂ comes not near it. All my house,
  But now, steamed like a bath with her thick breath;
  A lawyer could not have been heard; nor scarce
  Another woman, such a hail of words
  She has let fall. For hell's sake, rid her hence.
*Mosca.*    Has she presented? ˣ
*Volpone.*                    O, I do not care!
  I'll take her absence upon any price,              170
  With any loss.
*Mosca.*          Madam—
*Lady Wouldbe.*          I ha' brought your patron
  A toy, a cap here, of mine own work—
*Mosca.*                              'Tis well.
  I had forgot to tell you I saw your knight,
  Where you'd little think it—
*Lady Wouldbe.*                    Where?
*Mosca.*                              Marry,
  Where yet, if you make haste, you may apprehend him;
  Rowing upon the water in a gondole,
  With the most cunning ʸ courtesan of Venice.
*Lady Wouldbe.*    Is't true?
*Mosca.*                    Pursue 'em, and believe your eyes.
  Leave me to make your gift. [*Exit* Lady Wouldbe
    *hastily.*] I knew 'twould take.
  For lightly,ᶻ they that use themselves most license    180
  Are still most jealous.
*Volpone.*                Mosca, hearty thanks
  For thy quick fiction, and delivery of me.
  Now to my hopes, what sayst thou?

[*Re-enter* Lady Wouldbe.]

*Lady Wouldbe.*                    But do you hear, sir?
*Volpone.*    Again! I fear a paroxysm.
*Lady Wouldbe.*                    Which way

---

ᵂ place for cockfights    ˣ i.e., her gift    ʸ knowing    ᶻ generally

Rowed they together?
*Mosca.*                          Toward the Rialto.
*Lady Wouldbe.*    I pray you lend me your dwarf.
*Mosca.*                                    I pray you take him.
                                         [*Exit* Lady Wouldbe.]
Your hopes, sir, are like happy blossoms, fair,
And promise timely fruit, if you will stay
But the maturing. Keep you at your couch;
Corbaccio will arrive straight, with the will.             190
When he is gone, I'll tell you more.          [*Exit.*]
*Volpone.*                          My blood,
My spirits are returned; I am alive.
And, like your wanton gamester at primero,[a]
Whose thought had whispered to him, not go less,
Methinks I lie, and draw—for an encounter.[b]
                               [Volpone *closes the curtain.*]

[*Enter* Mosca *with* Bonario.]

*Mosca.*    Sir, here concealed [*pointing to a curtain*], you
     may hear all. But pray you
Have patience, sir. (*One knocks.*) The same's your father
     knocks.
I am compelled to leave you.                    [*Exit.*]
*Bonario.*                          Do so. Yet
Cannot my thought imagine this a truth. [*Conceals
     himself.*]

[*Enter* Mosca, Corvino, *followed by* Celia.]

*Mosca.*    Death on me! You are come too soon, what
     meant you?                                        200
Did not I say I would send?
*Corvino.*                          Yes, but I fear'd
You might forget it, and then they prevent us.
*Mosca.* [*Aside.*]    Prevent? Did e'er man haste so for his
     horns?
A courtier would not ply it so for a place.[c]—
Well, now there's no helping it, stay here;
I'll presently return.                              [*Exit.*]
*Corvino.*                    Where are you, Celia?
You know not wherefore I have brought you hither?
*Celia.*    Not well, except you told me.
*Corvino.*                          Now I will:

---

[a] a card game   [b] i.e., with Celia   [c] i.e., at court

    Hark hither.

[*Whispers to her.*]


*Mosca.* [*Appears at* Bonario's *curtain.*]   Sir, your father
    hath sent word
    It will be half an hour ere he come.           210
    And therefore, if you please to walk the while
    Into that gallery—at the upper end
    There are some books to entertain the time—
    And I'll take care no man shall come unto you, sir.
*Bonario.*   Yes, I will stay there. [*Aside.*] I do doubt
    this fellow.                                [*Exit.*]
*Mosca.*   There, he is far enough; he can hear nothing;
    And for his father, I can keep him off.


[*Withdraws to* Volpone's *couch.*]


*Corvino.*   Nay, now there is no starting back, and there-
    fore
    Resolve upon it; I have so decreed.
    It must be done. Nor would I move't [d] afore,       220
    Because I would avoid all shifts and tricks
    That might deny me.
*Celia.*                Sir, let me beseech you,
    Affect not these strange trials. If you doubt
    My chastity, why, lock me up forever;
    Make me the heir of darkness. Let me live
    Where I may please your fears, if not your trust.
*Corvino.*   Believe it, I have no such humor, I.
    All that I speak I mean; yet I am not mad,
    Not horn-mad, see you? Go to, show yourself
    Obedient, and a wife.
*Celia.*             O heaven!
*Corvino.*             I say it,       230
    Do so.
*Celia.*   Was this the train? [e]
*Corvino.*           I've told you reasons:
    What the physicians have set down, how much
    It may concern me, what my engagements are,
    My means, and the necessity of those means
    For my recovery. Wherefore, if you be
    Loyal, and mine, be won, respect my venture.
*Celia.*   Before your honor?


[d] propose it  [e] snare

*Corvino.*                    Honor! Tut, a breath;
    There's no such thing in nature: a mere term
    Invented to awe fools. What is my gold
    The worse for touching? Clothes for being looked on?    240
    Why, this 's no more. An old, decrepit wretch,
    That has no sense, no sinew; takes his meat
    With others' fingers; only knows to gape
    When you do scald his gums; a voice, a shadow;
    And what can this man hurt you?
*Celia.* [*Aside.*]                    Lord! What spirit
    Is this hath entered him?
*Corvino.*                    And for your fame,
    That's such a jig; [f] as if I would go tell it,
    Cry it on the Piazza! Who shall know it
    But he that cannot speak it, and this fellow,
    Whose lips are i' my pocket? Save yourself—    250
    If you'll proclaim't, you may. I know no other
    Should come to know it.
*Celia.*                    Are heaven and saints then nothing?
    Will they be blind or stupid?
*Corvino.*                    How?
*Celia.*                    Good sir,
    Be jealous still, emulate them; and think
    What hate they burn with toward every sin.
*Corvino.*    I grant you. If I thought it were a sin,
    I would not urge you. Should I offer this
    To some young Frenchman, or hot Tuscan blood,
    That had read Aretine, conned [g] all his prints,[h]
    Knew every quirk within lust's labyrinth,    260
    And were professed critic [i] in lechery;
    And I would look upon him, and applaud him—
    This were a sin. But here 'tis contrary:
    A pious work, mere charity, for physic,
    And honest polity [j] to assure mine own.
*Celia.*    O heaven! Canst thou suffer such a change?
*Volpone.*    Thou art mine honor, Mosca, and my pride,
    My joy, my tickling, my delight! Go bring 'em.
*Mosca.*    Please you draw near, sir.
*Corvino.*                    Come on, what—
    You will not be rebellious? By that light—    270
*Mosca.*    Sir, Signor Corvino, here, is come to see you.
*Volpone.*    Oh!
*Mosca.*                    And hearing of the consultation had,
    So lately, for your health, is come to offer,

---

[f] farce    [g] perused    [h] Aretino's sonnets were accompanied by porno-
graphic drawings    [i] specialist    [j] policy

      Or rather, sir, to prostitute—
*Corvino.*                        Thanks, sweet Mosca.
*Mosca.*   Freely, unasked, or unentreated—
*Corvino.*                                      Well!
*Mosca.*   As the true, fervent instance of his love,
      His own most fair and proper wife, the beauty
      Only of price ᵏ in Venice—
*Corvino.*                        'Tis well urged.
*Mosca.*   To be your comfortress, and to preserve you.
*Volpone.*   Alas, I am past, already! Pray you thank him     280
      For his good care and promptness; but for that,
      'Tis a vain labor e'en to fight 'gainst heaven,
      Applying fire to stone—uh, uh, uh, uh!—
      Making a dead leaf grow again. I take
      His wishes gently, though; and you may tell him
      What I've done for him. Marry, my state is hopeless!
      Will him to pray for me, and t' use his fortune
      With reverence when he comes to 't.
*Mosca.*                        Do you hear, sir?
      Go to him with your wife.
*Corvino.*                  Heart of my father!
      Wilt thou persist thus? Come, I pray thee, come.     290
      Thou seest 'tis nothing, Celia. By this hand,
      I shall grow violent. Come, do't, I say.
*Celia.*   Sir, kill me, rather. I will take down poison,
      Eat burning coals, do anything—
*Corvino.*                        Be damned!
      Heart, I will drag thee hence home by the hair,
      Cry thee a strumpet through the streets, rip up
      Thy mouth unto thine ears, and slit thy nose
      Like a raw rocket ˡ—Do not tempt me, come!
      Yield, I am loath—Death! I will buy some slave,
      Whom I will kill, and bind thee to him alive,     300
      And at my window hang you forth; devising
      Some monstrous crime, which I, in capital letters,
      Will eat into thy flesh with acquafortis ᵐ
      And burning corsives,ⁿ on this stubborn breast.
      Now, by the blood thou has incensed, I'll do't!
*Celia.*   Sir, what you please, you may; I am your martyr.
*Corvino.*   Be not thus obstinate; I ha' not deserved it.
      Think who it is entreats you. Pray thee, sweet—
      Good faith, thou shalt have jewels, gowns, attires,
      What thou wilt think, and ask. Do but go kiss him.     310
      Or touch him but. For my sake. At my suit.

ᵏ the most precious   ˡ a fish   ᵐ acid   ⁿ corrosives

This once. No? Not? I shall remember this!
Will you disgrace me thus? D'you thirst my undoing?

*Mosca.*    Nay, gentle lady, be advised.

*Corvino.*                                                      No, no.
She has watched her time. God's precious, this is
    scurvy,
'Tis very scurvy; and you are—

*Mosca.*                          Nay, good sir.

*Corvino.*    An arrant locust,° by heaven, a locust! Whore,
    Crocodile, that hast thy tears prepared,
    Expecting how thou'lt bid 'em flow.

*Mosca.*                              Nay, pray you, sir
She will consider.

*Celia.*                  Would my life would serve                    320
    To satisfy.

*Corvino.*    'Sdeath! If she would but speak to him,
    And save my reputation, 't were somewhat;
    But spitefully to affect my utter ruin!

*Mosca.*    Aye, now you've put your fortune in her hands.
    Why, i'faith, it is her modesty; I must quit ᵖ her.
    If you were absent, she would be more coming; �q
    I know it, and dare undertake ʳ for her.
    What woman can before her husband? Pray you,
    Let us depart, and leave her here.

*Corvino.*                          Sweet Celia,
    Thou mayst redeem all yet; I'll say no more.          330
    If not, esteem yourself as lost. Nay, stay there.
                                        [*Exit with* Mosca.]

*Celia.*    O God and his good angels! Whither, whither
    Is shame fled human breasts, that with such ease,
    Men dare put off your honors, and their own?
    Is that ˢ which ever was a cause of life
    Now placed beneath the basest circumstance,
    And modesty an exile made, for money?

*Volpone.* (*Leaps off from his couch.*)    Aye, in Corvino,
        and such earth-fed minds,
    That never tasted the true heav'n of love.
    Assure thee, Celia, he that would sell thee          340
    Only for hope of gain, and that uncertain,
    He would have sold his part of paradise
    For ready money, had he met a cope-man.ᵗ
    Why art thou 'mazed to see me thus revived?
    Rather applaud thy beauty's miracle;
    'Tis thy great work that hath, not now alone,

° downright plague  ᵖ acquit  �q willing  ʳ vouch  ˢ i.e., marriage  ᵗ merchant

But sundry times raised me in several shapes,
And, but this morning, like a mountebank,
To see thee at thy window. Aye, before
I would have left my practice ᵘ for thy love,          350
In varying figures I would have contended
With the blue Proteus,ᵛ or the hornèd flood.ʷ
Now art thou welcome.

*Celia.*                    Sir!
*Volpone.*                         Nay, fly me not.
Nor let thy false imagination
That I was bed-rid, make thee think I am so.
Thou shalt not find it. I am now as fresh,
As hot, as high, and in as jovial plight,
As when, in that so celebrated scene,
At recitation of our comedy
For entertainment of the great Valois,ˣ          360
I acted young Antinous; ʸ and attracted
The eyes and ears of all the ladies present,
T' admire each grateful gesture, note, and footing.

### Song.

"Come, my Celia, let us prove,ᶻ
    While we can, the sports of love.
    Time will not be ours forever,
    He at length our good will sever;
    Spend not then his gifts in vain.
    Suns that set may rise again;
    But if once we lose this light,          370
    'Tis with us perpetual night.
    Why should we defer our joys?
    Fame and rumor are but toys.

    Cannot we delude the eyes
    Of a few poor household spies?
    Or his easier ears beguile,
    Thus removèd by our wile?
    'Tis no sin love's fruits to steal,
    But the sweet thefts to reveal:
    To be taken, to be seen,          380
    These have crimes accounted been."

*Celia.*    Some sèrene ᵃ blast me, or dire lightning strike
    This my offending face.

u plotting  ᵛ a sea god who could change his shape at will  ʷ a river
god  ˣ Henry III of France, who visited Venice in 1574  ʸ favorite of the
Emperor Hadrian  ᶻ try  ᵃ infectious evening mist

*Volpone.*                     Why droops my Celia?
  Thou hast, in place of a base husband, found
  A worthy lover; use thy fortune well,
  With secrecy and pleasure. See, behold
  What thou art queen of, not in expectation—
  As I feed others—but possessed and crowned.
  See, here, a rope of pearl, and each more orient
  Than that the brave Egyptian queen caroused [b]——      390
  Dissolve and drink 'em. See, a carbuncle,
  May put out both the eyes of our St. Mark;
  A diamond would have bought Lollia Paulina, [c]
  When she came in like starlight, hid with jewels
  That were the spoils of provinces—take these
  And wear, and lose 'em; yet remains an earring
  To purchase them again, and this whole state.
  A gem but worth a private patrimony
  Is nothing; we will eat such at a meal.
  The heads of parrots, tongues of nightingales,      400
  The brains of peacocks, and of estriches,
  Shall be our food; and, could we get the phoenix, [d]
  Though nature lost her kind, [e] she were our dish.
*Celia.*   Good sir, these things might move a mind af-
    fected
  With such delights; but I, whose innocence
  Is all I can think wealthy, or worth th' enjoying,
  And which, once lost, I have nought to lose beyond it,
  Cannot be taken with these sensual baits.
  If you have conscience—
*Volpone.*                  'Tis the beggar's virtue.
  If thou hast wisdom, hear me, Celia.               410
  Thy baths shall be the juice of julyflowers, [f]
  Spirit of roses, and of violets,
  The milk of unicorns, and panthers' breath
  Gathered in bags, and mixed with Cretan wines.
  Our drink shall be preparèd gold and amber,
  Which we will take until my roof whirl round
  With the vertigo; and my dwarf shall dance,
  My eunuch sing, my fool make up the antic. [g]
  Whilst we, in changèd shapes, act Ovid's tales, [h]
  Thou like Europa [i] now, and I like Jove,         420
  Then I like Mars, and thou like Erycine; [j]
  So of the rest, till we have quite run through

---

  [b] Cleopatra, who drank pearls dissolved in vinegar   [c] wife of a Roman
governor   [d] mythical bird, of which only one existed   [e] species   [f] gilly-
flowers   [g] grotesque dance   [h] *Metamorphoses*   [i] abducted by Jove in the
form of a bull   [j] Venus

And wearied all the fables of the gods.
Then will I have thee in more modern forms,
Attirèd like some sprightly dame of France,
Brave Tuscan lady, or proud Spanish beauty;
Sometimes unto the Persian Sophy's [k] wife,
Or the Grand Signor's [l] mistress; and for change,
To one of our most artful courtesans,
Or some quick [m] Negro, or cold Russian.                    430
And I will meet thee in as many shapes;
Where we may so transfuse our wand'ring souls
Out at our lips, and score up sums of pleasures,

   "That the curious shall not know
     How to tell [n] them as they flow;
    And the envious, when they find
     What their number is, be pined." [o]

*Celia.*   If you have ears that will be pierced, or eyes
  That can be opened, a heart may be touched,
  Or any part that yet sounds man about you;                 440
  If you have touch of holy saints, or heaven,
  Do me the grace to let me 'scape. If not,
  Be bountiful and kill me. You do know
  I am a creature hither ill betrayed,
  By one whose shame I would forget it were.
  If you will deign me neither of these graces,
  Yet feed your wrath, sir, rather than your lust—
  It is a vice comes nearer manliness—
  And punish that unhappy crime of nature
  Which you miscall my beauty. Flay my face,                 450
  Or poison it with ointments, for seducing
  Your blood to this rebellion. Rub these hands
  With what may cause an eating leprosy,
  E'en to my bones and marrow—anything
  That may disfavor [p] me, save in my honor.
  And I will kneel to you, pray for you, pay down
  A thousand hourly vows, sir, for your health;
  Report and think you virtuous—
*Volpone.*             Think me cold,
  Frozen, and impotent, and so report me?
  That I had Nestor's hernia [q] thou wouldst think.         460
  I do degenerate, and abuse my nation,
  To play with opportunity thus long.
  I should have done the act, and then have parleyed.

[k] Shah  [l] Turkish Sultan  [m] lively  [n] count  [o] i.e., with envy  [p] disfigure  [q] i.e., so old as to be impotent

Yield, or I'll force thee.
*Celia.*                    O! Just God!
*Volpone.*                            In vain—
*Bonario.* (*Leaps out from where* Mosca *had placed him.*)
        Forbear, foul ravisher! Libidinous swine!
    Free the forced lady or thou diest, impostor.
    But that I am loath to snatch thy punishment
    Out of the hand of justice, thou shouldst yet
    Be made the timely sacrifice of vengeance,
    Before this altar, and this dross, thy idol.                    470
    Lady, let's quit the place; it is the den
    Of villainy. Fear nought, you have a guard;
    And he ere long shall meet his just reward.
                            [*Exeunt* Bonario *and* Celia.]
*Volpone.*    Fall on me, roof, and bury me in ruin!
    Become my grave, that wert my shelter! O!
    I am unmasked, unspirited,[r] undone,
    Betrayed to beggary, to infamy—


[*Enter* Mosca, *wounded*.]


*Mosca.*    Where shall I run, most wretched shame of men,
    To beat out my unlucky brains?
*Volpone.*                            Here, here.
    What! Dost thou bleed?
*Mosca.*                        O that his well-driv'n sword            480
    Had been so courteous to have cleft me down
    Unto the navel, ere I lived to see
    My life, my hopes, my spirits, my patron, all
    Thus desperately engagèd[s] by my error.
*Volpone.*    Woe on thy fortune.
*Mosca.*                            And my follies, sir.
*Volpone.*    Th'ast made me miserable.
*Mosca.*                                And myself, sir.
    Who would have thought he would have hearkened so?
*Volpone.*    What shall we do?
*Mosca.*                        I know not; if my heart
    Could expiate the mischance, I'd pluck it out.
    Will you be pleased to hang me, or cut my throat?            490
    And I'll requite[t] you, sir. Let's die like Romans,[u]
    Since we have lived like Grecians.[v]


(*They knock without.*)


[r] despondent    [s] caught    [t] reciprocate    [u] i.e., commit suicide    [v] i.e., dissolutely

*Volpone.*                                     Hark! Who's there?
  I hear some footing; officers, the *Saffi*,[w]
  Come to apprehend us! I do feel the brand
  Hissing already at my forehead; now
  Mine ears are boring.[x]
*Mosca.*                          To your couch, sir; you
  Make that place good, however.[y] [*Volpone lies down as
    before.*] Guilty men
  Suspect what they deserve still. Signor Corbaccio!

[*Enter* Corbaccio.]

*Corbaccio.*   Why, how now, Mosca?
*Mosca.*                              O, undone, amazed, sir!
  Your son—I know not by what accident—                    500
  Acquainted with your purpose to my patron,
  Touching your will, and making him your heir,
  Entered our house with violence, his sword drawn,
  Sought for you, called you wretch, unnatural,
  Vowed he would kill you.
*Corbaccio.*                  Me?
*Mosca.*                              Yes, and my patron.
*Corbaccio.*   This act shall disinherit him indeed!
  Here is the will.
*Mosca.*           'Tis well, sir.
*Corbaccio.*                        Right and well.
  Be you as careful [z] now for me.

[*Enter* Voltore, *behind.*]

*Mosca.*                              My life, sir,
  Is not more tendered; [a] I am only yours.
*Corbaccio.*   How does he? Will he die shortly, think'st
    thou?
*Mosca.*   I fear                                           510
  He'll outlast May.
*Corbaccio.*           Today?
*Mosca.*                        No, last out May, sir.
*Corbaccio.*   Couldst thou not gi' him a dram?
*Mosca.*                              O, by no means, sir.
*Corbaccio.*   Nay, I'll not bid you.
*Voltore.*                        This is a knave, I see.
*Mosca.* [*Aside.*]  How! Signor Voltore! Did he hear
    me?
*Voltore.*   Parasite!

---

[w] Venetian bailiffs     [x] being punctured     [y] in any case     [z] concerned
[a] cared for

*Mosca.*    Who's that? O sir, most timely welcome—
*Voltore.*                                          Scarce,
    To the discovery of your tricks, I fear.
    You are his only? And mine also, are you not?
*Mosca.*    Who? I, sir!
*Voltore.*                    You, sir. What device is this
    About a will?
*Mosca.*                A plot for you, sir.
*Voltore.*                                  Come,
    Put not your foists ᵇ upon me; I shall scent 'em.                    520
*Mosca.*    Did you not hear it?
*Voltore.*                            Yes, I hear Corbaccio
    Hath made your patron there his heir.
*Mosca.*                                    'Tis true;
    By my device, drawn to it by my plot,
    With hope—
*Voltore.*          Your patron should reciprocate?
    And you have promised?
*Mosca.*                        For your good I did, sir.
    Nay more, I told his son, brought, hid him here,
    Where he might hear his father pass the deed;
    Being persuaded to it by his thought, sir:
    That the unnaturalness, first, of the act,
    And then his father's oft disclaiming ᶜ in him—                    530
    Which I did mean t'help on—would sure enrage him
    To do some violence upon his parent;
    On which the law should take sufficient hold,
    And you be stated ᵈ in a double hope.
    Truth be my comfort, and my conscience,
    My only aim was to dig you a fortune
    Out of these two old rotten sepulchers—
*Voltore.*    I cry thee mercy, Mosca.
*Mosca.*                                Worth your patience,
    And your great merit, sir. And see the change!
*Voltore.*    Why, what success? ᵉ
*Mosca.*                        Most hapless! You must help, sir. 540
    Whilst we expected th' old raven, in comes
    Corvino's wife, sent hither by her husband—
*Voltore.*    What, with a present?
*Mosca.*                            No, sir, on visitation—
    I'll tell you how anon—and staying long,
    The youth he grows impatient, rushes forth,
    Seizeth the lady, wounds me, makes her swear—
    Or he would murder her, that was his vow—
    T' affirm my patron to have done her rape;

ᵇ (i) schemes (ii) stenches   ᶜ rejecting   ᵈ placed   ᵉ result

    Which how unlike it is, you see! And hence
    With that pretext he's gone, t' accuse his father,     550
    Defame my patron, defeat you—
*Voltore.*                   Where's her husband?
    Let him be sent for straight.
*Mosca.*             Sir, I'll go fetch him.
*Voltore.*   Bring him to the *Scrutineo*.[f]
*Mosca.*                Sir, I will.
*Voltore.*   This must be stopped.
*Mosca.*           O, you do nobly, sir.
    Alas, 'twas labored all, sir, for your good;
    Nor was there want of counsel in the plot.
    But fortune can, at any time, o'erthrow
    The projects of a hundred learnèd clerks,[g] sir.
*Corbaccio.*   What's that?
*Voltore.*           Will't please you, sir, to go along?
            [*Exit* Voltore, *followed by* Corbaccio.]
*Mosca.*   Patron, go in and pray for our success.     560
*Volpone.*   Need makes devotion. Heaven your labor bless!
                   [*Exeunt.*]


# ACT IV

### Scene I

### [*A street*]

[*Enter* Sir Politic Wouldbe *and* Peregrine.]

*Sir Politic.*    I told you, sir, it was a plot. You see
    What observation is. You mentioned [h] me
    For some instructions: I will tell you, sir,
    Since we are met here in this height of Venice,
    Some few particulars I have set down,
    Only for this meridian, fit to be known
    Of your crude traveler; and they are these.
    I will not touch, sir, at your phrase, or clothes,
    For they are old.
*Peregrine.*        Sir, I have better
*Sir Politic.*              Pardon,
    I meant, as they are themes.[i]

[f] Senate House   [g] scholars   [h] asked   [i] subjects to discuss

*Peregrine.*                    O sir, proceed.
    I'll slander you no more of wit, good sir.
*Sir Politic.*    First, for your garb,[j] it must be grave and
    serious,
    Very reserved and locked; not tell a secret
    On any terms, not to your father; scarce
    A fable, but with caution; make sure choice
    Both of your company and discourse; beware
    You never speak a truth—
*Peregrine.*                    How?
*Sir Politic.*                        Not to strangers,
    For those be they you must converse with most;
    Others I would not know,[k] sir, but at distance,
    So as I still might be a saver in 'em;[l]                    20
    You shall have tricks else passed upon you hourly.
    And then, for your religion, profess none,
    But wonder at the diversity of all;
    And, for your part, protest, were there no other
    But simply the laws o' th' land, you could content you.
    Nick Machiavel and Monsieur Bodin [m] both
    Were of this mind. Then must you learn the use
    And handling of your silver fork at meals,
    The metal [n] of your glass—these are main matters
    With your Italian—and to know the hour                    30
    When you must eat your melons and your figs.
*Peregrine.*    Is that a point of state, too?
*Sir Politic.*                        Here it is
    For your Venetian, if he see a man
    Preposterous [o] in the least, he has [p] him straight.
    He has; he strips him. I'll acquaint you, sir,
    I now have lived here 'tis some fourteen months,
    Within the first week of my landing here,
    All took me for a citizen of Venice.
    I knew the forms so well—
*Peregrine.* [*Aside.*]             And nothing else.
*Sir Politic.*    I had read Contarene,[q] took me a house,      40
    Dealt with my Jews to furnish it with movables—
    Well, if I could but find one man, one man
    To mine own heart, whom I durst trust, I would—
*Peregrine.*    What, what, sir?
*Sir Politic.*                    Make him rich; make him a
    fortune.
    He should not think [r] again. I would command it.
*Peregrine.*    As how?
*Sir Politic.*                    With certain projects that I have,

---

[j] outward bearing  [k] greet  [l] i.e., still retain their acquaintance  [m] a
French political philosopher  [n] material  [o] eccentric  [p] knows  [q] Con-
tarini, wrote a work on Venice  [r] i.e., about money

Which I may not discover.[s]

*Peregrine.* [*Aside.*]            If I had
But one [t] to wager with, I would lay odds now,
He tells me instantly.

*Sir Politic.*            One is—and that
I care not greatly who knows—to serve the state        50
Of Venice with red herrings for three years,
And at a certain rate, from Rotterdam,
Where I have correspondence. There's a letter,
Sent me from one o' th' States,[u] and to that purpose.
He cannot write his name, but that's his mark.

*Peregrine.*   He is a chandler?[v]

*Sir Politic.*                No, a cheesemonger.[w]
There are some other, too, with whom I treat
About the same negotiation;
And I will undertake it. For 'tis thus:
I'll do't with ease, I've cast [x] it all. Your hoy [y]     60
Carries but three men in her, and a boy,
And she shall make me three returns a year;
So if there come but one of three, I save;
If two, I can defalc.[z] But this is now,
If my main project fail.

*Peregrine.*            Then you have others?

*Sir Politic.*   I should be loath to draw the subtle air
Of such a place, without my thousand aims.
I'll not dissemble, sir, where'er I come,
I love to be considerative;[a] and 'tis true
I have at my free hours thought upon              70
Some certain goods unto the state of Venice,
Which I do call my cautions; and, sir, which
I mean, in hope of pension, to propound
To the Great Council, then unto the Forty,
So to the Ten. My means are made already—

*Peregrine.*   By whom?

*Sir Politic.*            Sir, one that though his place be
    obscure,
Yet he can sway, and they will hear him. He's
A *commendadore.*

*Peregrine.*            What! A common sergeant?

*Sir Politic.*   Sir, such as they are, put it in their mouths,
What they should say, sometimes, as well as greater.        80
I think I have my notes to show you—

*Peregrine.*                Good, sir.

---

[s] reveal  [t] someone  [u] a member of the States General of Holland
[v] candle merchant  [w] cheese merchant  [x] figured out  [y] small sloop
[z] reduce expenses  [a] thoughtful

*Sir Politic.*   But you shall swear unto me, on your
     gentry,
   Not to anticipate—
*Peregrine.*   I, sir?
*Sir Politic.*                    Nor reveal
   A circumstance—My paper is not with me.
*Peregrine.*   O, but you can remember, sir.
*Sir Politic.*                              My first is
   Concerning tinder-boxes. You must know,
   No family is here without its box.
   Now, sir, it being so portable a thing,
   Put case ᵇ that you or I were ill affected
   Unto the state; sir, with it in our pockets,          90
   Might not I go into the Arsenal?
   Or you? Come out again? And none the wiser?
*Peregrine.*   Except yourself, sir.
*Sir Politic.*                    Go to, then. I therefore
   Advertise to the state, how fit it were
   That none but such as were known patriots,
   Sound lovers of their country, should be suffered
   T' enjoy them in their houses; and even those
   Sealed at some office, and at such a bigness
   As might not lurk in pockets.
*Peregrine.*                    Admirable!
*Sir Politic.*   My next is, how t' inquire, and be resolved    100
   By present demonstration, whether a ship,
   Newly arrivèd from Soria,ᶜ or from
   Any suspected part of all the Levant,
   Be guilty of the plague. And, where they use
   To lie out forty, fifty days, sometimes,
   About the *Lazaretto,*ᵈ for their trial;
   I'll save that charge and loss unto the merchant,
   And in an hour clear the doubt.
*Peregrine.*                    Indeed, sir!
*Sir Politic.*   Or—I will lose my labor.
*Peregrine.*                              My faith, that's much.
*Sir Politic.*   Nay, sir, conceive me. 'Twill cost me, in    110
     onions,
   Some thirty livres ᵉ—
*Peregrine.*              Which is one pound sterling.
*Sir Politic.*   Beside my waterworks. For this I do, sir:
   First, I bring in your ship 'twixt two brick walls—
   But those the state shall venture. On the one
   I strain ᶠ me a fair tarpaulin, and in that

   ᵇ assume   ᶜ Syria   ᵈ place of quarantine   ᵉ French money   ᶠ stretch

　　I stick my onions, cut in halves; the other
　　Is full of loopholes, out at which I thrust
　　The noses of my bellows; and those bellows
　　I keep, with waterworks, in perpetual motion,
　　Which is the easiest matter of a hundred.　　　　　120
　　Now, sir, your onion, which doth naturally
　　Attract th' infection, and your bellows blowing
　　The air upon him,[g] will show instantly,
　　By his changed color, if there be contagion;
　　Or else remain as fair as at the first.
　　Now 'tis known, 'tis nothing.

*Peregrine.*　　　　　　　　You are right, sir.
*Sir Politic.*　I would I had my note.

*Peregrine.*　　　　　　　　Faith, so would I.
　　But you ha' done well for once, sir.

*Sir Politic.*　　　　　　　　Were I false,
　　Or would be made so, I could show you reasons
　　How I could sell this state now to the Turk,　　　130
　　Spite of their galleys, or their—

*Peregrine.*　　　　　　　　Pray you, Sir Poll.
*Sir Politic.*　I have 'em not about me.

*Peregrine.*　　　　　　　　That I feared.
　　They 're there, sir?

*Sir Politic.*　　　　　　No, this is my diary,
　　Wherein I note my actions of the day.

*Peregrine.*　Pray you let's see, sir. What is here?—
　　　"*Notandum.*
　　A rat had gnawn my spur-leathers; notwithstanding,
　　I put on new, and did go forth; but first
　　I threw three beans over the threshold. Item,
　　I went and bought two toothpicks, whereof one
　　I burst immediately, in a discourse　　　　　140
　　With a Dutch merchant, 'bout *ragion del stato*.[h]
　　From him I went and paid a *muccinigo*
　　For piecing [i] my silk stocking; by the way
　　I cheapened sprats; [j] and at St. Mark's I urined."
　　Faith these are politic notes!

*Sir Politic.*　　　　　　Sir, I do slip[k]
　　No action of my life, thus, but I quote it.

*Peregrine.*　Believe me, it is wise!
*Sir Politic.*　　　　　　　Nay, sir, read forth.

[*Enter* Lady Wouldbe, Nano, *and two* Women.]

[g] it　　[h] affairs of state　　[i] sewing　　[j] bargained for herrings　　[k] overlook

*Lady Wouldbe.*    Where should this loose knight be,
    trow? Sure, he's housed.
*Nano.*    Why, then he's fast.
*Lady Wouldbe.*                        Aye, he plays both [1] with me.
  I pray you stay. This heat will do more harm                    150
  To my complexion than his heart is worth.
  I do not care to hinder, but to take him.
  How it comes off!
*1st Woman.*    My master's yonder.
*Lady Wouldbe.*                        Where?
*2nd Woman.*    With a young gentleman.
*Lady Wouldbe.*                        That same's the party,
  In man's apparel! Pray you, sir, jog my knight.
  I will be tender to his reputation,
  However he demerit.[m]
*Sir Politic.*            My lady!
*Peregrine.*                        Where?
*Sir Politic.*    'Tis she indeed, sir, you shall know her.
    She is,
  Were she not mine, a lady of that merit,
  For fashion and behavior; and for beauty                          160
  I durst compare—
*Peregrine.*        It seems you are not jealous,
  That dare commend her.
*Sir Politic.*                        Nay, and for discourse—
*Peregrine.*    Being your wife, she cannot miss that.
*Sir Politic.*                                    Madam,
  Here is a gentleman, pray you, use him fairly;
  He seems a youth, but he is—
*Lady Wouldbe.*                    None?
*Sir Politic.*                            Yes, one
  Has put his face as soon into the world—
*Lady Wouldbe.*    You mean, as early? But today?
*Sir Politic.*                                How's this?
*Lady Wouldbe.*    Why, in this habit, sir, you apprehend
    me.
  Well, Master Wouldbe, this doth not become you.
  I had thought the odor, sir, of your good name                    170
  Had been more precious to you; that you would not
  Have done this dire massàcre on your honor;
  One of your gravity, and rank besides!
  But knights, I see, care little for the oath
  They make to ladies, chiefly their own ladies.
*Sir Politic.*    Now, by my spurs, the symbol of my
    knighthood—

---

[1] i.e., both fast and loose    [m] however he is undeserving

*Peregrine*. [*Aside*].    Lord, how his brain is humbled for
    an oath!
*Sir Politic*.    I reach ⁿ you not.
*Lady Wouldbe*.                    Right, sir, your polity °
    May bear it through thus. [*To* Peregrine.] Sir, a word
      with you.
    I would be loath to còntest publicly                    180
    With any gentlewoman, or to seem
    Froward, or violent, as the courtier ᵖ says—
    It comes too near rusticity in a lady,
    Which I would shun by all means. And, however
    I may deserve from Master Wouldbe, yet
    T' have one fair gentlewoman thus be made
    Th' unkind instrument to wrong another,
    And one she knows not, aye, and to persèver,
    In my poor judgment, is not warranted
    From being a solecism �q in our sex,                    190
    If not in manners.
*Peregrine*.        How is this!
*Sir Politic*.                    Sweet madam,
    Come nearer to your aim.
*Lady Wouldbe*.                    Marry, and will, sir.
    Since you provoke me with your impudence,
    And laughter of your light ʳ land-siren here,
    Your Sporus,ˢ your hermaphrodite—
*Peregrine*.                    What's here?
    Poetic fury and historic storms!
*Sir Politic*.    The gentleman, believe it, is of worth,
    And of our nation.
*Lady Wouldbe*.    Aye, your Whitefriars ᵗ nation!
    Come, I blush for you, Master Wouldbe, I;
    And am ashamed you should ha' no more forehead ᵘ    200
    Than thus to be the patron, or St. George,
    To a lewd harlot, a base fricatrice,ᵛ
    A female devil in a male outside.
*Sir Politic*.                    Nay,
    And you be such a one, I must bid adieu
    To your delights. The case appears too liquid.ʷ

                             [*Exit*.]
*Lady Wouldbe*.    Aye, you may carry't clear, with your
    state-face! ˣ
    But for your carnival concupiscence,ʸ

---

ⁿ understand  ° shrewdness  ᵖ i.e., Castiglione, author of the courtesy
book, *The Courtier*  q i.e., it would be a breach of etiquette  ʳ loose
ˢ Nero's eunuch  ᵗ a section of London inhabited by criminals  ᵘ shame
ᵛ prostitute  ʷ clear  ˣ official countenance  ʸ i.e., the flamboyant object
of your lust

Who here is fled for liberty of conscience.
From furious persecution of the Marshal,ᶻ
Her will I disc'ple.ᵃ
*Peregrine.*      This is fine, i' faith!     210
And do you use this often? Is this part
Of your wit's exercise, 'gainst ᵇ you have occasion?
Madam—
*Lady Wouldbe.*   Go to, sir.
*Peregrine.*      Do you hear me, lady?
Why, if your knight have set you to beg shirts,
Or to invite me home, you might have done it
A nearer way ᶜ by far.
*Lady Wouldbe.*   This cannot work you
Out of my snare.
*Peregrine.*     Why, am I in it, then?
Indeed your husband told me you were fair,
And so you are; only your nose inclines—
That side that's next the sun—to the queen-apple.ᵈ   220
*Lady Wouldbe.*   This cannot be endured by any
patience.

[*Enter* Mosca.]

*Mosca.*   What's the matter, madam?
*Lady Wouldbe.*      If the Senate
Right not my quest in this, I will protest 'em
To all the world no aristocracy.
*Mosca.*   What is the injury, lady?
*Lady Wouldbe.*      Why, the callet ᵉ
You told me of, here I have ta'en disguised.
*Mosca.*   Who? This! What means your ladyship? The
creature
I mentioned to you is apprehended now
Before the Senate. You shall see her—
*Lady Wouldbe.*      Where?
*Mosca.*   I'll bring you to her. This young gentleman,   230
I saw him land this morning at the port.
*Lady Wouldbe.*   Is't possible? How has my judgment
wandered!
Sir, I must, blushing, say to you I have erred,
And plead your pardon.
*Peregrine.*      What, more changes yet?
*Lady Wouldbe.*   I hope y' ha' not the malice to remember
A gentlewoman's passion. If you stay
In Venice here, please you to use me, sir—

ᶻ an officer of an English court of law ᵃ punish ᵇ when ᶜ more directly ᵈ i.e., your nose is apple-red ᵉ harlot

*Mosca.*   Will you go, madam?
*Lady Wouldbe.*                    Pray you, sir, use me. In faith,
  The more you see me, the more I shall conceive
  You have forgot our quarrel.
        [*Exeunt* Lady Wouldbe, Mosca, Nano, *and* Women.]
*Peregrine.*                    This is rare!                    240
  Sir Politic Wouldbe? No, Sir Politic Bawd,
  To bring me thus acquainted with his wife!
  Well, wise Sir Poll, since you have practiced ᶠ thus
  Upon my freshmanship, I'll try your salt-head,ᵍ
  What proof it is against a counter-plot.          [*Exit.*]


## Scene II

### [*The Scrutineo.*]

[*Enter* Voltore, Corbaccio, Corvino, *and* Mosca.]


*Voltore.*   Well, now you know the carriage ʰ of the
      business,
  Your constancy is all that is required
  Unto the safety of it.
*Mosca.*                    Is the lie
  Safely conveyed amongst us? Is that sure?
  Knows every man his burden? ⁱ
*Corvino.*                    Yes.
*Mosca.*                                Then shrink not.
*Corvino.* [*Aside to* Mosca.]   But knows the advocate
      the truth?
*Mosca.*                    O sir,
  By no means. I devised a formal ʲ tale
  That salved your reputation. But be valient, sir.
*Corvino.*   I fear no one but him, that this his pleading
  Should make him stand for a co-heir—                    10
*Mosca.*                                Co-halter!
  Hang him, we will but use his tongue, his noise,
  As we do Croaker's ᵏ here.
*Corvino.*                    Aye, what shall he do?
*Mosca.*   When we have done, you mean?
*Corvino.*                                Yes.
*Mosca.*                                Why, we'll think:
  Sell him for mummia; ˡ he's half dust already. (*To*
      Voltore.)

---

ᶠ schemed   ᵍ test your sophistication   ʰ purpose   ⁱ i.e., role   ʲ cred-
ible   ᵏ i.e., Corbaccio   ˡ medicine made from mummies

Do not you smile to see this buffalo,[m]
How he doth sport it with his head? I should,
If all were well and past. (*To* Corbaccio.)     Sir, only you
Are he that shall enjoy the crop of all,
And these not know for whom they toil.

*Corbaccio.*                              Aye, peace.

*Mosca.* (*To* Corvino.)     But you shall eat it. [*Aside.*]
    Much! (*To* Voltore.) Worshipful sir,          20
  Mercury [n] sit upon your thund'ring tongue,
  Or the French Hercules,[o] and make your language
  As conquering as his club, to beat along,
  As with a tempest, flat, our adversaries;
  But much more yours, sir.

*Voltore.*                              Here they come, ha' done.

*Mosca.*     I have another witness, if you need, sir,
  I can produce.

*Voltore.*          Who is it?

*Mosca.*                    Sir, I have her.

[*Enter four* Avocatori, Bonario, Celia, Notario,
    Commendadori, *etc.*]

*1st Avocatore.*     The like of this the Senate never heard
    of.

*2nd Avocatore.*     'Twill come most strange to them,
  when we report it.

*4th Avocatore.*     The gentlewoman has been ever held
  Of unreprovèd name.                          30

*3rd Avocatore.*     So the young man.

*4th Avocatore.*     The more unnatural part that of his
  father.

*2nd Avocatore.*     More of the husband.

*1st Avocatore.*                         I not know to give
  His act a name, it is so monstrous!

*4th Avocatore.*     But the impostor, he is a thing created
  T' exceed example!

*1st Avocatore.*     And all after-times!

*2nd Avocatore.*     I never heard a true voluptuary
  Described, but him.

*3rd Avocatore.*     Appear yet those were cited?

*Notario.*     All but the old magnifico,[p] Volpone.

*1st Avocatore.*     Why is not he here?

*Mosca.*                    Please your fatherhoods,     40
  Here is his advocate. Himself's so weak,
  So feeble—

*4th Avocatore.*     What are you?

---

[m] i.e., Corvino, because of his horns   [n] god of eloquence   [o] Ogmius,
Celtic symbol of eloquence   [p] Venetian nobleman

*Bonario*.                              His parasite,
　His knave, his pander. I beseech the court
　He may be forced to come, that your grave eyes
　May bear strong witness of his strange impostures.
*Voltore*.    Upon my faith and credit with your virtues,
　He is not able to endure the air.
*2nd Avocatore*.    Bring him, however.
*3rd Avocatore*.                          We will see him.
*4th Avocatore*.    Fetch him.        [*Exeunt* Officers.]
*Voltore*.    Your fatherhoods' fit pleasures be obeyed,
　But sure the sight will rather move your pities        50
　Than indignation. May it please the court,
　In the meantime, he may be heard in me:
　I know this place most void of prejudice,
　And therefore crave it, since we have no reason
　To fear our truth should hurt our cause.
*3rd Avocatore*.                          Speak free.
*Voltore*.    Then know, most honored fathers, I must now
　Discover to your strangely abusèd ᑫ ears
　The most prodigious and most frontless ʳ piece
　Of solid impudence and treachery                      60
　That ever vicious nature yet brought forth
　To shame the state of Venice. This lewd woman,
　That wants no artificial looks or tears
　To help the visor she has now put on,
　Hath long been known a close ˢ adulteress
　To that lascivious youth there; not suspected,
　I say, but known, and taken in the act
　With him; and by this man, the easy husband,
　Pardoned; whose timeless bounty ᵗ makes him now
　Stand here, the most unhappy, innocent person
　That ever man's own goodness made accused.             70
　For these, not knowing how to owe ᵘ a gift
　Of that dear grace, but with their shame; being placed
　So above all powers of their gratitude,
　Began to hate the benefit; and in place
　Of thanks, devise t' extirp ᵛ the memory
　Of such an act. Wherein, I pray your fatherhoods
　To observe the malice, yea, the rage of creatures
　Discovered in their evils; and what heart
　Such take, even from their crimes. But that anon
　Will more appear. This gentleman, the father,        80
　Hearing of this foul fact, ʷ with many others,
　Which daily struck at his too tender ears,

---

ᑫ deceived    ʳ shameless    ˢ secret    ᵗ untimely
mercy    ᵘ value    ᵛ tear
out    ʷ crime

And grieved in nothing more than that he could not
Preserve himself a parent—his son's ills
Growing to that strange flood—at last decreed
To disinherit him.
*1st Avocatore.*    These be strange turns!
*2nd Avocatore.*    The young man's fame was ever fair
   and honest.
*Voltore.*    So much more full of danger is his vice,
   That can beguile so, under shade of virtue.
   But, as I said, my honored sires, his father          90
   Having this settled purpose—by what means
   To him betrayed, we know not—and this day
   Appointed for the deed; that parricide,
   I cannot style him better, by confederacy
   Preparing this his paramour to be there,
   Entered Volpone's house—who was the man,
   Your fatherhoods must understand, designed
   For the inheritance—there sought his father.
   But with what purpose sought he him, my lords?
   I tremble to pronounce it, that a son          100
   Unto a father, and to such a father,
   Should have so foul, felonious intent:
   It was to murder him! When, being prevented
   By his more happy absence, what then did he?
   Not check his wicked thoughts; no, now new deeds—
   Mischief doth never end where it begins—
   An act of horror, fathers! He dragged forth
   The agèd gentleman that had there lain bed-rid
   Three years and more, out off his innocent couch,
   Naked, upon the floor, there left him; wounded          110
   His servant in the face; and with this strumpet,
   The stale [x] to his forged practice, who was glad
   To be so active—I shall here desire
   Your fatherhoods to note but my collections,[y]
   As most remarkable—thought at once to stop
   His father's ends, discredit his free choice
   In the old gentleman, redeem themselves
   By laying infamy upon this man,
   To whom, with blushing, they should owe their lives.
*1st Avocatore.*    What proofs have you of this?
*Bonario.*                        Most honored fathers,  120
   I humbly crave there be no credit given
   To this man's mercenary tongue.
*2nd Avocatore.*                        Forbear.
*Bonario.*    His soul moves in his fee.

   [x] decoy    [y] evidence

*3rd Avocatore.*                        O, sir!
*Bonario.*                                    This fellow,
  For six sols ᶻ more would plead against his Maker.
*1st Avocatore.*    You do forget yourself.
*Voltore.*                            Nay, nay, grave fathers,
  Let him have scope. Can any man imagine
  That he will spare 's accuser, that would not
  Have spared his parent?
*1st Avocatore*            Well, produce your proofs.
*Celia.*    I would I could forget I were a creature!
*Voltore.*    Signor Corbaccio!
*4th Avocatore.*                    What is he?
*Voltore.*                            The father.                    130
*2nd Avocatore.*    Has he had an oath?
*Notario.*                            Yes.
*Corbaccio.*                        What must I do now?
*Notario.*    Your testimony's craved.
*Corbaccio.*                        Speak to the knave?
  I'll ha' my mouth first stopped with earth. My heart
  Abhors his knowledge. I disclaim in ᵃ him.
*1st Avocatore.*    But for what cause?
*Corbaccio.*                    The mere portent ᵇ of nature.
  He is an utter stranger to my loins.
*Bonario.*    Have they made ᶜ you to this?
*Corbaccio.*                        I will not hear thee,
  Monster of men, swine, goat, wolf, parricide!
  Speak not, thou viper.
*Bonario.*                Sir, I will sit down,
  And rather wish my innocence should suffer,            140
  Than I resist the authority of a father.
*Voltore.*    Signor Corvino!
*2nd Avocatore.*        This is strange.
*1st Avocatore.*                        Who's this?
*Notario.*    The husband.
*4th Avocatore.*            Is he sworn?
*Notario.*                        He is.
*3rd Avocatore.*                        Speak, then.
*Corvino.*    This woman, please your fatherhoods, is a
      whore
  Of most hot exercise, more than a partridge,
  Upon recòrd—
*1st Avocatore.*    No more.
*Corvino.*                Neighs like a jennet. ᵈ
*Notario.*    Preserve the honor of the court.
*Corvino.*                            I shall,

ᶻ halfpennies   ᵃ disown   ᵇ complete   monster   ᶜ coached   ᵈ horse   (in
heat)

And modesty of your most reverend ears.
And yet I hope that I may say these eyes
Have seen her glued unto that piece of cedar,                    150
That fine, well-timbered gallant; and that here
The letters may be read, thorough ᵉ the horn [*making the
  cuckold's sign*],
That make the story perfect.ᶠ

*Mosca.* [*Aside.*]                        Excellent, sir!
*Corvino.* [*Aside.*]    There is no shame in this now, is
  there?
*Mosca.* [*Aside.*]                                    None
*Corvino.*    Or if I said, I hoped that she were onward
  To her damnation, if there be a hell
  Greater than whore and woman; a good Catholic
  May make the doubt.
*3rd Avocatore.*            His grief hath made him frantic.
*1st Avocatore.*    Remove him hence.

(Celia *swoons.*)

*2nd Avocatore.*                        Look to the woman.
*Corvino.*                                        Rare!
  Prettily feigned again!
*4th Avocatore.*                Stand from about her.        160
*1st Avocatore.*    Give her the air.
*3rd Avocatore.* [*To* Mosca.]    What can you say?
*Mosca.*                                    My wound,
  May 't please your wisdoms, speaks for me, received
  In aid of my good patron, when he missed
  His sought-for father, when that well-taught dame
  Had her cue given her to cry out a rape.
*Bonario.*    O most laid ᵍ impudence! Fathers—
*3rd Avocatore.*                            Sir, be silent;
  You had your hearing free, so must they theirs.
*2nd Avocatore.*    I do begin to doubt ʰ th' imposture
  here.
*4th Avocatore.*    This woman has too many moods.
*Voltore.*                            Grave fathers,        170
  She is a creature of a most professed
  And prostituted lewdness.
*Corvino.*                        Most impetuous,
  Unsatisfied, grave fathers!
*Voltore.*                        May her feignings
  Not take your widsoms; but this day she baited
  A stranger, a grave knight, with her loose eyes

  ᵉ through    ᶠ complete    ᵍ contrived    ʰ suspect

    And more lascivious kisses. This man saw 'em
    Together on the water in a gondola.
*Mosca.*    Here is the lady herself, that saw 'em too,
    Without; who then had in the open streets
    Pursued them, but for saving her knight's honor.
*1st Avocatore.*    Produce that lady.
*2nd Avocatore.*             Let her come. [*Exit* Mosca.]
*4th Avocatore.*                 These things,  180
    They strike with wonder!
*3rd Avocatore*          I am turned a stone!

[*Re-enter* Mosca *with* Lady Wouldbe.]

*Mosca.*    Be resolute, madam.
*Lady Wouldbe.*          Aye, this same is she.
    Out, thou chameleon harlot! Now thine eyes
    Vie tears with the hyena.[1] Dar'st thou look
    Upon my wrongèd face? I cry your pardons.
    I fear I have forgettingly transgressed
    Against the dignity of the court—
*2nd Avocatore.*           No, madam,
*Lady Wouldbe.*    And been exorbitant[j]—
*4th Avocatore.*           You have not, lady,
    These proofs are strong.
*Lady Wouldbe.*        Surely, I had no purpose
    To scandalize your honors, or my sex's.  190
*3rd Avocatore.*    We do believe it.
*Lady Wouldbe.*         Surely you may believe it.
*2nd Avocatore.*    Madam, we do.
*Lady Wouldbe.*         Indeed you may, my breeding
    Is not so coarse—
*4th Avocatore.*    We know it.
*Lady Wouldbe.*         To offend
    With pertinacy[k]—
*3rd Avocatore.*    Lady—
*Lady Wouldbe.*         Such a presence!
    No surely.
*1st Avocatore.*    We well think it.
*Lady Wouldbe.*          You may think it.
*1st Avocatore.*    Let her o'ercome. What witnesses
    have you,
    To make good your report?
*Bonario.*         Our consciences.
*Celia.*    And heaven, that never fails the innocent.
*4th Avocatore.*    These are no testimonies.

[1] a hyena supposedly shed false tears to attract its prey   [j] out of order  [k] pertinacity

*Bonario.*                                        Not in your courts,
    Where multitude and clamor overcomes.                    200
*1st Avocatore.*    Nay, then you do wax insolent.


*Volpone is brought in, as impotent.*


*Voltore.*                                        Here, here
    The testimony comes that will convince,
    And put to utter dumbness their bold tongues!
    See here, grave fathers, here's the ravisher,
    The rider on men's wives, the great impostor,
    The grand voluptuary! Do you not think
    These limbs should affect venery? [1] Or these eyes
    Covet a concubine? Pray you mark these hands;
    Are they not fit to stroke a lady's breasts?
    Perhaps he doth dissemble?
*Bonario.*                          So he does.                    210
*Voltore.*    Would you ha' him tortured?
*Bonario.*                          I would have him proved.
*Voltore.*    Best try him then with goads, or burning irons;
    Put him to the strappado.[m] I have heard
    The rack hath cured the gout—faith, give it him,
    And help him of a malady; be courteous.
    I'll undertake, before these honored fathers,
    He shall have yet as many left diseases
    As she has known adulterers, or thou strumpets.
    O my most equal [n] hearers, if these deeds,
    Acts of this bold and most exorbitant strain,                    220
    May pass with sufferance, what one citizen
    But owes the forfeit of his life, yea, fame,
    To him that dares traduce him? Which of you
    Are safe, my honored fathers? I would ask,
    With leave of your grave fatherhoods, if their plot
    Have any face or color like to truth?
    Or if, unto the dullest nostril here,
    It smell not rank and most abhorrèd slander?
    I crave your care of this good gentleman,
    Whose life is much endangered by their fable;                    230
    And as for them, I will conclude with this:
    That vicious persons, when they are hot, and fleshed [o]
    In impious acts, their constancy abounds.
    Damned deeds are done with greatest confidence.
*1st Avocatore.*    Take 'em to custody, and sever [p]
    them.

---

[1] licentiousness    [m] form of torture    [n] just    [o] satiated    [p] separate

*2nd Avocatore.*    'Tis pity two such prodigies should
    live.
*1st Avocatore.*    Let the old gentleman be returned with
    care.                          [*Exeunt* Officers *with* Volpone.]
    I'm sorry our credulity wronged him.
*4th Avocatore.*    These are two creatures!
*3rd Avocatore.*                    I have an earthquake in me!
*2nd Avocatore.*    Their shame, even in their cradles, fled
    their faces.                                               240
*4th Avocatore.* [*To* Voltore.]    You've done a worthy
    service to the state, sir,
    In their discovery.
*1st Avocatore.*    You shall hear ere night
    What punishment the court decrees upon 'em.
            [*Exeunt* Avocatori, Notario, *and* Commendadori
                            *with* Bonario *and* Celia.]
*Voltore.*    We thank your fatherhoods. How like you it?
*Mosca.*                                      Rare.
    I'd ha' your tongue, sir, tipped with gold for this;
    I'd ha' you be the heir to the whole city;
    The earth I'd have want [q] men, ere you want living.
    They're bound to erect your statue in St. Mark's.
    Signor Corvino, I would have you go
    And show yourself, that you have conquered.
*Corvino.*                                      Yes.        250
*Mosca.*    It was much better that you should profess
    Yourself a cuckold thus, than that the other
    Should have been proved.
*Corvino.*                    Nay, I considered that.
    Now it is her fault.
*Mosca.*                    Then it had been yours.
*Corvino.*    True. I do doubt this advocate still.
*Mosca.*                                      I' faith,
    You need not; I dare ease you of that care.
*Corvino.*    I trust thee, Mosca.                    [*Exit.*]
*Mosca.*                    As your own soul, sir.
*Corbaccio.*                                      Mosca!
*Mosca.*    Now for your business, sir.
*Corbaccio.*                    How! Ha' you business?
*Mosca.*    Yes, yours, sir.
*Corbaccio.*                    O, none else?
*Mosca.*                    None else, not I.
*Corbaccio.*    Be careful, then.
*Mosca.*                    Rest you with both your eyes, [r] sir.  260

[q] lack    [r] i.e., leave it to me

*Corbaccio.*    Dispatch it.
*Mosca.*                        Instantly.
*Corbaccio.*                        And look that all
  Whatever be put in, jewels, plate, moneys,
  Household stuff, bedding, curtains.
*Mosca.*                        Curtain-rings, sir;
  Only the advocate's fee must be deducted.
*Corbaccio.*    I'll pay him now; you'll be too prodigal.
*Mosca.*    Sir, I must tender it.
*Corbaccio.*                    Two *cecchines* is well?
*Mosca.*    No, six, sir.
*Corbaccio.*            'Tis too much.
*Mosca.*                        He talked a great while,
  You must consider that, sir.
*Corbaccio.*                    Well, there's three—
*Mosca.*    I'll give it him.
*Corbaccio.*            Do so, and there's for thee.
                                              *[Exit.]*

*Mosca.* [*Aside.*]    Bountiful bones! What horrid                    270
    strange offense
  Did he commit 'gainst nature, in his youth,
  Worthy this age? [*To* Voltore.] You see, sir, how I work
  Unto your ends; take you no notice.
*Voltore.*                    No,
  I'll leave you.                    *[Exit.]*
*Mosca.*            All is yours, the devil and all,
  Good advocate! Madam, I'll bring you home.
*Lady Wouldbe.*    No, I'll go see your patron.
*Mosca.*                        That you shall not.
  I'll tell you why: my purpose is to urge
  My patron to reform [8] his will, and for
  The zeal you've shown today, whereas before
  You were but third or fourth, you shall be now                    280
  Put in the first; which would appear as begged
  If you were present. Therefore—
*Lady Wouldbe.*    You shall sway me.            *[Exeunt.]*

    [8] alter

# ACT V

## *Scene I*

### [Volpone's *house*]

[*Enter* Volpone.]

*Volpone.*   Well, I am here, and all this brunt [t] is past.
　I ne'er was in dislike with my disguise
　Till this fled moment. Here 'twas good, in private;
　But in your public—*Cavè*,[u] whilst I breathe.
　'Fore God, my left leg 'gan to have the cramp,
　And I apprehended straight some power had struck me
　With a dead palsy. Well, I must be merry,
　And shake it off. A many of these fears
　Would put me into some villainous disease,
　Should they come thick upon me. I'll prevent 'em.　　　　10
　Give me a bowl of lusty wine, to fright
　This humor from my heart. (*Drinks.*) Hum, hum, hum!
　'Tis almost gone already; I shall conquer.
　Any device, now, of rare, ingenious knavery,
　That would possess me with a violent laughter,
　Would make me up again. (*Drinks again.*) So, so, so, so!
　This heat is life; 'tis blood by this time! Mosca!

[*Enter* Mosca.]

*Mosca.*   How now, sir? Does the day look clear again?
　Are we recovered, and wrought out of error,
　Into our way, to see our path before us?　　　　20
　Is our trade free once more?
*Volpone.*　　　　　　　　　　Exquisite Mosca!
*Mosca.*   Was it not carried learnedly?
*Volpone.*　　　　　　　　　　　　And stoutly.
　Good wits are greatest in extremities.
*Mosca.*   It were a folly beyond thought, to trust
　Any grand act unto a cowardly spirit.
　You are not taken with it enough, methinks.
*Volpone.*   O, more than if I had enjoyed the wench.
　The pleasure of all womankind's not like it.
*Mosca.*   Why, now you speak, sir. We must here be
　fixed;

[t] crisis　[u] Beware

Here we must rest. This is our masterpiece;                    30
We cannot think to go beyond this.

*Volpone.*                              True,
Th'ast played thy prize, my precious Mosca.

*Mosca.*                                    Nay, sir,
To gull the court—

*Volpone.*            And quite divert the torrent
Upon the innocent.

*Mosca.*                    Yes, and to make
So rare a music out of discords—

*Volpone.*                          Right.
That yet to me's the strangest; how th'ast borne it!
That these, being so divided 'mongst themselves,
Should not scent somewhat, or in me or thee,
Or doubt their own side.

*Mosca.*                        True, they will not see't.
Too much light blinds 'em, I think. Each of 'em          40
Is so possessed and stuffed with his own hopes
That anything unto the contrary,
Never so true, or never so apparent,
Never so palpable, they will resist it—

*Volpone.*    Like a temptation of the devil.

*Mosca.*                                Right, sir.
Merchants may talk of trade, and your great signors
Of land that yields well; but if Italy
Have any glebe ⱽ more fruitful than these fellows,
I am deceived. Did not your advocate rare?

*Volpone.*    O—"My most honored fathers, my grave fa-
      thers,                                              50
Under correction of your fatherhoods,
What face of truth is here? If these strange deeds
May pass, most honored fathers"—I had much ado
To forbear laughing.

*Mosca.*                    'T seemed to me you sweat, sir.

*Volpone.*    In troth, I did a little.

*Mosca.*                          But confess, sir,
Were you not daunted?

*Volpone.*            In good faith, I was
A little in a mist, but not dejected;
Never, but still myself.

*Mosca.*                    I think it, sir.
Now, so truth help me, I must needs say this, sir,
And out of conscience for your advocate:                  60
He's taken pains, in faith, sir, and deserved,
In my poor judgment, I speak it under favor,

ⱽ soil

Not to contrary you, sir, very richly—
Well—to be cozened.[w]

*Volpone.*          Troth, and I think so too,
By that I heard him in the latter end.

*Mosca.*    O, but before, sir, had you heard him first
Draw it to certain heads,[x] then aggravate,
Then use his vehement figures [y]—I looked still
When he would shift a shirt; [z] and doing this
Out of pure love, no hope of gain—

*Volpone.*          'Tis right.       70
I cannot answer [a] him, Mosca, as I would,
Not yet; but for thy sake, at thy entreaty,
I will begin ev'n now—to vex 'em all,
This very instant.

*Mosca.*        Good, sir.

*Volpone.*         Call the dwarf
And eunuch forth.

*Mosca.*       Castrone! Nano!

[*Enter* Castrone *and* Nano.]

*Nano.*              Here.

*Volpone.*    Shall we have a jig now?

*Mosca.*        What you please, sir.

*Volpone.*            Go,
Straight give out about the streets, you two,
That I am dead; do it with constancy,
Sadly, do you hear? Impute it to the grief
Of this late slander.     [*Exeunt* Castrone *and* Nano.]

*Mosca.*        What do you mean, sir?     80

*Volpone.*          O,
I shall have instantly my vulture, crow,
Raven, come flying hither, on the news,
To peck for carrion, my she-wolf and all,
Greedy and full of expectation—

*Mosca.*    And then to have it ravished from their mouths?

*Volpone.*    'Tis true. I will ha' thee put on a gown,
And take upon thee as thou wert mine heir;
Show 'em a will. Open that chest, and reach
Forth one of those that has the blanks. I'll straight
Put in thy name.

*Mosca.*       It will be rare, sir.

*Volpone.*           Aye,       90
When they e'en gape, and find themselves deluded—

*Mosca.*    Yes.

---

[w] duped    [x] i.e., organize his case by topics    [y] i.e., of speech    [z] i.e., because of his flailing about    [a] repay

*Volpone.*        And thou use them scurvily! Dispatch,
   Get on thy gown.
*Mosca.*                    But what, sir, if they ask
   After the body?
*Volpone.*              Say it was corrupted.
*Mosca.*     I'll say it stunk, sir; and was fain t' have it
   Coffined up instantly, and sent away.
*Volpone.*     Anything, what thou wilt. Hold, here's my
      will.
   Get thee a cap, a count-book, pen and ink,
   Papers afore thee; sit as thou wert taking
   An inventory of parcels. I'll get up                      100
   Behind the curtain, on a stool, and hearken;
   Sometime peep over, see how they do look,
   With what degrees their blood doth leave their faces.
   O, 'twill afford me a rare meal of laughter!
*Mosca.*     Your advocate will turn stark dull upon it.
*Volpone.*     It will take off his oratory's edge.
*Mosca.*     But your *clarissimo,*[b] old round-back, he
   Will crump you [c] like a hog-louse with the touch.
*Volpone.*     And what Corvino?
*Mosca.*                         O sir, look for him
   Tomorrow morning, with a rope and dagger,                 110
   To visit all the streets; he must run mad.
   My lady too, that came into the court
   To bear false witness for your worship—
*Volpone.*                              Yes,
   And kissed me 'fore the fathers, when my face
   Flowed all with oils—
*Mosca.*                      And sweat, sir. Why, your gold
   Is such another med'cine, it dries up
   All those offensive savors! It transforms
   The most deformèd, and restores 'em lovely
   As 'twere the strange poetical girdle.[d] Jove
   Could not invent t' himself a shroud more subtle          120
   To pass Acrisius'[e] guards. It is the thing
   Makes all the world her grace, her youth, her beauty.
*Volpone.*     I think she loves me.
*Mosca.*                         Who? The lady, sir?
   She's jealous of you.
*Volpone.*             Dost thou say so? [*Knocking without.*]
*Mosca.*                        Hark,
   There's some already.

---

[b] Venetian grandee (i.e., Corbaccio)   [c] curl up for you   [d] belt worn
by Venus   [e] Danaë's father, who locked her up in a tower. Jove came
to her as a shower of gold.

*Volpone.*                    Look.
*Mosca.*                              It is the vulture;
    He has the quickest scent.
*Volpone.*                    I'll to my place,
    Thou to thy posture.
*Mosca.*              I am set.
*Volpone.*                        But, Mosca,
    Play the artificer, now, torture 'em rarely.

[*Enter* Voltore.]

*Voltore.*    How now, my Mosca?
*Mosca.* [*Writing.*]                  "Turkey carpets, nine—"
*Voltore.*    Taking an inventory? That is well.          130
*Mosca.*    "Two suits ᶠ of bedding, tissue ᵍ—"
*Voltore.*                              Where's the will?
    Let me read that the while.

[*Enter* Servitori *with* Corbaccio *in a chair.*]

*Corbaccio.*                    So, set me down,
    And get you home.                    [*Exeunt* Servitori.]
*Voltore.*      Is he come now, to trouble us?
*Mosca.*    "Of cloth of gold, two more—"
*Corbaccio.*                              Is it done, Mosca?
*Mosca.*    "Of several velvets, eight—"
*Voltore.*                              I like his care.
*Corbaccio.*    Dost thou not hear?

[*Enter* Corvino.]

*Corvino.*                    Ha! Is the hour come, Mosca?
*Volpone.* [*Peeps from behind a traverse.*ʰ] Aye,
    now they muster.
*Corvino.*                    What does the advocate here,
    Or this Corbaccio?
*Corbaccio.*                    What do these here?

[*Enter* Lady Wouldbe.]

*Lady Wouldbe.*                              Mosca!
    Is his thread spun?
*Mosca.*    "Eight chests of linen—"
*Volpone.*                          O,

----

ᶠ sets    ᵍ gold brocade    ʰ curtain

My fine Dame Wouldbe, too!
*Corvino.*                    Mosca, the will,                    140
  That I may show it these, and rid 'em hence.
*Mosca.*   "Six chests of diaper,[1] four of damask—" There.

[*Gives them the will carelessly.*]

*Corbaccio.*   Is that the will?
*Mosca.*                    "Down-beds, and bolsters—"
*Volpone.*                                        Rare!
  Be busy still. Now they begin to flutter;
  They never think of me. Look, see, see, see!
  How their swift eyes run over the long deed,
  Unto the name, and to the legacies,
  What is bequeathed them there—
*Mosca.*                    "Ten suits of hangings—"
*Volpone.*   Aye, i' their garters,[j] Mosca. Now their hopes
  Are at the gasp.
*Voltore.*        Mosca the heir!
*Corbaccio.*                    What's that?                    150
*Volpone.*   My advocate is dumb; look to my merchant,
  He has heard of some strange storm, a ship is lost,
  He faints; my lady will swoon. Old glazen-eyes
  He hath not reached his despair yet.
*Corbaccio.*                    All these
  Are out of hope; I'm sure the man.
*Corvino.*                    But, Mosca—
*Mosca.*   "Two cabinets—"
*Corvino.*                    Is this in earnest?
*Mosca.*                                        "One
  Of ebony—"
*Corvino.*        Or do you but delude me?
*Mosca.*   "The other, mother of pearl"—I am very busy.
  Good faith, it is a fortune thrown upon me—
  "Item, one salt [k] of agate"—not my seeking.        160
*Lady Wouldbe.*   Do you hear, sir?
*Mosca.*                    "A perfumed box"—Pray you forbear,
  You see I'm troubled—"made of an onyx—"
*Lady Wouldbe.*                    How!
*Mosca.*   Tomorrow or next day, I shall be at leisure
  To talk with you all.
*Corvino.*                    Is this my large hope's issue?[l]
*Lady Wouldbe.*   Sir, I must have a fairer answer.
*Mosca.*                                        Madam!
  Marry, and shall: pray you, fairly quit my house.

[1] a kind of damask   [j] i.e., with which to hang themselves   [k] saltcellar
[l] outcome

Nay, raise no tempest with your looks; but hark you,
Remember what your ladyship offered me
To put you in an heir; go to, think on 't;
And what you said e'en your best madams did        170
For maintenance, and why not you? Enough.
Go home, and use the poor Sir Poll, your knight, well,
For fear I tell some riddles. Go, be melancholic.

                         [*Exit* Lady Wouldbe.]

*Volpone.*     O my fine devil!
*Corvino.*                  Mosca, pray you a word.
*Mosca.*     Lord! Will not you take your dispatch hence yet?
Methinks of all you should have been th' example.
Why should you stay here? With what thought? What
     promise?
Hear you, do not you know I know you an ass,
And that you would most fain have been a wittol ᵐ
If fortune would have let you? That you are         180
A declared cuckold, on good terms? This pearl,
You'll say, was yours? Right. This diamond?
I'll not deny't, but thank you. Much here else?
It may be so. Why, think that these good works
May help to hide your bad. I'll not betray you;
Although you be but extraordinary,
And have it only in title, it sufficeth.
Go home, be melancholic too, or mad.   [*Exit* Corvino.]
*Volpone.*     Rare, Mosca! How his villainy becomes him!
*Voltore.*     Certain, he doth delude all these for me.      190
*Corbaccio.*     Mosca the heir?
*Volpone.*                 O, his four eyes ⁿ have found it!
*Corbaccio.*     I'm cozened, cheated, by a parasite slave!
Harlot,° th'ast gulled me.
*Mosca.*                 Yes, sir. Stop your mouth,
Or I shall draw the only tooth is left.
Are not you he, that filthy, covetous wretch,
With the three legs,ᵖ that here, in hope of prey,
Have, any time this three year, snuffed about
With your most grov'ling nose; and would have hired
Me to the pois'ning of my patron, sir?
Are not you he that have today in court         200
Professed the disinheriting of your son?
Perjured yourself? Go home, and die, and stink;
If you but croak a syllable, all comes out.
Away, and call your porters! [*Exit* Corbaccio.] Go, go,
     stink.
*Volpone.*     Excellent varlet!

ᵐ willing  cuckold  ⁿ Corbaccio  wears  glasses  ° rogue  ᵖ i.e.,  using
a cane

*Voltore.*                    Now, my faithful Mosca,
  I find thy constancy—
*Mosca.*                Sir?
*Voltore.*                    Sincere.
*Mosca.*                              "A table
  Of porphyry"—I mar'l [q] you'll be thus troublesome.
*Voltore.*    Nay, leave off now, they are gone.
*Mosca.*                              Why, who are you?
  What! Who did send for you? O, cry you mercy,
  Reverend sir! Good faith, I am grieved for you,                    210
  That any chance of mine should thus defeat
  Your—I must needs say—most deserving travails.
  But I protest, sir, it was cast upon me,
  And I could almost wish to be without it,
  But that the will o' th' dead must be observed.
  Marry, my joy is that you need it not;
  You have a gift, sir—thank your education—
  Will never let you want, while there are men
  And malice to breed causes.[r] Would I had
  But half the like, for all my fortune, sir.                    220
  If I have any suits—as I do hope,
  Things being so easy and direct, I shall not—
  I will make bold with your obstreperous aid,
  Conceive me, for your fee, sir. In meantime,
  You that have so much law, I know ha' the conscience
  Not to be covetous of what is mine.
  Good sir, I thank you for my plate; 'twill help
  To set up a young man. Good faith, you look
  As you were costive; [s] best go home and purge, sir.
                                        [*Exit* Voltore.]
*Volpone.*    Bid him eat lettuce [t] well. My witty mischief,    230
  Let me embrace thee. O that I could now
  Transform thee to a Venus—Mosca, go,
  Straight take my habit [u] of *clarissimo,*
  And walk the streets; be seen, torment 'em more.
  We must pursue as well as plot. Who would
  Have lost this feast?
*Mosca.*                I doubt [v] it will lose them.
*Volpone.*    O, my recovery shall recover all.
  That I could now but think on some disguise
  To meet 'em in, and ask 'em questions;
  How I would vex 'em still at every turn!                    240
*Mosca.*    Sir, I can fit you.
*Volpone.*                Canst thou?

  [q] marvel   [r] lawsuits   [s] constipated   [t] i.e., as a laxative   [u] garb   [v] suspect

*Mosca.*                              Yes, I know
   One o' th' *commendadori*, sir, so like you,
   Him will I straight make drunk, and bring you his habit.
*Volpone.*   A rare disguise, and answering thy brain!
   O, I will be a sharp disease unto 'em.
*Mosca.*   Sir, you must look for curses—
*Volpone.*                         Till they burst;
   The fox fares ever best when he is curst.     [*Exeunt.*]


### Scene II

#### [*Sir Politic's residence.*]

[*Enter* Peregrine *disguised, and three* Mercatori.]

*Peregrine.*   Am I enough disguised?
*1st Mercatore.*          I warrant you.
*Peregrine.*   All my ambition is to fright him only.
*2nd Mercatore.*   If you could ship him away, 'twere ex-
      cellent.
*3rd Mercatore.*   To Zant,ʷ or to Aleppo!ˣ
*Peregrine.*                         Yes, and ha' his
   Adventures put i' th' book of voyages,ʸ
   And his gulled story ᶻ registered for truth.
   Well, gentlemen, when I am in a while,
   And that you think us warm in our discourse,
   Know your approaches.
*1st Mercatore.*          Trust it to our care.
                              [*Exeunt* Mercatori.]


[*Enter* Woman.]

*Peregrine.*   Save you, fair lady! Is Sir Poll within?     10
*Woman.*   I do not know, sir.
*Peregrine.*                    Pray you say unto him,
   Here is a merchant, upon earnest business,
   Desires to speak with him.
*Woman.*              I will see, sir.     [*Exit.*]
*Peregrine.*                    Pray you.
   I see the family is all female here.

[*Re-enter* Woman.]

*Woman.*   He says, sir, he has weighty affairs of state
   That now require him whole; some other time

────────

ʷ a Greek island   ˣ Syrian city   ʸ i.e., in one of the contemporary travel
books   ᶻ story of his gulling

You may possess him.
*Peregrine.*                    Pray you say again,
   If those require him whole, these will exact him,
   Whereof I bring him tidings. [*Exit* Woman.] What might
      be
   His grave affair of state now? How to make                        20
   Bolognian sausages here in Venice, sparing
   One o' th' ingredients?

[*Re-enter* Woman.]

*Woman.*                    Sir, he says he knows
   By your word "tidings" that you are no statesman,[a]
   And therefore wills you stay.
*Peregrine.*                    Sweet, pray you return him,
   I have not read so many proclamations,
   And studied them for words, as he has done,
   But—Here he deigns to come.          [*Exit* Woman.]

[*Enter* Sir Politic.]

*Sir Politic.*                         Sir, I must crave
   Your courteous pardon. There hath chanced today
   Unkind disaster 'twixt my lady and me,
   And I was penning my apology                                      30
   To give her satisfaction, as you came now.
*Peregrine.*    Sir, I am grieved I bring you worse disaster:
   The gentleman you met at th' port today,
   That told you he was newly arrived—
*Sir Politic.*                    Aye, was
   A fugitive punk?[b]
*Peregrine.*            No, sir, a spy set on you;
   And he has made relation to the Senate
   That you professed to him to have a plot
   To sell the state of Venice to the Turk.
*Sir Politic.*    O me!
*Peregrine.*            For which warrants are signed by this
      time,
   To apprehend you, and to search your study                       40
   For papers—
*Sir Politic.*    Alas, sir, I have none but notes
   Drawn out of play-books—
*Peregrine.*                    All the better, sir.
*Sir Politic.*    And some essays. What shall I do?
*Peregrine.*                              Sir, best

   [a] statesmen said "intelligence"      [b] prostitute

Convey yourself into a sugar-chest,
Or, if you could lie round, a frail $^e$ were rare;
And I could send you aboard.
Sir Politic.                    Sir, I but talked so,
For discourse sake merely.

(*They knock without.*)

Peregrine.                    Hark! They are there.
Sir Politic.   I am a wretch, a wretch!
Peregrine.                         What will you do, sir?
Ha' you ne'er a currant-butt $^d$ to leap into?
They'll put you to the rack; you must be sudden.      50
Sir Politic.   Sir, I have an engine $^e$—
3rd Merchant. [*Within.*]          Sir Politic Wouldbe!
2nd Merchant. [*Within.*]   Where is he?
Sir Politic.              That I have thought upon beforetime.
Peregrine.   What is it?
Sir Politic.              I shall ne'er endure the torture!
Marry, it is, sir, of a tortoise-shell,
Fitted for these extremities. Pray you, sir, help me. [*Gets
     into shell.*]
Here I've a place, sir, to put back my legs;
Please you to lay it on, sir. With this cap,
And my black gloves, I'll lie, sir, like a tortoise,
Till they are gone.
Peregrine.              And call you this an engine?
Sir Politic.   Mine own device—Good sir, bid my wife's      60
     women
To burn my papers.

*The Three* Mercatori *rush in.*

1st Mercatore.   Where's he hid?
3rd Mercatore.                    We must,
And will sure find him.
2nd Mercatore.              Which is his study?
1st Mercatore.                              What
Are you, sir?
Peregrine.   I'm a merchant, that came here
To look upon this tortoise.
3rd Mercatore.              How!
1st Mercatore.                    St. Mark!
What beast is this?
Peregrine.         It is a fish.

$^e$ straw basket   $^d$ cask   $^e$ contraption

*2nd Mercatore.*                    Come out here!

*Peregrine.*   Nay, you may strike him, sir, and tread upon
    him.

    He'll bear a cart.

*1st Mercatore.*   What, to run over him?

*Peregrine.*                              Yes.

*3rd Mercatore.*   Let's jump upon him.

*2nd Mercatore.*                       Can he not go?

*Peregrine.*                              He creeps, sir.

*1st Mercatore.*   Let's see him creep.

*Peregrine.*                  No, good sir, you will hurt him.

*2nd Mercatore.*   Heart, I'll see him creep, or prick his      70
    guts!

*3rd Mercatore.*   Come out here!

*Peregrine.*   Pray you, sir.        [*Aside to* Sir Politic.]
    Creep a little.

*1st Mercatore.*                              Forth.

*2nd Mercatore.*   Yet further.

*Peregrine.*                  Good sir!—Creep.

*2nd Mercatore.*                       We'll see his legs.

*They pull off the shell and discover* Sir Politic.

*3rd Mercatore.*   God's so', he has garters!

*1st Mercatore.*                       Ay, and gloves!

*2nd Mercatore.*                              Is this
    Your fearful tortoise?

*Peregrine.*                  Now, Sir Poll, we are even;
    For your next project I shall be prepared.
    I am sorry for the funeral of your notes, sir.

*1st Mercatore.*   'Twere a rare motion [f] to be seen in
    Fleet Street.[g]

*2nd Mercatore.*   Aye, i' the term.[h]

*2nd Mercatore.*                  Or Smithfield, in the fair.[i]

*3rd Mercatore.*   Methinks 'tis but a melancholic sight.

*Peregrine.*   Farewell, most politic tortoise!
                    [*Exeunt* Peregrine *and* Mercatori.]

*Sir Politic.* [*Re-enter* Woman.]       Where's my lady?   80
    Knows she of this?

*Woman.*              I know not, sir.

*Sir Politic.*                  Inquire. [*Exit* Woman.]
    O, I shall be the fable of all feasts,
    The freight of the *gazetti*,[j] ship-boys' tale,
    And, which is worst, even talk for ordinaries.[k]

[f] puppet show   [g] noted for exhibitions of freaks   [h] season of the law
courts   [i] Bartholomew Fair   [j] subject of newspapers   [k] taverns

[*Re-enter* Woman.]

*Woman.*   My lady's come most melancholic home,
   And says, sir, she will straight to sea, for physic.
*Sir Politic.*   And I, to shun this place and clime forever,
   Creeping with house on back, and think it well
   To shrink my poor head in my politic shell.   [*Exeunt.*]


### Scene III

[Volpone's *house.*]

[*Enter* Volpone *in the habit of a commendadore, and*
   Mosca *in that of a clarissimo.*]


*Volpone.*   Am I then like him?
*Mosca.*                      O sir, you are he;
   No man can sever you.
*Volpone.*            Good.
*Mosca.*                      But what am I?
*Volpone.*   'Fore heav'n, a brave *clarissimo*, thou becom'st
      it!
   Pity thou wert not born one.
*Mosca.* [*Aside.*]            If I hold
   My made one, 'twill be well.
*Volpone.*                  I'll go and see
   What news first at the court.            [*Exit.*]
*Mosca.*                  Do so. My fox
   Is out on [1] his hole, and ere he shall re-enter,
   I'll make him languish in his borrowed case,[m]
   Except he come to composition [n] with me.
   Androgyno, Castrone, Nano!

[*Enter* Androgyno, Castrone, *and* Nano.]

*All.*                      Here.                      10
*Mosca.*   Go, recreate yourselves abroad; go, sport.
                                          [*Exeunt.*]
   So, now I have the keys, and am possessed.
   Since he will needs be dead afore his time,
   I'll bury him or gain by him. I'm his heir,
   And so will keep me, till he share at least.
   To cozen him of all were but a cheat

---

[1] of   [m] disguise   [n] unless he comes to terms

Well placed; no man would construe it a sin.
Let his sport pay for 't. This is called the fox-trap.

                                         *[Exit.]*

### Scene IV

#### [A street.]

[*Enter* Corbaccio *and* Corvino.]

*Corbaccio.*    They say the court is set.
*Corvino.*                    We must maintain
  Our first tale good, for both our reputations.
*Corbaccio.*  Why, mine's no tale! My son would there
  have killed me.
*Corvino.*  That's true, I had forgot. [*Aside.*] Mine is,
  I'm sure.—
  But for your will, sir.
*Corbaccio.*          Aye, I'll come upon him
  For that hereafter, now his patron's dead.

[*Enter* Volpone.]

*Volpone.*  Signor Corvino! And Corbaccio! Sir,
  Much joy unto you.
*Corvino.*          Of what?
*Volpone.*              The sudden good
  Dropped down upon you—
*Corbaccio.*           Where?
*Volpone.*              And none knows how,
  From old Volpone, sir.
*Corbaccio.*         Out, arrant knave!       10
*Volpone.*  Let not your too much wealth, sir, make you
  furious.
*Corbaccio.*  Away, thou varlet.
*Volpone.*           Why, sir?
*Corbaccio.*         Dost thou mock me?
*Volpone.*  You mock the world, sir; did you not change
  wills?
*Corbaccio.*  Out, harlot!
*Volpone.*            O! Belike ° you are the man,
  Signor Corvino? Faith, you carry it well;
  You grow not mad withal. I love your spirit.
  You are not over-leavened with your fortune.

   ° perhaps

You should ha' some would swell now, like a wine-vat,
With such an autumn—Did he gi' you all, sir?
*Corvino.*     Avoid,[p] you rascal.
*Volpone.*                         Troth, your wife has shown   20
Herself a very woman! But you are well,
You need not care; you have a good estate,
To bear it out, sir, better by this chance—
Except Corbaccio have a share.
*Corbaccio.*                Hence, varlet.
*Volpone.*   You will not be a'known,[q] sir? Why, 'tis wise.
Thus do all gamesters, at all games, dissemble.
No man will seem to win. [*Exeunt* Corvino *and* Corbac-
   cio.] Here comes my vulture,
Heaving his beak up i' the air, and snuffing.

[*Enter* Voltore.]

*Voltore.*   Outstripped thus, by a parasite! A slave,
Would run on errands, and make legs for crumbs!   30
Well, what I'll do—
*Volpone.*             The court stays for your worship.
I e'en rejoice, sir, at your worship's happiness,
And that it fell into so learnèd hands,
That understand the fingering—
*Voltore.*                    What do you mean?
*Volpone.*   I mean to be a suitor to your worship,
For the small tenement, out of reparations,[r]
That at the end of your long row of houses,
By the *Piscaria* [s]—it was, in Volpone's time,
Your predecessor, ere he grew diseased,
A handsome, pretty, customed [t] bawdy-house   40
As any was in Venice, none dispraised;
But fell with him. His body and that house
Decayed together.
*Voltore.*          Come, sir, leave your prating.
*Volpone.*   Why, if your worship give me but your hand,[u]
That I may ha' the refusal, I have done.
'Tis a mere toy to you, sir, candle-rents.[v]
As your learned worship knows—
*Voltore.*                    What do I know?
*Volpone.*   Marry, no end of your wealth, sir, God decrease
   it!
*Voltore.*   Mistaking knave! What, mock'st thou my mis-
   fortune?                                [*Exit.*]

[p] begone   [q] acknowledged   [r] in poor condition   [s] fish market   [t] well-
attended   [u] signature   [v] rents from deteriorating property

*Volpone.*   His blessing on your heart, sir; would 'twere
        more!                                                        50
    Now to my first again, at the next corner.         [*Exit.*]


                        *Scene V*


                    [*Another corner.*]


[*Enter* Corbaccio *and* Corvino. Mosca *passes over the*
    *stage.*]

*Corbaccio.*   See, in our habit! See the impudent varlet!
*Corvino.*   That I could shoot mine eyes at him, like gun-
        stones! ᵂ

[*Enter* Volpone.]

*Volpone.*   But is this true, sir, of the parasite?
*Corbaccio.*   Again, t' afflict us? Monster!
*Volpone.*                            In good faith, sir,
    I'm heartily grieved, a beard of your grave length
    Should be so over-reached.ˣ I never brooked
    That parasite's hair; methought his nose should cozen.
    There still was somewhat in his look, did promise
    The bane of a *clarissimo.*
*Corbaccio.*                    Knave—
*Volpone.*                            Methinks
    Yet you, that are so traded i' the world,                       10
    A witty merchant, the fine bird, Corvino,
    That have such normal emblems ʸ on your name,
    Should not have sung your shame; and dropped your
        cheese,
    To let the fox laugh at your emptiness.
*Corvino.*   Sirrah, you think the privilege of the place,
    And your red saucy cap, that seems to me
    Nailed to your jolt-head ᶻ with those two *cecchines,*ᵃ
    Can warrant your abuses. Come you hither.
    You shall perceive, sir, I dare beat you. Approach.
*Volpone.*   No haste, sir, I do know your valor well,              20
    Since you durst publish what you are, sir.
*Corvino.*                                    Tarry,
    I'd speak with you.
*Volpone.*            Sir, sir another time—
*Corvino.*   Nay, now.

─────────────
    ᵂ stone cannon balls   ˣ duped   ʸ allegorical pictures with mottoes
ᶻ blockhead   ᵃ gilt buttons

*Volpone.*                    O God, sir! I were a wise man,
  Would stand the fury of a distracted cuckold.

(Mosca *walks by them.*)

*Corbaccio.*   What, come again!
*Volpone.*                        Upon 'em, Mosca; save me.
*Corbaccio.*   The air's infected where he breathes.
*Corvino.*                            Let's fly him.
                  [*Exeunt* Corvino *and* Corbaccio.]
*Volpone.*   Excellent basilisk! [b] Turn upon the vulture.

[*Enter* Voltore.]

*Voltore.*   Well, flesh-fly, it is summer with you now;
  Your winter will come on.
*Mosca.*                        Good advocate,
  Pray thee not rail, nor threaten out of place thus;     30
  Thou'lt make a solecism, as Madam says.
  Get you a biggen [c] more; your brain breaks loose. [*Exit.*]
*Voltore.*   Well, sir.
*Volpone.*                Would you ha' me beat the insolent
    slave?
  Throw dirt upon his first good clothes?
*Voltore.*                      This same
  Is doubtless some familiar! [d]
*Volpone.*                    Sir, the court,
  In troth, stays for you. I am mad, a mule
  That never read Justinian, [e] should get up
  And ride an advocate. Had you no quirk [f]
  To avoid gullage, sir, by such a creature?
  I hope you do but jest; he has not done 't;     40
  This's but confederacy to blind the rest.
  You are the heir?
*Voltore.*            A strange, officious,
  Troublesome knave! Thou dost torment me.
*Volpone.*                        I know—
  It cannot be, sir, that you should be cozened;
  'Tis not within the wit of man to do it.
  You are so wise, so prudent; and 'tis fit
  That wealth and wisdom still should go together.
                              [*Exeunt.*]

[b] mythical beast whose look would kill   [c] lawyer's skull cap   [d] attendant spirit   [e] Emperor who codified Roman law   [f] trick

## Scene VI

### [*The Scrutineo.*]

[*Enter four* Avocatori, Notario, Bonario, Celia, Corbaccio, Corvino, Commendadori, *etc.*]

*1st Avocatore.*    Are all the parties here?
*Notario.*                            All but the advocate.
*2nd Avocatore.*    And here he comes.

[*Enter* Voltore *and* Volpone.]

*1st Avocatore.*    Then bring 'em forth to sentence.
*Voltore.*    O my most honored fathers, let your mercy
  Once win upon your justice, to forgive—
  I am distracted—
*Volpone.* [*Aside.*] What will he do now?
*Voltore.*                            O,
  I know not which t' address myself to first;
  Whether your fatherhoods, or these innocents—
*Corvino.* [*Aside.*]    Will he betray himself?
*Voltore.*                            Whom equally
  I have abused, out of most covetous ends—
*Corvino.*    The man is mad!
*Corbaccio.*                  What's that?
*Corvino.*                                  He is possessed.    10
*Voltore.*    For which, now struck in conscience, here I
    prostrate
  Myself at your offended feet, for pardon.
*1st, 2nd Avocatori.*    Arise.
*Celia.*                  O heav'n, how just thou art!
*Volpone.* [*Aside.*]                        I'm caught
  I' mine own noose—
*Corvino.* [*Aside to Corbaccio.*]    Be constant, sir; nought
    now
  Can help but impudence.
*1st Avocatore.*            Speak forward.
*Commendadore.*                        Silence!
*Voltore.*    It is not passion in me, reverend fathers,
  But only conscience, conscience, my good sires,
  That makes me now tell truth. That parasite,
  That knave, hath been the instrument of all.
*1st Avocatore.*    Where is that knave? Fetch him.
*Volpone.*                  I go.                        [*Exit.*]

*Corvino*.                                    Grave fathers,   20
  This man's distracted; he confessed it now.
  For, hoping to be old Volpone's heir,
  Who now is dead—
*3rd Avocatore*.        How?
*2nd Avocatore*.              Is Volpone dead?
*Corvino*. Dead since, grave fathers—
*Bonario*.                              O sure vengeance!
*1st Avocatore*.                                Stay,
  Then he was no deceiver?
*Voltore*.                O, no, none;
  The parasite, grave fathers.
*Corvino*.                        He does speak
  Out of mere envy, 'cause the servant's made
  The thing he gaped for. Please your fatherhoods,
  This is the truth; though I'll not justify
  The other, but he may be some-deal faulty.        30
*Voltore*.   Ay, to your hopes, as well as mine, Corvino.
  But I'll use modesty.[g] Pleaseth your wisdoms
  To view these certain [h] notes, and but confer [i] them;
  As I hope favor, they shall speak clear truth.
*Corvino*.   The devil has entered him!
*Bonario*.                              Or bides in you.
*4th Avocatore*.   We have done ill, by a public officer
  To send for him, if he be heir.
*2nd Avocatore*.                  For whom?
*4th Avocatore*.   Him that they call the parasite.
*3rd Avocatore*.                              'Tis true,
  He is a man of great estate now left.
*4th Avocatore*.   Go you, and learn his name, and say        40
    the court
  Entreats his presence here, but to the clearing
  Of some few doubts.          [*Exit* Notario.]
*2nd Avocatore*.   This same's a labyrinth!
*1st Avocatore*.   Stand you unto your first report?
*Corvino*.                              My state,
  My life, my fame—
*Bonario*.          Where is't?
*Corvino*.                    Are at the stake.
*1st Avocatore*.   Is yours so too?
*Corbaccio*.                  The advocate's a knave,
  And has a forkèd tongue—
*2nd Avocatore*.          Speak to the point.

[g] moderation   [h] particular   [i] compare

*Corbaccio.*   So is the parasite too.
*1st Avocatore.*                       This is confusion.
*Voltore.*   I do beseech you fatherhoods, read but those—
*Corvino.*   And credit nothing the false spirit hath writ.
     It cannot be but he is possessed, grave fathers.          50
                                             *Exeunt.*


                              *Scene VII*

                             [*A street.*]


[*Enter* Volpone.]

*Volpone.*   To make a snare for mine own neck! And run
     My head into it wilfully, with laughter!
     When I had newly 'scaped, was free and clear!
     Out of mere wantonness! O, the dull devil
     Was in this brain of mine when I devised it,
     And Mosca gave it second; he must now
     Help to sear up this vein, or we bleed dead.


[*Enter* Nano, Androgyno, *and* Castrone.]

     How now! Who let you loose? Whither go you now?
     What, to buy gingerbread, or to drown kitlings?[j]
*Nano.*   Sir, Master Mosca called us out of doors,          10
     And bid us all go play, and took the keys.
*Androgyno.*                                        Yes.
*Volpone.*   Did Master Mosca take the keys? Why, so!
     I am farther in. These are my fine conceits![k]
     I must be merry, with a mischief to me!
     What a vile wretch was I, that could not bear
     My fortune soberly. I must ha' my crotchets
     And my conundrums!—Well, go you and seek him.—
     His meaning may be truer than my fear.[l]—
     Bid him, he straight come to me to the court;
     Thither will I, and, if't be possible,                    20
     Unscrew my advocate, upon new hopes.
     When I provoked him, then I lost myself.     [*Exeunt.*]

     [j] kittens   [k] ideas   [l] his purpose may be more honest than I think

## Scene VIII

### [The Scrutineo.]

[*Four* Avocatori, Notario, Voltore, Bonario, Celia, Corbaccio, Corvino, *etc., as before.*]

*1st Avocatore.*    These things can ne'er be reconciled.
    He here
  Professeth that the gentleman was wronged,
  And that the gentlewoman was brought thither,
  Forced by her husband, and there left.
*Voltore.*               Most true.
*Celia.*   How ready is heav'n to those that pray!
*1st Avocatore.*            But that
  Volpone would have ravished her, he holds
  Utterly false, knowing his impotence.
*Corvino.*   Grave fathers, he is possessed; again, I say,
  Possessed. Nay, if there be possession and
  Obsession,[m] he has both.
*3rd Avocatore.*       Here comes our officer.       10

[*Enter* Volpone.]

*Volpone.*   The parasite will straight be here, grave
    fathers.
*4th Avocatore.*   You might invent some other name, sir
    varlet.
*3rd Avocatore.*   Did not the notary meet him?
*Volpone.*               Not that I know.
*4th Avocatore.*   His coming will clear all.
*2nd Avocatore.*           Yet it is misty.
*Voltore.*   May't please your fatherhoods—
*Volpone.* [*Whispers to* Voltore.]    Sir, the parasite
  Willed me to tell you that his master lives;
  That you are still the man; your hopes the same;
  And this was only a jest—
*Voltore.*      How?
*Volpone.*          Sir, to try
  If you were firm, and how you stood affected.
*Voltore.*   Art sure he lives?
*Volpone.*         Do I live, sir?
*Voltore.*             O me!     20

[m] the attack of the devil from outside the body, as opposed to "possession," the attack from within

I was too violent.

*Volpone.*         Sir, you may redeem it:
They said you were possessed; fall down, and seem so.
I'll help to make it good. (Voltore *falls*.) God bless the
    man! [*Aside to* Voltore.]
Stop your wind hard, and swell—See, see, see, see!
He vomits crooked pins! [n] His eyes are set,
Like a dead hare's hung in a poulter's [o] shop!
His mouth's running away! [p] Do you see, signor?
Now 'tis in his belly.

*Corvino.*         Aye, the devil!

*Volpone.*    Now in his throat.

*Corvino.*              Aye, I perceive it plain.

*Volpone.*    'Twill out, 'twill out! Stand clear. See where
    it flies,                                                    30
    In shape of a blue toad, with a bat's wings!
    Do not you see it, sir?

*Corbaccio.*    What? I think I do.

*Corvino.*    'Tis too manifest.

*Volpone.*              Look! He comes t' himself!

*Voltore.*    Where am I?

*Volpone.*    Take good heart, the worst is past, sir.
    You are dispossessed.

*1st Avocatore.*    What accident is this?

*2nd Avocatore.*    Sudden, and full of wonder!

*3rd Avocatore.*              If he were
    Possessed, as it appears, all this is nothing.

*Corvino.*    He has been often subject to these fits.

*1st Avocatore.*    Show him that writing. Do you know
    it, sir?

*Volpone.* [*Aside to* Voltore.]    Deny it, sir, forswear it,    40
    know it not.

*Voltore.*    Yes, I do know it well, it is my hand;
    But all that it contains is false.

*Bonario.*              O practice!

*2nd Avocatore.*    What maze is this!

*1st Avocatore.*              Is he not guilty then,
    Whom you there name the parasite?

*Voltore.*              Grave fathers,
    No more than his good patron, old Volpone.

*4th Avocatore.*    Why, he is dead.

*Voltore.*              O, no, my honored fathers,
    He lives—

*1st Avocatore.*    How! Lives?

[n] Voltore's symptoms are drawn from contemporary accounts of
witchcraft   [o] poultry and game seller   [p] distorted

*Voltore.*                    Lives.
*2nd Avocatore.*                        This is subtler yet!
*3rd Avocatore.*   You said he was dead.
*Voltore.*                            Never.
*3rd Avocatore.*                          You said so.
*Corvino.*                                I heard so.
*4th Avocatore.*   Here comes the gentleman; make him
    way.
*3rd Avocatore.*   A stool!

[*Enter* Mosca.]

*4th Avocatore.* [*Aside.*]    A proper �q man and, were          50
    Volpone dead,
  A fit match for my daughter.
*3rd Avocatore.*                  Give him way.
*Volpone.* [*Aside to* Mosca.]   Mosca, I was almost
    lost; the advocate
  Had betrayed all; but now it is recovered.
  All's o' the hinge again—Say I am living.
*Mosca.*   What busy knave is this? Most reverend
    fathers,
  I sooner had attended your grave pleasures,
  But that my order for the funeral
  Of my dear patron did require me—
*Volpone.* [*Aside.*]                  Mosca!
*Mosca.*   Whom I intend to bury like a gentleman.
*Volpone.* [*Aside.*]   Aye, quick,ʳ and cozen me of all.
*2nd Avocatore.*                  Still stranger!   60
  More intricate!
*1st Avocatore.*   And come about again!
*4th Avocatore.* [*Aside.*]   It is a match, my daughter
    is bestowed.
*Mosca.* [*Aside to* Volpone.]   Will you gi' me half?
*Volpone.*                      First I'll be hanged.
*Mosca.*                                I know
  Your voice is good, cry not so loud.
*1st Avocatore.*                  Demand ˢ
  The advocate. Sir, did not you affirm
  Volpone was alive?
*Volpone.*           Yes, and he is;
  This gent'man told me so. [*Aside to* Mosca.] Thou shalt
    have half.
*Mosca.*   Whose drunkard is this same? Speak, some that
    know him.

  �q handsome   ʳ alive   ˢ question

I never saw his face. [*Aside to* Volpone.] I cannot
  now
Afford it you so cheap.
*Volpone.*                         No?
*1st Avocatore.*                    What say you?                70
*Voltore.*   The officer told me.
*Volpone.*                          I did, grave fathers,
  And will maintain he lives, with mine own life,
  And that this creature told me. [*Aside.*] I was born
  With all good stars my enemies.
*Mosca.*                            Most grave fathers,
  If such an insolence as this must pass
  Upon me, I am silent; 'twas not this
  For which you sent, I hope.
*2nd Avocatore.*              Take him away.
*Volpone.*   Mosca!
*3rd Avocatore.*   Let him be whipped.
*Volpone.*                      Wilt thou betray me?
  Cozen me?
*3rd Avocatore.*   And taught to bear himself
  Toward a person of his rank.
*4th Avocatore.* [*The officers seize* Volpone.]   Away.   80
*Mosca.*   I humbly thank your fatherhoods.
*Volpone.* [*Aside.*]              Soft, soft. Whipped!
  And lose all that I have! If I confess,
  It cannot be much more.
*4th Avocatore.*           Sir, are you married?
*Volpone.*   They'll be allied anon; I must be resolute:
  The fox shall here uncase.         *Puts off his disguise.*
*Mosca.*                      Patron!
*Volpone.*                         Nay, now
  My ruins shall not come alone; your match
  I'll hinder sure; my substance shall not glue you
  Nor screw you into a family.
*Mosca.*                      Why, patron!
*Volpone.*   I am Volpone, and this [*Points to* Mosca] is my
    knave;
  This, [*To* Voltore.] his own knave; this, [*To* Corbaccio.]
    avarice's fool;                                        90
  This, [*To* Corvino.] a chimera[t] of wittol, fool, and
    knave.
  And, reverend fathers, since we all can hope
  Nought but a sentence, let's not now despair it.
  You hear me brief.
*Corvino.*            May it please your fatherhoods—

[t] mythological monster

*Commendatore.*                                    Silence!

*1st Avocatore.*   The knot is now undone by miracle.

*2nd Avocatore.*   Nothing can be more clear.

*3rd Avocatore.*                          Or can more prove
   These innocent.

*1st Avocatore.*   Give 'em their liberty.

*Bonario.*   Heaven could not long let such gross crimes be
   hid.

*2nd Avocatore.*   If this be held the highway to get
   riches,
   May I be poor!

*3rd Avocatore.*   This's not the gain, but torment.          100

*1st Avocatore.*   These possess wealth, as sick men
   possess fevers,
   Which trulier may be said to possess them.

*2nd Avocatore.*   Disrobe that parasite.

*Corvino, Mosca.*                     Most honored fathers—

*1st Avocatore.*   Can you plead aught to stay the course
   of justice?
   If you can, speak.

*Corvino, Voltore.*   We beg favor.

*Celia.*                          And mercy.

*1st Avocatore.*   You hurt your innocence, suing for the
   guilty.
   Stand forth; and first the parasite. You appear
   T'have been the chiefest minister, if not plotter,
   In all these lewd impostures; and now, lastly,
   Have with your impudence abused the court          110
   And habit of a gentleman of Venice,
   Being a fellow of no birth or blood;
   For which our sentence is, first thou be whipped;
   Then live perpetual prisoner in our galleys.

*Volpone.*   I thank you for him.

*Mosca.*                     Bane to thy wolfish nature!

*1st Avocatore.*   Deliver him to the *Saffi.* [*Mosca is carried
   out.*] Thou, Volpone,
   By blood and rank a gentleman, canst not fall
   Under like censure; but our judgment on thee
   Is that thy substance all be straight confiscate
   To the hospital of the *Incurabili.*[u]          120
   And since the most was gotten by imposture,
   By feigning lame, gout, palsy, and such diseases,
   Thou art to lie in prison, cramped with irons,
   Till thou be'st sick and lame indeed. Remove him.

[u] incurables

*Volpone.*   This is called mortifying [v] of a fox.
*1st Avocatore.*   Thou, Voltore, to take away the scandal
   Thou hast giv'n all worthy men of thy profession,
   Art banished from their fellowship, and our state.
   Corbaccio, bring him near! We here possess
   Thy son of all thy state, and confine thee          130
   To the monastery of San Spirito;
   Where, since thou knew'st not how to live well here,
   Thou shalt be learned to die well.
*Corbaccio.*                     Ha! What said he?
*Commendatore.*   You shall know anon, sir.
*1st Avocatore.*                     Thou, Corvino, shalt
   Be straight embarked from thine own house, and rowed
   Round about Venice, through the Grand Canal,
   Wearing a cap, with fair long ass's ears
   Instead of horns; and so to mount, a paper
   Pinned on thy breast, to the *berlino* [w]—
*Corvino.*                          Yes,
   And have mine eyes beat out with stinking fish,    140
   Bruised fruit, and rotten eggs—'Tis well. I'm glad
   I shall not see my shame yet.
*1st Avocatore.*                And to expiate
   Thy wrongs done to thy wife, thou art to send her
   Home to her father, with her dowry trebled.
   And these are all your judgments.
*All.*                     Honored fathers.
*1st Avocatore.*   Which may not be revoked. Now you
      begin,
   When crimes are done and past, and to be punished,
   To think what your crimes are. Away with them.
   Let all that see these vices thus rewarded,
   Take heart, and love to study 'em. Mischiefs feed   150
   Like beasts, till they be fat, and then they bleed.
                                    [*Exeunt.*]


[Volpone *comes forward.*]


*Volpone.*   The seasoning of a play is the applause.
   Now, though the fox be punished by the laws,
   He yet doth hope there is no suff'ring due,
   For any fact which he hath done 'gainst you.
   If there be, censure him; here he doubtful stands.
   If not, fare jovially, and clap your hands.       [*Exit.*]

---

   [v] chastening; also, a cooking term: to mortify a fowl was to
store it until tender enough for cooking   [w] pillory

# John Milton:

## *Samson Agonistes*

"Division into act and scene, referring chiefly to the stage (to which this work never was intended), is here omitted." These are forbidding words; a play not intended for the stage is rarely stageable and only a little less rarely is it readable. Probably there are not half a dozen English dramatic works that were written without an eye to the stage and that nevertheless may be read with pleasure. Whatever the virtues of *Samson* on the stage (perhaps no one alive today has seen it done by professionals), to exclude it from *The Genius of the English Theater* would be to deny that there is a theater under one's own hat in which *Samson* may be nobly performed.

For Milton, drama was of two sorts—ancient and modern. Toward modern drama on the whole he seems to have been casual. The second edition of Shakespeare's complete plays (1632) received from him a polite poem of sixteen lines, and Shakespeare's comedies along with Jonson's received an elegant tribute in "L'Allegro":

> Then to the well-trod stage anon,
> If Jonson's learned sock be on,
> Or sweetest Shakespeare, Fancy's child,
> Warble his native wood-notes wild.

A passage in "Il Penseroso" suggests that an occasional modern tragedy deserves praise, but no authors are singled out:

> Sometime let gorgeous Tragedy
> In sceptered pall come sweeping by,
> Presenting Thebes, or Pelops' line,
> Or the tale of Troy divine,
> Or what (though rare) of later age
> Ennobled hath the buskined stage.

Mention, too, should be made of the "Elegia Prima," a Latin poem in which Milton speaks of the delights of the theater; it is apparent in this poem that he has in mind the ancient theater, with its plays set in Troy and Thebes, not the modern theater, with its plays set in Elsinore, Birnam Wood, and Bohemia.

It is not surprising, then, that when he set out to write a tragedy he took as his models Aeschylus, Sophocles, and Euripides, whom he rated "the three tragic poets unequaled yet by any, and the best rule to all who endeavor to write tragedy." When one considers the tedious plays written in imitation of Shakespeare—plays written, for example, by Wordsworth, Coleridge, Lamb, Tennyson—with their lifeless Elizabethan echoes, vapid young ladies, villainous young men, and clownish servants who speak prose while their masters speak verse, one is thankful that Milton looked elsewhere for a model. About the time Milton was probably writing *Samson,* John Dryden saw the impossibility of imitating Shakespeare:

> But Shakespeare's magic could not copied be;
> Within that circle none durst walk but he.

The Greeks to whom Milton turned were better models if only because they were more remote. The difference in language, for example, prevented him from feebly echoing them. Most obviously, Milton's Greek models taught him to present only a single action (i.e., to avoid a subplot, such as the story of Gloucester in *King Lear*), to exclude comic material (though perhaps Harapha, the blustering giant, verges on the comic), to include a chorus, to have the entire action cover less than a day, and to keep to a single locale throughout. Why should a writer obey the so-called Three Unities, of action, time, and place? Perhaps the chief value of the unities is that they help provide restraints within which the writer must work, as the rules of the sonnet (fourteen lines, iambic pentameter, rhyming in a fixed pattern) can help a writer mold his material into shape. André Gide suggests that submission to the unities is both a sign of the artist's strength and an aid: "Art is always the result of constraint. To believe that it rises higher as it becomes freer is to believe that what keeps a kite from rising is its string. Kant's dove, which thought it could fly better without the air to trouble its wings, did not realize that in order to fly, it had to have the air's resistance to support its wings." Milton's choice of a subject, too, shows the influence of Greek drama: he selects a hero from the body of sacred legend. The Hebrew word *shimshon* means "solar." Samson is ultimately a sun hero; his long hair doubtless represented the sun's

rays, and perhaps his task of turning the mill was a vestige of
the sun's course through the heavens. Milton's Samson is
drawn from the Old Testament, mainly from Judges 12–16, but the
Biblical Samson is something of a barbarian and buffoon. In
Judges, Samson visited the harlot at Gaza and carried off the
gates of the city; when his wife was given to another, "Samson
went and caught three hundred foxes, and took firebrands, and
turned tail to tail, and put a firebrand in the midst between
two tails. And when he had set the brands on fire, he let them
go into the standing corn of the Philistines." Milton's Samson is
different. "Agonistes" is the Greek word for an athlete contending for a prize, but to anyone who knows of Christ's
"agony in the garden" it necessarily suggests a spiritual as well
physical conflict. The conflict in *Samson Agonistes* is not simply
between Samson and his Philistine captors but within Samson
himself. His insistence that he has been subjected to captivity
not by Dalila but by himself ("I to myself was false ere thou to
me") has brought on a despair that must be overcome if he is
to be reconciled with God:

> Nor am I in the list of them that hope;
> Hopeless are all my evils, all remediless.

The arrival of Dalila stirs him at least to anger, and the arrival
of Harapha stirs him not only to anger but also to renewed
thought of God's goodness:

> All these indignities, for such they are
> From thine, these evils I deserve and more,
> Acknowledge them from God inflicted on me
> Justly, yet despair not of his final pardon,
> Whose ear is ever open, and his eye
> Gracious to re-admit the suppliant.

The Chorus perceives that Samson is "With plain heroic magnitude of mind/ And celestial vigor armed"; a little later Samson says,

>                 I begin to feel
> Some rousing motions in me, which dispose
> To something extraordinary my thoughts. . . .
> If there be aught of presage in the mind,
> This day will be remarkable in my life
> By some great act, or of my days the last.

We have known all along, of course, what the "great act" will
be, but Milton's play is not about a man who pulls a temple

down; rather, it is about a man who, having violated a Divine trust, matched punishment of his body with punishment of his mind and finally was brought, by God's grace (and with no violence to psychology) and by his own effort, back to triumph, joy, and sanctity.

Milton so insists on the triumph of the conclusion that one can ask if *Samson* is really "of that sort of dramatic poem which is called tragedy." At least two replies can be made. First, the Greeks themselves did not insist that a tragedy necessarily end unhappily. Sophocles' *Oedipus at Colonus* ends with a death that is something of an apotheosis; Aeschylus' *Oresteia* concludes not with a death but with a triumphal procession honoring new, benevolent deities. Second, there is the problem of exactly how unhappy the ending of any tragedy is. It is true that tragedy customarily shows us suffering and death, but it is also true that there is commonly an exhilarating nobility in these sufferings and deaths. W. B. Yeats only slightly overstates what most spectators and readers feel to be a basic truth: "The arts are all the bridal chambers of joy. No tragedy is legitimate unless it leads some great character to his final joy. Polonius may go out wretchedly, but I can hear the dance music in 'Absent thee from felicity awhile,' or in Hamlet's speech over the dead Ophelia, and what of Cleopatra's last farewells, Lear's rage under the lightning, Oedipus sinking down at the story's end into an earth 'riven' by love?"

The joy of tragedy may be touched on in the *Poetics,* where Aristotle speaks cryptically of tragedy effecting a purgation (catharsis) of pity and terror. His words have been variously interpreted, but there is wide agreement that the spectators at a tragedy leave with a sense not of despair but of heightened awareness. Milton, with Aristotle in mind, is saying something like this in his preface, in Manoa's last words, and, most notably, in the Chorus' final assertion that the Israelites (like the audience)

> With peace and consolation [are] dismissed,
> And calm of mind, all passions spent.

## Biographical Note

John Milton (1608–1674) was early dedicated to a career as an interpreter of God to man, but he did not seek a position in the church, apparently because he was intensely aware of its corruptions. He chose, instead, to be a poet; in his greatest work, *Paradise Lost* (1667), he set out to "justify the ways of God to men." During the Commonwealth Period (1649–1660), he had gone blind in the

service of his country, expending his failing eyesight as
Latin Secretary to Cromwell's Council of State; with the
restoration of Charles II in 1660, the republic for which
he had struggled vanished, and he must have felt rather
like the blind Samson whose fellow Israelites did not retain
the liberty he had helped them to win, but were conquered
by the Philistines (see especially lines 692-704). *Samson
Agonistes,* published in 1671, was probably written in the
years immediately preceding, though for some thirty
years Milton had contemplated writing a drama on the
subject.

# Samson Agonistes:

## A DRAMATIC POEM

# OF THAT SORT OF DRAMATIC POEM
# WHICH IS CALLED TRAGEDY

Tragedy, as it was anciently composed, hath been ever held the gravest, moralest, and most profitable of all other poems: therefore said by Aristotle to be of power, by raising pity and fear, or terror, to purge the mind of those and such-like passions,—that is, to temper and reduce them to just measure with a kind of delight, stirred up by reading or seeing those passions well imitated. Nor is Nature wanting in her own effects to make good his assertion; for so, in physic,[a] things of melancholic hue and quality are used against melancholy, sour against sour, salt to remove salt humors. Hence philosophers and other gravest writers, as Cicero, Plutarch, and others, frequently cite out of tragic poets, both to adorn and illustrate their discourse. The Apostle Paul himself thought it not unworthy to insert a verse of Euripides into the text of Holy Scripture, I Cor. xv. 33; and Pareus,[b] commenting on the *Revelation*, divides the whole book, as a tragedy, into acts, distinguished each by a Chorus of heavenly harpings and song between. Heretofore men in highest dignity have labored not a little to be thought able to compose a tragedy. Of that honor Dionysius the elder [c] was no less ambitious than before his attaining to the tyranny. Augustus Caesar also had begun his *Ajax*, but unable to please his own judgment with what he had begun, left it unfinished. Seneca, the philosopher, is by some thought the author of those tragedies (at least the best of them) that go under that name. Gregory Nazianzen, a Father of the Church,

[a] medicine   [b] David Pareus, 16th-century German Calvinist theologian
[c] ancient ruler of Syracuse

thought it not unbeseeming the sanctity of his person to write a tragedy, which he entitled *Christ Suffering*. This is mentioned to vindicate tragedy from the small esteem, or rather infamy, which in the account of many it undergoes at this day, with other common interludes: happening through the poet's error of intermixing comic stuff with tragic sadness and gravity, or introducing trivial and vulgar persons: which by all judicious hath been counted absurd, and brought in without discretion, corruptly to gratify the people. And, though ancient tragedy use no Prologue, yet using sometimes, in case of self-defense or explanation, that which Martial calls an Epistle, in behalf of this tragedy, coming forth after the ancient manner, much different from what among us passes for best, thus much beforehand may be *epistled*—that Chorus is here introduced after the Greek manner, not ancient only, but modern, and still in use among the Italians. In the modeling therefore of this poem, with good reason, the Ancients and Italians are rather followed, as of much more authority and fame. The measure of verse used in the Chorus is of all sorts, called by the Greeks *Monostrophic*, or rather *Apolelymenon*,[d] without regard had to strophe, antistrophe, or epode—which were a kind of stanzas framed only for the music, then used with the Chorus that sung; not essential to the poem, and therefore not material: or, being divided into stanzas or pauses, they may be called *Allaeostropha*.[e] Division into act and scene, referring chiefly to the stage (to which this work never was intended), is here omitted.

It suffices if the whole drama be found not produced beyond the fifth act. Of the style and uniformity, and that commonly called the plot, whether intricate or explicit—which is nothing indeed but such economy, or disposition of the fable, as may stand best with verisimilitude and decorum—they only will best judge who are not unacquainted with Aeschylus, Sophocles, and Euripides, the three tragic poets unequaled yet by any, and the best rule to all who endeavor to write tragedy. The circumscription of time wherein the whole drama begins and ends is, according to ancient rule and best example, within the space of twenty-four hours.

[d] free   [e] irregular

# THE ARGUMENT[f]

*Samson, made captive, blind, and now in the prison at Gaza,[g] there to labor as in a common workhouse, on a festival day, in the general cessation from labor, comes forth into the open air, to a place nigh, somewhat retired, there to sit a while and bemoan his condition. Where he happens at length to be visited by certain friends and equals[h] of his tribe, which make the Chorus, who seek to comfort him what they can; then by his old father, Manoa, who endeavors the like, and withal tells him his purpose to procure his liberty by ransom; lastly, that this feast was proclaimed by the Philistines as a day of thanksgiving for their deliverance from the hands of Samson—which yet more troubles him. Manoa then departs to prosecute his endeavor with the Philistian lords for Samson's redemption; who, in the meanwhile, is visited by other persons, and, lastly, by a public officer to require his coming to the feast before the lords and people, to play or show his strength in their presence. He at first refuses, dismissing the public officer with absolute denial to come; at length persuaded inwardly that this was from God, he yields to go along with him, who came now the second time with great threatenings to fetch him. The Chorus yet remaining on the place, Manoa returns full of joyful hope to procure ere long his son's deliverance: in the midst of which discourse an Ebrew comes in haste, confusedly at first, and afterwards more distinctly, relating the catastrophe—what Samson had done to the Philistines, and by accident to himself; wherewith the tragedy ends.*

## The Persons

| | |
|---|---|
| Samson | Harapha of Gath |
| Manoa, the father of | Public Officer |
| Samson | Messenger |
| Dálila, his wife | Chorus of Danites[i] |

The Scene, before the Prison in Gaza.

---

[f] summary  [g] Gaza, Ekron, Ashdod, Gath, and Ashkelon were the chief Philistine cities  [h] men of his own age  [i] members of the tribe of Dan, to which Manoa belonged

*Samson.*   A little onward lend thy guiding hand
     To these dark steps, a little further on;
     For yonder bank hath choice of sun or shade.
     There I am wont to sit, when any chance
     Relieves me from my task of servile toil,
     Daily in the common prison else enjoined me,
     Where I, a prisoner chained, scarce freely draw
     The air, imprisoned also, close and damp,
     Unwholesome draught. But here I feel amends—
     The breath of heaven fresh blowing, pure and sweet,      10
     With day-spring ʲ born; here leave me to respire.
     This day a solemn feast the people hold
     To Dagon,ᵏ their sea-idol, and forbid
     Laborious works. Unwillingly this rest
     Their superstition yields me; hence, with leave
     Retiring from the popular noise,ˡ I seek
     This unfrequented place, to find some ease—
     Ease to the body some, none to the mind
     From restless thoughts, that, like a deadly swarm
     Of hornets armed, no sooner found alone      20
     But rush upon me thronging, and present
     Times past, what once I was, and what am now.
     Oh, wherefore was my birth from Heaven foretold
     Twice by an Angel, who at last, in sight
     Of both my parents, all in flames ascended
     From off the altar where an offering burned,
     As in a fiery column charioting
     His godlike presence, and from some great act
     Or benefit revealed to Abraham's race?
     Why was my breeding ᵐ ordered and prescribed      30
     As of a person separate to ⁿ God,
     Designed for great exploits, if I must die
     Betrayed, captíved, and both my eyes put out,
     Made of my enemies the scorn and gaze,
     To grind in brazen fetters under task
     With this heaven-gifted strength? O glorious strength,
     Put to the labor of a beast, debased
     Lower than bond-slave! Promise was that I
     Should Israel from Philistian yoke deliver;
     Ask for this great deliverer now, and find him      40

ʲ daybreak   ᵏ god of the Philistines, part man, part fish   ˡ noise of
the populace   ᵐ training   ⁿ set apart for (see Judges 13:7)

Eyeless in Gaza, at the mill with slaves,
Himself in bonds under Philistian yoke.
Yet stay; let me not rashly call in doubt
Divine prediction. What if all foretold
Had been fulfilled but through mine own default?
Whom have I to complain of but myself,
Who this high gift of strength committed to me,
In what part lodged, how easily bereft me,
Under the seal of silence could not keep,
But weakly to a woman must reveal it,                           50
O'ercome with importunity and tears?
O impotence of mind in body strong!
But what is strength without a double share
Of wisdom? Vast, unwieldy, burdensome,
Proudly secure,° yet liable to fall
By weakest subtleties; not made to rule,
But to subserve where wisdom bears command.
God, when he gave me strength, to show withal,
How slight the gift was, hung it in my hair.
But peace! I must not quarrel ᵖ with the will                   60
Of highest dispensation, which herein
Haply had ends above my reach to know.
Suffices that to me strength is my bane,
And proves the source of all my miseries—
So many, and so huge, that each apart
Would ask �q a life to wail. But, chief of all,
O loss of sight, of thee I must complain!
Blind among enemies! O worse than chains,
Dungeon, or beggary, or decrepit age!
Light, the prime work of God, to me is extinct,ʳ              70
And all her various objects of delight
Annulled, which might in part my grief have eased.
Inferior to the vilest now become
Of man or worm, the vilest here excel me:
They creep, yet see, I, dark in light, exposed
To daily fraud, contempt, abuse, and wrong,
Within doors, or without, still ˢ as a fool,
In power of others, never in my own—
Scarce half I seem to live, dead more than half.
O dark, dark, dark, amid the blaze of noon,                    80
Irrecoverably dark, total eclipse
Without all ᵗ hope of day!
O first-created beam, and thou great Word,
"Let there be light, and light was over all,"

---

° heedless of danger    ᵖ find fault     q require    ʳ extinguished    ˢ always
ᵗ any

Why am I thus bereaved <sup>u</sup> thy prime decree?
The Sun to me is dark
And silent <sup>v</sup> as the Moon,
When she deserts the night,
Hid in her vacant interlunar cave.<sup>w</sup>                          90
Since light so necessary is to life,
And almost life itself, if it be true
That light is in the soul,
She all in every part, why was the sight
To such a tender ball as th' eye confined,
So obvious <sup>x</sup> and so easy to be quenched,
And not, as feeling, through all parts diffused,
That she might look at will through every pore?
Then had I not been thus exiled from light,
As in the land of darkness, yet in light,
To live a life half dead, a living death,                            100
And buried; but, O yet more miserable!
Myself my sepulcher, a moving grave;
Buried, yet not exempt,
By privilege of death and burial,
From worst of other evils, pains, and wrongs;
But made hereby obnoxious <sup>y</sup> more
To all the miseries of life,
Life in captivity
Among inhuman foes.
But who are these? for with joint pace I hear                        110
The tread of many feet steering this way;
Perhaps my enemies, who come to stare
At my affliction, and perhaps to insult—
Their daily practice to afflict me more.

*Chorus.*  This, this is he; softly a while;
Let us not break in upon him.
O change beyond report, thought, or belief!
See how he lies at random, carelessly diffused,<sup>z</sup>
With languished <sup>a</sup> head unpropped,
As one past hope, abandoned,                                         120
And by himself given over,
In slavish habit,<sup>b</sup> ill-fitted weeds <sup>c</sup>
O'er-worn and soiled.
Or do my eyes misrepresent? Can this be he,
That heroic, that renowned,
Irresistible Samson? whom, unarmed,

<sup>u</sup> robbed of  <sup>v</sup> inactive  <sup>w</sup> the cave in which the moon supposedly hid
when invisible between its old and new phases  <sup>x</sup> exposed  <sup>y</sup> liable  <sup>z</sup> i.e.,
stretched out  <sup>a</sup> relaxed  <sup>b</sup> dress  <sup>c</sup> clothes

No strength of man, or fiercest wild beast, could with-
    stand;
Who tore the lion as the lion tears the kid;
Ran on embattled armies clad in iron,
And, weaponless himself,                                    130
Made arms ridiculous, useless the forgery
Of brazen shield and spear, the hammered cuirass,
Chalybean-tempered [d] steel, and frock of mail
Adamantean proof; [e]
But safest he who stood aloof,
When insupportably [f] his foot advanced,
In scorn of their proud arms and warlike tools, [g]
Spurned them to death by troops. The bold Ascalonite [h]
Fled from his lion ramp; [i] old warriors turned
Their plated [j] backs under his heel,                      140
Or groveling soiled their crested helmets in the dust.
Then with what trivial weapon came to hand,
The jaw of a dead ass, his sword of bone,
A thousand foreskins [k] fell, the flower of Palestine, [l]
In Ramath-lechi, [m] famous to this day:
Then by main force pulled up, and on his shoulders bore,
The gates of Azza, [n] post and massy bar,
Up to the hill by Hebron, seat of giants old [o]—
No journey of a Sabbath-day, [p] and loaded so—
Like whom [q] the Gentiles feign to bear up Heaven.        150
Which shall I first bewail,
Thy bondage or lost sight,
Prison within prison
Inseparably dark?
Thou art become (O worst imprisonment!)
The dungeon of thyself; thy soul,
(Which men enjoying sight oft without cause complain)
Imprisoned now indeed,
In real darkness of the body dwells,                        160
Shut up from outward light
To incorporate with gloomy night;
For inward light, alas!
Puts forth no visual beam. [r]
O mirror of our fickle state,
Since man on earth, unparalleled!

[d] the Chalybes of the Black Sea were famed for their skill in forging
metal   [e] proof against the hardest steel   [f] irresistibly   [g] weapons   [h] citizen of Ashkelon   [i] spring   [j] armored   [k] i.e., Philistines, who were uncircumcised   [l] Philistia   [m] Judges 15:17   [n] Gaza   [o] city about 40 miles
east of Gaza (see Numbers 13:22, 33)   [p] Mosaic law, as interpreted by
the rabbis, forbade travel on the Sabbath beyond some 3000 feet   [q] i.e.,
Atlas   [r] sense of sight

The rarer thy example stands,
By how much from the top of wondrous glory,
Strongest of mortal men,
To lowest pitch of abject fortune thou art fallen!
For him I reckon not in high estate                          170
Whom long descent of birth,
Or the sphere of fortune,ˢ raises;
But thee, whose strength, while virtue was her mate,
Might have subdued the Earth,
Universally crowned with highest praises.
*Samson.*   I hear the sound of words; their sense the air
Dissolves unjointed ere it reach my ear.
*Chorus.*   He speaks: let us draw nigh. Matchless in might,
The glory late of Israel, now the grief!
We come, thy friends and neighbors not unknown,             180
From Eshtaol and Zora'sᵗ fruitful vale,
To visit or bewail thee; or, if better,
Counsel or consolation we may bring,
Salve to thy sores: apt words have power to swage ᵘ
The tumors of a troubled mind,
And are as balm to festered wounds.
*Samson.*   Your coming, friends, revives me; for I learn
Now of my own experience, not by talk,
How counterfeit a coin they are who "friends"
Bear in their superscription ᵛ (of the most               190
I would be understood). In prosperous days
They swarm, but in adverse withdraw their head,
Not to be found, though sought. Ye see, O friends,
How many evils have enclosed me round;
Yet that which was the worst now least afflicts me,
Blindness; for, had I sight, confused with shame,
How could I once look up, or heave the head,
Who, like a foolish pilot, have shipwrecked
My vessel trusted to me from above,
Gloriously rigged, and for a word, a tear,                  200
Fool! have divulged the secret gift of God
To a deceitful woman? Tell me, friends,
Am I not sung and proverbed for a fool
In every street? Do they not say, "How well
Are come upon him his deserts"? Yet why?
Immeasurable strength they might behold
In me; of wisdom nothing more than mean.ʷ
This with the other should at least have paired; ˣ
These two, proportioned ill, drove me transverse.ʸ

ˢ wheel of fortune—the medieval idea that men rise and fall as the
wheel turns    ᵗ Israelite towns    ᵘ assuage    ᵛ value engraved on a coin
ʷ average    ˣ equaled    ʸ off the course

*Chorus.*    Tax [z] not divine disposal. Wisest men                210
   Have erred, and by bad women been deceived;
   And shall again, pretend they ne'er so wise. [a]
   Deject not, then, so overmuch thyself,
   Who hast of sorrow thy full load besides.
   Yet, truth to say, I oft have heard men wonder
   Why thou should'st wed Philistian women rather
   Than of thine own tribe fairer, or as fair,
   At least of thy own nation, and as noble.
*Samson.*    The first I saw at Timna, [b] and she pleased
   Me, not my parents, that I sought to wed                        220
   The daughter of an infidel. They knew not
   That what I motioned was of God; I knew
   From intimate [c] impulse, and therefore urged
   The marriage on, that, by occasion hence,
   I might begin Israel's deliverance—
   The work to which I was divinely called.
   She proving false, the next I took to wife
   (O that I never had! fond [d] wish too late!)
   Was in the vale of Sorec, Dálila,
   That specious monster, my accomplished snare.                   230
   I thought it lawful from my former act,
   And the same end, still watching to oppress
   Israel's oppressors. Of what now I suffer
   She was not the prime cause, but I myself,
   Who, vanquished with a peal of words (O weakness!),
   Gave up my fort of silence to a woman.
*Chorus.*    In seeking just occasion to provoke
   The Philistine, thy country's enemy,
   Thou never wast remiss, I bear thee witness;
   Yet Israel still serves [e] with all his sons. [f]              240
*Samson.*    That fault I take not on me, but transfer
   On Israel's governors and heads of tribes,
   Who, seeing those great acts which God had done
   Singly by me against their conquerors,
   Acknowledged not, or not at all considered, [g]
   Deliverance offered. I, on th' other side,
   Used no ambition [h] to commend my deeds;
   The deeds themselves, though mute, spoke loud the doer.
   But they persisted deaf, and would not seem
   To count them things worth notice, till at length              250
   Their lords, the Philistines, with gathered powers, [i]

---

[z] blame    [a] i.e., however wisely they may intend    [b] Timnath, a Philistine city    [c] inward    [d] foolish    [e] is in bondage    [f] i.e., Israel's twelve tribes    [g] appreciated    [h] attempt to seek public support    [i] troops

Entered Judea seeking me, who then
Safe to the rock of Etham [j] was retired—
Not flying, but forecasting in what place
To set upon them, what advantaged best.
Meanwhile the men of Judah, to prevent
The harass of their land, beset me round;
I willingly on some conditions [k] came
Into their hands, and they as gladly yield me
To the uncircumcised a welcome prey,                         260
Bound with two cords. But cords to me were threads
Touched with the flame: on their whole host I flew
Unarmed, and with a trivial weapon [l] felled
Their choicest youth; they only lived who fled.
Had Judah that day joined, or one whole tribe,
They had by this [m] possessed the towers of Gath,[n]
And lorded over them whom now they serve.
But what more oft, in nations grown corrupt,
And by their vices brought to servitude,
Than to love bondage more than liberty—                      270
Bondage with ease than strenuous liberty—
And to despise, or envy, or suspect,
Whom God hath of his special favor raised
As their deliverer? If he aught begin,
How frequent to desert him, and at last
To heap ingratitude on worthiest deeds!
*Chorus.*    Thy words to my remembrance bring
How Succoth and the fort of Penuel
Their great deliverer contemned,
The matchless Gideon, in pursuit                             280
Of Madian, and her vanquished kings; [o]
And how ingrateful Ephraim
Had dealt with Jephtha, who by argument,
Not worse than by his shield and spear,
Defended Israel from the Ammonite,
Had not his prowess quelled their pride
In that sore battle when so many died
Without reprieve, adjudged to death
For want of well pronouncing *Shibboleth.*[p]
*Samson.*    Of such examples add me to the roll.            290
Me easily indeed mine [q] may neglect,
But God's proposed deliverance not so.
*Chorus.*    Just are the ways of God,
And justifiable to men,
Unless there be who think not [r] God at all.

---

[j] Etam, a hill town   [k] Judges 15: 12–13   [l] the jawbone of an ass   [m] i.e.,
by this time   [n] i.e., all Philistia   [o] Judges 8:4–9   [p] Judges 11:12–33;
12:5–6   [q] i.e., my own people   [r] do not believe in

If any be, they walk obscure; [s]
For of such doctrine never was there school,
But the heart of the fool,
And no man therein doctor [t] but himself.
    Yet more there be who doubt his ways not just,                   300
As to his own edicts found contradicting;
Then give the reins to wandering thought,
Regardless of his glory's diminution,
Till, by their own perplexities involved,
They ravel [u] more, still [v] less resolved,
But never find self-satisfying solution.
    As if they would confine th' Interminable, [w]
And tie him to his own prescript,
Who made our laws to bind us, not himself,
And hath full right to exempt                                              310
Whomso it pleases him by choice
From national obstriction, [x] without taint
Of sin, or legal debt;
For with his own laws he can best dispense.
    He would not else, who never wanted means,
Nor in respect of the enemy just cause,
To set his people free,
Have prompted this heroic Nazarite, [y]
Against his vow of strictest purity,
To seek in marriage that fallacious [z] bride,                            320
Unclean, unchaste.
    Down, Reason, then; at least, vain reasonings down;
Though Reason here aver
That moral verdict quits [a] her of unclean:
Unchaste was subsequent; her stain, not his.
    But see! here comes thy reverend sire,
With careful [b] step, locks white as down,
Old Manoa: advise [c]
Forthwith how thou ought'st to receive him.

*Samson.*   Ay me! another inward grief, awaked                        330
    With mention of that name, renews th' assault.

*Manoa.*   Brethren and men of Dan (for such ye seem,
    Though in this uncouth [d] place), if old respect,
    As I suppose, towards your once gloried friend,
    My son, now captive, hither hath informed [e]
    Your younger feet, while mine, cast back with age,

---

[s] in darkness  [t] authoritative teacher  [u] entangle  [v] always  [w] Infinite
[x] obligation (here, Mosaic law forbidding marriage with Gentiles)  [y] one
who, consecrated to God, abstained from wine, unclean food, and hair-
cuts  [z] deceitful  [a] acquits  [b] sorrowful  [c] consider  [d] unfamiliar  [e] guided

Came lagging after, say if he be here.
*Chorus.* As signal [f] now in low dejected state
As erst [g] in highest, behold him where he lies.
*Manoa.* O miserable change! Is this the man, 340
That invincible Samson, far renowned,
The dread of Israel's foes, who with a strength
Equivalent to Angels' walked their streets,
None offering fight; who, single combatant,
Dueled their armies ranked in proud array,
Himself an army—now unequal match
To save himself against a coward armed
At one spear's length? O ever-failing trust
In mortal strength! and, oh, what not in man
Deceivable and vain? Nay, what thing good 350
Prayed for, but often proves our woe, our bane?
I prayed for children, and thought barrenness
In wedlock a reproach; I gained a son,
And such a son as all men hailed me happy:
Who would be now a father in my stead?
Oh, wherefore did God grant me my request,
And as a blessing with such pomp adorned?
Why are his gifts desirable, to tempt
Our earnest prayers, then, given with solemn hand
As graces,[h] draw a scorpion's tail behind? 360
For this did the Angel twice descend? for this
Ordained thy nurture holy, as of a plant
Select and sacred? glorious for a while,
The miracle of men; then in an hour
Ensnared, assaulted, overcome, led bound,
Thy foes' derision, captive, poor and blind,
Into a dungeon thrust, to work with slaves!
Alas! methinks whom God hath chosen once
To worthiest deeds, if he through frailty err,
He should not so o'erwhelm, and as a thrall 370
Subject him to so foul indignities,
Be it but for honor's sake of former deeds.
*Samson.* Appoint [i] not heavenly disposition, Father.
Nothing of all these evils hath befallen me
But justly; I myself have brought them on;
Sole author I, sole cause. If aught seem vile,
As vile hath been my folly, who have profaned
The mystery of God, given me under pledge
Of vow, and have betrayed it to a woman,
A Canaanite, my faithless enemy. 380
This well I knew, nor was at all surprised,

[f] conspicuous  [g] formerly  [h] favors  [i] direct

But warned by oft experience. Did not she
Of Timna first betray me, and reveal
The secret wrested from me in her height
Of nuptial love professed, carrying it straight
To them who had corrupted her, my spies
And rivals? In this other was there found
More faith, who, also in her prime of love,
Spousal embraces, vitiated with gold,
Though offered only, by the scent conceived,                    390
Her spurious first-born, treason against me?
Thrice she assayed, with flattering prayers and sighs,
And amorous reproaches, to win from me
My capital [j] secret, in what part my strength
Lay stored, in what part summed, that she might know;
Thrice I deluded her, and turned to sport
Her importunity, each time perceiving
How openly and with what impudence
She purposed to betray me, and (which was worse
Than undissembled hate) with what contempt                    400
She sought to make me traitor to myself.
Yet, the fourth time, when, mustering all her wiles,
With blandished parleys, feminine assaults,
Tongue-batteries, she surceased not day nor night
To storm me, over-watched and wearied out,
At times when men seek most repose and rest,
I yielded, and unlocked her all my heart,
Who, with a grain of manhood well resolved,
Might easily have shook off all her snares;
But foul effeminacy held me yoked                             410
Her bond-slave. O indignity, O blot
To honor and religion! servile mind
Rewarded well with servile punishment!
The base degree to which I now am fallen,
These rags, this grinding, is not yet so base
As was my former servitude, ignoble,
Unmanly, ignominious, infamous,
True slavery; and that blindness worse than this,
That saw not how degenerately I served.
_Manoa._   I cannot praise thy marriage-choices, son—          420
Rather approved them not; but thou didst plead
Divine impulsion prompting how thou might'st
Find some occasion to infest [k] our foes.
I state not that; this I am sure—our foes
Found soon occasion thereby to make thee
Their captive, and their triumph; thou the sooner

[j] chief (a pun alluding to Samson's hair: Latin _caput_, "head")   [k] harass

Temptation found'st, or over-potent charms,
To violate the sacred trust of silence
Deposited within thee—which to have kept
Tacit was in thy power. True; and thou bear'st          430
Enough, and more, the burden of that fault;
Bitterly hast thou paid, and still art paying,
That rigid score.[1] A worse thing yet remains:—
This day the Philistines a popular feast
Here celebrate in Gaza, and proclaim
Great pomp, and sacrifice, and praises loud,
To Dagon, as their god who hath delivered
Thee, Samson, bound and blind, into their hands—
Them out of thine, who slew'st them many a slain.
So Dagon shall be magnified, and God,          440
Besides whom is no god, compared with idols,
Disglorified, blasphemed, and had in scorn
By th' idolatrous rout amidst their wine;
Which to have come to pass by means of thee,
Samson, of all thy sufferings think the heaviest,
Of all reproach [m] the most with shame that ever
Could have befallen thee and thy father's house.
*Samson.*   Father, I do acknowledge and confess
That I this honor, I this pomp, have brought
To Dagon, and advanced his praises high          450
Among the heathen round—to God have brought
Dishonor, obloquy, and oped the mouths
Of idolists and atheists; have brought scandal
To Israel, diffidence[n] of God, and doubt
In feeble hearts, propense [o] enough before
To waver, or fall off and join with idols;
Which is my chief affliction, shame and sorrow,
The anguish of my soul, that suffers not
Mine eye to harbor sleep, or thoughts to rest.
This only hope relieves me, that the strife          460
With me hath end. All the contést is now
'Twixt God and Dagon. Dagon hath presumed,
Me overthrown, to enter lists with God,
His deity comparing and preferring
Before the God of Abraham. He, be sure,
Will not connive,[p] or linger, thus provoked,
But will arise, and his great name assert.
Dagon must stoop, and shall ere long receive
Such a discomfit as shall quite despoil him
Of all these boasted trophies won on [q] me,          470
And with confusion blank [r] his worshipers.

[1] record of debts   [m] dishonor   [n] distrust   [o] inclined   [p] ignore   [q] over confound

*Manoa.*     With cause this hope relieves thee; and these
          words
     I as a prophecy receive; for God,
     Nothing more certain, will not long defer
     To vindicate the glory of his name
     Against all competition, nor will long
     Endure it doubtful whether God be Lord
     Or Dagon. But for thee what shall be done?
     Thou must not in the meanwhile, here forgot,
     Lie in this miserable loathsome plight                         480
     Neglected. I already have made way
     To some Philistian lords, with whom to treat
     About thy ransom. Well they may by this
     Have satisfied their utmost of revenge,
     By pains and slaveries, worse than death, inflicted
     On thee, who now no more canst do them harm.
*Samson.*    Spare that proposal, Father; spare the trouble
     Of that solicitation. Let me here,
     As I deserve, pay on[s] my punishment,
     And expiate, if possible, my crime,                            490
     Shameful garrulity. To have revealed
     Secrets of men, the secrets of a friend,
     How heinous had the fact[t] been, how deserving
     Contempt and scorn of all—to be excluded
     All friendship, and avoided as a blab,
     The mark of fool set on his front! But I
     God's counsel have not kept, his holy secret
     Presumptuously have published, impiously,
     Weakly at least and shamefully—a sin
     That Gentiles in their parables condemn                        500
     To their abyss and horrid pains confined.[u]
*Manoa.*    Be penitent, and for thy fault contrite;
     But act not in[v] thy own affliction, son.
     Repent the sin; but, if the punishment
     Thou canst avoid, self-preservation bids;
     Or th' execution leave to high disposal,
     And let another hand, not thine, exact
     Thy penal forfeit from thyself. Perhaps
     God will relent, and quit thee all his debt;[w]
     Who ever more approves and more accepts                        510
     (Best pleased with humble and filial submission)
     Him who, imploring mercy, sues for life,
     Than who, self-rigorous, chooses death as due;
     Which argues over-just, and self-displeased
     For self-offense more than for God offended.

[s] continue to pay   [t] deed   [u] an allusion to Prometheus and Tantalus
[v] i.e., to bring about   [w] i.e., cancel all your debt to him

Reject not, then, what offered means who knows
But God hath set before us to return thee
Home to thy country and his sacred house,
Where thou may'st bring thy offerings, to avert
His further ire, with prayers and vows renewed. 520
*Samson.*  His pardon I implore; but, as for life,
To what end should I seek it? When in strength
All mortals I excelled, and great in hopes,
With youthful courage, and magnanimous thoughts
Of birth from Heaven foretold and high exploits,
Full of divine instinct, after some proof
Of acts indeed heroic, far beyond
The sons of Anak,ˣ famous now and blazed,
Fearless of danger, like a petty god
I walked about, admired of all, and dreaded 530
On hostile ground, none daring my affront ʸ—
Then, swoll'n with pride, into the snare I fell
Of fair fallacious looks, venereal trains,ᶻ
Softened with pleasure and voluptuous life,
At length to lay my head and hallowed pledge
Of all my strength in the lascivious lap
Of a deceitful concubine, who shore me,
Like a tame wether, all my precious fleece,
Then turned me out ridiculous, despoiled,
Shaven, and disarmed among my enemies. 540
*Chorus.*  Desire of wine and all delicious drinks,
Which many a famous warrior overturns,
Thou could'st repress; nor did the dancing ruby,
Sparkling out-poured, the flavor or the smell,
Or taste, that cheers the heart of gods and men,
Allure thee from the cool crystalline stream.
*Samson.*  Wherever fountain or fresh current flowed
Against ᵃ the eastern ray, translucent, pure ᵇ
With touch ethereal of Heaven's fiery rod,ᶜ
I drank, from the clear milky juice ᵈ allaying 550
Thirst, and refreshed; nor envied them the grape
Whose heads that turbulent liquor fills with fumes.
*Chorus.*  O madness! to think use of strongest wines
And strongest drinks our chief support of health,
When God with these forbidden made choice to rear
His mighty champion, strong above compare,
Whose drink was only from the liquid brook!
*Samson.*  But what availed this temperance, not complete
Against another object more enticing?

ˣ giants (see Numbers 13:33)  ʸ to encounter me  ᶻ sexual attractions
ᵃ toward  ᵇ water flowing eastward was thought purest  ᶜ the sun's rays
ᵈ fresh water

What boots [e] it at one gate to make defense,                        560
And at another to let in the foe,
Effeminately vanquished? by which means,
Now blind, disheartened, shamed, dishonored, quelled,
To what can I be useful? wherein serve
My nation, and the work from Heaven imposed?
But to sit idle on the household hearth,
A burdenous drone; to visitants a gaze,
Or pitied object; these redundant [f] locks,
Robustious [g] to no purpose, clustering down,
Vain monument of strength; till length of years                        570
And sedentary numbness craze [h] my limbs
To a contemptible old age obscure.
Here rather let me drudge, and earn my bread,
Till vermin, or the draff [i] of servile food,
Consume me, and oft-invocated death
Hasten the welcome end of all my pains.

*Manoa.*   Wilt thou then serve the Philistines with that
    gift
Which was expressly given thee to annoy [j] them?
Better at home lie bed-rid, not only idle,
Inglorious, unemployed, with age outworn.                        580
But God, who caused a fountain at thy prayer
From the dry ground to spring,[k] thy thirst to allay
After the brunt of battle, can as easy
Cause light again within thy eyes to spring,
Wherewith to serve him better than thou hast.
And I persuade me so. Why else this strength
Miraculous yet remaining in those locks?
His might continues in thee not for naught,
Nor shall his wondrous gifts be frustrate thus.

*Samson.*   All otherwise to me my thoughts portend,—                        590
That these dark orbs no more shall treat with light,
Nor th' other light of life continue long,
But yield to double darkness [l] nigh at hand;
So much I feel my genial [m] spirits droop,
My hopes all flat: Nature within me seems
In all her functions weary of herself;
My race of glory run, and race of shame,
And I shall shortly be with them that rest.

*Manoa.*   Believe not these suggestions, which proceed
From anguish of the mind, and humors black [n]                        600
That mingle with thy fancy. I, however,
Must not omit a father's timely care
To prosecute the means of thy deliverance

[e] avails   [f] flowing   [g] vigorous   [h] impair   [i] dregs   [j] damage   [k] Judges
15:18–19   [l] i.e., blindness and death   [m] natural   [n] i.e., melancholy

By ransom or how else: meanwhile be calm,
And healing words from these thy friends admit.
*Samson.* Oh, that torment should not be confined
To the body's wounds and sores,
With maladies innumerable
In heart, head, breast, and reins,°
But must secret passage find                    610
To th' inmost mind,
There exercise all his fierce accidents,ᵖ
And on her purest spirits prey,
As on entrails, joints, and limbs,
With answerable ᑫ pains, but more intense,
Though void of corporal sense!
   My griefs not only pain me
As a lingering disease,
But, finding no redress, ferment and rage;
Nor less than wounds immedicable           620
Rankle, and fester, and gangrene,
To black mortification,
Thoughts, my tormentors, armed with daily stings,
Mangle my apprehensive ʳ tenderest parts,
Exasperate, exulcerate, and raise
Dire inflammation, which no cooling herb
Or med'cinal liquor can assuage,
Nor breath of vernal air from snowy Alp.
Sleep hath forsook and given me o'er
To death's benumbing opium as my only cure;   630
Thence faintings, swoonings of despair,
And sense of Heaven's desertion.
   I was his nursling once and choice delight,
His destined from the womb,
Promised by heavenly message ˢ twice descending.
Under his special eye
Abstemious I grew up and thrived amain;
He led me on to mightiest deeds,
Above the nerve ᵗ of mortal arm,
Against the uncircumcised, our enemies:        640
But now hath cast me off as never known,
And to those cruel enemies,
Whom I by his appointment had provoked,
Left me, all helpless with th' irreparable loss
Of sight, reserved alive to be repeated
The subject of their cruelty or scorn.
Nor am I in the list of them that hope;

° loins  ᵖ symptoms of disease  ᑫ corresponding  ʳ sensitive  ˢ messenger  ᵗ sinew

Hopeless are all my evils, all remediless.
This one prayer yet remains, might I be heard,
No long petition—speedy death,                                    650
The close of all my miseries and the balm.
*Chorus.*   Many are the sayings of the wise,
In ancient and in modern books enrolled,
Extolling patience as the truest fortitude,
And to the bearing well of all calamities,
All chances incident to man's frail life,
Consolatories writ
With studied argument, and much persuasion sought,
Lenient of ᵘ grief and anxious thought.
But with th' afflicted in his pangs their sound          660
Little prevails, or rather seems a tune
Harsh, and of dissonant mood ᵛ from his complaint,
Unless he feel within
Some source of consolation from above,
Secret refreshings that repair his strength
And fainting spirits uphold.
   God of our fathers! what is Man,
That thou towards him with hand so various—
Or might I say contrarious?—
Temper'st thy providence through his short course:        670
Not evenly, as thou rul'st
The angelic orders, and inferior creatures mute,
Irrational and brute?
Nor do I name of men the common rout,
That, wandering loose about,
Grow up and perish as the summer fly,
Heads ʷ without name, no more remembered;
But such as thou hast solemnly elected,
With gifts and graces eminently adorned,
To some great work, thy glory,                            680
And people's safety, which in part they effect.
Yet toward these, thus dignified, thou oft,
Amidst their height of noon,
Changest thy countenance and thy hand, with no
   regard
Of highest favors past
From thee on them, or them to thee of service.
   Nor only dost degrade them, or remit
To life obscured,ˣ which were a fair dismission,
But throw'st them lower than thou didst exalt them
   high—

ᵘ allaying   ᵛ mode (in music)   ʷ persons   ˣ disgraced

Unseemly falls in human eye,                                          690
Too grievous for the trespass or omission;
Oft leav'st them to the hostile sword
Of heathen and profane, their carcasses
To dogs and fowls a prey, or else captíved,
Or to the unjust tribunals, under change of times,
And condemnation of the ingrateful multitude.
If these they scape, perhaps in poverty
With sickness and disease thou bow'st them down,
Painful diseases and deformed,
In crude ʸ old age;                                                   700
Though not disordinate,ᶻ yet causeless suffering
The punishment of dissolute days. In fine,
Just or unjust alike seem miserable,
For oft alike both come to evil end.
    So deal not with this once thy glorious champion,
The image of thy strength, and mighty minister.
What do I beg? how hast thou dealt already!
Behold him in this state calamitous, and turn
His labors, for thou canst, to peaceful end.
    But who is this? what thing of sea or land—          710
Female of sex it seems—
That, so bedecked, ornate, and gay,
Comes this way sailing,
Like a stately ship
Of Tarsus,ᵃ bound for th' isles
Of Javan ᵇ or Gadire,ᶜ
With all her bravery ᵈ on, and tackle trim,
Sails filled, and streamers waving,
Courted by all the winds that hold them play;
An amber ᵉ scent of odorous perfume                        720
Her harbinger, a damsel train behind?
Some rich Philistian matron she may seem;
And now, at nearer view, no other certain
Than Dálila thy wife.
*Samson.*    My wife! my traitress! let her not come near me.
*Chorus.*    Yet on she moves; now stands and eyes thee
        fixed,
About t' have spoke; but now, with head declined,
Like a fair flower surcharged with dew, she weeps,
And words addressed ᶠ seem into tears dissolved,
Wetting the borders of her silken veil.                       730
But now again she makes address to speak.
*Dálila.*    With doubtful feet and wavering resolution

ʸ premature   ᶻ intemperate   ᵃ seaport in Asia Minor   ᵇ Ionian islands
ᶜ Cadiz   ᵈ finery   ᵉ ambergris   ᶠ prepared for utterance

I came, still dreading thy displeasure, Samson;
Which to have merited, without excuse,
I cannot but acknowledge. Yet, if tears
May expiate (though the fact [g] more evil drew
In the perverse event [h] than I foresaw),
My penance [i] hath not slackened, though my pardon
No way assured. But conjugal affection,
Prevailing over fear and timorous doubt,                    740
Hath led me on, desirous to behold
Once more thy face, and know of thy estate,[j]
If aught in my ability may serve
To lighten what thou suffer'st, and appease
Thy mind with what amends is in my power—
Though late, yet in some part to recompense
My rash but more unfortunate misdeed.

*Samson.*    Out, out, hyena! [k] These are thy wonted arts,
And arts of every woman false like thee—
To break all faith, all vows, deceive, betray;            750
Then, as repentant, to submit, beseech,
And reconcilement move [l] with feigned remorse,
Confess, and promise wonders in her change—
Not truly penitent, but chief to try
Her husband, how far urged his patience bears,
His virtue or weakness which way to assail:
Then, with more cautious and instructed skill,
Again transgresses, and again submits;
That wisest and best men, full oft beguiled,
With goodness principled not to reject                     760
The penitent, but ever to forgive,
Are drawn to wear out miserable days,
Entangled with a poisonous bosom-snake,
If not by quick destruction soon cut off,
As I by thee, to ages an example.

*Dálila.*    Yet hear me, Samson, not that I endeavor
To lessen or extenuate my offense,
But that, on th' other side, if it be weighed
By itself, with aggravations not surcharged,
Or else with just allowance counterpoised,                770
I may, if possible, thy pardon find
The easier towards me, or thy hatred less.
First granting, as I do, it was a weakness
In me, but incident to all our sex,
Curiosity, inquisitive, importune [m]
Of secrets, then with like infirmity

To publish ⁿ them—both common female faults—
Was it not weakness also to make known,
For importunity, that is for naught,
Wherein consisted all thy strength and safety?          780
To what I did thou show'dst me first the way.
But I to enemies revealed, and should not!
Nor should'st thou have trusted that to woman's frailty:
Ere I to thee, thou to thyself wast cruel.
Let weakness, then, with weakness come to parle, °
So near related, or the same of kind; ᴾ
Thine forgive mine, that men may censure thine
The gentler, if severely thou exact not
More strength from me than in thyself was found.
And what if love, which thou interpret'st hate,          790
The jealousy of love, powerful of sway
In human hearts, nor less in mine towards thee,
Caused what I did? I saw thee mutable
Of fancy; �q feared lest one day thou would'st leave me,
As her at Timna; sought by all means, therefore,
How to endear, and hold thee to me firmest:
No better way I saw than by importuning
To learn thy secrets, get into my power
Thy key of strength and safety. Thou wilt say,
"Why, then, revealed?" I was assured by those          800
Who tempted me that nothing was designed
Against thee but safe custody and hold.
That made for me; ʳ I knew that liberty
Would draw thee forth to perilous enterprises,
While I at home sat full of cares and fears,
Wailing thy absence in my widowed bed;
Here I should still enjoy thee, day and night,
Mine and love's prisoner, not the Philistines',
Whole to myself, unhazarded abroad,
Fearless at home of partners in my love.          810
These reasons in love's law have passed for good,
Though fond ˢ and reasonless to some perhaps;
And love hath oft, well meaning, wrought much woe,
Yet always pity or pardon hath obtained.
Be not unlike all others, not austere
As thou art strong, inflexible as steel.
If thou in strength all mortals dost exceed.
In uncompassionate anger do not so.

*Samson.*      How cunningly the sorceress displays
Her own trangressions, to upbraid me mine!          820

ⁿ make public  ° parley  ᴾ nature  q affection  ʳ that was to my advantage  ˢ foolish

That malice, not repentance, brought thee hither,
By this appears. I gave, thou say'st, th' example,
I led the way—bitter reproach, but true;
I to myself was false ere thou to me.
Such pardon, therefore, as I give my folly
Take to thy wicked deed; which when thou seest
Impartial, self-severe, inexorable,
Thou wilt renounce thy seeking, and much rather
Confess it feigned. Weakness is thy excuse,
And I believe it—weakness to resist                    830
Philistian gold. If weakness may excuse,
What murderer, what traitor, parricide,
Incestuous, sacrilegious, but may plead it?
All wickedness is weakness; that plea, therefore,
With God or man will gain thee no remission.
But love constrained thee! Call it furious rage
To satisfy thy lust. Love seeks to have love;
My love how could'st thou hope, who took'st the way
To raise in me inexpiable hate,
Knowing, as needs I must, by thee betrayed?           840
In vain thou striv'st to cover shame with shame,
Or by evasions thy crime uncover'st more.
*Dálila.*    Since thou determin'st weakness for no plea
In man or woman, though to thy own condemning,
Hear what assaults I had, what snares besides,
What sieges girt me round, ere I consented;
Which might have awed the best-resolved of men,
The constantest, to have yielded without blame.
It was not gold, as to my charge thou lay'st,
That wrought with me. Thou know'st the magistrates    850
And princes of my country came in person,
Solicited, commanded, threatened, urged,
Adjured by all the bonds of civil duty
And of religion—pressed how just it was,
How honorable, how glorious, to entrap
A common enemy, who had destroyed
Such numbers of our nation: and the priest
Was not behind, but ever at my ear,
Preaching how meritorious with the gods
It would be to ensnare an irreligious                 860
Dishonorer of Dagon. What had I
To oppose against such powerful arguments?
Only my love of thee held long debate,
And combated in silence all these reasons
With hard contest. At length, that grounded maxim,
So rife and celebrated in the mouths

Of wisest men, that to the public good
Private respects <sup>t</sup> must yield, with grave authority
Took full possession of me, and prevailed;
Virtue, as I thought, truth, duty, so enjoining.                    870
*Samson.*    I thought where all thy circling <sup>u</sup> wiles
      would end—
In feigned religion, smooth hypocrisy!
But, had thy love, still odiously pretended,
Been, as it ought, sincere, it would have taught thee
Far other reasonings, brought forth other deeds.
I, before all the daughters of my tribe
And of my nation, chose thee from among
My enemies, loved thee, as too well thou knew'st;
Too well; unbosomed all my secrets to thee,
Not out of levity, but overpowered                    880
By thy request, who could deny thee nothing;
Yet now am judged an enemy. Why, then,
Didst thou at first receive me for thy husband—
Then, as since then, thy country's foe professed?
Being once a wife, for me thou wast to leave
Parents and country; nor was I their subject,
Nor under their protection, but my own;
Thou mine, not theirs. If aught against my life
Thy country sought of thee, it sought unjustly,
Against the law of nature, law of nations;                    890
No more thy country, but an impious crew
Of men conspiring to uphold their state
By worse than hostile deeds, violating the ends
For which our country is a name so dear;
Not therefore to be obeyed. But zeal moved thee;
To please thy gods thou didst it! Gods unable
To acquit themselves and prosecute their foes
But by ungodly deeds, the contradiction
Of their own deity, gods cannot be—
Less therefore to be pleased, obeyed, or feared.                    900
These false pretexts and varnished colors failing,
Bare in thy guilt, how foul must thou appear!
*Dálila.*    In argument with men a woman ever
Goes by <sup>v</sup> the worse, whatever be her cause.
*Samson.*    For want of words, no doubt, or lack of breath!
Witness when I was worried with thy peals.
*Dálila.*    I was a fool, too rash, and quite mistaken
In what I thought would have succeeded best.
Let me obtain forgiveness of thee, Samson;

<sup>t</sup> interests    <sup>u</sup> devious    <sup>v</sup> comes off

Afford me place to show what recompense                                            910
Towards thee I intend for what I have misdone,
Misguided. Only what remains past cure
Bear not too sensibly,<sup>w</sup> nor still insist
To afflict thyself in vain. Though sight be lost,
Life yet hath many solaces, enjoyed
Where other senses want <sup>x</sup> not their delights—
At home, in leisure and domestic ease,
Exempt from many a care and chance to which
Eyesight exposes, daily, men abroad.<sup>y</sup>
I to the lords will intercede, not doubting                                        920
Their favorable ear, that I may fetch thee
From forth this loathsome prison-house, to abide
With me, where my redoubled love and care,
With nursing diligence, to me glad office,<sup>z</sup>
May ever tend about thee to old age,
With all things grateful <sup>a</sup> cheered, and so supplied
That what by me thou hast lost thou least shalt miss.
*Samson.*    No, no; of my condition take no care;
It fits not; thou and I long since are twain;                                      930
Nor think me so unwary or accursed
To bring my feet again into the snare
Where once I have been caught. I know thy trains,<sup>b</sup>
Though dearly to my cost, thy gins, and toils.<sup>c</sup>
Thy fair enchanted cup,<sup>d</sup> and warbling charms,<sup>e</sup>
No more on me have power; their force is nulled;
So much of adder's wisdom <sup>f</sup> I have learned,
To fence my ear against thy sorceries.
If in my flower of youth and strength, when all men
Loved, honored, feared me, thou alone could hate me,
Thy husband, slight me, sell me, and forgo me,                                     940
How would'st thou use me now, blind, and thereby
Deceivable, in most things as a child
Helpless, thence easily contemned and scorned,
And last neglected! How would'st thou insult,
When I must live uxorious to thy will
In perfect thraldom! how again betray me,
Bearing my words and doings to the lords
To gloss <sup>g</sup> upon, and, censuring,<sup>h</sup> frown or smile!
This jail I count the house of liberty
To thine, whose doors my feet shall never enter.                                   950
*Dálila.*    Let me approach at least, and touch thy hand.
*Samson.*    Not for thy life, lest fierce remembrance wake

<sup>w</sup> sensitively    <sup>x</sup> lack    <sup>y</sup> outdoors    <sup>z</sup> responsibility    <sup>a</sup> comforting
<sup>b</sup> schemes    <sup>c</sup> traps and nets    <sup>d</sup> Jeremiah 51:7    <sup>e</sup> songs    <sup>f</sup> adders were
supposedly deaf to charmers (see Psalms 58:4–5)    <sup>g</sup> comment    <sup>h</sup> judg-
ing

My sudden rage to tear thee joint by joint.
At distance I forgive thee, go with that;
Bewail thy falsehood, and the pious works
It hath brought forth to make thee memorable
Among illustrious women, faithful wives;
Cherish thy hastened widowhood with the gold
Of matrimonial treason: so farewell.

*Dálila.*    I see thou art implacable, more deaf          960
To prayers than winds and seas. Yet winds to seas
Are reconciled at length, and sea to shore:
Thy anger, unappeasable, still rages,
Eternal tempest never to be calmed.
Why do I humble thus myself, and, suing
For peace, reap nothing but repulse and hate,
Bid go with evil omen, and the brand
Of infamy upon my name denounced?
To mix with thy concernments I desist
Henceforth, nor too much disapprove my own.          970
Fame,[1] if not double-faced, is double-mouthed,
And with contrary blast proclaims most deeds;
On both his wings, one black, th' other white,
Bears greatest names in his wild airy flight.
My name, perhaps, among the circumcised
In Dan, in Judah, and the bordering tribes,
To all posterity may stand defamed,
With malediction mentioned, and the blot
Of falsehood most unconjugal traduced.
But in my country, where I most desire,          980
In Ecron, Gaza, Asdod, and in Gath,
I shall be named among the famousest
Of women, sung at solemn festivals,
Living and dead recorded, who to save
Her country from a fierce destroyer chose
Above the faith of wedlock bands; my tomb
With odors[j] visited and annual flowers;
Not less renowned than in Mount Ephraim
Jael, who, with inhospitable guile,
Smote Sisera sleeping, through the temples nailed.[k]          990
Nor shall I count it heinous to enjoy
The public marks of honor and reward
Conferred upon me for the piety
Which to my country I was judged to have shown.
At this whoever envies or repines,
I leave him to his lot, and like my own.

[1] rumor   [j] spices   [k] Judges 4–5

*Chorus.*   She's gone—a manifest serpent by her sting
    Discovered in the end, till now concealed.
*Samson.*   So let her go. God sent her to debase me,
    And aggravate my folly, who committed.          1000
    To such a viper his most sacred trust
    Of secrecy, my safety, and my life.
*Chorus.*   Yet beauty, though injurious, hath strange
      power,
    After offense returning, to regain
    Love once possessed, nor can be easily
    Repulsed, without much inward passion [1] felt,
    And secret sting of amorous remorse.[m]
*Samson.*   Love-quarrels oft in pleasing concord end;
    Not wedlock-treachery, endangering life.
*Chorus.*   It is not virtue, wisdom, valor, wit,          1010
    Strength, comeliness of shape, or amplest merit,
    That woman's love can win, or long inherit;[n]
    But what it is hard is to say,
    Harder to hit,
    Which way soever men refer it
    (Much like thy riddle, Samson), in one day
    Or seven though one should musing sit.
      If any of these, or all, the Timnian bride
    Had not so soon preferred
    Thy paranymph,[o] worthless to thee compared,      1020
    Successor in thy bed,
    Nor both so loosely disallied
    Their nuptials, nor this last so treacherously
    Had shorn the fatal harvest of thy head.
    Is it for that [p] such outward ornament
    Was lavished on their sex, that inward gifts
    Were left for haste unfinished, judgment scant,
    Capacity not raised to apprehend
    Or value what is best
    In choice, but oftest to affect [q] the wrong?       1030
    Or was too much of self-love mixed,
    Of constancy no root infixed,
    That either they love nothing, or not long?
      Whate'er it be, to wisest men and best,
    Seeming at first all heavenly under virgin veil,
    Soft, modest, meek, demure,
    Once joined, the contrary she proves—a thorn
    Intestine,[r] far within defensive arms
    A cleaving [s] mischief, in his way to virtue
    Adverse and turbulent; or by her charms       1040

[1] emotion   [m] pity   [n] possess   [o] best man (see Judges 14:20)   [p] because   [q] strongly desire   [r] i.e., domestic   [s] clinging

Draws him awry, enslaved
With dotage, and his sense depraved
To folly and shameful deeds, which ruin ends.
What pilot so expert but needs must wreck,
Embarked with such a steers-mate at the helm?
 Favored of Heaven who finds
One virtuous, rarely found,
That in domestic good combines: [t]
Happy that house! his way to peace is smooth:
But virtue which breaks through all opposition,     1050
And all temptation can remove,
Most shines and most is acceptable above.
 Therefore God's universal law
Gave to the man despotic [u] power
Over his female in due awe,
Nor from that right to part an hour,
Smile she or lour:
So shall he least confusion draw
On his whole life, not swayed
By female usurpation, nor dismayed.     1060
 But had we best retire? I see a storm.

*Samson.* Fair days have oft contracted [v] wind and rain.

*Chorus.* But this another kind of tempest brings.

*Samson.* Be less abstruse; my riddling days are past.

*Chorus.* Look now for no enchanting voice, nor fear
The bait of honeyed words; a rougher tongue
Draws hitherward; I know him by his stride,
The giant Harapha of Gath, his look
Haughty, as is his pile [w] high-built and proud.
Comes he in peace? What wind hath blown him hither   1070
I less conjecture than when first I saw
The sumptuous Dálila floating this way:
His habit carries peace, his brow defiance.

*Samson.* Or peace or not, alike to me he comes.

*Chorus.* His fraught [x] we soon shall know: he now ar-
 rives.

*Harapha.* I come not, Samson, to condole thy chance,
As these [y] perhaps, yet wish it had not been,
Though for no friendly intent. I am of Gath;
Men call me Harapha, of stock renowned
As Og, or Anak, and the Emims [z] old     1080
That Kiriathaim [a] held. Thou know'st me now,
If thou at all art known. Much I have heard

---

[t] i.e., who unites with her husband for the good of the home [u] absolute [v] drawn together [w] towerlike body [x] freight (i.e., purpose)
[y] i.e., the Chorus [z] various giants [a] the place where the Emims were
defeated

Of thy prodigious might and feats performed,
Incredible to me, in this displeased,—
That I was never present on the place
Of those encounters, where we might have tried
Each other's force in camp [b] or listed field; [c]
And now am come to see of whom such noise [d]
Hath walked about, and each limb to survey,
If thy appearance answer loud report.                          1090
*Samson.*    The way to know were not to see, but taste. [e]
*Harapha.*    Dost thou already single [f] me? I thought
Gyves [g] and the mill had tamed thee. O that fortune
Had brought me to the field where thou art famed
To have wrought such wonders with an ass's jaw!
I should have forced thee soon with [h] other arms
Or left thy carcass where the ass lay thrown;
So had the glory of prowess been recovered
To Palestine, won by a Philistine
From the unforeskinned race, of whom thou bear'st          1100
The highest name for valiant acts. That honor,
Certain to have won by mortal duel from thee,
I lose, prevented by thy eyes put out.
*Samson.*    Boast not of what thou would'st have done, but
do
What then thou would'st; thou seest it in thy hand. [i]
*Harapha.*    To combat with a blind man I disdain,
And thou hast need much washing to be touched.
*Samson.*    Such usage as your honorable lords
Afford me, assassinated [j] and betrayed;
Who durst not with their whole united powers              1110
In fight withstand me single and unarmed,
Nor in the house with chamber ambushes
Close-banded [k] durst attack me, no, not sleeping,
Till they had hired a woman with their gold,
Breaking her marriage-faith, to circumvent me.
Therefore, without feign'd shifts, let be assigned
Some narrow place enclosed, where sight may give thee,
Or rather flight, no great advantage on me;
Then put on all thy gorgeous arms, thy helmet
And brigandine [l] of brass, thy broad habergeon, [m]       1120
Vant-brace and greaves [n] and gauntlet; add thy spear,
A weaver's beam, and seven-times-folded shield:
I only with an oaken staff will meet thee,

[b] battlefield   [c] tournament   [d] rumor   [e] test   [f] challenge to single combat   [g] shackles   [h] perhaps a misprint for "wish" (i.e., wish for)   [i] power   [j] ambushed   [k] secretly united   [l] body armor   [m] sleeveless coat of mail   [n] forearm armor and shin armor

And raise such outcries on thy clattered iron,
Which long shall not withhold me from thy head,
That in a little time, while breath remains thee,
Thou oft shalt wish thyself at Gath, to boast
Again in safety what thou would'st have done
To Samson, but shalt never see Gath more.

*Harapha.*    Thou durst not thus disparage glorious arms,    1130
Which greatest heroes have in battle worn,
Their ornament and safety, had not spells
And black enchantments, some magician's art,
Armed thee or charmed thee strong, which thou from
   Heaven
Feign'dst at thy birth was given thee in thy hair,
Where strength can least abide, though all thy hairs
Were bristles ranged like those that ridge the back
Of chafed wild boars or ruffled porcupines.

*Samson.*    I know no spells, use no forbidden arts;
My trust is in the Living God, who gave me,    1140
At my nativity, this strength, diffused
No less through all my sinews, joints, and bones,
Than thine, while I preserved these locks unshorn,
The pledge of my unviolated vow.
For proof hereof, if Dagon be thy god,
Go to his temple, invocate his aid
With solemnest devotion, spread before him
How highly it concerns his glory now
To frustrate and dissolve these magic spells,
Which I to be the power of Israel's God    1150
Avow, and challenge Dagon to the test,
Offering to combat thee, his champion bold,
With th' utmost of his godhead seconded:
Then thou shalt see, or rather to thy sorrow
Soon feel, whose God is strongest, thine or mine.

*Harapha.*    Presume not on thy God. Whate'er he be,
Thee he regards not, owns not, hath cut off
Quite from his people, and delivered up
Into thy enemies' hand; permitted them
To put out both thine eyes, and fettered send thee    1160
Into the common prison, there to grind
Among the slaves and asses, thy comrádes,
As good for nothing else, no better service
With those thy boisterous ° locks; no worthy match
For valor to assail, nor by the sword
Of noble warrior, so to stain his honor,

° thick

But by the barber's razor best subdued.
*Samson.*    All these indignities, for such they are
From thine,[p] these evils I deserve and more,
Acknowledge them from God inflicted on me                    1170
Justly, yet despair not of his final pardon,
Whose ear is ever open, and his eye
Gracious to re-admit the suppliant;
In confidence whereof I once again
Defy thee to the trial of mortal fight,
By combat to decide whose god is God,
Thine, or whom I with Israel's sons adore.
*Harapha.*    Fair honor that thou dost thy God, in trusting
He will accept thee to defend his cause,
A murderer, a revolter, and a robber!                        1180
*Samson.*    Tongue-doughty giant, how dost thou prove me
these?
*Harapha.*    Is not thy nation subject to our lords?
Their magistrates confessed it when they took thee
As a league-breaker, and delivered bound
Into our hands; for hadst not committed
Notorious murder on those thirty men
At Ascalon,[q] who never did thee harm,
Then, like a robber, stripp'dst them of their robes?
The Philistines, when thou hadst broke the league,
Went up with armèd powers thee only seeking,                 1190
To others did no violence nor spoil.
*Samson.*    Among the daughters of the Philistines
I chose a wife, which argued me no foe,
And in your city held my nuptial feast;
But your ill-meaning politician lords,
Under pretense of bridal friends and guests,
Appointed to await me thirty spies,
Who, threatening cruel death, constrained the bride
To wring from me, and tell to them, my secret,
That solved the riddle which I had proposed.                 1200
When I perceived all set on enmity,
As on my enemies, wherever chanced,
I used hostility, and took their spoil,
To pay my underminers in their coin.
My nation was subjected to your lords!
It was the force of conquest; force with force
Is well ejected when the conquered can.
But I, a private person, whom my country
As a league-breaker gave up bound, presumed

---

[p] i.e., thy people    [q] see Judges 14:19

Single rebellion, and did hostile acts!                1210
I was no private, but a person raised,
With strength sufficient, and command from Heaven,
To free my country. If their servile minds
Me, their deliverer sent, would not receive,
But to their masters gave me up for nought,
Th' unworthier they; whence to this day they serve.
I was to do my part from Heaven assigned,
And had performed it if my known offense
Had not disabled me, not all your force.
These shifts<sup>r</sup> refuted, answer thy appellant,<sup>s</sup>    1220
Though by his blindness maimed for high attempts,
Who now defies thee thrice<sup>t</sup> to single fight,
As a petty enterprise of small enforce.<sup>u</sup>

*Harapha.*     With thee, a man condemned, a slave enrolled,
Due by the law to capital punishment!
To fight with thee no man of arms will deign.

*Samson.*     Cam'st thou for this, vain boaster, to survey me,
To descant on<sup>v</sup> my strength, and give thy verdict?
Come nearer; part not hence so slight informed;
But take good heed my hand survey not thee.      1230

*Harapha.*     O Baal-zebub!<sup>w</sup> can my ears unused<sup>x</sup>
Hear these dishonors, and not render death?

*Samson.*     No man withholds thee; nothing from thy hand
Fear I incurable; bring up thy van;<sup>y</sup>
My heels are fettered, but my fist is free.

*Harapha.*     This insolence other kind of answer fits.

*Samson.*     Go, baffled coward, lest I run upon thee,
Though in these chains, bulk without spirit vast,
And with one buffet lay thy structure low,
Or swing thee in the air, then dash thee down,      1240
To the hazard of thy brains and shattered sides.

*Harapha.*     By Astaroth,<sup>z</sup> ere long thou shalt lament
These braveries,<sup>a</sup> in irons loaden on thee.

*Chorus.*     His giantship is gone somewhat crestfallen,
Stalking with less unconscionable strides,
And lower looks, but in a sultry chafe.

*Samson.*     I dread him not, nor all his giant brood,
Though fame divulge him father of five sons,
All of gigantic size, Goliah chief.

*Chorus.*     He will directly to the lords, I fear,      1250
And with malicious counsel stir them up
Some way or other yet further to afflict thee.

*Samson.*     He must allege some cause, and offered fight

<sup>r</sup> evasions  <sup>s</sup> challenger  <sup>t</sup> for the third time  <sup>u</sup> effort  <sup>v</sup> criticize  <sup>w</sup> Philistine god  <sup>x</sup> unaccustomed  <sup>y</sup> vanguard  <sup>z</sup> goddess of fertility and passion  <sup>a</sup> boasts

Will not dare mention, lest a question rise
Whether he durst accept the offer or not;
And that he durst not plain enough appeared.
Much more affliction than already felt
They cannot well impose, nor I sustain,
If they intend advantage of my labors,
The work of many hands, which earns my keeping,        1260
With no small profit daily to my owners.
But come what will; my deadliest foe will prove
My speediest friend, by death to rid me hence;
The worst that he can give to me the best.
Yet so it may fall out, because their end
Is hate, not help to me, it may with mine
Draw their own ruin who attempt the deed.
*Chorus.*    O, how comely it is, and how reviving
To the spirits of just men long oppressed,
When God into the hands of their deliverer        1270
Puts invincible might,
To quell the mighty of the earth, th' oppressor,
The brute and boisterous force of violent men,
Hardy and industrious to support
Tyrannic power, but raging to pursue
The righteous, and all such as honor truth!
He all their ammunition[b]
And feats of war defeats,
With plain heroic magnitude of mind
And celestial vigor armed;        1280
Their armories and magazines contemns,
Renders them useless, while
With wingèd expedition[c]
Swift as the lightning glance he executes
His errand[d] on the wicked, who, surprised,
Lose their defense, distracted and amazed.
      But patience is more oft the exercise
Of saints,[e] the trial of their fortitude,
Making them each his own deliverer,
And victor over all        1290
That tyranny or fortune can inflict.
Either of these is in thy lot,
Samson, with might endued
Above the sons of men; but sight bereaved
May chance to number thee with those
Whom patience finally must crown.
      This Idol's day hath been to thee no day of rest,

[b] war supplies    [c] speed    [d] i.e., of vengeance    [e] godly persons

Laboring thy mind
More than the working day thy hands.
And yet, perhaps, more trouble is behind;                    1300
For I descry this way
Some other tending; in his hand
A scepter or quaint<sup>f</sup> staff he bears,—
Comes on amain, speed in his look.
By his habit I discern him now
A public officer, and now at hand.
His message will be short and voluble.<sup>g</sup>

*Officer.*    Ebrews, the prisoner Samson here I seek.
*Chorus.*    His manacles remark<sup>h</sup> him; there he sits.
*Officer.*    Samson, to thee our lords thus bid me say:          1310
  This day to Dagon is a solemn feast,
  With sacrifices, triumph, pomp, and games;
  Thy strength they know surpassing human rate,
  And now some public proof thereof require
  To honor this great feast, and great assembly.
  Rise, therefore, with all speed, and come along,
  Where I will see thee heartened and fresh clad,
  To appear as fits before th' illustrious lords.
*Samson.*    Thou know'st I am an Ebrew; therefore tell
    them
  Our law forbids at their religious rites                       1320
  My presence; for that cause I cannot come.
*Officer.*    This answer, be assured, will not content them.
*Samson.*    Have they not sword-players, and every sort
  Of gymnic artists, wrestlers, riders, runners,
  Jugglers and dancers, antics, mummers, mimics,<sup>i</sup>
  But they must pick me out, with shackles tired,
  And over-labored at their public mill,
  To make them sport with blind activity?
  Do they not seek occasion of new quarrels,
  On my refusal, to distress me more,                           1330
  Or make a game of my calamities?
  Return the way thou cam'st; I will not come.
*Officer.*    Regard thyself;<sup>j</sup> this will offend them highly.
*Samson.*    Myself? my conscience, and internal peace.
  Can they think me so broken, so debased
  With corporal servitude, that my mind ever
  Will condescend to such absurd commands?
  Although their drudge, to be their fool or jester,
  And, in my midst of sorrow and heart-grief,
  To show them feats, and play before their god—              1340

<sup>f</sup> intricately decorated  <sup>g</sup> concise  <sup>h</sup> mark out  <sup>i</sup> clowns, masqueraders,
actors  <sup>j</sup> take care what you do

The worst of all indignities, yet on me
Joined[k] with supreme contempt! I will not come.
*Officer.*    My message was imposed on me with speed,
Brooks no delay: is this thy resolution?
*Samson.*    So take it with what speed thy message needs.
*Officer.*    I am sorry what this stoutness[l] will produce.
*Samson.*    Perhaps thou shalt have cause to sorrow indeed.
*Chorus.*    Consider, Samson; matters now are strained
Up to the height, whether to hold or break.
He's gone, and who knows how he may report            1350
Thy words by adding fuel to the flame?
Expect another message, more imperious,
More lordly thundering than thou well wilt bear.
*Samson.*    Shall I abuse this consecrated gift
Of strength, again returning with my hair
After my great transgression—so requite
Favor renewed, and add a greater sin
By prostituting holy things to idols,
A Nazarite, in place abominable,
Vaunting[m] my strength in honor to their Dagon?            1360
Besides how vile, contemptible, ridiculous,
What act more execrably unclean, profane?
*Chorus.*    Yet with this strength thou serv'st the Philis-
tines,
Idolatrous, uncircumcised, unclean.
*Samson.*    Not in their idol-worship, but by labor
Honest and lawful to deserve my food
Of those who have me in their civil power.
*Chorus.*    Where the heart joins not, outward acts defile
not.
*Samson.*    Where outward force constrains, the sentence[n]
holds:
But who constrains me to the temple of Dagon,            1370
Not dragging? The Philistian lords command:
Commands are no constraints. If I obey them,
I do it freely, venturing to displease
God for the fear of man, and man prefer,
Set God behind; which, in his jealousy,
Shall never, unrepented, find forgiveness.
Yet that he may dispense with[o] me, or thee,
Present in temples at idolatrous rites
For some important cause, thou need'st not doubt.
*Chorus.*    How thou wilt here come off surmounts my
reach.            1380

---

[k] enjoined    [l] arrogance    [m] displaying  proudly    [n] maxim    [o] grant  dispensation to

*Samson.*  Be of good courage; I begin to feel
 Some rousing motions in me, which dispose
 To something extraordinary my thoughts.
 I with this messenger will go along—
 Nothing to do, be sure, that may dishonor
 Our Law, or stain my vow of Nazarite.
 If there be aught of presage in the mind,
 This day will be remarkable in my life
 By some great act, or of my days the last.
*Chorus.* In time thou hast resolved; the man returns.  1390
*Officer.* Samson, this second message from our lords
 To thee I am bid say: Art thou our slave,
 Our captive, at the public mill our drudge,
 And dar'st thou, at our sending and command,
 Dispute thy coming? Come without delay;
 Or we shall find such engines <sup>p</sup> to assail
 And hamper <sup>q</sup> thee, as thou shalt come of force,
 Though thou wert firmlier fastened than a rock.
*Samson.* I could be well content to try their art,
 Which to no few of them would prove pernicious; <sup>r</sup>  1400
 Yet, knowing their advantages too many,
 Because <sup>s</sup> they shall not trail me through their streets
 Like a wild beast, I am content to go.
 Masters' commands come with a power resistless
 To such as owe them absolute subjection;
 And for a life who will not change his purpose?
 (So mutable are all the ways of men!)
 Yet this be sure, in nothing to comply
 Scandalous or forbidden in our Law.
*Officer.* I praise thy resolution. Doff these links:  1410
 By this compliance thou wilt win the lords
 To favor, and perhaps to set thee free.
*Samson.* Brethren, farewell. Your company along
 I will not wish, lest it perhaps offend them
 To see me girt with friends, and how the sight
 Of me, as of a common enemy,
 So dreaded once, may now exasperate them
 I know not. Lords are lordliest in their wine;
 And the well-feasted priest then soonest fired
 With zeal, if aught religion seem concerned;  1420
 No less the people, on their holy-days,
 Impetuous, insolent, unquenchable.
 Happen what may, of me expect to hear

<sup>p</sup> instruments <sup>q</sup> fetter <sup>r</sup> deadly <sup>s</sup> so that

Nothing dishonorable, impure, unworthy
Our God, our Law, my nation, or myself;
The last of me or no I cannot warrant.
*Chorus.*   Go, and the Holy One
     Of Israel be thy guide
     To what may serve his glory best, and spread his name
     Great among the heathen round;                          1430
     Send thee the Angel of thy birth, to stand
     Fast by thy side, who from thy father's field
     Rode up in flames after his message told
     Of thy conception, and be now a shield
     Of fire; that Spirit that first rushed on thee
     In the camp of Dan,
     Be efficacious in thee now at need!
     For never was from Heaven imparted
     Measure of strength so great to mortal seed
     As in thy wondrous actions hath been seen.            1440
     But wherefore comes old Manoa in such haste
     With youthful steps? Much livelier than erewhile
     He seems: supposing here to find his son,
     Or of him bringing to us some glad news?
*Manoa.*   Peace with you, brethren! My inducement hither
     Was not at present here to find my son,
     By order of the lords new parted[t] hence
     To come and play before them at their feast.
     I heard all as I came; the city rings,
     And numbers thither flock: I had no will,            1450
     Lest I should see him forced to things unseemly.
     But that which moved my coming now was chiefly
     To give ye part with me what hope I have
     With good success to work his liberty.
*Chorus.*   That hope would much rejoice us to partake
     With thee. Say, reverend sire; we thirst to hear.
*Manoa.*   I have attempted,[u] one by one, the lords,
     Either at home, or through the high street passing,
     With supplication prone and father's tears,
     To accept of ransom for my son, their prisoner.      1460
     Some much averse I found, and wondrous harsh,
     Contemptuous, proud, set on revenge and spite;
     That part most reverenced Dagon and his priests:
     Others more moderate seeming, but their aim
     Private reward, for which both God and State
     They easily would set to sale: a third
     More generous far and civil, who confessed

     [t] just departed     [u] appealed to

They had enough revenged, having reduced
Their foe to misery beneath their fears;
The rest<sup>v</sup> was magnanimity to remit,                                1470
If some convenient ransom were proposed.
What noise or shout was that? It tore the sky.
*Chorus.*    Doubtless the people shouting to behold
  Their once great dread, captive and blind before them,
  Or at some proof of strength before them shown.
*Manoa.*    His ransom, if my whole inheritance
  May compass it, shall willingly be paid
  And numbered down. Much rather I shall choose
  To live the poorest in my tribe, than richest
  And he in that calamitous prison left.                                 1480
  No, I am fixed not to part hence without him.
  For his redemption all my patrimony,
  If need be, I am ready to forgo
  And quit.<sup>w</sup> Not wanting<sup>x</sup> him, I shall want nothing.
*Chorus.*    Fathers are wont to lay up for their sons;
  Thou for thy son art bent to lay out all:
  Sons wont to nurse their parents in old age;
  Thou in old age car'st how to nurse thy son,
  Made older than thy age through eye-sight lost.
*Manoa.*    It shall be my delight to tend his eyes,                       1490
  And view him sitting in his house, ennobled
  With all those high exploits by him achieved,
  And on his shoulders waving down those locks
  That of a nation armed the strength contained.
  And I persuade me God had not permitted
  His strength again to grow up with his hair
  Garrisoned round about him like a camp
  Of faithful soldiery, were not his purpose
  To use him further yet in some great service—
  Not to sit idle with so great a gift                                   1500
  Useless, and thence ridiculous, about him.
  And, since his strength with eye-sight was not lost,
  God will restore him eye-sight to his strength.
*Chorus.*    Thy hopes are not ill founded, nor seem vain,
  Of his delivery, and thy joy thereon
  Conceived, agreeable<sup>y</sup> to a father's love;
  In both which we, as next,<sup>z</sup> participate.
*Manoa.*    I know your friendly minds, and—O, what
    noise!
  Mercy of Heaven! what hideous noise was that?
  Horribly loud, unlike the former shout.                                1510

<sup>v</sup> i.e., of their revenge    <sup>w</sup> release    <sup>x</sup> lacking    <sup>y</sup> appropriate    <sup>z</sup> i.e., of
kin

*Chorus.*    Noise call you it, or universal groan,
  As if the whole inhabitation perished?
  Blood, death, and deathful deeds, are in that noise,
  Ruin, [a] destruction at the utmost point.
*Manoa.*    Of ruin indeed methought I heard the noise.
  Oh! it continues; they have slain my son.
*Chorus.*    Thy son is rather slaying them; that outcry
  From slaughter of one foe could not ascend.
*Manoa.*    Some dismal accident it needs must be.
  What shall we do—stay here, or run and see?                    1520
*Chorus.*    Best keep together here, lest, running thither,
  We unawares run into danger's mouth.
  This evil on the Philistines is fallen:
  From whom could else a general cry be heard?
  The sufferers then will scarce molest us here;
  From other hands we need not much to fear.
  What if, his eye-sight (for to Israel's God
  Nothing is hard) by miracle restored,
  He now be dealing dole [b] among his foes,
  And over heaps of slaughtered walk his way?                    1530
*Manoa.*    That were a joy presumptuous to be thought.
*Chorus.*    Yet God hath wrought things as incredible
  For his people of old; what hinders now?
*Manoa.*    He can, I know, but doubt to think he will;
  Yet hope would fain subscribe, and tempts belief.
  A little stay will bring some notice hither.
*Chorus.*    Of good or bad so great, of bad the sooner;
  For evil news rides post, [c] while good news baits. [d]
  And to our wish I see one hither speeding—
  An Ebrew, as I guess, and of our tribe.                        1540
*Messenger.*    O, whither shall I run, or which way fly
  The sight of this so horrid spectacle,
  Which erst [e] my eyes beheld, and yet behold?
  For dire imagination still pursues me.
  But providence or instinct of nature seems,
  Or reason, though disturbed, and scarce consulted,
  To have guided me aright, I know not how,
  To thee first, reverend Manoa, and to these
  My countrymen, whom here I knew remaining,
  As at some distance from the place of horror,                  1550
  So in the sad event too much concerned.
*Manoa.*    The accident was loud, and here before thee
  With rueful cry; yet what it was we hear not.
  No preface needs; thou seest we long to know.

---

  [a] collapse   [b] grief   [c] on post horses (i.e., speedily)   [d] delays   [e] not
long ago

*Messenger.*   It would burst forth, but I recover breath,
  And sense distract, to know well what I utter.
*Manoa.*   Tell us the sum; the circumstance defer.
*Messenger.*   Gaza yet stands; but all her sons are fallen,
  All in a moment overwhelmed and fallen.
*Manoa.*   Sad! but thou know'st to Israelites not saddest   1560
  The desolation of a hostile city.
*Messenger.*   Feed on that first; there may in grief be
    surfeit.
*Manoa.*   Relate by whom.
*Messenger.*                   By Samson.
*Manoa.*                           That still lessens
  The sorrow, and coverts it nigh to joy.
*Messenger.*   Ah! Manoa, I refrain too suddenly
  To utter what will come at last too soon,
  Lest evil tidings, with too rude irruption
  Hitting thy agèd ear, should pierce too deep.
*Manoa.*   Suspense in news is torture; speak them out.
*Messenger.*   Then take the worst in brief: Samson is dead. 1570
*Manoa.*   The worst indeed! O, all my hopes defeated
  To free him hence! but Death, who sets all free,
  Hath paid his ransom now and full discharge.
  What windy[f] joy this day had I conceived,
  Hopeful of his delivery, which now proves
  Abortive as the first-born bloom of spring
  Nipt with the lagging rear of winter's frost!
  Yet, ere I give the reins to grief, say first
  How died he; death to life is crown or shame.
  All by him fell, thou say'st; by whom fell he?       1580
  What glorious hand gave Samson his death's wound?
*Messenger.*   Unwounded of his enemies he fell.
*Manoa.*   Wearied with slaughter, then, or how? explain.
*Messenger.*   By his own hands.
*Manoa.*                   Self-violence! What cause
  Brought him so soon at variance with himself
  Among his foes?
*Messenger.*                   Inevitable cause—
  At once both to destroy and be destroyed.
  The edifice, where all were met to see him,
  Upon their heads and on his own he pulled.
*Manoa.*   O lastly over-strong against thyself!       1590
  A dreadful way thou took'st to thy revenge.
  More than enough we know; but, while things yet
  Are in confusion, give us, if thou canst,

[f] empty

Eye-witness of what first or last was done,
Relation more particular and distinct.
*Messenger.*    Occasions[g] drew me early to this city;
    And, as the gates I entered with sun-rise,
    The morning trumpets festival proclaimed
    Through each high street. Little I had dispatched,
    When all abroad was rumored that this day                1600
    Samson should be brought forth, to show the people
    Proof of his mighty strength in feats and games.
    I sorrowed at his captive state, but minded[h]
    Not to be absent at that spectacle.
    The building was a spacious theater,
    Half round on two main pillars vaulted high,
    With seats where all the lords, and each degree
    Of sort,[i] might sit in order to behold;
    The other side was open, where the throng
    On banks[j] and scaffolds under sky might stand:          1610
    I among these aloof obscurely stood.
    The feast and noon grew high, and sacrifice
    Had filled their hearts with mirth, high cheer, and wine,
    When to their sports they turned. Immediately
    Was Samson as a public servant brought,
    In their state livery clad: before him pipes
    And timbrels; on each side went armèd guards;
    Both horse and foot before him and behind,
    Archers and slingers, cataphracts and spears.[k]
    At sight of him the people with a shout                   1620
    Rifted[l] the air, clamoring their god with praise,
    Who had made their dreadful enemy their thrall.
    He patient, but undaunted, where they led him,
    Came to the place; and what was set before him,
    Which without help of eye might be assayed,[m]
    To heave, pull, draw, or break, he still[n] performed
    All with incredible, stupendious force,
    None daring to appear antagonist.
    At length, for intermission sake, they led him
    Between the pillars; he his guide requested               1630
    (For so from such as nearer stood we heard),
    As over-tired, to let him lean a while
    With both his arms on those two massy pillars,
    That to the archèd roof gave main support.
    He unsuspicious led him; which when Samson
    Felt in his arms, with head a while inclined,
    And eyes fast fixed, he stood, as one who prayed,

---

[g] business   [h] determined   [i] rank   [j] benches   [k] armored cavalry and
spearmen   [l] rent   [m] attempted   [n] always

Or some great matter in his mind revolved:
At last, with head erect, thus cried aloud:—
"Hitherto, Lords, what your commands imposed          1640
I have performed, as reason was, obeying,
Not without wonder or delight beheld;
Now, of my own accord, such other trial
I mean to show you of my strength yet greater
As with amaze shall strike all who behold."
This uttered, straining all his nerves, he bowed;
As with the force of winds and waters pent
When mountains tremble, those two massy pillars
With horrible convulsion to and fro
He tugged, he shook, till down they came, and drew    1650
The whole roof after them with burst of thunder
Upon the heads of all who sat beneath,
Lords, ladies, captains, counselors, or priests,
Their choice nobility and flower, not only
Of this, but each Philistian city round,
Met from all parts to solemnize this feast.
Samson, with these immixed, inevitably
Pulled down the same destruction on himself;
The vulgar° only scaped, who stood without.
*Chorus.*   O dearly bought revenge, yet glorious!     1660
Living or dying thou hast fulfilled
The work for which thou wast foretold
To Israel, and now li'st victorious
Among thy slain self-killed;
Not willingly, but tangled in the fold
Of dire Necessity, whose law in death conjoined
Thee with thy slaughtered foes, in number more
Than all thy life had slain before.
*Semichorus.*   While their hearts were jocund and
            sublime,ᵖ
Drunk with idolatry, drunk with wine                   1670
And fat regorged of bulls and goats,
Chaunting their idol, and preferring
Before our living Dread, who dwells
In Silo,�q his bright sanctuary,
Among them he a spirit of frenzy sent,
Who hurt their minds,
And urged them on with mad desire
To call in haste for their destroyer.
They, only set on sport and play,
Unweetinglyʳ importuned                                1680

° common people   ᵖ uplifted   q Shiloh, where the Tabernacle was lo-
cated (see Joshua 18:1)   ʳ unwittingly

Their own destruction to come speedy upon them.
So fond<sup>s</sup> are mortal men,
Fallen into wrath divine,<sup>t</sup>
As their own ruin on themselves to invite,
Insensate left, or to sense reprobate,
And with blindness internal struck.

*Semichorus.*   But he, though blind of sight,
Despised, and thought extinguished quite,
With inward eyes illuminated,
His fiery virtue roused                                    1690
From under ashes into sudden flame,
And as an evening dragon<sup>u</sup> came,
Assailant on the perchèd roosts
And nests in order ranged
Of tame villatic<sup>v</sup> fowl, but as an eagle
His cloudless thunder bolted on their heads.
So Virtue, given for lost,
Depressed and overthrown, as seemed,
Like that self-begotten bird,<sup>w</sup>
In the Arabian woods embossed,<sup>x</sup>                  1700
That no second knows nor third,
And lay erewhile a holocaust,<sup>y</sup>
From out her ashy womb now teemed,<sup>z</sup>
Revives, reflourishes, then vigorous most
When most unactive deemed;
And, though her body die, her fame survives,
A secular<sup>a</sup> bird, ages of lives.

*Manoa.*   Come, come; no time for lamentation now,
Nor much more cause. Samson hath quit<sup>b</sup> himself
Like Samson, and heroicly hath finished          1710
A life heroic, on his enemies
Fully revenged—hath left them years of mourning
And lamentation to the sons of Caphtor<sup>c</sup>
Through all Philistian bounds; to Israel
Honor hath left and freedom, let but them
Find courage to lay hold on this occasion;
To himself and father's house eternal fame;
And, which is best and happiest yet, all this
With God not parted from him, as was feared,
But favoring and assisting to the end.           1720
Nothing is here for tears, nothing to wail

---

<sup>s</sup> foolish   <sup>t</sup> i.e., divinely inspired   <sup>u</sup> serpent   <sup>v</sup> farmyard   <sup>w</sup> i.e., the phoenix, which supposedly is consumed in fire every 500 years, only to renew itself out of its own ashes   <sup>x</sup> hidden in a thicket   <sup>y</sup> a sacrifice burnt whole   <sup>z</sup> born   <sup>a</sup> living for centuries   <sup>b</sup> acquitted   <sup>c</sup> Crete, the Philistines' original home

Or knock the breast; no weakness, no contempt,
Dispraise, or blame; nothing but well and fair,
And what may quiet us in a death so noble.
Let us go find the body where it lies
Soaked in his enemies' blood, and from the stream
With lavers pure, and cleansing herbs, wash off
The clotted gore. I, with what speed[d] the while
(Gaza is not in plight to say us nay),
Will send for all my kindred, all my friends,          1730
To fetch him hence, and solemnly attend,
With silent obsequy and funeral train,
Home to his father's house. There will I build him
A monument, and plant it round with shade
Of laurel ever green and branching palm,
With all his trophies hung, and acts enrolled
In copious legend, or sweet lyric song.
Thither shall all the valiant youth resort,
And from his memory inflame their breasts
To matchless valor and adventures high;                1740
The virgins also shall, on feastful days,
Visit his tomb with flowers, only bewailing
His lot unfortunate in nuptial choice,
From whence captivity and loss of eyes.
*Chorus.*   All is best, though we oft doubt
What th' unsearchable dispose[e]
Of Highest Wisdom brings about,
And ever best found in the close.
Oft he seems to hide his face,
But unexpectedly returns,                               1750
And to his faithful champion hath in place[f]
Bore witness gloriously; whence Gaza mourns,
And all that band[g] them to resist
His uncontrollable intent.
His servants he, with new acquist[h]
Of true experience from this great event,
With peace and consolation hath dismissed,
And calm of mind, all passion spent.

[d] as fast as possible   [e] dispensation   [f] on this spot   [g] bound   [h] acquisition

# Part Two

❧

# THE ESSAYS

❧

## Anonymous:

## *A TREATISE AGAINST MIRACLE PLAYS*

Know ye, Christian men, that, as Christ, who is God and man, is also the way, the truth, and the life, as says the gospel of John (the way to the erring, the truth to the ignorant and doubting, and the life to those climbing to heaven and growing weary), so Christ did nothing for us but was effective in the way of mercy, in the truth of righteousness, and in a life yielding everlasting joy in return for our continual mourning and sorrowing in this vale of tears. The miracles, therefore, that Christ did here on earth, either through himself or through his saints, were so effectual and done in such earnest, that, to sinful men who err, they brought forgiveness of sin, setting them again on the path of true faith; to doubting men, who were not steadfast, they brought knowledge of how to please God better, and true hope in God, to be steadfast in him; and to those

This anonymous treatise in the form of a sermon is from the late fourteenth century. Its attitude suggests a Lollard, i.e., a religious reformer whose doctrines in large measure anticipate those of the Protestant Reformation. In the first half of the sixteenth century his descendants were loud, and doubtless contributed substantially to the extermination of miracle plays. The treatise is printed in Middle English in *A Literary Middle English Reader,* ed. Albert S. Cook (Boston: Ginn and Co., 1915, 1943).

who were weary in God's way, because of the great penance and suffering arising from the tribulation that must needs be therein, they brought the love of burning charity, which makes all things easy (even if a man were to suffer death, which men most dread) in comparison with the everlasting life and joy that men most love and desire, the true hope of which puts away all weariness here in the way to God.

Then, since the miracles of Christ and of his saints were thus effectual, as our religion assures us, no man should use in jest and play the miracles and works that Christ so earnestly wrought for our salvation. For, whosoever so doth, errs in the faith, contradicts Christ, and scorns God. He errs in the faith, in that he takes the most precious works of God in play and jest; he takes his name in vain, and so misuses our faith. Ah, Lord, since an earthly servant dare not take in play and jest that which his earthly lord takes seriously, so much the more should we not make our play and jest of those miracles and works that God so earnestly wrought for us; for, truly, when we so do, the dread of sin is taken away—as a servant, when he jokes about his master, loses his dread of offending him, particularly when he jokes about that which his master takes seriously....

Now then, since these players of miracles take in jest the serious works of God, there is no doubt that they scorn God, as did the Jews who mocked Christ; for they laughed at his passion, as these laugh and poke fun at the miracles of God. Therefore, as they scorned Christ, so these scorn God; and even as Pharaoh, hating to do as God bade him, displeased God, so these miracle-players, and those who defend them, omitting for the sake of pleasure to do what God bade them, scorn God. He indeed has commanded us to hallow his name, showing fear and reverence at every remembrance of his works, without any playing or joking, as all holiness lies in very earnest men; then, playing on the name of God's miracles, for fun, they cease to do what God commands them; so they scorn his name, and so scorn him.

But in reply to these things they say that they play these miracles to the worship of God, as did not those Jews that mocked Christ. Also, oftentimes by such miracle playing men are converted to good living, as when men and women, seeing in miracle plays that the devil, through those acts by which they incite each other to lechery and pride, makes them his servants, to bring them and many others to hell, and to have far more suffering hereafter, because of their proud conduct here, than they have honor here; and seeing, furthermore, that all these worldly things are but passing vanities—as in the playing of miracles—they will leave their pride, and take for themselves afterwards the meek conversation of Christ and of his saints; and so miracle playing turns men to the faith, and does not turn them away.

Also, oftentimes by such miracle playing men and women, seeing the passion of Christ and of his saints, are moved to compassion and devotion, weeping bitter tears; then are they not scornful of God, but reverent. Also, it is profitable to men and to the worship of God, to present fully and to seek out all the means by which men flee sin and draw them to virtue. And, since there are men who only by serious action will be converted to God, so there are other men who will be turned to God only by game and play; and nowadays men are not turned by the serious actions of either God or man. Therefore, it is timely and reasonable to try to turn the people by play and game, as by miracle playing, and other kinds of entertainment.

Also, men must have some recreation, and it is better, or less evil, that they have their recreation by the playing of miracles than by the playing of other jokes. Also, since it is permissible to make paintings of the miracles of God, why is it not also permissible to have the miracles of God played, since men may the better explain the will of God and his marvelous works, in the acting of them than in painting them? And they are better held in mind, and rehearsed the more often by the acting of them than by representing them in painting, since the latter is a dead book, the other a living.

To the first argument we answer, saying that such miracle playing is not to the worship of God, for they are performed more to be seen of the world, and to please the world, than to be seen of God, or to please him, as Christ never taught their use by example, but only heathens, who evermore dishonor God, declaring that to be to the worship of God which is the greatest debasing of him. Therefore, as the wickedness of the false belief of heathens deceives them, when they say that the worship of idols is conducive to the worship of God, so men's lechery nowadays, to the having of their own lusts, deceives them, when they say that such miracle playing is to the worship of God. . . .

In the same manner, miracle playing, although it be sin, is sometimes the occasion for converting men; but as it is sin, it is far more an occasion for perverting men, not only one individual person, but a whole community, as it makes a whole people to be occupied with vanities, contrary to the command of the Psalter Book, which says to all men, and specially to priests, who read it each day in their services, "Turn away mine eyes from beholding vanities," and again, "Lord, thou hatest all ensnaring vanities." How then may a priest play in interludes, or give himself to the sight of them? . . .

Miracle playing, since it is contrary to the commandment of God, which bids that we take not God's name in vain, is contrary to our faith, and so it cannot offer an occasion for turning men to the faith, but of turning them aside; and, therefore, many men believe that there is no hell of everlasting pain, but that God threatens us, and will not actually enact it, as in the playing of miracles, symbolically and not actually.

A priest of the New Testament, who has passed the age of childhood, and who should maintain not only chastity but all the other virtues, administers not only the sacrament of matrimony, but all other sacraments, and, specially, since he ought administer to all the people the precious body of Christ, ought to abstain from all idle play, both of miracles and other things. . . .

These men that say, "Let us play a play of Antichrist and of the Day of Judgment, that some man may be converted thereby," fall into the heresy of them that, reversing the Apostle, said, "Let us do evil that good may come thereof"—"of whom," as saith the Apostle, "damnation is just."

By this do we answer the third argument, saying that such acting of miracles gives no occasion of true and profitable weeping; but the weeping that befalls men and women at the sight of such acting of plays, as it is not principally for their own sins, nor inwardly, of their own good faith, but more because of their beholding that which is outside, is not acceptable before God, but the more odious; for, since Christ himself reproved the women who wept for him at his passion, much more are they to be reproved who weep because of a play on Christ's passion, omitting to weep for their own sins and those of their children, as Christ bade the women who wept for him.

And by this do we answer the fourth argument, replying that no man can be converted to God except by the earnest working on God's part, and by no vain acting; for that which neither the word of God nor his sacraments can effect, how should acting bring about, which is of no power, but only of error? . . . The weeping that men weep often in such a play is commonly false, witnessing that they love more the delights of their body and the welfare of this world than delight in God and the virtuous welfare of the soul; and, therefore, having more consciousness of pain than of sin, they falsely weep more for the lack of bodily welfare than for the loss of spiritual welfare. . . .

And hereby do we answer the fifth argument, saying that

true recreation is the lawful occupying of oneself in lesser works, so that one may more ardently perform the greater works. Therefore, neither acting in miracle plays nor watching them is true recreation, but false and worldly, as prove the deeds of the supporters of such plays. . . . And if one were to ask what recreation men should have for the holiday, after their holy contemplation in church, we say to them two things: first, that if he had truly busied himself before in contemplation, he would neither ask that question nor desire to witness vanity; second, that his recreation should be in works of mercy toward his neighbor, and in taking pleasure in all good communication with his neighbor, as before he took pleasure in God, and in all other needful works that are reasonable and natural.

And to the last argument we reply that paintings, if they are true, without admixture of falsehood, and not intent upon greatly feeding men's wits, and not an occasion of idolatry for the people, are but as naked letters for a clerk to read the truth; but many miracle plays are not so, which are made more to delight men bodily than to be books for uneducated men, and, therefore, if they are living books, they are living books of wickedness more than of goodness. Good men, therefore, seeing the day of their reckoning draw quickly near, and not knowing when they must go hence, flee all such idleness, hastening that they might be with their spouse, Christ, in the bliss of heaven. . . .

If thou hadst had a father, who had suffered a cruel death to get thee thine heritage, and if after that thou wouldst so lightly hold it in mind as to make a play out of it, for thyself and for all people, no doubt all good men would think thee unnatural. Much more, God and all his saints would judge all those Christian men unnatural who play or favor the acting of the death or of the miracles of their most kind Father, Christ, who died and wrought miracles to bring men to the everlasting heritage of heaven.

But, possibly, here thou mayst say that, if the acting of miracles be sin, nevertheless it is but a little sin. But on this point, dear friend, know ye that each sin, be it never so little, if it be continued and preached as good and profitable, is deadly sin. And on this saith the prophet, "Woe to them who call good evil and evil good"; and therefore the wise man condemneth them who rejoice when they do evil. And therefore all saints say that it is human to fall, but devilish to abide still therein. Therefore, since this performance of miracles is sin, as thou dost acknowledge, and it is steadfastly supported, and also men delight themselves therein, there is no doubt that it is mortal sin, damnable, devilish, not human. . . .

As it is indeed a lie to say that, for the love of God, one will be a good fellow with the devil, so it is indeed a lie to say that, for the love of God, one will act his miracles, for in neither is the love of God shown, but his commandments are broken. And since the ceremonies of the Old Law, albeit they were given by God, because they were of the flesh cannot be ranked with the New Testament, because it is of the spirit, much more, acting, because it is of the flesh, and never commanded by God, should never be applied to the marvelous works of God, since they are of the spirit. For, as the playing of Ishmael with Isaac might have taken from Isaac of his heritage, so the keeping of the ceremonies of the Old Law in the New Testament might have taken from men their belief in Christ, and have made men go backwards, that is, from the spiritual life of the New Testament to the fleshly life of the Old Testament. . . .

This acting of miracles is indeed witness to men's avarice, and covetousness before, which is idolatry, as saith the Apostle; for that which they should spend upon the needs of their neighbors, they spend upon plays; to pay their rent and their debt, they will complain; but to spend twice as much upon the play, they make no complaint. Furthermore, to gather men together, so as to buy their food the dearer, and to stir men to gluttony and to pride and to boasting, they perform these miracles; and also, to have money to spend on these miracles, and to hold fellowship with gluttony and lechery on such days as plays are given, they busy themselves beforehand, more greedily to beguile their neighbors, in buying and selling; and so this performing of miracle plays nowadays is true evidence of hideous covetousness, which is idolatry.

# Sir Philip Sidney:

# From *THE DEFENSE OF POESY*

Perchance it is the comic [which is disliked], whom naughty play-makers and stage-keepers have justly made odious. To the arguments of abuse I will after answer. Only thus much now is to be said, that the comedy is an imitation of the common errors of our life, which he representeth in the most ridiculous and scornful sort that may be, so as it is impossible that any beholder can be content to be such a one. Now, as in geometry the oblique must be known as well as the right, and in arithmetic the odd as well as the even, so in the actions of our life who seeth not the filthiness of evil wanteth a great foil to perceive the beauty of virtue. This doth the comedy handle so in our private and domestical matters, as with hearing it we get as it were an experience, what is to be looked for of a niggardly Demea, of a crafty Davus, of a flattering Gnatho, of a vainglorious Thraso;[a] and not only to know what effects are to be expected, but to know who be such, by the signifying badge given them by the comedian. And little reason hath any man to say that men learn evil by seeing it so set out; since, as I said before, there is no man living but, by the force truth hath in nature, no sooner seeth these men play their parts, but wisheth them in *pistrinum*;[b] although perchance the sack of his own faults lie so behind his back that he seeth not himself dance the same measure; whereto yet nothing can more open his eyes than to see his own actions contemptibly set forth.

[a] stock characters in Roman comedies   [b] mill to which Roman slaves were condemned to heavy labor

Sir Philip Sidney (1554–1586) was considered the ideal Renaissance gentleman: scholar, poet, courtier, soldier. He wrote his treatise on literature about 1583, but it was not published until 1595, when it was published twice, once entitled *The Defense of Poesy* and once entitled *An Apology for Poetry*. Sidney ranges over a good deal of material; the following selection includes virtually all that he wrote on the drama.

So that the right use of comedy will (I think) by nobody be blamed; and much less of the high and excellent tragedy, that openeth the greatest wounds, and showeth forth the ulcers that are covered with tissue, that maketh kings fear to be tyrants, and tyrants manifest their tyrannical humors; that with stirring the affects of admiration and commiseration teacheth the uncertainty of this world, and upon how weak foundations gilden roofs are builded, that maketh us know,

> *Qui sceptra saevus duro imperio regit,*
> *Timet timentes, metus in auctorem redit.*[c]

But how much it can move, Plutarch yieldeth a notable testimony of the abominable tyrant Alexander Pheraeus, from whose eyes a tragedy, well made and represented, drew abundance of tears, who without all pity had murdered infinite numbers, and some of his own blood, so as he that was not ashamed to make matters for tragedies yet could not resist the sweet violence of a tragedy. And if it wrought no further good in him, it was that he, in despite of himself, withdrew himself from hearkening to that which might mollify his hardened heart. But it is not the tragedy they do mislike; for it were too absurd to cast out so excellent a representation of whatsoever is most worthy to be learned. . . .

Our tragedies and comedies not without cause cried out against, observing rules neither of honest civility nor skillful poetry, excepting *Gorboduc*[d] (again, I say, of those that I have seen), which notwithstanding, as it is full of stately speeches and well-sounding phrases, climbing to the height of Seneca's style, and as full of notable morality, which it doth most delightfully teach, and so obtain the very end of poesy, yet in truth it is very defective in the circumstances, which grieves me, because it might not remain as an exact model of all tragedies. For it is faulty both in place and time, the two necessary companions of all corporal actions. For where the stage should always represent but one place, and the uttermost time presupposed in it should be, both by Aristotle's precept and common reason, but one day, there is both many days and many places, inartificially imagined. But if it be so in *Gorboduc,* how much more in all the rest, where you shall have Asia of the one side and Afric of the other, and so many other underkingdoms, that the player, when he comes in, must ever begin

[c] "He who rules with a heavy hand fears the fearful; the fear returns upon its author" (Seneca).
[d] First English tragedy in blank verse, by Thomas Sackville and Thomas Norton (published in 1565)

with telling where he is, or else the tale will not be conceived?
Now ye shall have three ladies walk to gather flowers, and
then we must believe the stage to be a garden. By and by we
hear news of shipwreck in the same place, and then we are to
blame if we accept it not for a rock. Upon the back of that
comes out a hideous monster, with fire and smoke, and then
the miserable beholders are bound to take it for a cave. While in
the meantime two armies fly in, represented with four swords
and bucklers, and then what hard heart will not receive it for a
pitched field? Now of time they are much more liberal, for ordinary it is that two young princes fall in love. After many trav-
erses, she is got with child, delivered of a fair boy; he is lost,
groweth a man, falleth in love, and is ready to get another
child; and all this in two hours' space; which how absurd it is in
sense, even sense may imagine, and art hath taught, and all
ancient examples justified, and, at this day, the ordinary players in Italy will not err in. Yet will some bring in an example of
*Eunuchus* in Terence,[e] that containeth matter of two days,
yet far short of twenty years. True it is, and so was it to be
played in two days, and so fitted to the time it set forth. And
though Plautus have in one place done amiss, let us hit with
him, and not miss with him. But they will say, How then shall
we set forth a story, which contains both many places and
many times? And do they not know that a tragedy is tied to
the laws of poesy, and not of history; not bound to follow the
story, but having liberty either to feign a quite new matter or
to frame the history to the most tragical conveniency? Again,
many things may be told which cannot be showed, if they know
the difference betwixt reporting and representing. As for example, I may speak (though I am here) of Peru, and in speech
digress from that to the description of Calicut; but in action I
cannot represent it without Pacolet's horse.[f] And so was the
manner the ancients took, by some *Nuntius*[g] to recount
things done in former time or other place. Lastly, if they will
represent an history, they must not (as Horace saith) begin
*ab ovo,*[h] but they must come to the principal point of that one
action which they will represent. By example this will be best
expressed. I have a story of young Polydorus, delivered for
safety's sake, with great riches, by his father Priam to Polym-
nestor, king of Thrace, in the Trojan war time. He, after some
years, hearing the overthrow of Priam, for to make the treasure
his own, murdereth the child. The body of the child is taken
up by Hecuba. She, the same day, findeth a slight to be revenged

[e] Sidney confused *Eunuchus* with *Heautontimorumenos,* another play
by Terence (c. 190–159 B.C.), a Roman dramatist.   [f] a magic horse in
the tale of *Valentine and Orson,* a French romance   [g] messenger
[h] Latin, "from the egg," i.e., from the beginning

most cruelly of the tyrant. Where now would one of our tragedy writers begin, but with the delivery of the child? Then
should he sail over into Thrace, and so spend I know not how
many years, and travel numbers of places. But where doth
Euripides? Even with the finding of the body, leaving the rest
to be told by the spirit of Polydorus. This needs no further to
be enlarged; the dullest wit may conceive it.

But besides these gross absurdities, how all their plays be
neither right tragedies nor right comedies, mingling kings and
clowns, not because the matter so carrieth it, but thrust in the
clown by head and shoulders to play a part in majestical matters, with neither decency [1] nor discretion, so as neither the
admiration and commiseration nor the right sportfulness is by
their mongrel tragicomedy obtained. I know Apuleius did
somewhat so, but that is a thing recounted with space of time,
not represented in one moment: and I know the ancients have
one or two examples of tragicomedies, as Plautus hath *Amphitryo*. But if we mark them well we shall find that they never,
or very daintily, match hornpipes and funerals. So falleth it out
that, having indeed no right comedy, in that comical part of
our tragedy we have nothing but scurrility unworthy of any
chaste ears, or some extreme show of doltishness, indeed fit to
lift up a loud laughter, and nothing else; where the whole tract
of a comedy should be full of delight, as the tragedy should be
still maintained in a well-raised admiration.

But our comedians think there is no delight without laughter; which is very wrong, for though laughter may come with
delight, yet cometh it not of delight, as though delight should
be the cause of laughter; but well may one thing breed both
together. Nay rather in themselves they have, as it were, a
kind of contrariety; for delight we scarcely do but in things
that have a conveniency to ourselves or to the general nature;
laughter almost ever cometh of things most disproportioned
to ourselves and nature. Delight hath a joy in it, either permanent or present. Laughter hath only a scornful tickling. For
example, we are ravished with delight to see a fair woman,
and yet are far from being moved to laughter. We laugh at deformed creatures, wherein certainly we cannot delight. We delight in good chances, we laugh at mischances; we delight to
hear the happiness of our friends and country, at which he
were worthy to be laughed at that would laugh. We shall, con-
trarily, laugh sometimes to find a matter quite mistaken and
go down the hill against the bias, in the mouth of some such
men as for the respect of them one shall be heartily sorry,

---

[1] fitness

yet he cannot choose but laugh; and so is rather pained than delighted with laughter. Yet deny I not but that they may go well together. For as in Alexander's picture well set out we delight without laughter, and in twenty mad antics we laugh without delight, so in Hercules, painted with his great beard and furious countenance, in woman's attire, spinning at Omphale's commandment, it breeds both delight and laughter. For the representing of so strange a power in love procures delight; and the scornfulness of the action stirreth laughter. But I speak to this purpose, that all the end of the comical part be not upon such scornful matters as stir laughter only, but mix with it that delightful teaching which is the end of poesy. And the great fault even in that point of laughter, and forbidden plainly by Aristotle, is that they stir laughter in sinful things, which are rather execrable than ridiculous; or in miserable, which are rather to be pitied than scorned. For what is it to make folks gape at a wretched beggar or a beggarly clown; or against law of hospitality to jest at strangers, because they speak not English so well as we do? What do we learn? since it is certain

> *Nil habet infelix paupertas durius in se,*
> *Quam quod ridiculos homines facit.*[1]

But rather a busy loving courtier, a heartless threatening Thraso, a self-wise-seeming schoolmaster, a wry transformed traveler—these if we saw walk in stage names, which we play naturally, therein were delightful laughter, and teaching delightfulness; as in the other, the tragedies of Buchanan do justly bring forth a divine admiration. But I have lavished out too many words of this play matter. I do it because, as they are excelling parts of poesy, so is there none so much used in England, and none can be more pitifully abused; which, like an unmannerly daughter showing a bad education, causeth her mother Poesy's honesty to be called in question.

---

[1] "Unhappy poverty has nothing in it worse than this, that it makes men ridiculous" (Juvenal).

# Thomas Heywood:

# From *AN APOLOGY FOR ACTORS*

Tragedies and comedies, saith Donatus,[a] had their beginning *a rebus divinis*, from divine sacrifices. They differ thus: in comedies *turbulenta prima, tranquilla ultima;* in tragedies *tranquilla prima, turbulenta ultima;* comedies begin in trouble and end in peace; tragedies begin in calms and end in tempest. . . . The definition of the comedy according to the Latins: a discourse consisting of divers institutions comprehending civil and domestic things, in which is taught what in our lives and manners is to be followed, what to be avoided. The Greeks define it thus: Κωμωδία ἔστιν ἰδιωτικῶν καὶ πολιτικῶν πραγμάτων ἀκίνδυνος περιοχή.[b] Cicero saith a comedy is the imitation of life, the glass of custom, and the image of truth. In Athens they had their first original. . . .

I hope there is no man of so unsensible a spirit that can inveigh against the true and direct use of this quality.[c] Oh but, say they, the Romans in their time and some in these days have abused it, and therefore we volley out our exclamations against the use. Oh shallow! because such a man hath his house burned we shall quite condemn the use of fire; because one man quaffed poison we must forbear to drink; because some have been shipwrecked no man shall hereafter traffic by sea. Then I may as well argue thus: he cut his finger, therefore must I wear no knife; yond man fell from his horse, therefore must I

---

[a] Latin grammarian  [b] "Comedy is a portion, involving no danger, of the affairs of ordinary men and citizens."  [c] i.e., the profession of the actor

Thomas Heywood (*c.* 1573–1641) was a younger contemporary of Shakespeare. He says he had "either an entire hand or at least a main finger" in the composition of some 220 plays. Perhaps two dozen survive, the best-known of which is *A Woman Killed with Kindness*. The following selection, first published in 1612, is drawn from one of the longest defenses of the English stage.

travel a foot; that man surfeited, therefore I dare not eat. What can appear more absurd than such a gross and senseless assertion? I could turn this unpointed weapon against his breast that aims it at mine, and reason thus: Roscius had a large pension allowed him by the senate of Rome; why should not an actor of the like desert have the like allowance now? Or this: The most famous city and nation in the world held plays in great admiration. *Ergo*—but it is a rule in logic, *ex particularibus nihil fit.*[d] These are not the bases we must build upon nor the columns that must support our architecture.

> *Et latro et cautus precingitur ense viator;*
> *Ille sed insidias, hic sibi portat opem.* [*Ovid*]

> Both thieves and true men weapons wear alike;
> The one to defend, the other comes to strike.

Let us use fire to warm us, not to scorch us, to make ready our necessaries, not to burn our houses; let us drink to quench our thirst, not to surfeit; and eat to satisfy nature, not to gourmandize.

> *Comaedia, recta si mente legatur,*
> *Constabit nulli posse nocere.* [Ovid]

> Plays are in use as they are understood,
> Spectators' eyes may make them bad or good.

Shall we condemn a generality for any one particular misconstruction? Give me then leave to argue thus. Among kings have there not been some tyrants? Yet the office of a king is the image of the majesty of God. Among true subjects have there not crept in some false traitors? Even among the twelve there was one Judas, but shall we for his fault censure worse of the eleven? God forbid. Art thou prince or peasant? Art thou of the nobility or commonalty? Art thou merchant or soldier? Of the city or country? Art thou preacher or auditor? Art thou tutor or pupil? There have been of thy function bad and good, profane and holy. I adduce these instances to confirm this common argument that the use of any general thing is not for any one particular abuse to be condemned, for if that assertion stood firm we should run into many notable inconveniences.

> *Quis locus est templis augustior? haec quoque vitet,*
> *In culpam si qua est ingeniosa suam!* [e]

[d] from individual cases, nothing can be concluded    [e] "What place is more august than temples? but these should be shunned by any woman inclined to fault" (Ovid).

To proceed to the matter. First, playing is an ornament
to the city, which strangers of all nations repairing hither report of in their countries, beholding them here with some
admiration; for what variety of entertainment can there be in
any city of Christendom more than in London? But some will
say this dish might be very well spared out of the banquet.
To him I answer: Diogenes, that used to feed on roots, cannot
relish a marchpane.

Secondly, our English tongue, which has been the most
harsh, uneven, and broken language of the world, part Dutch,
part Irish, Saxon, Scotch, Welsh, and indeed a gallimaufry of
many but perfect in none, is now by this secondary means of
playing continually refined, every writer striving in himself to
add a new flourish unto it, so that in process from the most
rude and unpolished tongue it is grown to a most perfect and
composed language, and many excellent works and elaborate
poems written in the same, that many nations grow enamored
of our tongue (before despised). . . . Thus you see to what excel-
lency our refined English is brought, that in these days we
are ashamed of that euphony and eloquence which within
these sixty years the best tongues in the land were proud to
pronounce.

Thirdly, plays have made the ignorant more apprehensive, taught the unlearned the knowledge of many famous
histories, instructed such as cannot read in the discovery of
all our English chronicles, and what man have you now
of that weak capacity that cannot discourse of any notable
thing recorded even from William the Conqueror, nay from
the landing of Brute, until this day? being possessed of their
true use; for or because plays are written with this aim and
carried with this method: to teach subjects obedience to their
king, to show the people the untimely ends of such as have
moved tumults, commotions, and insurrections; to present
them with the flourishing estate of such as live in obedience,
exhorting them to allegiance, dehorting them from all traitor-
ous and felonious stratagems.

*Omne genus scripti gravitate tragedia vincit.*[f]

If we present a tragedy, we include the fatal and abortive
ends of such as commit notorious murders, which is aggra-
vated [g] and acted with all the art that may be, to terrify men
from the like abhorred practices. If we present a foreign history, the subject is so intended that in the lives of Romans

[f] "Tragedy surpasses in seriousness every kind of writing" (Ovid)
[g] made more striking

Grecians, or others, either the virtues of our countrymen are
extolled or their vices reproved, as thus by the example of
Caesar to stir soldiers to valor and magnanimity, by the fall of
Pompey that no man trust in his own strength; we present
Alexander killing his friend in his rage, to reprove rashness;
Midas choked with his gold, to tax covetousness; Nero against
tyranny; Sardanapalus against luxury; Ninus against ambition;
with infinite others by sundry instances either animating men
to noble attempts or attacking the consciences of the spectators, finding themselves touched in presenting the vices of
others.

If a moral,[h] it is to persuade men to humanity and good
life, to instruct them in civility and good manners, showing
them the fruits of honesty and the end of villany.

*Versibus exponi tragicis res comica non vult.*[i]

Again Horace, *Arte poetica,*

> *At vestri proavi Plautinos et numeros et*
> *Laudavere sales.*[j]

If a comedy, it is pleasantly contrived with merry accidents
and intermixt with apt and witty jests to present before the
prince at certain times of solemnity, or else merrily fitted
to the stage. And what is then the subject of this harmless
mirth? Either in the shape of a clown to show others their
slovenly and unhandsome behavior, that they may reform that
simplicity in themselves which others make their sport, lest
they happen to become the like subject of general scorn to an
auditory; else it entreats of love, deriding foolish enamorates
who spend their ages, their spirits, nay themselves, in the servile
and ridiculous employments of their mistresses; and these are
mingled with sportful accidents to recreate such as of themselves are wholly devoted to melancholy, which corrupts the
blood, or to refresh such weary spirits as are tired with labor or
study, to moderate the cares and heaviness of the mind, that
they may return to their trades and faculties with more zeal
and earnestness after some small, soft and pleasant retirement.
Sometimes they discourse of pantaloons, usurers that have unthrifty sons, which both the fathers and sons may behold to
their instruction, sometimes of courtesans, to divulge their subtleties and snares in which young men may be entangled, showing them the means to avoid them.

---

[h] morality play; see *Everyman*, p. 66    [i] "A comic affair should not
be set forth in tragic verses."    [j] "Your fathers praised the verses of
Plautus for both their meter and wit."

If we present a pastoral we show the harmless love of shepherds diversely moralized, distinguishing between the craft of the city and the innocence of the sheep-cote.

Briefly there is neither tragedy, history, comedy, moral, or pastoral from which an infinite use cannot be gathered. I speak not in the defense of any lascivious shows, scurrilous jests, or scandalous invectives. If there be any such I banish them quite from my patronage. . . .

Eupolis, Cratinus, Aristophanes, and other comic poets in the time of Horace, with large scope and unbridled liberty, boldly and plainly scourged all such abuses as in their ages were generally practised to the staining and blemishing of a fair and beautiful commonweal. Likewise a learned gentleman [k] in his *Apology for Poetry* speaks thus: Tragedies well handled be a most worthy kind of poesie. Comedies make men see and shame at their faults, and proceeding further among other university plays he remembers the Tragedy of Richard the Third acted in St. John's in Cambridge so essentially that had the tyrant Phalaris beheld his bloody proceedings, it had mollified his heart and made him relent at sight of his inhuman massacres. Further he commends of comedies the Cambridge *Pedantius* and the Oxford *Bellum grammaticale* and leaving them passes on to our public plays, speaking liberally in their praise and what commendable use may be gathered of them. If you peruse *Margarita poetica* you may see what excellent uses and sentences he hath gathered out of Terence's *Andria, Eunuchus*, and the rest; likewise out of Plautus's *Amphitryo, Asinaria.* . . .

Is thy mind noble and wouldst thou be further stirred up to magnanimity? Behold, upon the stage thou mayst see Hercules, Achilles, Alexander, Caesar, Alcibiades, Lysander, Sertorious, Hannibal, Antigonus, Philip of Macedon, Mithridates of Pontus, Pyrrhus of Epirus, Agesilaus among the Lacedemonians, Epaminondas among the Thebans, Scaevola alone entering the armed tents of Porsenna, Horatius Cocles alone withstanding the whole army of the Etrurians, Leonidas of Sparta choosing a lion to lead a band of deer rather than one deer to conduct an army of lions, with infinite others in their own persons, qualities, and shapes, animating thee with courage, deterring thee from cowardice. Hast thou of thy country well deserved and art thou of thy labor evil requited? To associate [1] thee thou mayst see the valiant Roman Marcellus pursue Hannibal at Nola, conquering Syracusa, vanquishing the Gauls at Padua, and presently (for his reward) banished

---

[k] Sir John Harrington (1561–1612)     [1] accompany

his country into Greece. There thou mayest see Scipio Afri-
canus, now triumphing for the conquest of all Africa and immediately exiled the confines of Romania. Art thou inclined
to lust? Behold the falls of the Tarquins in the rape of
Lucrece; the guerdon of luxury in the death of Sardanapalus;
Appius destroyed in the ravishing of Virginia; and the destruction of Troy in the lust of Helena. Art thou proud? Our scene
presents thee with the fall of Phaeton; Narcissus pining in the
love of his shadow; ambitious Haman now calling himself a
god, and by and by thrust headlong among the devils. We present men with the ugliness of their vices to make them the more
to abhor them, as the Persians use, who, above all sins loathing drunkenness, accustomed in their solemn feasts to make
their servants and captives extremely overcome with wine and
then call their children to view their nasty and loathsome behavior, making them hate that sin in themselves which showed
so gross and abominable in others. The like use may be gathered of the drunkards so naturally imitated in our plays, to the
applause of the actor, content of the auditory, and reproving
of the vice. Art thou covetous? Go no further than Plautus'
comedy called *Euclio*.

> *Dum fallax servus, durus pater, improba lena*
> *Vixerit, et meretrix blanda, Menandros erit.* [Ovid]

> While there's false servant, or obdurate sire,
> Sly bawd, smooth whore, Menandros we'll admire.

To end in a word, art thou addicted to prodigality, envy,
cruelty, perjury, flattery, or rage? Our scenes afford thee store
of men to shape your lives by, who be frugal, loving, gentle,
trusty, without soothing, and in all things temperate. Wouldst
thou be honorable, just, friendly, moderate, devout, merciful, and loving concord? Thou mayest see many of their fates
and ruins who have been dishonorable, unjust, false, glutton-
ous, sacrilegious, bloody-minded, and broachers of dissention.
Women likewise that are chaste are by us extolled and encouraged in their virtues, being instanced by Diana, Bel-
phoebe, Matilda, Lucrece, and the Countess of Salisbury. The
unchaste are by us shown their errors in the persons of Phryne,
Lais, Thais, Flora, and among us Rosamond and Mistress
Shore. What can sooner print modesty in the souls of the
wanton than by discovering unto them the monstrousness of
their sin?

It follows that we prove these exercises to have been the
discoverers of many notorious murders long concealed from

the eyes of the world. To omit all far-fetched instances, we will prove it by a domestic and home-born truth which within these few years happened. At Lynn, in Norfolk, the then Earl of Sussex' players acting the old History of Fair Francis and presenting a woman who, insatiately doting on a young gentleman, the more securely to enjoy his affection, mischievously and secretly murdered her husband; whose ghost haunted her, and at divers times, in her most solitary and private contemplations, in most horrid and fearful shapes appeared and stood before her. As this was acted, a town's-woman (till then of good estimation and report), finding her conscience (at this presentment) extremely troubled, suddenly screeched and cried out: "Oh, my husband, my husband! I see the ghost of my husband fiercely threatening and menacing me." At which shrill and unexpected outcry, the people about her, moved to a strange amazement, inquired the reason of her clamor, when presently, un-urged, she told them that seven years ago she, to be possessed of such a gentleman (meaning him), had poisoned her husband, whose fearful image personated itself in the shape of that ghost. Whereupon the murderess was apprehended, before the justices further examined, and by her voluntary confession after condemned. That this is true, as well by the report of the actors as the records of the town, there are many eyewitnesses of this accident yet living vocally to confirm it. . . .

The Cardinal at Brussels has at this time in pay a company of our English comedians. The French king allows certain companies in Paris, Orleans, besides other cities: so does the King of Spain, in Seville, Madrid, and other provinces. But in no country they are of that eminence that ours are: so our most royal and ever renowned sovereign has licensed us in London: so did his predecessor, the thrice virtuous virgin, Queen Elizabeth; and before her, her sister, Queen Mary, Edward the Sixth, and their father, Henry the Eighth: and before these, in the tenth year of the reign of Edward the Fourth, Anno 1490. John Stowe, an ancient and grave chronicler, records (amongst other varieties tending to the like effect) that a play was acted at a place called Skinner's-well, fast by Clerkenwell, which continued eight days, and was of matter from Adam and Eve (the first creation of the world). The spectators were no worse than the royalty of England. . . . Moreover, to this day in divers places of England there be towns that hold the privilege of their fairs, and other charters by yearly stage plays, as at Manningtree in Suffolk, Kendall in the north, and others. To let these pass, as things familiarly known to all men. . . .

# Alfred Harbage:

# From *SHAKESPEARE'S AUDIENCE*

We have nearly exhausted the supply of direct evidence on the nature of Shakespeare's audience. There remain the diverse elements to be found in the plays themselves. But here we confront a difficulty. Any approach to the audience through the plays must be highly subjective; conclusions are as apt to reflect the nature of the reader as of what he reads. That Shakespeare's plays mirror the audience for which they were written, except in their defects, has as often as not been dismissed as an impractical notion. The reason is understandable. The defects are irritating, but it would be ungrateful merely to say so, with the audience available as whipping boy. Of course, the subjective element is bound to obtrude no matter what type of evidence is being interpreted, including the figures in Henslowe's *Diary*. The best we can do is to collect it and leave the issue to debate.

What follows is my contribution to the debate. It is mainly rebuttal, but its intention is constructive. Sarcastic allusions to "commentators" come without grace from those who themselves are commenting. Shakespeare like Falstaff is the cause that wit is in other men, and the most brilliant criticism in English has been provoked by Shakespeare's plays. But the least brilliant of this criticism is, I believe, that which relates the plays to their audience. It is usually incidental; and it is often careless, cynical, or marked by an incredible condescension. The Elizabethan stratum of humanity is divested of mystery, its common sense assessed at the rate of some early treatise on physiology, its perceptive range simplified to "two

Alfred Harbage (1901–    ) holds degrees from the University of Pennsylvania, where he taught from 1924 to 1947. Later he taught at Columbia University; he is now the Henry B. and Anne M. Cabot Professor of English Literature at Harvard University. The following essay is drawn from *Shakespeare's Audience*, available in paperback. Mr. Harbage's *As They Liked It: An Essay on Shakespeare and Morality* has also been issued as a paperback.

levels of intelligence," while whole battalions of our former fellow mortals are dismissed with placid allusions to "groundlings" or "a motley crew." At the safe remove of three centuries the nature of a generation collectively has even been deduced from a heap of nutshells. Sometimes distance lends courage also to the idealist, and the Globe is filled with mute inglorious Shakespeares, but normally we hear the voice of derision and disdain. Not all of the critical attitudes toward the audience are uncongenial, but none of them need be taken on faith.

We are familiar with the tendency in others (and ourselves) to apply colors recklessly to any part of a canvas depicting the lusty age of Elizabeth. Enthusiastic brushwork transforms human beings into Elizabethans. A brief description of Shakespeare's audience by Brander Matthews contains the following phrases: "superabundant energy," "soaring imagination," "puffed with pride," "reckless daredevil," "sensuous and sensual," "furious in hate and love," "avid of swift sensation," "primitive savagery of manners," "violently passionate," "frankly brutal." [1] * The portrait is exhiliarating but conducive at last to sober reflection. Were Shakespeare's contemporaries truly such galvanic creatures? Imagine, if you will, some London carter plodding beside his oxen on the road to Hackney, some London housewife sewing a fine seam, some London mason patiently, skillfully pointing the stones of Bridge Gate at Is. 4d. a long, long day. Imagine entering some Bread Street shop in 1601, fixing the proprietor with your eye, and saying: "You are puffed with pride, a reckless daredevil, furious in hate and love, violently passionate, and frankly brutal." Would he not reply with pardonable dismay: "Who? Me!" Nothing we can discover from examining their daily routine, their frugal expense accounts, and their quiet and sensible letters suggests that Elizabethans, individually or collectively, were vastly different from us. Their nature cannot be deduced from the defeat of the Armada or the public hangings in Tyburn. We ourselves live in a spectacular age, without being individually spectacular.

The kinship we feel with the old playgoers, those of us who love their drama, must not be confined to the upper classes, no matter what our own social allegiances or aspirations may be. I have previously quoted the statement that while Heywood wrote for apprentices and shopkeepers, Shakespeare "kept in his mind's eye the approval of the lordly patrons of Blackfriars." The writer, I suspect, would indignantly repudiate the implica-

* Notes are printed at the end of this selection.

tions of the statement if put in bald terms—the fine things in Elizabethan drama were written for the fine people, for lords. So prevalent is the notion that óne is apt to countenance it through sheer inadvertence; the cloven hoof flashes out in half the Shakespearean criticism being written. Inadvertence can scarcely be the explanation for the following: "The movie seems to be quite as capable of proceeding on two levels as the Elizabethan tragedy: poetry and psychology for the gentleman's galleries, action and blood for the pit." [2] The writer is a careful investigator in a modern field, repeating something evidently conceived to be a critical truism. But if we are to confuse social with spiritual distinction, we may as well subscribe at once to the belief that Shakespeare's plays were written by the Earl of Oxford, or Southampton, or Rutland, or whoever the current candidate may be.

Misconceptions are prevalent concerning the intellectual and artistic attainments of the Elizabethan nobleman. One suspects that he is often patterned in the image of Sir Philip Sidney and the Earl of Southampton, the latter generously endowed with the qualities found in the literary works dedicated to him. It is true that the English Renaissance brought forth lords, knights, and gentlemen with literary gifts, in greater number, perhaps, than any comparable span of years, but it was a great age and the law of averages was operating. It is doubtful if the proportion of the genteel classes displaying such gifts, creative or appreciative, was higher than that of the literate ungenteel. That the nobility could produce a Sidney is the less remarkable in view of the ability of the middle classes to produce a Spenser and a Milton. Marlowe and Shakespeare illustrate the remarkable efficaciousness of extraction from workers in leather. Many men of high birth still looked with disdain upon anything so clerkly as literature, while many others, including nominal patrons of now famous dramatic companies, displayed simply a depressing indifference. The Elizabethan great world from the queen down, let the truth be told, was mean to its poets and dramatists.

As we read Sir Edmund Chambers's fine volumes on the Elizabethan stage, we come first to the queen, then to the royal household, then to the Revels Office, until by this magnificent route we arrive at the theatres and the acting companies. All is relevant and all is revealing, but, unless we are wary, we may gather the impression that the drama of the age was an appendage of the court. An equally valid approach to the stage would be a chronicle of London taverns and of enterprisers before James Burbage. Sir Edmund writes:

It will be manifest, in the course of the present treatise, that the palace was the point of vantage from which the stage won its way, against the linked opposition of an alienated pulpit and an alienated municipality, to an ultimate entrenchment of economic independence.[3]

Let us not forget the spadesmen who dug that entrenchment, the anonymous thousands who dropped their pennies in the gatherer's box: these were the true patrons of Elizabethan drama. The queen, the Privy Council, and the (bribed) officials of the Revels Office sponsored a working arrangement whereby one minor means of her majesty's "solace" could be maintained at the public expense. It was quite unconsciously that the court performed its great service to art: poetry like Protestantism entered the palace through a postern gate.

Sir Edmund continues:

> On the literary side, the milieu of the Court had its profound effect in helping to determine the character of the Elizabethan play as a psychological hybrid, in which the romance and erudition, dear to the bower and the library, interact at every turn with the robust popular elements of farce and melodrama.

But the specifications of the habitué of bower and library had to be modified by something other than farce and melodrama before great drama could result. The appearance of its qualities of greatness awaited that "ultimate entrenchment in economic independence" provided by the populace of London. The names of great lords had been associated with acting companies for generations before plays show signs of poetic or other artistic worth. The drama was as popular at court before the eighties as after, and, for all we know otherwise, *Herpetulus the Blue Knight and Perobia* was as cordially received there in 1574 as *King Lear* in 1606. No great Elizabethan play was written by a sojourner in the great world, and, so far as we know, such plays appealed no more to that world than to the public at large. In fact, the highborn as a class showed a preference for pageantry and pedantry, for pastoral and mask, and the body of drama they ultimately created for themselves was, above all else, fantastic. The bane upon Renaissance drama in Italy was its failure to escape from the palace and the library. Elizabeth and James permitted Shakespeare to write, but there was another kind of permission not within the royal gift—permission to write as he did.

In one sense Elizabethan drama was lordly indeed, or kingly: a throne was the one indispensable piece of theatrical property. Thoughts flew upward, and the multitude had to be treated to displays of majesty. Playwrights shared this taste for grandeur, and the fine people in their audience must have been stimulating. Noble auditors, like command performances, would have given a cachet to dramatic activity. The lordly ones were still lordly; their functions were not all deputized: they were lawgivers and leaders in battle. They were personally imposing, so clad and attended as to give visible token of their power and affluence. They were distinguishable and on view —we may owe them something for that. Playwrights would have been conscious of their presence, and ambition and vanity are great releasers of energy.

It is even conceivable that some playwrights then, like some critics now, assumed the minds of lordly patrons to be as elegantly furnished as their bodies and for them, especially, hung out their "richest words as polish't jewels." But it is hard to believe that we owe the poetry and psychology of the drama to the accident of the writers' having been dazzled. Shakespeare knew an Osric when he saw one, and he knew that Osrics were more plentiful than Sidneys. *Hamlet* itself would not have been written for such courtiers as it portrays. Assuming among the writers a willingness to let the "candied tongue lick absurd pomp," would poetry and psychology have resulted? or satire, "wantonness," pomposity itself? We do not know as we read what sad jest may have been designed to tickle the Earl of Rutland, or what lovely song to charm the groundlings. "Why should the poor be flattered?" to ask Hamlet's question. Because in Shakespeare's theatre there were so many of them.

This is not to imply that poetry and psychology were wasted upon the "gentlemen's galleries." The patrician was as capable of rising above his class as the plebeian. It is only to insist, with weariness, that mentality should not be measured in terms of caste. If we substitute the word "taste" for "mentality," we must reckon with what has been deduced as to the essential "unity of taste" among all castes, and among playwrights and playgoers together, in Elizabethan times.[4] To assume that action and bloodshed (or farce and wordplay) were intended exclusively for the pit is simply not feasible. The disparate elements in the drama—the bloodshed and sweeping action on the one hand and poetry and psychology on the other—are explainable on a sounder principle than that of dual appeal to social levels in the audience. The disparity may result from nothing more than a theatrical heightening of the actual contrast in life—between the constantly observable crudity of human action and refinement of human thought. Elizabethan

drama is not the only great literature where the contrast is
glaringly reflected. The soul stirrings of Achilles, kin of the
gods, were necessarily infinite, but what he actually did was
sulk in his tent or slay Trojans. The balance between the tendency to action and the tendency to reflection is more apt to
be disturbed in favor of reflection among modern critical readers of Shakespeare than among Elizabethan playgoers (or human beings generally), so that the action of the plays is apt to
seem intrusive. Naturally we wish to think of the nobility as
sharing our tastes: we invite only the best people to join our
club.

Sometimes Shakespeare's spectators are graded not according to a social hierarchy in his day but an intellectual hierarchy
in ours. The "judicious" spectator is newly invoked, and he is
endowed with the ability to discern in the play esoteric meanings not intended for the audience as a whole; in default of
either his or the playwright's having left a commentary, the
modern critic supplies it. Spectacular results can be achieved
by this method, and, strangely enough, the most spectacular of
all has been achieved by one of the most meticulous of scholars.
W. W. Greg distinguishes between the "bulk" or "generality"
of Shakespeare's audience and the "humaner minds" and
argues that the playwright wrote two meanings into *Hamlet:*
the "humaner minds" perceived that Claudius was no murderer
and the Ghost's accusations were "a mere figment of Hamlet's
brain." Greg presents this theory with earnestness and skill;
then later he defends it, although he has "never discovered"
whether he believes in it himself.[5] These are baffling tactics.
If one were to describe a newly found quarto of the play with a
title page bearing an unknown printer's device, stipulating that
what appeared to be the device might be after all only the stain
of a crushed roach, Greg's indignation can be imagined.

Evidently it is only with the "unknowable," with the meaning of the book rather than with the book as a physical fact,
that we may take liberties. Whether Greg believes in his theory
is immaterial; he certainly believes in the two levels of intelligence and in the "judicious" spectator. Yet his theory has dem-
onstrated once and for all the slippery nature of this person:
we never know when we have him in hand. Originally, he was
the occult friend of the playwright; he now serves the critic in
a like capacity. So far as the meaning of *Hamlet* is concerned,
Adams, Schücking, Granville-Barker, W. W. Lawrence,[6]
and presumably most others are content to stand with the
"bulk" of the audience. But even if Greg had only a single
opponent, J. Dover Wilson let us say, we should have to recognize that among the "humaner minds" in the audience, some

were more human than others, and we should have to postulate not two levels of intelligence but three at least—Greg's, Wilson's, and the "generality's."

W. W. Lawrence has said that Shakespeare "provided for the more intellectual spectators something which the groundlings, with their imperfect mentality and defective education, could not perceive, but this was an extension of the simple meaning of his play, and not at variance with it." [7] With the main bearing of this statement, one must certainly agree. It is unfortunate, however, that perfection of mentality and adequacy of education seem still to be measured in ratio to distance from the ground. Are we not too facile in our generalizations about the education and mentality of the penny playgoers? It seems probable that the rank and file were more literate in the sixteenth century than in the eighteenth. In view of the profusion of schools,[8] of the tendency of the trade guilds to make literacy a qualification even for entrance into apprenticeship,[9] and of the manifest interest in self-instruction, we must revise any impressions we may ever have had that London workmen were "nine-tenths illiterate." In a period of eight months during the single year 1585, the publishers disposed of ten thousand copies of their reading primer, *The A B C and Little Catechism*.[10] Using this book, women at their wheels and men at their looms taught, for a pittance, the children of other workers how to read. In the opinion of the one who has most carefully investigated the subject, the people of London constituted "by no means an illiterate society." [11] It would be impossible to prove that more than a fraction even of the groundlings in Shakespeare's audience had no passport to books.

The groundlings, nevertheless, like the audience in general, did not read much: books, candles, and daylight leisure were all hard to come by. The great majority of men and women were "ignorant." But we must ask whether ignorance was so crippling in the time of Shakespeare as it is today. There were, without doubt, more unlighted chambers in the mind of the average spectator than in our own, and creatures of darkness found a dwelling there, but we are likely to overestimate the degree of this benightedness. Miss Doran, in her excellent attempt to discover the Elizabethan attitude toward the ghost in *Hamlet*, has mentioned the "lack of relevance between fact and theory" [12] in Renaissance science. Cannot one say, without casuistry, that when theory is fallacious, the ignorant benefit by their enforced reliance upon observable fact? The burned child who shuns the fire has been an inductive philosopher for ages. It was the learned ones who needed Bacon's

422              ALFRED HARBAGE

recommendations. Edward Topsell was more "learned" about beasts than other Englishmen in 1607. But observe his earnest belief in the existence of the unicorn and his contempt for ignorant unbelievers:

> the vulgar sort of infidell people which scarcely beleeue any hearbe but such as they see in their owne Gardens, or any beast but such as in their own flocks, or any knowledge but such as in their own braines, or any birds which are not hatched in their own Nests.[13]

We must score one for the "vulgar." Topsell was relying upon authority, the rank and file upon experience. We must not decide upon the attitudes and beliefs held by the rank and file of Elizabethans through reading their authorities. We must not assume that credulity, concerning unicorns, satyrs, or even ghosts and demons, was then the especial mark of the uncultivated as it is now.

J. Dover Wilson is quite assured in his pronouncements on what Shakespeare's audience believed about various things.[14] It would be folly to ignore the erudition and analysis of so talented a writer. Inquiry into contemporary point of view is the current fashion in Shakespearean criticism, and a wholesome one, but we must look twice at all the conclusions. The difficulty is that we cannot consult the spectators at the Globe and make sure they had read the right books. If a critic quotes selected passages from selected works to prove what the audience thought upon selected topics, we are likely to witness only a sinister alliance between the pedantry of two ages. The following passage, I believe, does not aid in demonstrating that Hamlet was a man of action and would be so regarded by Shakespeare's audience:

> Perhaps most significant is the statement by the illustrious French physician Laurentius, whose works were read throughout Western Europe: "The melancholike are accounted as most fit to undertake matters of weightie charge and high attempt. Aristotle in his Problemes sayeth that the melancholike are most wittie and ingenious. . . ." If then ability to transact important business was one result assigned to the melancholy temperament, this temperament could hardly have been looked upon as causing morbid inaction. Why then did Shakespeare make Hamlet melancholy?[15]

There is always the possibility that both Shakespeare and his audience had formed an opinion about melancholy otherwise than by reading Laurentius.

An amusing revelation of the practical responses of the audience is offered by the fate of *The Faithful Shepherdess*. Fletcher complained that the audience, noting that the characters were shepherds, but "missing whitsun ales, creame, wasiel & morris-dances, began to be angry." [16] In a word, they wanted the shepherds to behave like shepherds. To them it meant nothing that the play obeyed, in Chapman's words of praise, "the holy lawes of homely pastorall." Unlike Chapman, they were ignorant of such laws. We see the force in operation again in *The Knight of the Burning Pestle*. When Merrythought in the play says, "Never trust a Tailor that does not sing at his work; his mind is of nothing but filching," the Grocer's wife in the audience comments, "Mark this George, 'tis worth noting: Godfrey my Tailor, you know never sings, and he had fourteen yards to make this gown; and I'll be sworn, Mistress Penistone the Draper's Wife had one made with twelve." [17] Here is dramatic criticism in its purest form.

The most invidious modern charge against Shakespeare's audience is that it was primitive, brutal, in some way spiritually debased. It is not infrequently made. In mild form the charge appears in the following passage forming part of an otherwise closely reasoned treatise on the acting time of Elizabethan plays:

> Would this audience, composed largely of illiterate Londoners, be able without excess of mental and physical fatigue, to concentrate its undivided attention for three hours without a break upon such an enthralling melodrama as *Richard III* or such a soul-stirring tragedy as *Othello*? Could such primitive beings pay out the nervous energy needed to endure three hours of imaginative exaltation? The very rapidity of the actors' utterance must have imposed a tiresome strain upon untrained minds, toiling in vain to keep pace with speeches not half understood. [18]

The atmosphere created is suggestive of the Old Stone Age; evolutionary processes seem to have been marvelously accelerated since Shakespeare's day. We may be dealing here only with indiscretion of speech. Such cannot be said of the following, included in the most recent study of Shakespeare's audience, and inspired by the putting out of Gloucester's eyes and by other "horrors" in the plays:

> What these horrors enable us to do is accurately to measure the sensibility of the audience and to gauge their imagina-

tive reaction. On that evidence we have no choice but to
rate both low. This deduction is, of course, amply borne
out by our knowledge of the time. A strong vein of brutality and an insensitiveness to physical suffering were part
and parcel of the mentality of the Elizabethan audience.

Miss Byrne's summing up presents the "psychological picture"
of "an audience primitive and undeveloped imaginatively."[19]
The most furious assault upon the audience on the grounds
of spiritual and moral depravity was made by Robert Bridges:

> Shakespeare should not be put into the hands of the young
> without the warning that the foolish things in his plays are
> for the foolish, the filthy for the filthy, and the brutal for
> the brutal; and that, if out of veneration for his genius we
> are led to admire or even tolerate such things, we may be
> thereby not conforming ourselves to him, but only degrad-
> ing ourselves to the level of his audience, and learning
> contamination from those wretched beings who can never
> be forgiven their share in preventing the greatest poet and
> dramatist of the world from being the best artist.[20]

A. C. Bradley, the poet laureate's good and even deferential
friend, could not let these words pass wholly unrebuked, although in the traditional manner of scholars, he placed the
disagreeable matter in a footnote and almost in Latin.[21]
Bridges's essay as a whole scarcely invites refutation. The details considered "filthy," "foolish," and "brutal" are of a type
to be found also in nondramatic works such as few members
of the popular audiences could have afforded to buy. The words
themselves are too harsh. To share Bridges's attitude toward
the audience, we must share his view that Falstaff was at last
bidden a "triumphant farewell" by a creator recoiling in moral
disgust; we must be willing to exchange Falstaff as he is for
Falstaff as Bridges would have him. There is an obvious risk in
endorsing a conception of the audience based upon such details of the plays as "most offend the simple taste" of a particular critic, no matter how eminent he may be; fortunately,
scolding the audience is an alternative to excising the plays.

That our "knowledge of the time," as Miss Byrne maintains,
establishes the presumption of "a strong vein of brutality and
an insensitiveness to physical suffering" is a courageous assertion, placing a tremendous burden upon our knowledge of
the time. Miss Byrne is identifying Elizabethans with certain
of their institutions. We must consent, presumably, to be identi-
fied with certain of ours. The children once harnessed to coal
carts in the tunnels of English mines should send us seeking

brutality in the poetry of Coleridge and Wordsworth. If we do not find it, perhaps we should wonder how these poets could have been so brutally aloof. It is easy to cast stones. Children are harnessed no more, but evils still are permitted to exist. It would be an indiscretion of taste to mention some of these evils, since we have become so sensitive, so ingenious in evading the spectacle of suffering, so convinced of the ethical superiority of looking the other way.

Each age has its own brutalities. The Elizabethans were forced to live more intimately with theirs, and they acceded to the conditions of their existence. Shakespeare's auditors look at Talbot spattered with stage blood; but as they look, they weep. Throngs gather to see the felons hanged at Tyburn, but "the criminals' friends come and draw them down by their feet, that they may die all the sooner." [22] Is this brutality or tenderness? Animals are baited and whipped in the pits, but voices are raised in protest and the sport is declining.[23] Beneath its "callouses" human nature must have been the same in Shakespeare's day as in ours. The range of feeling must have been the same. People are still compounded of heaven and earth: kind fathers are harsh creditors, decent folk exchange ribaldries, and ruffians rescue puppies. We need to know more about human impulses in all ages before we grow rash about the Elizabethans. We need to distinguish between what is fundamental in human nature and what is superficial adjustment to environment. Perhaps the whole range of impulses was more operative in the less comfortable age of Shakespeare and more apt to impress itself upon art. It is more accurate to say that the audience expected and accepted brutality than that they demanded and enjoyed it. There is a manifest injustice in charging Shakespeare's audience with brutality because of the putting out of Gloucester's eyes, unless we credit it with an exquisite tenderness because of Lear's words over the body of Cordelia.

Among the hosts of books about Shakespeare's plays, some are ignorant and foolish; one can always make a Roman holiday by quoting such books. I have avoided doing so, at the cost of comic relief. The only alternative has involved a certain injustice; one never represents fairly the views of responsible writers by quoting a few vulnerable statements. I have not pretended to evaluate in their entirety the essays I have quoted, but to illustrate from them some of the commoner attitudes toward Shakespeare's audience. That these attitudes may be mistaken is illustrated by opposing counsel. The treatment by Thorndike, although deficient in proof and perhaps mistaken in details, strikes me as essentially true.[24] Bradley, although almost in wonder, affirmed that "the audience had not only imagination and the power to sink its soul in the essence of drama. It had something else of scarcely less import for Shakespeare, the love of poetry." [25] Elmer E. Stoll, in his most recent utterance, rejects the judicious few:

> by ear the audience through lifelong attendance responded to the niceties of the different art in the Forum and the Athenian and London theatres. The technique as such they did not understand; but the ideas, sentiments, and morals, the language and situations, were not above their heads, and to what they heard they were accustomed, attuned.[26]

Felix E. Schelling holds no brief for lordly patrons:

> The drama of Shakespeare and his immediate fellows spoke to men by right of their manhood, not by virtue of their gentility. It stirred in its appeal the depths of a large and generous humanity.[27]

And Charles J. Sisson points out that most of those qualities with which Beaumont mockingly endowed his citizen-grocer— patriotism, personal pride, love of romance, and the rest—can, in the "spectateur représentatif," scarcely be considered undesirable.[28]

The "representative spectator" may be as much an abstraction as the "typical man," but conveniences must sometimes be used. We may say in the present case, quite apart from Beaumont's satirical use of them as the spectators in *The Knight of the Burning Pestle*, that a grocer, his wife, and their young apprentice form as acceptable an epitome of Shakespeare's audience as any the facts will warrant us to choose. If Shakespeare did not write to please such a little cockney family as this, he did not write to please his audience. But if he did so write, then there must be some correspondence in quality between the plays and our sample three—the grocer, his wife, and their young apprentice.

Reflection may reduce our amazement. That the potentialities of the human mind are unaffected by time, place, and social position is sound biology, and we may safely presume that our little group possessed human minds. We may even presume that they possessed the right kind of minds. We find them in the theatre separated from many of their neighbors— the stolid, the material, the bigoted, the folk of predominately animal appetite. That they had read few books is no stigma upon them. The modern correspondence between the reading habit and active mentality is a product of new folkways. Even complete illiteracy, when not the product of incapacity or indifference, but of mere conformity, may be consonant with the highest intelligence, sometimes even with heightened powers of memory and observation.

The minds of our spectators have been sharpened by urban life. The cockney as a type has seldom been accused of stupidity. In 1601 London is growing rapidly, teeming with life and variegated activity. As like as not our little group are first generation Londoners, as stimulated and knowledgeable as modern New Yorkers lately transplanted from their prairie homes. In any case, in the crowded London of 1601 alertness is a condition of survival.

They are easy in the company of the audible arts. Music, preaching, speechmaking, storytelling, disputation—these have been available even when food and warmth have not. There is lacking the tremendous range of diversions and distractions to be devised by later centuries, but there is always the spectacle of humanity, the balm of melody, the marvel of words. The theatres have been standing a lifetime, offering an education in literature and history. Wide vistas have been opened to the mind and have furnished it with powers of association. The unlearned have been taught "the knowledge of many famous histories" and few playgoers are "of that weake capacity that cannot discourse of any notable things." [29]

The factor above all else that we must reckon with in assessing the quality of our sample spectators is the almost incalculable effect of interest upon understanding. We have all been amazed at the proficiency of small boys in analyzing batting averages and of certain of their elders, dense in every other way, in moving easily through technical labyrinths concerning their business. Let us assume that our three spectators are intensely interested in plays. Of course, our instincts may still instruct us that no one out of a London shop could possibly have appreciated *Hamlet*—just as no one out of a Stratford shop could have written it.

### NOTES

1. In *Shakspere as a Playwright*, pp. 294-312.
2. Thorp, *America at the Movies*, p. 23
3. *Elizabethan Stage*, 1, 3.
4. See Bradley, "Shakespeare's Theatre and Audience, *Oxford Lectures on Poetry;* and, especially, Sisson, *Le Goût*

*public et le théâtre élisabéthain,* Chapter III (Unité du goût public).

5. "Hamlet's Hallucination," *Modern Language Review,* XII (1917), 393-421; "Re-Enter Ghost: a Reply to Mr. J. Dover Wilson, *ibid.,* XIV (1919), 353-69; "What Happens in 'Hamlet,' " *ibid.,* XXXI (1936), 145-54.

6. For a review of the controversy and a restatement of his own sound position, see Lawrence, "Hamlet and the Mouse-Trap," *PMLA,* LIV (1939), 709-35.

7. *Shakespeare's Problem Comedies,* p. 15.

8. Knights, "Education and the Drama in the Age of Shakespeare," *Criterion,* XI (1931-32), 599-625. Most of spectators at the Globe "were likely to have received an education of the Grammar school type" (p. 607), i.e., such as Shakespeare himself had received.

9. Dunlop, *English Apprenticeship and Child Labour,* pp. 45, 136.

10. Plant, *English Book Trade,* p. 40.

11. Adamson, "The Extent of Literacy in England in the Fifteenth and Sixteenth Centuries: Notes and Conjectures," *Library,* Ser. IV, X (1929), 163-93.

12. "On Elizabethan Credulity," *Journal of the History of Ideas,* I (1940), 166.

13. *The Historie of Foure-Footed Beastes* (1607), quoted in *ibid.,* p. 166.

14. *What Happens in Hamlet, passim.*

15. Draper, *The Hamlet of Shakespeare's Audience,* pp. 177-8. I question the premise of the concluding statement in the book: "Shakespeare's audience was an audience of men, and Shakespeare's Hamlet was a man's Hamlet."

16. To the Reader.

17. Act II, Scene i.

18. Hart, "The Time Allotted for Representation of Elizabethan and Jacobean Plays," *Review of English Studies,* VIII (1932), 412.

19. Byrne, "Shakespeare's Audience," in Shakespeare Association, *A Series of Papers on Shakespeare and the Theatre,* pp. 200, 215.

20. "On the Influence of the Audience," *The Works of William Shakespeare* (Shakespeare Head Press ed.), X, 334.

21. *Oxford Lectures on Poetry.* He is "not always repelled" by the things condemned in Mr. Bridges's "very interesting and original contribution" and suggests "reasons for at least diminishing the proportion of defect at-

tributable to a conscious sacrifice of art to the tastes of the audience" (p. 367, note 4).

22. *Thomas Platter's Travels in England, 1599*, p. 174.

23. Bearbaiting and bullbaiting were cruel, but they were enjoyed not as cruelty but as sport. There were a conflict of forces and sharing of risks. The activity was more lethal to the dogs than to the bulls, and even the men who whipped the bears took serious risks. Baiting was sometimes for "her Majesty's disport," and interest in it was not a matter of class distinction. Not the "brutal" element but the "sporting" element was attracted. The attitude toward animals, shared by Shakespeare himself, was still strictly utilitarian.

24. *Shakespeare's Theater*, pp. 404-31.

25. *Oxford Lectures on Poetry*, p. 392.

26. "Poetry and the Passions: an Aftermath," *PMLA*, LV (1940), 982-3

27. *Elizabethan Drama*, I, xxxviii.

28. *Le Goût public et le théâtre élisabéthain*, pp. 52-65.

29. Heywood, *Apology for Actors* (1612), Shakespeare Society Publications, No. III, pp. 52-3.

# Thomas De Quincey:

## *ON THE KNOCKING AT THE GATE IN* MACBETH

From my boyish days I had always felt a great perplexity on one point in *Macbeth*. It was this: the knocking at the gate, which succeeds to the murder of Duncan, produced to my feelings an effect for which I never could account. The effect was that it reflected back upon the murder a peculiar awfulness and a depth of solemnity; yet, however obstinately I endeavored with my understanding to comprehend this, for many years I could never see *why* it should produce such an effect.

Here I pause for one moment to exhort the reader never to pay any attention to his understanding when it stands in opposition to any other faculty of his mind. The mere understanding, however useful and indispensable, is the meanest faculty in the human mind and the most to be distrusted; and yet the great majority of people trust to nothing else; which may do for ordinary life, but not for philosophic purposes. Of this, out of ten thousand instances that I might produce, I will cite one. Ask of any person whatsoever, who is not previously prepared for the demand by a knowledge of perspective, to draw in the rudest way the commonest appearance which depends upon the laws of that science—as for instance, to represent the effect of two walls standing at right angles to each other, or the appearance of the houses on each side of a street, as seen by a person looking down the street from one extremity. Now in all cases, unless the person has happened to observe in pictures how it is that artists produce these effects, he will be utterly unable to make the smallest approximation to it. Yet why? For he

Thomas De Quincey (1785–1859) wrote voluminous literary criticism. The following essay on *Macbeth* II. ii. was first published in 1823; T. S. Eliot (p. 445) has said it is "perhaps the best known single piece of criticism of Shakespeare that has ever been written."

has actually seen the effect every day of his life. The reason is that he allows his understanding to overrule his eyes. His understanding, which includes no intuitive knowledge of the laws of vision, can furnish him with no reason why a line which is known and can be proved to be a horizontal line, should not *appear* a horizontal line: a line, that made any angle with the perpendicular less than a right angle, would seem to him to indicate that his houses were all tumbling down together. Accordingly he makes the line of his houses a horizontal line, and fails of course to produce the effect demanded. Here then is one instance out of many, in which not only the understanding is allowed to overrule the eyes, but where the understanding is positively allowed to obliterate the eyes as it were; for not only does the man believe the evidence of his understanding in opposition to that of his eyes, but (which is monstrous!) the idiot is not aware that his eyes ever gave such evidence. He does not know that he has seen (and therefore *quoad* his consciousness[a] has *not* seen) that which he *has* seen every day of his life. But to return from this digression. My understanding could furnish no reason why the knocking at the gate in *Macbeth* should produce any effect direct or reflected; in fact, my understanding said positively that it could *not* produce any effect. But I knew better; I felt that it did; and I waited and clung to the problem until further knowledge should enable me to solve it. At length, in 1812, Mr Williams made his *début* on the stage of Ratcliffe Highway,[b] and executed those unparalleled murders which have procured for him such a brilliant and undying reputation. On which murders, by the way, I must observe, that in one respect they have had an ill effect, by making the connoisseur in murder very fastidious in his taste, and dissatisfied with any thing that has been since done in that line. All other murders look pale by the deep crimson of his: and, as an amateur once said to me in a querulous tone, "There has been absolutely nothing *doing* since his time, or nothing that's worth speaking of." But this is wrong, for it is unreasonable to expect all men to be great artists, and born with the genius of Mr Williams. Now it will be remembered that in the first of these murders (that of the Marrs) the same incident (of a knocking at the door soon after the work of extermination was complete) did actually occur which the genius of Shakespeare had invented; and all good judges and the most eminent dilettanti acknowledged the felicity of Shakespeare's suggestion as soon as it was actually realized. Here then was a fresh proof that I had been right in relying on my own feeling in opposition to my understanding; and again I set myself to study the problem. At length I solved it to my own satisfaction; and my solution is this. Murder in ordinary cases, where the sympathy is wholly directed to the case of the murdered person, is an incident of coarse and vulgar horror; and for this reason—that it flings the interest exclusively upon the natural but ignoble instinct by which we cleave to life; an instinct which, as being indispensable to the primal law of self-preservation, is the same in kind (though different in degree) amongst all living creatures; this instinct therefore, because it annihilates all distinctions, and degrades the greatest of men to the level of "the poor beetle that we tread on," exhibits human nature in its most abject and humiliating attitude. Such an attitude would little suit the purposes of the poet. What then must he do? He must throw the interest on the murderer. Our sympathy must be with *him* (of course I mean a sympathy of comprehension, a sympathy by which we enter into his feelings, and are made to understand them—not a sympathy ᶜ of pity or approbation). In the murdered person all strife of thought, all flux and reflux of passion and of purpose, are crushed by one overwhelming panic; the fear of instant death smites him "with its petrific mace." But in the murderer, such a murderer as a poet will condescend to, there must be raging some great storm of passion—jealousy, ambition, vengeance, hatred—which will create a hell within him; and into this hell we are to look.

In *Macbeth*, for the sake of gratifying his own enormous and teeming faculty of creation, Shakspeare has introduced two murderers: and, as usual in his hands, they are remarkably discriminated: but though in Macbeth the strife of mind is greater than in his wife, the tiger spirit not so awake, and his feelings caught chiefly by contagion from her, yet, as both were finally involved in the guilt of murder, the murderous mind of necessity is finally to be presumed in both. This was to be expressed; and on its own account, as well as to make it a more proportionable antagonist to the unoffending nature of their victim, "the gracious Duncan," and adequately to expound "the

ᶜ [De Quincey's note]  It seems almost ludicrous to guard and explain my use of a word in a situation where it should naturally explain itself. But it has become necessary to do so, in consequence of the unscholarlike use of the word sympathy, at present so general, by which, instead of taking it in its proper use, as the act of reproducing in our minds the feelings of another, whether for hatred, indignation, love, pity, or approbation, it is made a mere synonym of the word *pity;* and hence, instead of saying "sympathy *with* another," many writers adopt the monstrous barbarism of "sympathy *for* another."

deep damnation of his taking off," this was to be expressed with peculiar energy. We were to be made to feel that the human nature, *i.e.*, the divine nature of love and mercy, spread through the hearts of all creatures and seldom utterly withdrawn from man, was gone, vanished, extinct; and that the fiendish nature had taken its place. And, as this effect is marvelously accomplished in the dialogues and soliloquies themselves, so it is finally consummated by the expedient under consideration; and it is to this that I now solicit the reader's attention. If the reader has ever witnessed a wife, daughter, or sister, in a fainting fit, he may chance to have observed that the most affecting moment in such a spectacle is *that* in which a sigh and a stirring announce the recommencement of suspended life. Or, if the reader has ever been present in a vast metropolis on the day when some great national idol was carried in funeral pomp to his grave, and chancing to walk near to the course through which it passed, has felt powerfully in the silence and desertion of the streets and in the stagnation of ordinary business, the deep interest which at that moment was possessing the heart of man, if all at once he should hear the death-like stillness broken up by the sound of wheels rattling away from the scene, and making known that the transitory vision was dissolved, he will be aware that at no moment was his sense of the complete suspension and pause in ordinary human concerns so full and affecting as at that moment when the suspension ceases, and the goings-on of human life are suddenly resumed. All action in any direction is best expounded, measured, and made apprehensible, by reaction. Now apply this to the case in *Macbeth*. Here, as I have said, the retiring of the human heart and the entrance of the fiendish heart was to be expressed and made sensible. Another world has stepped in; and the murderers are taken out of the region of human things, human purposes, human desires. They are transfigured: Lady Macbeth is "unsexed"; Macbeth has forgot that he was born of woman; both are conformed to the image of devils; and the world of devils is suddenly revealed. But how shall this be conveyed and made palpable? In order that a new world may step in, this world must for a time disappear. The murderers, and the murder, must be insulated—cut off by an immeasurable gulf from the ordinary tide and succession of human affairs—locked up and sequestered in some deep recess; we must be made sensible that the world of ordinary life is suddenly arrested, laid asleep, tranced, racked into a dread armistice; time must be annihilated; relation to things without abolished; and all must pass self-withdrawn into a deep syncope and suspension of earthly passion. Hence it is that when the deed is done, when the work of darkness is perfect, then the world of darkness passes away like a pageantry in the clouds: the knocking at the gate is heard; and it makes known audibly that the reaction has commenced; the human has made its reflux upon the fiendish; the pulses of life are beginning to beat again; and the re-establishment of the goings-on of the world in which we live, first makes us profoundly sensible of the awful parenthesis that had suspended them.

O mighty poet! Thy works are not as those of other men, simply and merely great works of art; but are also like the phenomena of nature, like the sun and the stars and the flowers, like frost and snow, rain and dew, hail-storm and thunder, which are to be studied with entire submission of our own faculties, and in the perfect faith that in them there can be no too much or too little, nothing useless or inert but that, the further we press in our discoveries, the more we shall see proofs of design and self-supporting arrangement where the careless eye had seen nothing but accident!

N.B. In the above specimen of psychological criticism, I have purposely omitted to notice another use of the knocking at the gate, viz. the opposition and contrast which it produces in the porter's comments to the scenes immediately preceding; because this use is tolerably obvious to all who are accustomed to reflect on what they read.

# T. S. Eliot:

## *SHAKESPEARIAN CRITICISM: FROM DRYDEN TO COLERIDGE*

I do not propose in this brief sketch to offer a compendium of all that has been written about Shakespeare in three languages in the period I have to cover. For that the reader may turn to Mr Augustus Ralli's *History of Shakespearean Criticism* (Oxford: 2 volumes). The purpose of a contribution on "Shakespeare Criticism" to such a volume as this, as it seems to me, should be to provide a plan, or pattern, for the reading of the principal texts of Shakespeare criticism. Such a vast amount there is, such a sum of Shakespeare criticism increasing every day at compound interest, that the student of Shakespeare may well wonder whether he should consume his time over Shakespeare criticism at all. The first step, therefore, in offering a scheme of Shakespeare criticism is to give a reason why the student of Shakespeare should read what has been written about him. The second step is to make points of emphasis to show why he should read certain things first, and other things second; rather than occupy himself industriously reading everything that has been written about Shakespeare with equal attention and in perfect chronological order.

Why then, to begin with, should we read all that has been written about Shakespeare, in three hundred years, merely because we want to understand Shakespeare? Should we not rather just soak ourselves in the poetry and drama of Shakespeare, and produce our own opinions, unaided and unencumbered by antiquity, about Shakespeare? But when a poet is a

T. S. Eliot (1888–    ) is best known as a poet and playwright, but he has also written important essays on the Elizabethan and Jacobean dramatists. The following essay is drawn from *A Companion to Shakespeare Studies*, ed. H. Granville–Barker and G. B. Harrison (Cambridge University Press, 1934). This collection of essays on the Elizabethan drama has recently been revised and issued as a paperback.

great poet as Shakespeare is, we cannot judge of his greatness unaided; we need both the opinions of other poets, and the diverse views of critics who were not poets, in order to help us to understand. Every view of Shakespeare is an imperfect, because a partial, view. In order to understand these views, we need something more than a good memory. In order to make a pattern of Shakespeare criticism, we need to have some conception of the function of criticism. It is quite impossible to make anything of the history of Shakespeare criticism, unless we can come to some understanding of criticism in general. We have first to grasp what criticism is, and second to grasp the relation between literary and philosophical criticism on the one hand, and literary and textual criticism on the other. With the history of textual criticism, with our increasing knowledge of Shakespeare, of his times, of his texts, of his theater, I am not to be concerned; but I am concerned with (among other things) the general formulation of the relation between our literary criticism and our scholarly knowledge. In the history of the criticism of Shakespeare which is primarily or strictly literary and dramatic there is a certain "progress", but only such progress as is possible as a result of the improved texts, the increased knowledge about the conditions of the Elizabethan stage, about the life of Shakespeare himself, and about the times in which he lived. Otherwise, it would be imprudent to say that we are approximating towards a final goal of understanding, after which there will be nothing new to be said; or retrospectively, to assume that A. C. Bradley's criticism of Shakespeare is "better" than that of Dryden. Shakespeare criticism will always change as the world changes.

This point is really a very simple one, and easy to accept when our eye is on the history of criticism in general; but when we are confining our attention to the history of the criticism of a single great poet like Shakespeare, it is easy to slip into a different assumption. We find it difficult, of course, to believe that the view of Shakespeare to be taken 100 years hence can be very different from our own. On the other hand, we are inclined to assume that the criticism of Shakespeare written before the nineteenth century is less illuminating than that written since. Neither assumption is quite true. There is undeniably an aspect in which early criticism may be seen as the substructure of that of the nineteenth century. We have to admit that the fuller understanding of Shakespeare's greatness came slowly, just as it comes slowly, I believe, in the life of the individual reader. But Shakespeare criticism cannot be appreciated without some understanding of the time and of the place in which it is written, without allowing for its nearness or remoteness in place or time from the object, and for its inevitable development in the future. The views of Shakespeare taken by different men at different times in different places form an integral part of the development and change of European civilization during the last 300 years. Furthermore, in this study we should, I think, take an attitude which is represented by the popular word *Gestalt* or, as we might say, "pattern." That is, we should not begin by the attempt to decide which Shakespeare critics are most illuminating, and ignore the rest; what we have to study is the whole pattern formed by Shakespeare criticism from his own time to ours. In tracing this pattern, certainly, we must study some critics more closely than others, and we may for practical purposes select certain critics who serve to determine the main outline of the pattern; but it should be the whole pattern rather than the individual critic, in which we interest ourselves.

For this reason I shall not attempt, in this space, a compendious history of the subject. I shall simply select certain critics, according to the principle I have indicated above, and leave the reader to fill in the gaps by his own reading. There are obvious points of triangulation. First, there is the testimony of Shakespeare's contemporaries, of which, making due allowance for personal bias, that of Ben Jonson may be our specimen. Second, there is the criticism of the age of Dryden, regarding which, again, we make due allowance for the singular individual genius of Dryden. This is a period in which there is still a criticism of the *acted* play (as Pepys's *Diary* attests); when—so far as the distinction holds—there is still dramatic as well as literary criticism; it is still a period in which criticism is directly in simple relation to the object, in contrast with modern criticism which is necessarily as much in relation to other criticism as to the work of Shakespeare itself. In the time of Pope and his contemporaries we feel at once the greater distance of time between the critic and the object, and we begin to feel that criticism has already to take account of criticism as well as of the object criticised. (This period, by the way, has been somewhat maligned: there is no period in which Shakespeare has not been treated with the greatest respect.) Against this, we must offset the critical views of the French in the eighteenth century, where we find, not so much the conflict of one dramatic type with another, as the conflict of English drama with a critical theory which was *not contradicted* by French practice. The French views of the eighteenth century—for example those of Voltaire, Diderot and La Harpe—have again to be compared with the other French views of the nineteenth century—as those of Taine and Victor Hugo. Meanwhile we find English

criticism modified, during the later part of the eighteenth century, by the development of the sentimental attitude. English
criticism of the greater part of the nineteenth century is very
largely a development from the work of Coleridge, Lamb, Hazlitt and De Quincey; amongst these the influence of Coleridge
is very much the most significant; and the explanation of Coleridge is partly found in the German critical thought of the latter part of the eighteenth century.

The student of Shakespeare criticism will be aware of all
these views and developments, will endeavor to appreciate
their appropriateness each to its place and time, their relations
to each other, their limitations of time and cultural sympathy,
and will consequently recognize that at different places and
times criticism has different work to do. The contemporary
of the poet has both obvious limitations and obvious advantages; he is too near to the object to see it clearly or in perspective; his judgment may be distorted by enthusiasm or prejudice;
on the other hand he enjoys the advantage of a freshness un-
spoiled by generations of other men's views. The later critic has
both to try to see the object as if for the first time, without the
direction of the criticism which has intervened; and also, as I
have said, previous criticism is itself a part of the object of his
criticism. Hence the critic's problem becomes for every generation more complicated; but also, every generation has a better
opportunity for realizing how complicated the problem is.
At one time, the critical task may be the elaboration of a kind
of criticism already initiated; at another, its refutation; at another, the introduction of a new theory, that is to say the ex-
position of an aspect hitherto overlooked; or again, it may be
to combine and to display the pattern afforded by the diverse
voices. And in this Shakespeare pattern everything laudatory
must find a place, when it is a true praise not previously
sounded; and everything derogatory too, even when blunted
by misunderstanding, so long as it evinces the temper of an age
or a people, and not merely a personal whim.

Of the contemporary comment upon Shakespeare it is that of
Ben Jonson which is best remembered and most quoted; and
with justice, as Jonson not only had the finest critical mind of
his day, but as a dramatist and poet is of so different a kind
from Shakespeare that his opinion has a peculiar interest. We
may incline to think that Shakespeare's contemporaries under-
estimated his accomplishment, and were blind to his genius;
forgetting that greatness is in a sense the result of time. It has
again and again been illustrated that the opinion of contempo-
raneity is imperfect; and that even when it shows intelligent
appreciation and enjoyment, it is apt surprisingly to elevate

some quite insignificant figure above a very great one. Our opinions of our own contemporaries will probably seem grotesque to the future. I believe that if I had lived in the seventeenth century, it is quite likely that I should have preferred Beaumont and Fletcher to Shakespeare; though my estimate of their difference today is enough to satisfy the most fanatical Shakespearian. What I wish to do is to remove the *stigma* of being a contemporary, and to deprecate the complacency which attaches to being a member of posterity.

And I certainly do not mean to confound all distinctions, or to allow easily all opinions to be right. Whenever Dryden mentions Shakespeare, Dryden's opinion must be treated with respect. To understand his view of Shakespeare we must read *all* of his critical writing. And in particular, in weighing Dryden's opinions, we must spend some time over his collocation of Shakespeare and Fletcher, we must try to come to a point of understanding at which we *see* why it was natural and proper for him to make this frequent parallel and comparison. That is not so much a matter of wide reading or scholarship, although we must make ourselves very familiar with the plays of Fletcher, and with the plays, as well as the criticism, of Dryden: it is a matter of the exercise of the critical imagination. There are critics who are definitely wrong-headed. Thomas Rymer was a man of considerable learning, and not destitute of taste, when he left his taste to look after itself; but a false theory of what the drama should be, of what he *ought* to like, came very near to paralyzing that function altogether, and made him the butt of his own and subsequent times. Nevertheless, I believe that the falsity of his dramatic theory, and the absurdity of the conclusions he drew from it, have had the unfortunate effect—as the extremity of false theorizing is apt to do—of sometimes confirming people in their own false opinions merely because they assured themselves too confidently that whatever Rymer did not believe must be right.

As soon as we enter the eighteenth century we feel a change in the atmosphere of criticism; and in reading the criticism itself we are aware that Shakespeare is beginning to be more read than seen upon the stage. Addison calls attention to a point of detail (the crowing of the cock in *Hamlet*) which has probably, we feel, struck him rather in the reading than at a performance; the attention of the eighteenth-century critic in England is rather on the poetry than on the drama. The observations of Pope are of value and interest, because they are by Pope. If other eighteenth-century critics are to be read, it is not so much for their individual contributions, but as a reminder that there was no period in which Shakespeare fell into neglect. There is indeed some development. Shakespeare begins to be written about in greater detail and at greater length, and apart from any more general discussion of the drama; he is, in the eighteenth century, gradually *detached* from his environment, from the other dramatists, and from a time which had become unfamiliar. And it may be mentioned, though this is outside my province, that during the eighteenth century the standard of scholarship and editorship was rising. But the major part of eighteenth-century criticism down to Johnson, and almost all the French criticism of Shakespeare during this period, strike me as unprofitable reading unless we enlarge our interests. The criticism of Shakespeare at any epoch is a most useful means of inducting us into the way in which people of that time enjoyed their contemporary poetry; and the approval which they express of Shakespeare indicates that he possessed some of the qualities that they cultivated in their own verse, and perhaps other qualities that they would have liked to find there. A study of the opinions of Voltaire, La Harpe and Diderot about Shakespeare may help to increase our appreciation of Racine; it is quite certain that we can never make head or tail of these opinions unless we do enjoy Corneille and Racine. And I do not mean merely a polite acquaintance with their plays, or a fluent ability to declaim their verse; I mean the immediate delight in their poetry. That is an experience which may arrive late in life, or oftener not at all; if it comes— I am speaking, of course, of Anglo-Saxon experience only— it is an illumination. And it is far from corrupting our pleasure in Shakespeare, or reducing our admiration. Poetry does not do these things to other poetry: the beauty of one kind only exhances the lustre of another.

To pass from Dryden to Johnson is to make the journey from one oasis to another. After the critical essays of Dryden, the Preface to Shakespeare by Samuel Johnson is the next of the great pieces of criticism to read. One would willingly resign the honor of an Abbey burial for the greater honor of words like the following, from a man of the greatness of their author:

> The poet, of whose works I have undertaken the revision, may now begin to assume the dignity of an ancient, and claim the privilege of established fame and prescriptive veneration. He has long outlived his century, the term commonly fixed as the test of literary merit. Whatever advantages he might once derive from personal allusions, local customs, or temporary opinions, have for many years been lost; and every topic of merriment, or motive of sorrow, which the modes of artificial life afforded him, now only obscure the scenes which they once illuminated.

The effects of favor and competition are at an end; the tradition of his friendships and his enmities has perished; his works support no opinion with arguments, nor supply any faction with invectives; they can neither indulge vanity, nor gratify malignity; but are read without any other reason than the desire of pleasure, and are therefore praised only as pleasure is obtained; yet, thus unassisted by interest or passion, they have passed through variations of taste and changes of manners, and, as they devolved from one generation to another, have received new honors at every transmission.

What a valedictory and obituary for any man to receive! My point is that if you assume that the classical criticism of England was grudging in its praise of Shakespeare, I say that no poet can ask more of posterity than to be greatly honored by the great; and Johnson's words about Shakespeare are great honor.

Johnson refutes those critics—and only Johnson could do it —who had thought that Shakespeare violated propriety, here and there, with his observation that Shakespeare's "scenes are occupied only by men, who act and think as the reader thinks that he himself should have spoken or acted on the same occasion." But a little further Johnson makes another most remarkable (but not sufficiently remarked) observation, to which several subsequent editors and publishers, even to our own time, seem to have paid not sufficient deference:

> The players, who in their edition divided our author's works into comedies, histories, and tragedies, seem not to have defined the three kinds by any very exact or definite ideas.

To those who would divide periods, and segregate men, neatly into classical and romantic groups, I commend the study of this sentence, and of what Johnson says afterwards about the relation of the tragic to the comic. This Preface to Shakespeare was published in 1765, and Voltaire, still writing ten years and more after this event, was maintaining an opposite point of view. Johnson saw deeper than Voltaire, in this as in most matters. Johnson perceived, though not explicitly, that the distinctions of tragic and comic are superficial—for *us;* though he did not know how important they were for the Greeks; for he did not know that they sprang from a difference in ritual. As a poet—and he was a fine poet—Johnson is at the end of a tether. But as a critic—and he was greater as critic than as poet— Johnson has a place comparable to that of Cowley as poet: in that we cannot say whether to classify him as the last of one

kind or the first of another. There is one sentence which we
may boggle over. Johnson says:

> In tragedy he (*i.e.* Shakespeare) often writes, with great
> appearance of toil and study, what is written at last with
> little felicity; but, in his comic scenes, he seems to produce,
> without labor, what no labor can improve.

This is an opinion which we cannot lightly dismiss. Johnson is quite aware that the alternation of "tragic" and "comic"
is something more than an alternation; he perceives that
something different and new is produced. "The interchanges of
mingled scenes seldom fail to produce the intended vicissitudes
of passion." "*Through all these denominations of the drama
Shakespeare's mode of composition is the same.*" But why
should Johnson have thought that Shakespeare's comic parts
were spontaneous, and that his tragic parts were labored?
Here, it seems to me, Johnson, by his simple integrity, in being
wrong has happened upon some truth much deeper than he
knew. For to those who have experienced the full horror of life,
tragedy is still inadequate. Sophocles felt more of it than he
could express, when he wrote *Œdipus the King;* Shakespeare,
when he wrote *Hamlet;* and Shakespeare had the advantage of
being able to employ his grave-diggers. In the end, horror and
laughter may be one—only when horror and laughter have become as horrible and laughable as they can be; and—whatever the conscious intention of the authors—you may laugh
or shudder over *Œdipus* or *Hamlet* or *King Lear*—or both at
once: then only do you perceive that the aim of the comic and
the tragic dramatist is the same: they are equally serious. So
do the meanings of words change, as we inspect them, that we
may even come to see Molière in some lights as a more serious
dramatist than Corneille or Racine; Wycherley as equally serious (in this sense) with Marlowe. All this is suggested to me
by the words of Samuel Johnson which I have quoted. What
Plato perceived has not been noticed by subsequent dramatic
critics; the dramatic poet uses the conventions of tragic and
comic poetry, so far as these are the conventions of his day;
there is potential comedy in Sophocles and potential tragedy
in Aristophanes, and otherwise they would not be such good
tragedians or comedians as they are. It might be added that
when you have comedy and tragedy united in the wrong way, or
separated in the wrong way, you get sentiment or amusement.
The distinction between the tragic and the comic is an account of the way in which we try to live; when we get below it,
as in *King Lear,* we have an account of the way in which we do
live.

The violent change between one period and another is both progress and retrogression. I have quoted only a few sentences from Johnson's Preface to Shakespeare; but I think they represent the view of a mature, if limited, personality. The next phase of English criticism of Shakespeare is prefaced from Germany. I must add, however, that the influence of German criticism upon English at this point can easily be exaggerated. It is in no wise to belittle the value of this criticism, if we affirm that there was rather a similarity of outlook, and a natural sympathy between the German and the English mind, in approaching Shakespeare, which we do not find with the French critics. It would be rash to assert that the German mind is better qualified to appreciate Shakespeare than is the French; but one less comprehensive generalisation I believe can be made. For the French mind, the approach to Shakespeare has normally been by way of a comparison to Corneille and Racine, if not to Molière. Now for the Frenchman the plays of his classical age are primarily, to this day, plays to be acted; and his memories of them are of the theater at least as much as of the library. For the Englishman of the nineteenth century the plays of Shakespeare have been dramatic poems to be read, rather than plays to be seen; and for most of us today the great majority of the plays are solely literary acquaintances. Furthermore, the French have always had this background of their own great dramatic achievement. But the Germans have never had this background of native authority in the drama; their acquaintance with Shakespeare was formed in the study; and until the reputation of Goethe was firmly established throughout Europe they had no native dramatic author with whom to compare him. For these reasons alone, without any rash generalizations about the Gallic and the Teutonic mind, we should expect the German attitude to be more sympathetic.

But the kind of criticism which arises rather from reading than from attendance at the theater arose in England spontaneously. The first striking example of this sort of criticism, a remarkable piece of writing which deserves meditation, and which commands our respect whether we agree with its conclusions or not, is Morgann's Essay *On the Dramatic Character of Sir John Falstaff* (1777). For the case which Morgann attempts to make out, I refer the reader to Morgann himself. My point is that Morgann's essay is the first conspicuous member of a long line of criticism dealing with the characters of the personages in the plays, considering not only their actions within the play itself, but inferring from their behavior on the stage what their general character is, that is to say, how they would behave in other circumstances. This is a perfectly legitimate form of criticism, though liable to abuses; at its best, it can add

very much to our enjoyment of the moments of the characters'
life which are given in the scene, if we feel this richness of reality in them; and at its worst, it becomes an irrelevance and dis-
tracts us from our enjoyment of the play.

The first of the great German critics, Lessing, tended to make
of Shakespeare almost a national issue, for he it was who affirmed that English literature, and in particular Shakespeare,
was more congenial than French literature and drama to the
German taste. The German critics in general insist upon the
naturalness and fidelity to reality of Shakespeare's plays. Her-
der, a critic of considerable understanding, begins to appreciate
the existence of something like a poetic pattern, in calling attention to the fitness between the passions of the personages and the scenery in which these passions are enacted. But
what interests me in this place is not a detailed valuation of
the opinions of the German critics of this period—not even the
opinions of the Schlegels and Goethe—but a consideration of
the general tendency of their opinions. Neglecting the circumstances in which the plays were written—and indeed the historical information was not available—and paying little attention to their dramatic merits, the Germans concentrated their
attention chiefly upon the philosophical significance of character. They penetrate to a deeper level than that of the simple
moral values attributed to great literature by earlier times,
and foreshadow the "criticism of life" definition by Arnold.
Furthermore, it is not until this period that an element of "mystery" is recognized in Shakespeare. That is one of the gifts of
the Romantic Movement to Shakespeare criticism, and one for
which, with all its excesses, we have reason to be grateful. It is
hardly too much to say that the German critics and Coleridge,
by their criticism of Shakespeare, radically altered the reflec-
tive attitude of criticism towards poetry.

The writings of Coleridge upon Shakespeare must be read entire; for it is impossible to understand Shakespeare criticism to
this day, without a familiar acquaintance with Coleridge's lectures and notes. Coleridge is an authority of the kind whose influence extends equally towards good and bad. It would be unjust to father upon him, without further ceremony, the
psycho-analytic school of Shakespeare criticism; the study of
individual characters which was begun by Morgann, to the
neglect of the pattern and meaning of the whole play, was
bound to lead to some such terminus, and we do not blame
Morgann for that. But when Coleridge released the truth that
Shakespeare already in *Venus and Adonis* and *Lucrece* gave
proof of a "most profound, energetic and *philosophic* mind" he
was perfectly right, if we use these adjectives rightly, but he

supplied a dangerous stimulant to the more adventurous. "Philosophic" is of course not the right word, but it cannot simply be erased: you must find another word to put in its place, and the word has not yet been found. The sense of the profundity of Shakespeare's "thought," or of his thinking-in-images, has so oppressed some critics that they have been forced to explain themselves by unintelligibles.

I have not spoken of Hazlitt, Lamb and De Quincey; that is because I wished to isolate Coleridge as perhaps the greatest single figure in Shakespeare criticism down to the present day. In a conspectus like the present, only the most salient points can be more than mentioned; and Hazlitt, Lamb and De Quincey, for my present purposes, do but make a constellation about the primary star of Coleridge. Their work is chiefly important as reinforcing the influence of Coleridge; though De Quincey's *On the Knocking on the Gate in* Macbeth is perhaps the best known single piece of criticism of Shakespeare that has been written. But for the student of Shakespeare criticism, the writing of all of these men is among those documents that are to be read, and not merely read about.

# James Agate:

# *VOLPONE; OR THE FOX*
# BY BEN JONSON

*De gustibus* and so on. Speaking for myself, I had as lief see this comedy by Ben Jonson as any by Shakespeare. Perhaps liefer, though the unfamiliarity of the one and the overfamiliarity of the other may have something to do with it. But then I would sooner live surrounded by Hogarths than by Watteaus, since to me the English painter, despite the grossness of his subject, is warm and alive, while the Frenchman, despite the elegance of his, is cold and not so alive. And there the not very good analogy must end. Still holding each to his own taste, I submit that it is possible to prove Hazlitt all wrong about this play. Consider Volpone's speech, which begins: "Why droops my Celia?" and goes on:

> See, behold
> What thou art queen of, not in expectation—
> As I feed others—but possessed and crowned.
> See, here, a rope of pearl, and each more orient
> Than that the brave Egyptian queen caroused—
> Dissolve and drink 'em. See, a carbuncle,
> May put out both the eyes of our St. Mark;
> A diamond would have bought Lollia Paulina,
> When she came in like starlight, hid with jewels
> That were the spoils of provinces—take these
> And wear, and lose 'em; yet remains an earring
> To purchase them again, and this whole state.

James Agate (1877–1947) was dramatic critic for the *Manchester Guardian* and later for the *Saturday Review* (London). He published several volumes of his criticism; the following essay is from *Brief Chronicles* (Jonathan Cape, 1943), a collection of reviews of modern productions of Renaissance drama.

Look over the exquisite passage beginning:

> Thy baths shall be the juice of julyflowers,
> Spirit of roses, and of violets,
> The milk of unicorns, and panthers' breath
> Gathered in bags, and mixed with Cretan wines,
> Our drink shall be preparèd gold and amber,
> Which we will take until my roof whirl round
> With the vertigo

It seems to me that Faustus himself would not have disdained

> When she came in like starlight, hid with jewels,

and that Perdita would have been at home with

> The milk of unicorns, and panthers' breath.

Yet Hazlitt's adjectives for Jonson's verse are "dry," "literal," and "meager." The point is that the great essayist is a sentimentalist and will take no pleasure in a play unless he can find in it some nice person with whom to identify himself: "There is almost a total want of variety, fancy, relief, and of those delightful transitions which abound, for instance, in Shakespeare's tragi-comedy. In Ben Jonson, we find ourselves generally in low company, and we see no hope of getting out of it. He is like a person who fastens upon a disagreeable subject and cannot be persuaded to leave it." But, in heaven's name, who wants anybody to leave a disagreeable subject if he can make it more interesting than an agreeable one?

Hazlitt thinks that the trouble with Jonson's comedy is that it is mean. This is palpably absurd, since one of the concomitants of meanness is littleness. I would rather call Jonson's comedy riotous, and his humanity of the cartoonist's size. Volpone bestrides his world as Valmont bestrides that of Choderlos de Laclos and Vautrin that of Balzac; the lesser rogues have still something Michael-Angelesque about them. Hazlitt denies Jonson gusto because he does not like the things the gusto is about, and because, like every sentimental playgoer, he wants to warm himself at the spectacle of good men routing bad ones, and sees no fun in villains destroying one another. It dismays him that Volpone should be undone by Mosca, and that both should be punished by a bench of zanies. He dislikes the caperings of Volpone's minions because he would not have them behaving so in his own drawing-room. To sum up, Hazlitt desires that comedy should make him think better of mankind, whereas I demand of comedy only that it shall make

me think. So long as the comic dramatist is writing well and not
ill I am indifferent whether his characters behave well or ill.
"Jonson had a keen sense of what was true and false, but not of
the difference between the agreeable and disagreeable."
This proves my case against any playgoer demanding that the
things shown him in the theater shall be agreeable rather than
that they shall be true. Judged by the West-End standard of
popularity, *Volpone* is "cross-grained," "prolix," "improbable,"
"repulsive," and even "revolting." Yet in a critic as good as Hazlitt the critical habit dies hard, and he cannot help saying that
"this best play" of Jonson "is written *con amore.*" This sentence clinches my argument. It is all very well for its author to
attempt to recover by saying that the play "is made up of
cheats and dupes, and the author is at home among them." The
gibe comes too late; *the piece is written* con amore!

   In the revival at the Westminster the boundless spirit is at
large. Mr. Michael MacOwen has given their heads to Mr. Peter
Goffin and Mr. Edmund Rubbra, and, thus encouraged, Mr.
Goffin responds with a gold-encrusted Jacobean tableau which
Mr. Sickert ought to paint, and Mr. Rubbra, meeting his pro-
ducer more than half-way, conjures from the throats of clari-
net, oboe, and bassoon a concourse of sounds even more obnoxious, in a Hazlittean sense, than the scenes they accompany.
This spirit extends to the players. Mr. Donald Wolfit makes a
splendid mouthful of the Fox; he is right in presence, and he
speaks the verse as the actor of Jonson's day must have spoken
it. There must be many ways of playing Mosca, and Mr. Alan
Wheatley has chosen to be a silk thread among the hempen villainy. Mr. Mark Dignam is the vulture-lawyer of all time, and
Mr. Stanley Lathbury a most pointed, witless crow. As I wish
this revival immensely well, and as at this point the praise of
the acting must get thinner, I stop.

                                        January 30, 1938

# Selected Bibliography

## TO THE MID-SIXTEENTH CENTURY

Chambers, E. K. *The English Folk Play.* Oxford: Claren-
don Press, 1933; New York: Oxford University Press.
————. *English Literature at the Close of the Middle
Ages.* Oxford: Clarendon Press, 1945; New York:
Oxford University Press.
————. *The Mediaeval Stage.* 2 vols. London & New
York: Oxford University Press, 1903.
Craig, Hardin. *English Religious Drama of the Middle
Ages.* Oxford: Clarendon Press, 1955; New York:
Oxford University Press.
Farnham, Willard. *The Medieval Heritage of Elizabethan
Tragedy.* Oxford: Basil Blackwell, 1956; New York:
Barnes & Noble.
Gardiner, Harold C. *Mysteries' End.* London: Oxford
University Press, 1946; New Haven: Yale University
Press.
Hunningher, Benjamin. *The Origin of the Theater.* The
Hague: N. V. Nijhoff, 1955; London: B. T. Batsford.
Kernodle, George R. *From Art to Theatre.* University of
Chicago Press, 1944.
Nicoll, Allardyce. *Masks, Mimes and Miracles.* London:
G. G. Harrap, 1931; New York: Harcourt, Brace &
Company.
Prosser, Eleanor. *Drama and Religion in the English
Mystery Plays.* Stanford: Stanford University Press,
1961.
Rossiter, A. P. *English Drama from Early Times to the
Elizabethans.* London: Hutchinson's University Li-
brary, 1950.
Salter, F. M. *Mediaeval Drama in Chester.* Toronto:

University of Toronto Press, 1955; London: Oxford
University Press, 1956.

Spivack, Bernard. *Shakespeare and the Allegory of Evil.*
London: Oxford University Press, 1958; New York:
Columbia University Press.

Williams, Arnold. *The Drama of Medieval England.* East
Lansing: Michigan State University Press, 1961.

Young, Karl. *The Drama of the Medieval Church.* Oxford: Clarendon Press, 1933; New York: Oxford
University Press.

## FROM THE MIDDLE OF THE SIXTEENTH CENTURY
## TO THE CLOSING OF THE THEATERS

Baker, Howard. *Induction to Tragedy.* Baton Rouge:
Louisiana State University Press, 1939.

Bentley, Gerald Eades. *The Jacobean and Caroline Stage.*
5 vols. Oxford: Clarendon Press, 1941–1956; New
York: Oxford University Press.

Bluestone, Max, and Norman Rabkin, ed. *Shakespeare's
Contemporaries.* Englewood Cliffs: Prentice-Hall,
1961.

Boas, F. S. *An Introduction to Stuart Drama.* London
& New York: Oxford University Press, 1946.

———. *An Introduction to Tudor Drama.* Oxford:
Clarendon Press, 1933; New York: Oxford University
Press.

Bradbrook, M. C. *The Growth and Structure of Elizabethan Comedy.* London: Chatto and Windus, 1955;
Berkeley: University of California Press, 1956.

———. *Themes and Conventions in Elizabethan Tragedy.* Cambridge: Cambridge University Press, 1935.

Chambers, E. K. *The Elizabethan Stage.* 4 vols. Oxford:
Clarendon Press, 1923; New York: Oxford University
Press.

Clemen, Wolfgang. *English Tragedy before Shakespeare,*
trans. T. S. Dorsch. London: Methuen & Company,
1961.

Doran, Madeleine. *Endeavors of Art.* Madison: University of Wisconsin Press, 1954.

Eliot, T. S. *Elizabethan Essays.* London: Faber and Faber, 1934.

Fluchère, Henri. *Shakespeare,* trans. Guy Hamilton. New York: Longmans, Green & Company, 1953. Reprinted as *Shakespeare and the Elizabethans.* New York: Hill and Wang, 1956.

Ford, Boris, ed. *The Age of Shakespeare.* Baltimore: Penguin Books (Pelican A 291), 1955.

Harbage, Alfred. *Cavalier Drama.* London: Oxford University Press, 1936; New York: Modern Language Association.

————. *Shakespeare and the Rival Traditions.* New York: The Macmillan Company, 1952.

Harrison, G. B. *Elizabethan Plays and Players.* Ann Arbor: University of Michigan Press, 1956.

Hodges, C. Walter. *The Globe Restored.* London: Ernest Benn, 1953; New York: Coward-McCann, 1954.

Nagler, A. M. *Shakespeare's Stage.* New Haven: Yale University Press, 1958.

Parrott, Thomas Marc, and Robert Hamilton Ball. *A Short View of Elizabethan Drama.* New York: Charles Scribner's Sons, 1943.

Prior, Moody. *The Language of Tragedy.* London: The Oxford University Press, 1947; New York: Columbia University Press.

## THE PLAYS

### *Abraham and Isaac*

Craig, Hardin. *English Religious Drama.* Oxford: Clarendon Press, 1955; New York: Oxford University Press.

Severs, J. Burke. "The Relationship between the Brome and Chester Play of *Abraham and Isaac,*" *Modern Philology,* XLII (1945), 137-151.

### *The Second Shepherds' Play*

Carpenter, Nan Cooke. "Music in the *Secunda Pastorum,*" *Speculum,* XXVI (1951), 696-700.

Speirs, John. "The Towneley *Shepherds' Plays,*" in *The*

*Age of Chaucer,* ed. Boris Ford. Baltimore: Penguin Books (Pelican A 290), 1954.

Thompson, Francis J. "Unity in the Second Shepherds' Tale," *Modern Language Notes,* LXIV (1949), 302-306.

Watt, Homer A. "The Dramatic Unity of the *Secunda Pastorum,*" in *Essays and Studies in Honor of Carleton Brown.* London: Oxford University Press, 1940; New York: New York University Press.

*Everyman*

Brooks, Cleanth, and Robert B. Heilman. *Understanding Drama: Twelve Plays.* New York: Henry Holt, 1948.

Cormican, L. A. "Morality Tradition and the Interludes," in *The Age of Chaucer,* ed. Boris Ford. Baltimore: Penguin Books (Pelican A 290), 1954.

Spivack, Bernard. *Shakespeare and the Allegory of Evil.* London: Oxford University Press, 1958; New York: Columbia University Press.

Christopher Marlowe, *Doctor Faustus*

Bluestone, Max, and Norman Rabkin, ed. *Shakespeare's Contemporaries.* Englewood Cliffs: Prentice-Hall, 1961.

Kocher, Paul. *Christopher Marlowe.* Chapel Hill: University of North Carolina Press, 1946; London: Oxford University Press, 1947.

Levin, Harry. *The Overreacher.* Cambridge, Mass.: Harvard University Press, 1952.

William Shakespeare, *Macbeth*

Bradley, A. C. *Shakespearean Tragedy.* New York: The Macmillan Company, 1905.

Harbage, Alfred. *As They Liked It.* London & New York: The Macmillan Company, 1947.

Paul, Henry N. *The Royal Play of Macbeth.* New York: The Macmillan Company, 1950; London, 1951.

Rosen, William. *Shakespeare and the Craft of Tragedy.* London: Oxford University Press, 1960; Cambridge, Mass.: Harvard University Press.

Stauffer, Donald A. *Shakespeare's World of Images.* New York: W. W. Norton, 1949; London: Oxford University Press, 1952.

Traversi, D. A. *An Approach to Shakespeare,* 2nd ed. rev. New York: Doubleday Anchor Books, 1956.

Van Doren, Mark. *Shakespeare.* New York: Henry Holt, 1939; London: George Allen & Unwin, 1941.

Watkins, Ronald. *On Producing Shakespeare.* London: Michael Joseph, 1950; New York: W. W. Norton, 1951.

Ben Jonson, *Volpone*

Barish, Jonas A. *Ben Jonson and the Language of Prose Comedy.* Cambridge, Mass.: Harvard University Press, 1960.

Bluestone, Max, and Norman Rabkin, ed. *Shakespeare's Contemporaries.* Englewood Cliffs: Prentice-Hall, 1961.

Enck, John J. *Jonson and the Comic Truth.* Madison: University of Wisconsin Press, 1957.

Knights, L. C. *Drama and Society in the Age of Jonson.* New York: George W. Stewart, n.d.

Partridge, Edward Bellamy. *The Broken Compass.* London: Chatto & Windus, 1958; New York: Columbia University Press.

John Milton, *Samson Agonistes*

Hanford, James Holly. *John Milton, Englishman.* New York: Crown, 1949; London: Victor Gollancz, 1950.

Parker, William R. *Milton's Debt to Greek Tragedy in "Samson Agonistes."* London: Oxford University Press, 1937; Baltimore: Johns Hopkins University Press.

Stein, Arnold. *Heroic Knowledge.* London: Oxford University Press, 1957; Minneapolis: University of Minnesota Press.

Woodhouse, A. S. P. "Tragic Effect in *Samson Agonistes,*" *University of Toronto Quarterly,* XXVIII (1959), 205-222.

## MENTOR Books of Related Interest

☐ **THE BIRDS by Aristophanes: translated and with an introduction by William Arrowsmith.** THE BIRDS is a masterpiece of unforgettable commentary on human dreams and follies. (#MQ1320—95¢)

☐ **THE CLOUDS by Aristophanes: translated and with an introduction by William Arrowsmith.** Filled with parody, exaggeration, outrageous burlesque, masterfully juggling ideas and reputations, it triumphantly remains as a magnificent display of comic genius.
(#MQ1397—95¢)

☐ **EIGHT GREAT COMEDIES edited by Barnet, Berman and Burto.** Complete texts of plays by Aristophanes, Shakespeare, Molière, Gay, four other masters, with essays on the nature of comedy. (#ME1340—$1.75)

☐ **EIGHT GREAT TRAGEDIES edited by Barnet, Berman and Burto.** The Greek dramatists, Shakespeare, Ibsen, Strindberg, O'Neill, Yeats, and essays on tragedy.
(#ME1347—$1.75)

☐ **THE GOLDEN TREASURY OF F. T. PALGRAVE, enlarged and updated by Oscar Williams.** Great lyric poems of the English language from 1526 to the present.
(#MW1423—$1.50)

## Outstanding Contemporary Plays in SIGNET Editions

☐ **THE SANDBOX AND THE DEATH OF BESSIE SMITH by Edward Albee.** Two explosive off-Broadway hits, one about a scathing domestic tragedy, the other baring the ugly circumstances surrounding the death of a great Black blues singer. (#Q6189—95¢)

☐ **THE AMERICAN DREAM AND THE ZOO STORY by Edward Albee.** Two remarkably successful off-Broadway plays by the author of the prize-winning play, Who's Afraid of Virginia Woolf? (#Q6585—95¢)

☐ **A STREETCAR NAMED DESIRE by Tennessee Williams.** The Pulitzer Prize-winning play of a woman betrayed by love. Illustrated with scenes from the New York, London, and Paris productions. (#Y6178—$1.25)

☐ **THE NIGHT OF THE IGUANA by Tennessee Williams.** The emotion-charged drama about two women who vie for the affections of a defrocked minister. Now a motion picture starring Richard Burton, Ava Gardner, Deborah Kerr, and Sue Lyon. (#Q5684—95¢)

☐ **A RAISIN IN THE SUN and THE SIGN IN SIDNEY BRUSTEIN'S WINDOW by Lorraine Hansberry.** Two outstanding plays: One, winner of the New York Drama Critics Award, about a young Black father's struggle to break free from the barriers of prejudice, the other, portraying a modern-day intellectual's challenge of the negation and detachment of his fellow intellectuals. With a Foreword by John Braine and an Introduction by Robert Nemiroff. (#Q4111—95¢)

𝒞

## The SIGNET Classic Shakespeare

THE NEW AMERICAN LIBRARY, INC.,
P.O. Box 999, Bergenfield, New Jersey 07621